An Anthology of
Disability Literature

An Anthology of
Disability Literature

Edited by

Christy Thompson Ibrahim

CAROLINA ACADEMIC PRESS

Durham, North Carolina

Library of Congress Cataloging-in-Publication Data

An anthology of disability literature / [compiled by] Christy Thompson
Ibrahim.
    p. cm.
Includes bibliographical references and index.
ISBN 978-1-61163-057-2 (alk. paper)
1. People with disabilities in literature. 2. Mind and body in literature.
I. Ibrahim, Christy Thompson.
PN56.5.H35D57 2011
808.83'93527--dc23   2011031961

CAROLINA ACADEMIC PRESS
700 Kent Street
Durham, North Carolina 27701
Telephone (919) 489-7486
Fax (919) 493-5668
www.cap-press.com

Printed in the United States of America

Contents

Acknowledgments

Thank you to my husband Kevin; my children, Zach and Jared; my parents, Lorin and Margaret-Lee Thompson; and my brothers, Dan and John. Thank you to my mentors: Larry Jones, Pat Kuszler, Mary Hotchkiss, Cynthia Hallen, and Jane Ellis. Thank you to all of my great English teachers and professors, particularly Steve Arkle, Ray Williams, the late Bruce Clark, and Darrell Spencer. Thanks to Laura Harris, Sarah Harris, and Fran Platt for their advice on the book, and to Peter London, Lisa Barelli, and the other publishers and authors who helped with this project. Finally, thanks to Keith Sipe, Zoë Oakes, Tim Colton, Suzanne Morgen, and Martha Hopper at Carolina Academic Press for making this book a reality.

Permissions

"The Ones Who Walk Away From Omelas" by Ursula Le Guin. Copyright 1973, 2001 by Ursula K. Le Guin. First appeared in *The Winds Twelve Quarters: From New Dimensions* #3. Reprinted by permission of the author and the author's agents.

"The Treatment of Bibi Haldar" from *Interpreter of Maladies* by Jhumpa Lahiri. Copyright 1999 by Jhumpa Lahiri. Reprinted by permission of Houghton Mifflin Harcourt Publishing Company. All rights reserved.

"The Texas School for the Blind" from *Dogwalker* by Arthur Bradford, copyright 2001 by Arthur Bradford. Used by permission of Alfred A. Knopf, a division of Random House, Inc.

from *Tears of the Giraffe* by Alexander McCall Smith, copyright by Alexander McCall Smith. Used by permission of Random House, Inc.

from *The Maytrees*, copyright 2007 by Annie Dillard. Reprinted by permission of HarperCollins publishers.

from *The Bell Jar* by Sylvia Plath, copyright by Sylvia Plath. Reprinted by permission of HarperCollins publishers.

from *Icy Sparks* by Gwyn Hyman Rubio, copyright 1998 by Gwyn Hyman Rubio. Used by permission of Viking Penguin, a division of Penguin Group (USA) Inc.

from *The Speed of Dark* by Elizabeth Moon, copyright 2002 by Elizabeth Moon. Used by permission of Ballantine Books, a division of Random House, Inc.

"Too Late To Die Young" from *Too Late to Die Young*. Copyright 2005 by Harriet McBryde Johnson. Reprinted by permission of Henry Holt and Company, LLC.

"Politics" from the book *Always Looking Up* by Michael J. Fox. Copyright 2009 Michael J. Fox. Reprinted by permission of Hyperion. All rights reserved.

"Public Transit" and "Fear of Bees" from *Moving Violations* by John Hockenberry. Copyright 1995 by John Hockenberry. Reprinted by permission of Hyperion. All rights reserved.

"First Words" by Jennifer Graf Groneberg. Originally published by Woodbine House.

"How Mya Saved Jacob" by Kate Silver. Used with permission of the author.

Introduction

As a disability law attorney and the sister of someone with Down Syndrome, I love to read about disability. This book contains some of my favorite works. Each selection is preceded by a short author biography and is followed by a list of possible discussion questions and further readings. The bibliography at the end of the book contains full citations for each selection in the main text and for each work cited in the "For Further Reading" sections.

I welcome your comments about the book, and invite your suggestions for additional discussion questions and further readings.

Christy Thompson Ibrahim, J.D.

An Anthology of
Disability Literature

The Yellow Wallpaper

It is very seldom that mere ordinary people like John and myself secure ancestral halls for the summer.

A colonial mansion, a hereditary estate, I would say a haunted house, and reach the height of romantic felicity—but that would be asking too much of fate!

Still I will proudly declare that there is something queer about it.

Else, why should it be let so cheaply? And why have stood so long untenanted?

John laughs at me, of course, but one expects that in marriage.

John is practical in the extreme. He has no patience with faith, an intense horror of superstition, and he scoffs openly at any talk of things not to be felt and seen and put down in figures.

John is a physician, and *perhaps*—(I would not say it to a living soul, of course, but this is dead paper and a great relief to my mind)—*perhaps* that is one reason I do not get well faster.

You see, he does not believe I am sick! And what can one do?

If a physician of high standing, and one's own husband, assures friends and relatives that there is really nothing the matter with one but temporary nervous depression—a slight hysterical tendency—what is one to do?

My brother is also a physician, and also of high standing, and he says the same thing.

So I take phosphates or phosphites—whichever it is, and tonics, and air and exercise, and journeys, and am absolutely forbidden to "work" until I am well again.

Personally, I disagree with their ideas.

Personally, I believe that congenial work, with excitement and change, would do me good.

But what is one to do?

I did write for a while in spite of them; but it *does* exhaust me a good deal—having to be so sly about it, or else meet with heavy opposition.

I sometimes fancy that my condition, if I had less opposition and more society and stimulus—but John says the very worst thing I can do is to think about my condition, and I confess it always makes me feel bad.

So I will let it alone and talk about the house.

The most beautiful place! It is quite alone, standing well back from the road, quite three miles from the village. It makes me think of English places that you read about, for there are hedges and walls and gates that lock, and lots of separate little houses for the gardeners and people.

There is a *delicious* garden! I never saw such a garden—large and shady, full of box-bordered paths, and lined with long grape-covered arbors with seats under them.

There were greenhouses, too, but they are all broken now.

There was some legal trouble, I believe, something about the heirs and co-heirs; anyhow, the place has been empty for years.

That spoils my ghostliness, I am afraid, but I don't care—there is something strange about the house—I can feel it.

I even said so to John one moonlit evening, but he said what I felt was a draught, and shut the window.

I get unreasonably angry with John sometimes. I'm sure I never used to be so sensitive. I think it is due to this nervous condition.

But John says if I feel so, I shall neglect proper self-control; so I take pains to control myself—before him, at least, and that makes me very tired.

I don't like our room a bit. I wanted one downstairs that opened onto the piazza and had roses all over the window, and such pretty old-fashioned chintz hangings! But John would not hear of it.

He said there was only one window and not room for two beds, and no near room for him if he took another.

He is very careful and loving, and hardly lets me stir without special direction.

I have a schedule prescription for each hour in the day; he takes all care from me, and so I feel basely ungrateful not to value it more.

He said we came here solely on my account, that I was to have perfect rest and all the air I could get. "Your exercise depends on your strength, my dear," said he, "and your food somewhat on your appetite; but air you can absorb all the time." So we took the nursery at the top of the house.

It is a big, airy room, the whole floor nearly, with windows that look all ways, and air and sunshine galore. It was nursery first, and then playroom and gymnasium, I should judge, for the windows are barred for little children, and there are rings and things in the walls.

The paint and paper look as if a boys' school had used it. It is stripped off—the paper—in great patches all around the head of my bed, about as far as I can reach, and in a great place on the other side of the room low down. I never saw a worse paper in my life.

One of those sprawling flamboyant patterns committing every artistic sin.

It is dull enough to confuse the eye in following, pronounced enough to constantly irritate and provoke study, and when you follow the lame uncertain curves for a little distance they suddenly commit suicide—plunge off at outrageous angles, destroy themselves in unheard-of contradictions.

The color is repellent, almost revolting: a smoldering unclean yellow, strangely faded by the slow-turning sunlight. It is a dull yet lurid orange in some places, a sickly sulphur tint in others.

No wonder the children hated it! I should hate it myself if I had to live in this room long.

There comes John, and I must put this away—he hates to have me write a word.

We have been here two weeks, and I haven't felt like writing before, since that first day.

I am sitting by the window now, up in this atrocious nursery, and there is nothing to hinder my writing as much as I please, save lack of strength.

John is away all day, and even some nights when his cases are serious.

I am glad my case is not serious!

But these nervous troubles are dreadfully depressing.

John does not know how much I really suffer. He knows there is no reason to suffer, and that satisfies him.

Of course it is only nervousness. It does weigh on me so not to do my duty in any way!

I meant to be such a help to John, such a real rest and comfort, and here I am a comparative burden already!

Nobody would believe what an effort it is to do what little I am able—to dress and entertain, and order things.

It is fortunate Mary is so good with the baby. Such a dear baby!

And yet I *cannot* be with him, it makes me so nervous.

I suppose John never was nervous in his life. He laughs at me so about this wallpaper!

At first he meant to repaper the room, but afterwards he said that I was letting it get the better of me, and that nothing was worse for a nervous patient than to give way to such fancies.

He said that after the wallpaper was changed it would be the heavy bedstead, and then the barred windows, and then that gate at the head of the stairs, and so on.

"You know the place is doing you good," he said, "and really, dear, I don't care to renovate the house just for a three months' rental."

"Then do let us go downstairs," I said, "there are such pretty rooms there."

Then he took me in his arms and called me a blessed little goose, and said he would go down to the cellar, if I wished, and have it whitewashed into the bargain.

But he is right enough about the beds and windows and things.

It is an airy and comfortable room as anyone need wish, and, of course, I would not be so silly as to make him uncomfortable just for a whim.

I'm really getting quite fond of the big room, all but that horrid paper.

Out of one window I can see the garden, those mysterious deep-shaded arbors, the riotous old-fashioned flowers, and bushes and gnarly trees.

Out of another I get a lovely view of the bay and a little private wharf belonging to the estate. There is a beautiful shaded lane that runs down there from the house. I always fancy I see people walking in these numerous paths and arbors, but John has cautioned me not to give way to fancy in the least. He says that with my imaginative power and habit of story-making, a nervous weakness like mine is sure to lead to all manner of excited fancies, and that I ought to use my will and good sense to check the tendency. So I try.

I think sometimes that if I were only well enough to write a little it would relieve the press of ideas and rest me.

But I find I get pretty tired when I try.

It is so discouraging not to have any advice and companionship about my work. When I get really well, John says we will ask Cousin Henry and Julia down for a long visit; but he says he would as soon put fireworks in my pillow-case as to let me have those stimulating people about now.

I wish I could get well faster.

But I must not think about that. This paper looks to me as if it *knew* what a vicious influence it had!

There is a recurrent spot where the pattern lolls like a broken neck and two bulbous eyes stare at you upside down.

I get positively angry with the impertinence of it and the everlastingness. Up and down and sideways they crawl, and those absurd, unblinking eyes are everywhere. There is one place where two breadths didn't match, and the eyes go all up and down the line, one a little higher than the other.

I never saw so much expression in an inanimate thing before, and we all know how much expression they have! I used to lie awake as a child and get more entertainment and terror out of blank walls and plain furniture than most children could find in a toy store.

I remember what a kindly wink the knobs of our big, old bureau used to have, and there was one chair that always seemed like a strong friend.

I used to feel that if any of the other things looked too fierce I could always hop into that chair and be safe.

The furniture in this room is no worse than inharmonious, however, for we had to bring it all from downstairs. I suppose when this was used as a playroom they had to take the nursery things out, and no wonder! I never saw such ravages as the children have made here.

The wallpaper, as I said before, is torn off in spots, and it sticketh closer than a brother—they must have had perseverance as well as hatred.

Then the floor is scratched and gouged and splintered, the plaster itself is dug out here and there, and this great heavy bed, which is all we found in the room, looks as if it had been through the wars.

But I don't mind it a bit—only the paper.

There comes John's sister. Such a dear girl as she is, and so careful of me! I must not let her find me writing.

She is a perfect and enthusiastic housekeeper, and hopes for no better profession. I verily believe she thinks it is the writing which made me sick!

But I can write when she is out, and see her a long way off from these windows.

There is one that commands the road, a lovely shaded winding road, and one that just looks off over the country. A lovely country, too, full of great elms and velvet meadows.

This wallpaper has a kind of sub-pattern in a different shade, a particularly irritating one, for you can only see it in certain lights, and not clearly then.

But in the places where it isn't faded and where the sun is just so—I can see a strange, provoking, formless sort of figure that seems to skulk about behind that silly and conspicuous front design.

There's sister on the stairs!

Well, the Fourth of July is over! The people are gone and I am tired out. John thought it might do me good to see a little company, so we just had mother and Nellie and the children down for a week.

Of course I didn't do a thing. Jennie sees to everything now.

But it tired me all the same.

John says if I don't pick up faster he shall send me to Weir Mitchell in the fall.

But I don't want to go there at all. I had a friend who was in his hands once, and she says he is just like John and my brother, only more so!

Besides, it is such an undertaking to go so far.

I don't feel as if it was worthwhile to turn my hand over for anything, and I'm getting dreadfully fretful and querulous.

I cry at nothing, and cry most of the time.

Of course I don't when John is here, or anybody else, but when I am alone.

And I am alone a good deal just now. John is kept in town very often by serious cases, and Jennie is good and lets me alone when I want her to.

So I walk a little in the garden or down that lovely lane, sit on the porch under the roses, and lie down up here a good deal.

I'm getting really fond of the room in spite of the wallpaper. Perhaps *because* of the wallpaper.

It dwells in my mind so!

I lie here on this great immovable bed—it is nailed down, I believe—and follow that pattern about by the hour. It is as good as gymnastics, I assure you. I start, we'll say, at the bottom, down in the corner over there where it has not been touched, and I determine for the thousandth time that I *will* follow that pointless pattern to some sort of a conclusion.

I know a little of the principle of design, and I know this thing was not arranged on any laws of radiation, or alternation, or repetition, or symmetry, or anything else that I ever heard of.

It is repeated, of course, by the breadths, but not otherwise.

Looked at in one way, each breadth stands alone; the bloated curves and flourishes—a kind of "debased Romanesque" with delirium tremens—go waddling up and down in isolated columns of fatuity.

But, on the other hand, they connect diagonally, and the sprawling outlines run off in great slanting waves of optic horror, like a lot of wallowing seaweeds in full chase.

The whole thing goes horizontally, too, at least it seems so, and I exhaust myself trying to distinguish the order of its going in that direction.

They have used a horizontal breadth for a frieze, and that adds wonderfully to the confusion.

There is one end of the room where it is almost intact, and there, when the crosslights fade and the low sun shines directly upon it, I can almost fancy radiation after all—the interminable grotesque seems to form around a common center and rush off in headlong plunges of equal distraction.

It makes me tired to follow it. I will take a nap, I guess.

I don't know why I should write this.

I don't want to.

I don't feel able.

And I know John would think it absurd. But I *must* say what I feel and think in some way—it is such a relief!

But the effort is getting to be greater than the relief.

Half the time now I am awfully lazy, and lie down ever so much. John says I mustn't lose my strength, and has me take cod liver oil and lots of tonics and things, to say nothing of ale and wine and rare meat.

Dear John! He loves me very dearly, and hates to have me sick. I tried to have a real earnest reasonable talk with him the other day, and tell him how I wish he would let me go and make a visit to Cousin Henry and Julia.

But he said I wasn't able to go, nor able to stand it after I got there; and I did not make out a very good case for myself, for I was crying before I had finished.

It is getting to be a great effort for me to think straight. Just this nervous weakness, I suppose.

And dear John gathered me up in his arms, and just carried me upstairs and laid me on the bed, and sat by me and read to me till it tired my head.

He said I was his darling and his comfort and all he had, and that I must take care of myself for his sake, and keep well.

He says no one but myself can help me out of it, that I must use my will and self-control and not let any silly fancies run away with me.

There's one comfort—the baby is well and happy, and does not have to occupy this nursery with the horrid wallpaper.

If we had not used it, that blessed child would have! What a fortunate escape! Why, I wouldn't have a child of mine, an impressionable little thing, live in such a room for worlds. I never thought of it before, but it is lucky that John kept me here after all; I can stand it so much easier than a baby, you see. Of course I never mention it to them any more—I am too wise—but I keep watch for it all the same.

There are things in that paper that nobody knows but me, or ever will.

Behind that outside pattern the dim shapes get clearer every day.

It is always the same shape, only very numerous. And it is like a woman stooping down and creeping about behind that pattern. I don't like it a bit. I wonder—I begin to think—I wish John would take me away from here!

It is so hard to talk with John about my case, because he is so wise, and because he loves me so.

But I tried it last night.

It was moonlight. The moon shines in all around just as the sun does. I hate to see it sometimes, it creeps so slowly, and always comes in by one window or another. John was asleep and I hated to waken him, so I kept still and watched the moonlight on that undulating wallpaper till I felt creepy. The faint figure behind seemed to shake the pattern, just as if she wanted to get out.

I got up softly and went to feel and see if the paper *did* move, and when I came back John was awake.

"What is it, little girl?" he said. "Don't go walking about like that—you'll get cold."

I thought it was a good time to talk, so I told him that I really was not gaining here, and that I wished he would take me away.

"Why, darling!" said he. "Our lease will be up in three weeks, and I can't see how to leave before. The repairs are not done at home, and I cannot possibly leave town just now. Of course, if you were in any danger, I could and would, but you really are better, dear, whether you can see it or not. I am a doctor, dear, and I know. You are gaining flesh and color, your appetite is better, I feel really much easier about you."

"I don't weigh a bit more," said I, "nor as much; and my appetite may be better in the evening when you are here, but it is worse in the morning when you are away!"

"Bless her little heart!" said he with a big hug. "She shall be as sick as she pleases! But now let's improve the shining hours by going to sleep, and talk about it in the morning!"

"And you won't go away?" I asked gloomily.

"Why, how can I, dear? It is only three weeks more and then we will take a nice little trip of a few days while Jennie is getting the house ready. Really, dear, you are better!"

"Better in body perhaps—" I began, and stopped short, for he sat up straight and looked at me with such a stern, reproachful look that I could not say another word.

"My darling," said he, "I beg of you, for my sake and for our child's sake, as well as for your own, that you will never for one instant let that idea enter your mind! There is nothing so dangerous, so fascinating, to a temperament like yours. It is a false and foolish fancy. Can you not trust me as a physician when I tell you so?"

So of course I said no more on that score, and we went to sleep before long. He thought I was asleep first, but I wasn't, and lay there for hours trying to decide whether that front pattern and the back pattern really did move together or separately.

On a pattern like this, by daylight, there is a lack of sequence, a defiance of law, that is a constant irritant to a normal mind. The color is hideous enough, and unreliable enough, and infuriating enough, but the pattern is torturing.

You think you have mastered it, but just as you get well underway in following, it turns a back-somersault and there you are. It slaps you in the face, knocks you down, and tramples upon you. It is like a bad dream.

The outside pattern is a florid arabesque, reminding one of a fungus. If you can imagine a toadstool in joints, an interminable string of toadstools, budding and sprouting in endless convolutions—why, that is something like it.

That is, sometimes!

There is one marked peculiarity about this paper, a thing nobody seems to notice but myself, and that is that it changes as the light changes. When the sun shoots in through the east window—I always watch for that first long, straight ray—it changes so quickly that I never can quite believe it.

That is why I watch it always.

By moonlight—the moon shines in all night when there is a moon—I wouldn't know it was the same paper.

At night in any kind of light, in twilight, candlelight, lamplight, and worst of all by moonlight, it becomes bars! The outside pattern I mean, and the woman behind it is as plain as can be. I didn't realize for a long time what the thing was that showed behind, that dim sub-pattern, but now I am quite sure it is a woman. By daylight she is subdued, quiet. I fancy it is the pattern that keeps her so still. It is so puzzling. It keeps me quiet by the hour.

I lie down ever so much now. John says it is good for me, and to sleep all I can.

Indeed he started the habit by making me lie down for an hour after each meal. It is a very bad habit, I am convinced, for you see, I don't sleep. And that cultivates deceit, for I don't tell them I'm awake—oh, no!

The fact is I am getting a little afraid of John.

He seems very queer sometimes, and even Jennie has an inexplicable look.

It strikes me occasionally, just as a scientific hypothesis, that perhaps it is the paper!

I have watched John when he did not know I was looking, and come into the room suddenly on the most innocent excuses, and I've caught him several times *looking at the paper*! And Jennie too.

I caught Jennie with her hand on it once. She didn't know I was in the room, and when I asked her in a quiet, a very quiet voice, with the most restrained manner possible, what she was doing with the paper, she turned around as if she had been caught stealing, and looked quite angry—asked me why I should frighten her so! Then she said that the paper stained everything it touched, that she had found yellow smooches on all my clothes and John's, and she wished we would be more careful! Did not that sound innocent? But I know she was studying that pattern, and I am determined that nobody shall find it out but myself!

Life is very much more exciting now than it used to be. You see, I have something more to expect, to look forward to, to watch. I really do eat better, and am more quiet than I was. John is so pleased to see me improve! He laughed a little the other day, and said I seemed to be flourishing in spite of my wallpaper. I turned it off with a laugh. I had no intention of telling him it was *because* of the wallpaper—he would make fun of me. He might even want to take me away. I don't want to leave now until I have found it out. There is a week more, and I think that will be enough.

I'm feeling so much better!

I don't sleep much at night, for it is so interesting to watch developments; but I sleep a good deal in the daytime. In the daytime it is tiresome and perplexing. There are always new shoots on the fungus, and new shades of yellow all over it. I cannot keep count of them, though I have tried conscientiously.

It is the strangest yellow, that wallpaper! It makes me think of all the yellow things I ever saw—not beautiful ones like buttercups, but old foul, bad yellow things.

But there is something else about that paper—the smell! I noticed it the moment we came into the room, but with so much air and sun it was not bad. Now we have had a week of fog and rain, and whether the windows are open or not, the smell is here.

It creeps all over the house.

I find it hovering in the dining-room, skulking in the parlor, hiding in the hall, lying in wait for me on the stairs.

It gets into my hair.

Even when I go to ride, if I turn my head suddenly and surprise it—there is that smell! Such a peculiar odor, too! I have spent hours in trying to analyze it, to find what it smelled like. It is not bad—at first—and very gentle, but quite the subtlest, most enduring odor I ever met. In this damp weather it is awful. I wake up in the night and find it hanging over me. It used to disturb me at first. I thought seriously of burning the house—to reach the smell. But now I am used to it. The only thing I can think of that it is like is the *color* of the paper! A yellow smell.

There is a very funny mark on this wall, low down, near the mopboard. A streak that runs round the room. It goes behind every piece of furniture, except the bed, a long, straight, even *smooch*, as if it had been rubbed over and over. I wonder how it was done and who did it, and what they did it for. Round and round and round—round and round and round—it makes me dizzy!

I really have discovered something at last. Through watching so much at night, when it changes so, I have finally found out. The front pattern *does* move—and no wonder! The woman behind shakes it! Sometimes I think there are a great many women behind, and sometimes only one, and she crawls around fast, and her crawling shakes it all over. Then in the very bright spots she keeps still, and in the very shady spots she just takes hold of the bars and shakes them hard. And she is all the time trying to climb through. But nobody could climb through that pattern—it strangles so; I think that is why it has so many heads. They get through, and then the pattern strangles them off and turns them upside down, and makes their eyes white! If those heads were covered or taken off it would not be half so bad.

I think that woman gets out in the daytime!

And I'll tell you why—privately—I've seen her! I can see her out of every one of my windows! It is the same woman, I know, for she is always creeping, and most women do not creep by daylight.

I see her on that long road under the trees, creeping along, and when a carriage comes she hides under the blackberry vines. I don't blame her a bit. It must be very humiliating to be caught creeping by daylight!

I always lock the door when I creep by daylight. I can't do it at night, for I know John would suspect something at once.

And John is so queer now, that I don't want to irritate him. I wish he would take another room! Besides, I don't want anybody to get that woman out at night but myself.

I often wonder if I could see her out of all the windows at once. But, turn as fast as I can, I can only see out of one at a time. And though I always see her, she *may* be able to creep faster than I can turn! I have watched her sometimes away off in the open country, creeping as fast as a cloud shadow in a wind.

If only that top pattern could be gotten off from the under one! I mean to try it, little by little.

I have found out another funny thing, but I shan't tell it this time! It does not do to trust people too much.

There are only two more days to get this paper off, and I believe John is beginning to notice. I don't like the look in his eyes. And I heard him ask Jennie a lot of professional questions about me. She had a very good report to give. She said I slept a good deal in the daytime. John knows I don't sleep very well at night, for all I'm so quiet! He asked me all sorts of questions, too, and pretended to be very loving and kind. As if I couldn't see through him! Still, I don't wonder he acts so, sleeping under this paper for three months. It only interests me, but I feel sure John and Jennie are secretly affected by it.

Hurrah! This is the last day, but it is enough. John is to stay in town overnight, and won't be out until this evening. Jennie wanted to sleep with me—the sly thing!—but I told her I should undoubtedly rest better for a night all alone.

That was clever, for really I wasn't alone a bit! As soon as it was moonlight and that poor thing began to crawl and shake the pattern, I got up and ran to help her. I pulled and she shook, I shook and she pulled, and before morning we had peeled off yards of that paper. A strip about as high as my head and half around the room. And then when the sun came and that awful pattern began to laugh at me, I declared I would finish it today! We go away tomorrow, and they are moving all my furniture down again to leave things as they were before.

Jennie looked at the wall in amazement, but I told her merrily that I did it out of pure spite at the vicious thing. She laughed and said she wouldn't mind doing it herself, but I must not get tired.

How she betrayed herself that time!

But I am here, and no person touches this paper but me—not *alive*!

She tried to get me out of the room—it was too patent! But I said it was so quiet and empty and clean now that I believed I would lie down again and sleep all I could; and not to wake me even for dinner—I would call when I woke.

So now she is gone, and the servants are gone, and the things are gone, and there is nothing left but that great bedstead nailed down, with the canvas mattress we found on it.

We shall sleep downstairs tonight, and take the boat home tomorrow.

I quite enjoy the room, now it is bare again.

How those children did tear about here! This bedstead is fairly gnawed! But I must get to work. I have locked the door and thrown the key down into the front path. I don't want to go out, and I don't want to have anybody come in, till John comes.

I want to astonish him.

I've got a rope up here that even Jennie did not find. If that woman does get out, and tries to get away, I can tie her!

But I forgot I could not reach far without anything to stand on!

This bed will *not* move! I tried to lift and push it until I was lame, and then I got so angry I bit off a little piece at one corner—but it hurt my teeth.

Then I peeled off all the paper I could reach standing on the floor. It sticks horribly and the pattern just enjoys it! All those strangled heads and bulbous eyes and waddling fungus growths just shriek with derision!

I am getting angry enough to do something desperate. To jump out of the window would be admirable exercise, but the bars are too strong even to try.

Besides I wouldn't do it. Of course not. I know well enough that a step like that is improper and might be misconstrued.

I don't like to *look* out of the windows even—there are so many of those creeping women, and they creep so fast. I wonder if they all come out of that wallpaper as I did?

But I am securely fastened now by my well-hidden rope—you don't get *me* out in the road there!

I suppose I shall have to get back behind the pattern when it comes night, and that is hard! It is so pleasant to be out in this great room and creep around as I please! I don't want to go outside. I won't, even if Jennie asks me to. For outside you have to creep on the ground, and everything is green instead of yellow. But here I can creep smoothly on the floor, and my shoulder just fits in that long smooch around the wall, so I cannot lose my way.

Why, there's John at the door!

It is no use, young man, you can't open it!

How he does call and pound! Now he's crying to Jennie for an axe.

It would be a shame to break down that beautiful door!

"John dear!" said I in the gentlest voice, "the key is down by the front steps, under a plantain leaf!"

That silenced him for a few moments.

Then he said, very quietly indeed, "Open the door, my darling!"

"I can't," said I. "The key is down by the front door under a plantain leaf!"

And then I said it again, several times, very gently and slowly, and said it so often that he had to go and see, and he got it of course, and came in. He stopped short by the door.

"What is the matter?" he cried. "For God's sake, what are you doing!"

I kept on creeping just the same, but I looked at him over my shoulder.

"I've got out at last," said I, "in spite of you and Jennie. And I've pulled off most of the paper, so you can't put me back!"

Now why should that man have fainted? But he did, and right across my path by the wall, so that I had to creep over him every time!

The Yellow Wallpaper

Questions for discussion

1. What is the main character's own view of her disability? Her husband's view? Which view do you believe is more accurate?

2. Did you like the ending? Was it what you expected? Why or why not? What do you think may have happened after the ending, if the story continued?

3. How has treatment for mental illness changed over time in the United States? In other parts of the world?

4. How does this story handle the issue of stigma? How does mental illness continue to be stigmatized today?

5. What women's issues overlap with disability issues in this story? What does the wallpaper represent?

6. If you were summarizing this story, what would you say?

7. Design your own discussion questions for this story.

For Further Reading

About mental illness and depression

Plath, Sylvia. *The Bell Jar.* A semi-autobiographical book about a young woman who becomes depressed and suicidal.

Kaysen, Susanna. *Girl, Interrupted.* An edgy, semi-autobiographical book about a teenage girl who is institutionalized for mental illness.

Packer, Ann. *Songs Without Words.* Two childhood friends, now adults, try to maintain their friendship throughout various obstacles, including one of the friend's anxiety issues.

Other works by Charlotte Perkins Gilman

You might enjoy *Herland*, her novella about an all-female society. How does this novella deal with disability issues?

Ursula K. Le Guin (1929–   ), a prolific science-fiction writer, has published twenty-one novels, eleven volumes of short stories, three collections of essays, twelve books for children, and six volumes of poetry. She has received many awards including the Hugo, Nebula, National Book Award, and PEN-Malamud. She lives in Portland, Oregon.

The Ones Who Walk Away From Omelas

With a clamor of bells that set the swallows soaring, the Festival of Summer came to the city Omelas, bright-towered by the sea. The ringing of the boats in harbor sparkled with flags. In the streets between houses with red roofs and painted walls, between old moss grown gardens and under avenues of trees, past great parks and public buildings, processions moved. Some were decorous: old people in long stiff robes of mauve and gray, grave master workmen, quiet, merry women carrying their babies and chatting as they walked. In other streets the music beat faster, a shimmering of gong and tambourine, and the people went dancing; the procession was a dance. Children dodged in and out, their high calls rising like the swallows' crossing flights over the music and the singing. All the processions wound towards the north side of the city, where on the great water-meadow called the Green Fields, boys and girls, naked in the bright air, with mud-stained feet and ankles and long, lithe arms, exercised their restive horses before the race. The horses wore no gear at all but a halter without bit. Their manes were braided with streamers of silver, gold, and green. They flared their nostrils and pranced and boasted to one another; they were vastly excited, the horse being the only animal who has adopted our ceremonies as his own.

Far off to the north and west the mountains stood up half encircling Omelas on her bay. The air of morning was so clear that the snow still crowning the Eighteen Peaks burned with white-gold fire across the miles of sunlit air, under the dark blue of the sky. There was just enough wind to make the banners that marked the race course snap and flutter now and then. In the silence of the broad green meadows one could hear the music winding throughout the city streets, farther and nearer and ever approaching, a cheerful faint sweetness of the air from time to time trembled and gathered together and broke out into the great joyous clanging of the bells.

Joyous! How is one to tell about joy? How describe the citizens of Omelas?

They were not simple folk, you see, though they were happy. But we do not say the words of cheer much anymore. All smiles have become archaic. Given a description such as this one tends to make certain assumptions. Given a description such as this one tends to look next for the king, mounted on a splendid stallion and surrounded by his noble knights, or perhaps in a golden litter borne by great-muscled slaves. But there was no king. They did not use swords, or keep slaves. They were not barbarians; I do not know the rules and laws of their society, but I suspect that they were singularly few. As they did without monarchy and slavery, so they also got on without the stock exchange, the advertisement, the secret police, and the bomb. Yet I repeat that these were not simple folk, not dulcet shepherds, noble savages, bland utopians. They were not less complex than us.

The trouble is that we have a bad habit, encouraged by pedants and sophisticates, of considering happiness as something rather stupid. Only pain is intellectual, only evil interesting. This is the treason of the artist: a refusal to admit the banality of evil and the terrible boredom of pain. If you can't lick 'em, join 'em. If it hurts, repeat it. But to praise despair is to condemn delight, to embrace violence is to lose hold of everything else. We have almost lost hold; we can no longer describe happy man, nor make any celebration of joy.

How can I tell you about the people of Omelas? They were not naive and happy children—though their children were, in fact, happy. They were mature, intelligent, passionate adults whose lives were not wretched. O miracle! But I wish I could describe it better. I wish I could convince you. Omelas sounds in my words like a city in a fairy tale, long ago and far away, once upon a time. Perhaps it would be best if you imagined it as your own fancy bids, assuming it will rise to the occasion, for certainly I cannot suit you all.

For instance, how about technology? I think that there would be no cars or helicopters in and above the streets; this follows from the fact that the people of Omelas are happy people. Happiness is based on a just discrimination of what is necessary, what is neither necessary nor destructive, and what is destructive. In the middle category, however—that of the unnecessary but undestructive, that of comfort, luxury, exuberance, etc.—they could perfectly well have central heating, subway trains, washing machines, and all kinds of marvelous devices not yet invented here, floating light-sources, fuelless power, a cure for the common cold. Or they could have none of that: it doesn't matter. As you like it. I incline to think that people from towns up and down the coast have been coming to Omelas during the last days before the Festival on very fast little trains and double-decked trams, and that the train station of Omelas is actually the handsomest building in town, though plainer than the magnificent Farmers' Market. But even granted trains, I fear that Omelas so far strikes some of you as goody-goody. Smiles, bells, parades, horses, bleh. If so, please add an orgy. If an orgy would help, don't hesitate. Let us not, however, have temples from which issue beautiful nude priests and priestesses already half in ecstasy and ready to copulate with any man or woman, lover or stranger, who desires union with the deep godhead of the blood, although that was my first idea. But really it would be better not to have any temples in Omelas—at least, not manned temples. Religion yes, clergy no. Surely the beautiful nudes can just wander about, offering themselves like divine souffles to the hunger of the needy and the rapture of the flesh. Let them join the processions. Let tambourines be struck above the copulations, and the glory of desire be proclaimed upon the gongs, and (a not unimportant point) let the offspring of these delightful rituals be beloved and looked after by all. One thing I know there is none of in Omelas is guilt.

But what else should there be? I thought at first there were no drugs, but that is puritanical. For those who like it, the faint insistent sweetness of drooz may perfume the ways of the city, drooz which first brings a great lightness and brilliance to the mind and limbs, and then after some hours a dreamy languor, and wonderful visions at last of the very arcane and inmost secrets of the Universe, as well as exciting the pleasure of sex beyond all belief; and it is not habit-forming. For more modest tastes I think there ought to be beer. What else, what else belongs in the joyous city? The sense of victory, surely, the celebration of courage. But as we did without clergy, let us do without soldiers. The joy built upon successful slaughter is not the right kind of joy; it will not do; it is fearful and it is trivial. A boundless and generous contentment, a magnanimous triumph felt not against some outer enemy but in communion with the finest and fairest in the souls of all men everywhere and the splendor of the world's summer: this is what swells the hearts of the people of Omelas, and the victory they celebrate is that of life. I don't think many of them need to take drooz.

Most of the processions have reached the Green Fields by now. A marvelous smell of cooking goes forth from the red and blue tents of the provisioners. The faces of small children are amiably sticky; in the benign gray beard of a man a couple of crumbs of rich pastry are entangled. The youths and girls have mounted their horses and are beginning to group around the starting line of the course. An old woman, small, fat, and laughing, is passing out flowers from a basket, and tall young men wear her flowers in their shining hair. A child of nine or ten sits at the edge of the crowd alone, playing on a wooden flute.

People pause to listen, and they smile, but they do not speak to him, for he never ceases playing and never sees them, his dark eyes wholly rapt in the sweet, thin magic of the tune. He finishes, and slowly lowers his hands holding the wooden flute. As if that little private silence were the signal, all at once a trumpet sounds from the pavilion near the starting line: imperious, melancholy, piercing. The horses rear on their slender legs, and some of them neigh in answer. Sober-faced, the young riders stroke the horses' necks and soothe them, whispering. "Quiet, quiet, there my beauty, my hope …" They begin to form in rank along the starting line. The crowds along the racecourse are like a field of grass and flowers in the wind. The Festival of Summer has begun.

Do you believe? Do you accept the festival, the city, the joy? No? Then let me describe one more thing.

In a basement under one of the beautiful public buildings of Omelas, or perhaps in the cellar of one of its spacious private homes, there is a room. It has one locked door, and no window. A little light seeps in dustily between cracks in the boards, secondhand from a cobwebbed window somewhere across the cellar. In one corner of the little room a couple of mops, with stiff, clotted, foul-smelling heads, stand near a rusty bucket. The floor is dirt, a little damp to the touch, as cellar dirt usually is.

The room is about three paces long and two wide: a mere broom closet or disused tool room. In the room, a child is sitting. It could be a boy or a girl. It looks about six, but actually is nearly ten. It is feeble-minded. Perhaps it was born defective, or perhaps it has become imbecile through fear, malnutrition, and neglect. It picks its nose and occasionally fumbles vaguely with its toes or genitals, as it sits hunched in the corner farthest from the bucket and the two mops. It is afraid of the mops. It finds them horrible. It shuts its eyes, but it knows the mops are still standing there; and the door is locked; and nobody will come. The door is always locked; and nobody ever comes, except that sometimes—the child has no understanding of time or interval—sometimes the door rattles terribly and opens, and a person, or several people, are there. One of them may come in and kick the child to make it stand up. The others never come close, but peer in at it with frightened, disgusted eyes. The food bowl and the water jug are hastily filled, the door is locked; the eyes disappear. The people at the door never say anything, but the child, who has not always lived in the tool room, and can remember sunlight and its mother's voice, sometimes speaks. "I will be good," it says. "Please let me out. I will be good!" They never answer. The child used to scream for help at night, and cry a good deal, but now it only makes a kind of whining, "eh-haa, eh-haa," and it speaks less and less often. It is so thin there are no calves to its legs; its belly protrudes; it lives on a half-bowl of corn meal and grease a day. It is naked. Its buttocks and thighs are a mass of festered sores, as it sits in its own excrement continually.

They all know it is there, all the people of Omelas. Some of them have come to see it, others are content merely to know it is there. They all know that it has to be there. Some of them understand why, and some do not, but they all understand that their happiness, the beauty of their city, the tenderness of their friendships, the health of their children, the wisdom of their scholars, the skill of their makers, even the abundance of their harvest and the kindly weathers of their skies, depend wholly on this child's abominable misery.

This is usually explained to children when they are between eight and twelve, whenever they seem capable of understanding; and most of those who come to see the child are young people, though often enough an adult comes, or comes back, to see the child. No matter how well the matter has been explained to them, these young spectators are always shocked and sickened at the sight. They feel disgust, which they had thought themselves superior to. They feel anger, outrage, impotence, despite all the explanations. They would like to do something for the child. But there is nothing they can do. If the child were brought up into the sunlight out of that vile place, if it were cleaned and fed and comforted, that would be a good thing, indeed; but if it were done, in that day and hour all the prosperity and beauty and delight of Omelas would wither and be destroyed. Those are the terms. To exchange all the goodness and grace of every life in Omelas for that single, small improvement: to throw away the happiness of thousands for the chance of happiness of one: that would be to let guilt within the walls indeed.

The terms are strict and absolute; there may not even be a kind word spoken to the child.

Often the young people go home in tears, or in a tearless rage, when they have seen the child and faced this terrible paradox. They may brood over it for weeks or years. But as time goes on they begin to realize that even if the child could be released, it would not get much good of its freedom: a little vague pleasure of warmth and food, no real doubt, but little more. It is too degraded and imbecile to know any real joy. It has been afraid too long ever to be free of fear. Its habits are too uncouth for it to respond to humane treatment. Indeed, after so long it would probably be wretched without walls about it to protect it, and darkness for its eyes, and its own excrement to sit in. Their tears at the bitter injustice dry when they begin to perceive the terrible justice of reality, and to accept it. Yet it is their tears and anger, the trying of their generosity and the acceptance of their helplessness, which are perhaps the true source of the splendor of their lives. Theirs is no vapid, irresponsible happiness. They know that they, like the child, are not free. They know compassion. It is the existence of the child, and their knowledge of its existence, that makes possible the nobility of their architecture, the poignancy of their music, the profundity of their science. It is because of the child that they are so gentle with children. They know that if the wretched one were not there sniveling in the dark, the other one, the flute-player, could make no joyful music as the young riders line up in their beauty for the race in the sunlight of the first morning of summer.

Now do you believe them? Are they not more credible? But there is one more thing to tell, and this is quite incredible.

At times one of the adolescent girls or boys who go see the child does not go home to weep or rage, does not, in fact, go home at all. Sometimes also a man or a woman much older falls silent for a day or two, then leaves home. These people go out into the street, and walk down the street alone. They keep walking, and walk straight out of the city of Omelas, through the beautiful gates. They keep walking across the farmlands of Omelas. Each one goes alone, youth or girl, man or woman. Night falls; the traveler must pass down village streets, between the houses with yellow-lit windows, and on out into the darkness of the fields. Each alone, they go west or north, towards the mountains. They go on. They leave Omelas, they walk ahead into the darkness, and they do not come back. The place they go towards is a place even less imaginable to most of us than the city of happiness. I cannot describe it at all. It is possible that it does not exist. But they seem to know where they are going, the ones who walk away from Omelas.

The Ones Who Walk Away From Omelas

Questions for discussion

1. Why do some people walk away from Omelas?

2. What does the child with a disability represent? Why do you think the author chose a disabled child for this character in the story?

3. Would you like to live in Omelas?

4. Why are the only alternatives to stay and accept the situation, or to walk away?

5. What do you think of the paragraph that says that after people visit the child, they realize that the child would not "get much good of its freedom" anyway? What assumptions do non-disabled people sometimes make about quality of life for people with disabilities? What do you think of the section later in that same paragraph that says the child has taught them compassion?

6. Design your own discussion questions for this story.

For Further Reading

About fictional societies with disability themes

Moon, Elizabeth. *The Speed of Dark.* A futuristic novel about a possible cure for autism and the narrator's dilemma: to cure or not to cure?

Wells, H.G. "Country of the Blind." A short story about a traveler who encounters a society where everyone is blind.

Other works by Ursula Le Guin

You might enjoy her book *The Lathe of Heaven,* about a man who has dreams that come true and change his society. As his society becomes more and more "pure," is it really a better place to live? How would disability issues figure in that society?

Jhumpa Lahiri (1967–) was born in London and grew up in Rhode Island. She has traveled several times to India, where both her parents were born and raised, and where a number of her stories are set. Lahiri received her B.A. from Barnard College; and from Boston University she has received an M.A. in English, an M.A. in Creative Writing, an M.A. in Comparative Studies in Literature and the Arts, and a Ph.D. in Renaissance Studies. She has taught creative writing at Boston University and the Rhode Island School of Design and has been a fellow at the Fine Arts Work Center in Provincetown, Massachusetts.

She has written two collections of short stories and a novel. Her first collection, *The Interpreter of Maladies*, which contains the Bibi Haldar story, won the Pulitzer Prize.

The Treatment of Bibi Haldar

For the greater number of her twenty-nine years, Bibi Haldar suffered from an ailment that baffled family, friends, priests, palmists, spinsters, gem therapists, prophets, and fools. In efforts to cure her, concerned members of our town brought her holy water from seven holy rivers. When we heard her screams and throes in the night, when her wrists were bound with ropes and stinging poultices pressed upon her, we named her in our prayers. Wise men had massaged eucalyptus balm into her temples, steamed her face with herbal infusions. At the suggestion of a blind Christian she was once taken by train to kiss the tombs of saints and martyrs. Amulets warding against the evil eye girded her arms and neck. Auspicious stones adorned her fingers.

Treatments offered by doctors only made matters worse. Allopaths, homeopaths, ayurvedics—over time, all branches of the medical arts had been consulted. Their advice was endless. After x-rays, probes, auscultations, and injections, some advised Bibi to gain weight, others to lose it. If one forbade her to sleep beyond dawn, another insisted she remain in bed till noon. This one told her to perform headstands, that one to chant Vedic verses at specified intervals throughout the day. "Take her to Calcutta for hypnosis," was a suggestion others would offer. Shuttled from one specialist to the next, the girl had been prescribed to shun garlic, consume disproportionate quantities of bitters, meditate, drink green coconut water, and swallow raw duck's eggs beaten

25

in milk. In short, Bibi's life was an encounter with one fruitless antidote after another.

The nature of her illness, which struck without warning, confined her world to the unpainted four-story building in which her only local family, an elder cousin and his wife, rented an apartment on the second floor. Liable to fall unconscious and enter, at any moment, into a shameless delirium, Bibi could be trusted neither to cross a street nor board a tram without supervision. Her daily occupation consisted of sitting in the storage room on the roof of our building, a space in which one could sit but not comfortably stand, featuring an adjoining latrine, a curtained entrance, one window without a grille, and shelves made from the panels of old doors. There, cross-legged on a square of jute, she recorded inventory for the cosmetics shop that her cousin Haldar owned and managed at the mouth of our courtyard. For her services, Bibi received no income but was given meals, provisions, and sufficient meters of cotton at every October holiday to replenish her wardrobe at an inexpensive tailor. At night she slept on a folding camp cot in the cousin's place downstairs.

In the mornings Bibi arrived in the storage room wearing cracked plastic slippers and a housecoat whose hem stopped some inches below the knee, a length we had not worn since we were fifteen. Her shins were hairless, and sprayed with a generous number of pallid freckles. She bemoaned her fate and challenged her stars as we hung our laundry or scrubbed scales from our fish. She was not pretty. Her upper lip was thin, her teeth too small. Her gums protruded when she spoke. "I ask you, is it fair for a girl to sit out her years, pass neglected through her prime, listing labels and prices without promise of a future?" Her voice was louder than necessary, as if she were speaking to a deaf person. "Is it wrong to envy you, all brides and mothers, busy with lives and cares? Wrong to want to shade my eyes, scent my hair? To raise a child and teach him sweet from sour, good from bad?"

Each day she unloaded her countless privations upon us, until it became unendurably apparent that Bibi wanted a man. She wanted to be spoken for, protected, placed on her path in life. Like the rest of us, she wanted to serve suppers, and scold servants, and set aside money in her *almari* to have her eyebrows threaded every three weeks at the Chinese beauty parlor. She pestered us for details of our own weddings: the jewels, the invitations, the scent of tuberoses strung over the nuptial bed. When, at her insistence, we showed our photo albums embossed with the designs of butterflies, she pored over the snapshots that chronicled the ceremony: butter poured in fires, garlands exchanged, vermilion-painted fish, trays of shells and silver coins. "An impressive number of guests," she would observe, stroking with her finger the misplaced faces that had surrounded us. "When it happens to me, you will all be present."

Anticipation began to plague her with such ferocity that the thought of a husband, on which all her hopes were pinned, threatened at times to send her into another attack. Amid tins of talc and boxes of bobby pins she would curl up on the floor of the storage room, speaking in non sequiturs. "I will never dip my feet in milk," she whimpered. "My face will never be painted with sandalwood paste. Who will rub me with tumeric? My name will never be printed with scarlet ink on a card."

Her soliloquies mawkish, her sentiments maudlin, malaise dripped like a fever from her pores. In her most embittered moments we wrapped her in shawls, washed her face from the cistern tap, and brought her glasses of yogurt and rosewater. In moments when she was less disconsolate, we encouraged her to accompany us to the tailor and replenish her blouses and petticoats, in part to provide her with a change of scenery, and in part because we thought it might increase whatever matrimonial prospects she had. "No man wants a woman who dresses like a dishwasher," we told her. "Do you want all that fabric of yours to go to the moths?" She sulked, pouted, protested, and sighed. "Where do I go, who would I dress for?" she demanded. "Who takes me to the cinema, the zoo-garden, buys me lime soda and cashews? Admit it, are these concerns of mine? I will never be cured, never married."

But then a new treatment was prescribed for Bibi, the most outrageous of them all. One evening on her way to dinner, she collapsed on the third-floor landing, pounding her fists, kicking her feet, sweating buckets, lost to this world. Her moans echoed throughout the stairwell, and we rushed out of our apartments to calm her at once, bearing palm fans and sugar cubes, and tumblers of refrigerated water to pour on her head. Our children clung to the banisters and witnessed her paroxysm; our servants were sent to summon her cousin. It was ten minutes before Haldar emerged from his shop, impassive apart from the red in his face. He told us to stop fussing, and then with no efforts to repress his disdain he packed her into a rickshaw bound for the polyclinic. It was there, after performing a series of blood tests, that the doctor in charge of Bibi's case, exasperated, concluded that a marriage would cure her.

News spread between our window bars, across our clotheslines, and over the pigeon droppings that plastered the parapets of our rooftops. By the next morning, three separate palmists had examined Bibi's hand and confirmed that there was, no doubt, evidence of an imminent union etched into her skin. Unsavory sorts murmured indelicacies at cutlet stands; grandmothers consulted almanacs to determine a propitious hour for the betrothal. For days afterward, as we walked our children to school, picked up our cleaning, stood in lines at the ration shop, we whispered. Apparently some activity was what the poor girl needed all along. For the first time we imagined the contours below her housecoat, and attempted to appraise the pleasures she could offer a man. For the first time we noted the clarity of her complexion, the length and languor of her eyelashes, the undeniably elegant armature of her hands. "They say it's the only hope. A case of overexcitement. They say"—and here we paused, blushing—"relations will calm her blood."

Needless to say, Bibi was delighted by the diagnosis, and began at once to prepare for conjugal life. With some damaged merchandise from Haldar's shop she polished her toenails and softened her elbows. Neglecting the new shipments delivered to the storage room, she began hounding us for recipes, for vermicelli pudding and papaya stew, and inscribed them in crooked letters in the pages of her inventory ledger. She made guest lists, dessert lists, listed lands in which she intended to honeymoon. She applied glycerine to smooth her lips, resisted sweets to reduce her measurements. One day she asked one of us to accompany her to the tailor, who stitched her a new *salwar-kameez* in an umbrella cut, the fashion that season. On the streets she dragged us to the counters of each and every jeweler, peering into glass cases, seeking our opinions of tiara designs and locket settings. In the windows of sari shops she pointed to a magenta Benarasi silk, and a turquoise one, and then one that was the color of marigolds. "The first part of the ceremony I will wear this one, then this one, then this."

But Haldar and his wife thought otherwise. Immune to her fancies, indifferent to our fears, they conducted business as usual, stuffed together in that cosmetic shop no bigger than a wardrobe, whose walls were crammed on three sides with hennas, hair oils, pumice stones, and fairness creams. "We have little time for indecent suggestions," replied Haldar to those who broached the subject of Bibi's health. "What won't be cured must be endured. Bibi has caused enough worry, added enough to expenses, sullied enough the family name." His wife, seated beside him behind the tiny glass counter, fanned the mottled skin above her breasts and agreed. She was a heavy woman whose powder, a shade too pale for her, caked in the creases of her throat. "Besides, who would marry her? The girl knows nothing about anything, speaks backward, is practically thirty, can't light a coal stove, can't boil rice, can't tell the difference between fennel and a cumin seed. Imagine her attempting to feed a man!"

They had a point. Bibi had never been taught to be a woman; the illness had left her naive in most practical matters. Haldar's wife, convinced that the devil himself possessed her, kept Bibi away from fire and flame. She had not been taught to wear a sari without pinning it in four different places, nor could she embroider slipcovers or crochet shawls with any exceptional talent. She was not allowed to watch the television (Haldar assumed its electronic properties would excite her), and was thus ignorant of the events and entertainments of our world. Her formal studies had ended after the ninth standard.

For Bibi's sake we argued in favor of finding a husband. "It's what she's wanted all along," we pointed out. But Haldar and his wife were impossible to reason with. Their rancor toward Bibi was fixed on their lips, thinner than the strings with which they tied our purchases. When we maintained that the new treatment deserved a chance, they contended, "Bibi possesses insufficient quantities of respect and self-control. She plays up her malady for the attention. The best thing is to keep her occupied, away from the trouble she invariably creates."

"Why not marry her off, then? It will get her off your hands, at least."

"And waste our profits on a wedding? Feeding guests, ordering bracelets, buying a bed, assembling a dowry?"

But Bibi's gripes persisted. Late one morning, dressed under our supervision in a sari of lavender eyelet chiffon and mirrored slippers lent to her for the occasion, she hastened in uneven steps to Haldar's shop and insisted on being taken to the photographer's studio so that her portrait, like those of other brides-in waiting, could be circulated in the homes of eligible men. Through the shutters of our balconies we watched her; perspiration had already left black moons beneath her armpits. "Apart from my x-rays I have never been photographed," she fretted. "Potential in-laws need to know what I look like." But Haldar refused. He said that anyone who wished to see her could observe her for themselves, weeping and wailing and warding off customers. She was a bane for business, he told her, a liability and a loss. Who in this town needed a photo to know that?

The next day Bibi stopped listing inventory altogether and regaled us, instead, with imprudent details about Haldar and his wife. "On Sundays he plucks hairs from her chin. They keep their money refrigerated under lock and key." For the benefit of neighboring rooftops she strutted and shrieked; with each proclamation her audience expanded. "In the bath she applies chickpea flour to her arms because she thinks it will make her paler. The third toe on her right foot is missing. The reason they take such long siestas is that she is impossible to please."

To get her to quiet down, Haldar placed a one-line advertisement in the town newspaper, in order to solicit a groom: "GIRL, UNSTABLE, HEIGHT 152 CENTIMETERS, SEEKS HUSBAND." The identity of the prospective bride was no secret to the parents of our young men, and no family was willing to shoulder so blatant a risk. Who could blame them? It was rumored by many that Bibi conversed with herself in a fluent but totally incomprehensible language, and slept without dreams. Even the lonely four-toothed widower who repaired our handbags in the market could not be persuaded to propose. Nevertheless, to distract her, we began to coach her in wifely ways. "Frowning like a rice pot will get you nowhere. Men require that you caress them with your expression." As practice for the event of encountering a possible suitor, we urged her to engage in small conversations with nearby men. When the water bearer arrived, at the end of his rounds, to fill Bibi's urn in the storage room, we instructed her to say "How do you do?" When the coal supplier unloaded his baskets on the roof, we advised her to smile and make a comment about the weather. Recalling our own experiences, we prepared her for an interview. "Most likely the groom will arrive with one parent, a grandparent, and either an uncle or aunt. They will stare, ask several questions. They will examine the bottoms of your feet, the thickness of your braid. They will ask you to name the prime minister, recite poetry, feed a dozen hungry people on half a dozen eggs."

When two months had passed without a single reply to the advertisement, Haldar and his wife felt vindicated. "Now do you see that she is unfit to marry? Now do you see no man of sane mind would touch her?"

Things had not been so bad for Bibi before her father died. (The mother had not survived beyond the birth of the girl.) In his final years, the old man, a teacher of mathematics in our elementary schools, had kept assiduous track of Bibi's illness in hopes of determining some logic to her condition. "To every problem there is a solution," he would reply whenever we inquired after his progress. He reassured Bibi. For a time he reassured us all. He wrote letters to doctors in England, spent his evenings reading casebooks at the library, gave up eating meat on Fridays in order to appease his household god. Eventually he gave up teaching as well, tutoring only from his room, so that he could monitor Bibi at all hours. But though in his youth he had received prizes for his ability to deduce square roots from memory, he was unable to solve the mystery of his daughter's disease. For all his work, his records led him to conclude only that Bibi's attacks occurred more frequently in summer than winter, and that she had suffered approximately twenty-five major attacks in all. He created a chart of her symptoms with directions for calming her, and distributed it throughout the neighborhood, but these were eventually lost, or turned into sailboats by our children, or used to calculate grocery budgets on the reverse side.

Apart from keeping her company, apart from soothing her woes, apart from keeping an occasional eye on her, there was little we could do to improve the situation. None of us were capable of understanding such desolation. Some days, after siesta, we combed out her hair, remembering now and then to change the part in her scalp so that it would not grow too broad.

At her request we powdered the down over her lips and throat, penciled definition into her brows, and walked her to the banks of the fish pond where our children played cricket in the afternoon. She was still determined to lure a man.

"Apart from my condition I am perfectly healthy," she maintained, seating herself on a bench along the footpath where courting men and women strolled hand in hand. "I have never had a cold or flu. I have never had jaundice. I have never suffered from colic or indigestion." Sometimes we brought her smoked corn on the cob sprinkled with lemon juice, or two *paisa* caramels. We consoled her; when she was convinced a man was giving her the eye, we humored her and agreed. But she was not our responsibility, and in our private moments we were thankful for it.

In November we learned that Haldar's wife was pregnant. That morning in the storage room, Bibi wept. "She says I'm contagious, like the pox. She says I'll spoil the baby." She was breathing heavily, her pupils fixed to a peeling spot on the wall. "What will become of me?" There was still no response to the advertisement in the newspaper. "Is it not punishment enough that I bear this curse alone? Must I also be blamed for infecting another?" Dissent within the Haldar household grew. The wife, convinced that Bibi's presence would infect the unborn child, began to wrap woolen shawls around her tumid belly. In the bathroom Bibi was given separate soaps and towels. According to the scullery maid, Bibi's plates were not washed with the others.

And then one afternoon, without word or warning, it happened again. On the banks of the fish pond, Bibi fell to the footpath. She shook. She shuddered. She chewed her lips. A group encircled the convulsing girl at once, eager to assist in whatever way possible. The opener of soda bottles pinned down her thrashing limbs. The vendor of sliced cucumbers attempted to unclasp her fingers. One of us doused her with water from the pond. Another wiped her mouth with a perfumed handkerchief. The seller of jackfruits was holding Bibi's head, which struggled to toss from side to side. And the man who cranked the sugarcane press gripped the palm fan that he ordinarily used to chase away flies, agitating the air from every conceivable angle.

"Is there a doctor in the crowd?"

"Watch that she doesn't swallow her tongue."

"Has anyone informed Haldar?"

"She's hotter than coals!"

In spite of our efforts, the tumult persisted. Wrestling with her adversary, wracked with anguish, she ground her teeth and twitched at the knees. Over two minutes had passed. We watched and worried. We wondered what to do.

"Leather!" someone cried suddenly. "She needs to smell leather." Then we remembered; the last time it had happened, a cowhide sandal held under her nostrils was what had finally freed Bibi from the clutches of her torment.

"Bibi, what happened? Tell us what happened," we asked when she opened her eyes.

"I felt hot, then hotter. Smoke passed before my eyes. The world went black. Didn't you see it?"

A group of our husbands escorted her home. Dusk thickened, conch shells were blown, and the air grew dense with the incense of prayers. Bibi muttered and staggered but said nothing. Her cheeks were bruised and nicked here and there. Her hair was matted, her elbows caked with dirt, and a small piece of one front tooth was missing. We followed behind, at what we assumed to be safe distances, holding our children by the hand.

She needed a blanket, a compress, a sedative tablet. She needed supervision. But when we reached the courtyard Haldar and his wife would not have her in the flat.

"The medical risk is too great for an expectant mother to be in contact with an hysterical person," he insisted.

That night Bibi slept in the storage room.

Their baby, a girl, was delivered by forceps at the end of June. By then Bibi was sleeping downstairs again, though they kept her camp cot in the corridor, and would not let her touch the child directly. Every day they sent her to the roof to record inventory until lunch, at which point Haldar brought her receipts from the morning's sales and a bowl of yellow split peas for her lunch. At night she ate milk and bread alone in the stairwell. Another seizure, and another, went unchecked.

When we voiced our concern, Haldar said it was not our business, and flatly refused to discuss the matter. To express our indignation we began to take our shopping elsewhere; this provided us with our only revenge. Over the weeks the products on Haldar's shelves grew dusty. Labels faded and colognes turned rank. Passing by in the evenings, we saw Haldar sitting alone, swatting moths with the sole of his slipper. We hardly saw the wife at all. According to the scullery maid she was still bedridden; apparently her labor had been complicated.

Autumn came, with its promise of the October holidays, and the town grew busy shopping and planning for the season. Film songs blared from amplifiers strung through trees. Arcades and markets stayed open all hours. We bought our children balloons and colored ribbons, purchased sweetmeats by the kilo, paid calls in taxis to relatives we had not seen throughout the year. The days grew shorter, the evenings colder. We buttoned our sweaters and pulled up our socks. Then a chill set in that made our throats itch. We made our children gargle with warm saltwater and wrap mufflers around their necks. But it was the Haldar baby who ended up getting sick.

A doctor was summoned in the middle of the night and commanded to reduce the fever. "Cure her," the wife pleaded. Her shrill commotion had woken us all. "We can give you anything, just cure my baby girl." The doctor prescribed a glucose formula, crushed aspirins in a mortar, and told them to wrap the child with quilts and covers.

Five days later the fever had not budged.

"It's Bibi," the wife wailed. "She's done it, she's infected our child. We should never have let her back down here. We should never have let her back into this house."

And so Bibi started to spend her nights in the storage room again. At the wife's insistence Haldar even moved her camp cot up there, along with a tin trunk that contained her belongings. Her meals were left covered with a colander at the top of the stairs.

"I don't mind," Bibi told us. "It's better to live apart from them, to set up house on my own." She unpacked the trunk—some housecoats, a framed portrait of her father, sewing supplies, and an assortment of fabrics—and arranged her things on a few empty shelves. By the week's end the baby had recuperated, but Bibi was not asked to return downstairs. "Don't worry, it's not as if they've locked me in here," she said in order to set us at ease. "The world begins at the bottom of the stairs. Now I am free to discover life as I please."

But in truth she stopped going out altogether. When we asked her to come with us to the fish pond or to go to see temple decorations she refused, claiming that she was stitching a new curtain to hang across the entrance of the storage room. Her skin looked ashen. She needed fresh air. "What about finding your husband?" we suggested. "How do you expect to charm a man sitting up here all day?"

Nothing persuaded her.

By mid-December, Haldar cleared all the unsold merchandise off the shelves of his beauty shop and hauled them in boxes up to the storage room. We had succeeded in driving him more or less out of business. Before the year's end the family moved away, leaving an envelope containing three hundred rupees under Bibi's door. There was no more news of them.

One of us had an address for a relation of Bibi's in Hyderabad, and wrote explaining the situation. The letter was returned unopened, address unknown. Before the coldest weeks set in, we had the shutters of the storage room repaired and attached a sheet of tin to the doorframe, so that she would at least have some privacy. Someone donated a kerosene lamp, another gave her some old mosquito netting and a pair of socks without heels. At every opportunity we reminded her that we surrounded her, that she could come to us if she ever needed advice or aid of any kind. For a time we sent our children to play on the roof in the afternoons, so that they could alert us if she was having another attack. But each night we left her alone.

Some months passed. Bibi had retreated into a deep and prolonged silence. We took turns leaving her plates of rice and glasses of tea. She drank little, ate less, and began to assume an expression that no longer matched her years. At twilight she circled the parapet once or twice, but she never left the rooftop. After dark she remained behind the tin door and did not come out for any reason. We did not disturb her. Some of us began to wonder if she was dying. Others concluded that she had lost her mind.

One morning in April, when the heat had returned for drying lentil wafers on the roof, we noticed that someone had vomited by the cistern tap. When we noticed this a second morning as well, we knocked on Bibi's tin door. When there was no answer we opened it ourselves, as there was no lock to fasten it.

We found her lying on the camp cot. She was about four months pregnant.

She said she could not remember what had happened. She would not tell us who had done it. We prepared her semolina with hot milk and raisins; still she would not reveal the man's identity. In vain we searched for traces of the assault, some sign of the intrusion, but the room was swept and in order. On the floor beside the cot, her inventory ledger, open to a fresh page, contained a list of names.

She carried the baby to full term, and one evening in September, we helped her deliver a son. We showed her how to feed him, and bathe him, and lull him to sleep. We bought her an oilcloth and helped her stitch clothes and pillowcases out of the fabric she had saved over the years. Within a month Bibi had recuperated from the birth, and with the money that Haldar had left her, she had the storage room whitewashed, and placed padlocks on the window and doors. Then she dusted the shelves and arranged the leftover potions and lotions, selling Haldar's old inventory at half price. She told us to spread word of the sale, and we did. From Bibi we purchased our soaps and kohl, our combs and powders, and when she had sold the last of her merchandise, she went by taxi to the wholesale market, using her profits to restock the shelves. In this manner she raised the boy and ran a business in the storage room, and we did what we could to help. For years afterward, we wondered who in our town had disgraced her. A few of our servants were questioned, and in tea stalls and bus stands, possible suspects were debated and dismissed. But there was no point carrying out an investigation. She was, to the best of our knowledge, cured.

The Treatment of Bibi Haldar

Questions for discussion

1. What do you think Bibi Haldar's disability was? What was her reaction to her disability? What was her cousin's reaction? The narrator's reaction? How did Bibi try to advocate for herself?

2. How can various assumptions and cultural expectations affect disability?

3. The story is told from the point of view of an unnamed narrator, who often refers to herself and her friends as "we." What can be done to eliminate "us/them" discourse? What, if anything, do you think the narrator and her friends learned from Bibi?

4. What do you think this author is saying about disability? Do you agree or disagree?

5. How do you think the story might have been different if Bibi were a male character with the same condition?

6. The word "treatment" in the title can, of course, have two connotations: the treatment she is prescribed by doctors, and the treatment she receives at the hands of her family and friends. How does Bibi cope with both kinds of treatment?

7. Contrast the care Bibi received from her father with the care she receives from the narrator and the other women, then compare both of these with the care she received from Haldar and his wife. What did you think when the narrator said, "At every opportunity we reminded her that we surrounded her, that she could come to us if she ever needed advice or aid of any kind"? Did you feel that they did enough to help her? What should be the extent of the obligations owed by neighbors and friends to those without sufficient family support?

8. Design your own discussion questions for this story.

For Further Reading

About defying assumptions

Dubus, Andre. "Dancing After Hours." Short story about a female bartender who spends an evening observing a customer in a wheelchair, and how her assumptions about him change over the course of the evening.

Hathaway, Katharine Butler. *The Little Locksmith.* Autobiography about a woman with a disability (perhaps polio) who, in the early 1900s, breaks the mold and buys herself a house.

About women with disabilities who are limited by society

Gilman, Charlotte Perkins. "The Yellow Wallpaper."

About communities who care for those with disabilities

Simon, Rachel. "It Takes a Village To Help a Sister."

About disability in other cultures

Bratt, Kay. *Silent Tears: A Journey of Hope in a Chinese Orphanage.* An American spends time volunteering in a Chinese orphanage, and meets and befriends many children with disabilities.

H.G. Wells (1866–1946) was an English novelist, journalist, sociologist, and historian. He is best known for his classic science fiction novels *The Time Machine* and *The War of the Worlds*.

The Country of the Blind

Three hundred miles and more from Chimborazo, one hundred from the snows of Cotopaxi, in the wildest wastes of Ecuador's Andes, there lies that mysterious mountain valley, cut off from the world of men, the Country of the Blind. Long years ago that valley lay so far open to the world that men might come at last through frightful gorges and over an icy pass into its equable meadows; and thither indeed men came, a family or so of Peruvian half-breeds fleeing from the lust and tyranny of an evil Spanish ruler. Then came the stupendous outbreak of Mindobamba, when it was night in Quito for seventeen days, and the water was boiling at Yaguachi and all the fish floating dying even as far as Guayaquil; everywhere along the Pacific slopes there were land-slips and swift thawings and sudden floods, and one whole side of the old Arauca crest slipped and came down in thunder, and cut off the Country of the Blind for ever from the exploring feet of men. But one of these early settlers had chanced to be on the hither side of the gorges when the world had so terribly shaken itself, and he perforce had to forget his wife and his child and all the friends and possessions he had left up there, and start life over again in the lower world. He started it again but ill, blindness overtook him, and he died of punishment in the mines; but the story he told begot a legend that lingers along the length of the Cordilleras of the Andes to this day.

He told of his reason for venturing back from that vastness, into which he had first been carried lashed to a llama, beside a vast bale of gear, when he was a child. The valley, he said, had in it all that the heart of man could desire—sweet water, pasture, and even climate, slopes of rich brown soil with tangles of a shrub that bore an excellent fruit, and on one side great hanging forests of pine that held the avalanches high. Far overhead, on three sides, vast cliffs of grey-green rock were capped by cliffs of ice; but the glacier stream came not to them but flowed away by the farther slopes, and only now and then huge ice masses fell on the valley side.

37

In this valley it neither rained nor snowed, but the abundant springs gave a rich green pasture, that irrigation would spread over all the valley space. The settlers did well indeed there. Their beasts did well and multiplied, and but one thing marred their happiness. Yet it was enough to mar it greatly. A strange disease had come upon them, and had made all the children born to them there—and indeed, several older children also—blind. It was to seek some charm or antidote against this plague of blindness that he had with fatigue and danger and difficulty returned down the gorge. In those days, in such cases, men did not think of germs and infections but of sins; and it seemed to him that the reason of this affliction must lie in the negligence of these priestless immigrants to set up a shrine so soon as they entered the valley. He wanted a shrine—a handsome, cheap, effectual shrine—to be erected in the valley; he wanted relics and such-like potent things of faith, blessed objects and mysterious medals and prayers. In his wallet he had a bar of native silver for which he would not account; he insisted there was none in the valley with something of the insistence of an inexpert liar. They had all clubbed their money and ornaments together, having little need for such treasure up there, he said, to buy them holy help against their ill. I figure this dim-eyed young mountaineer, sunburnt, gaunt, and anxious, hat-brim clutched feverishly, a man all unused to the ways of the lower world, telling this story to some keen-eyed, attentive priest before the great convulsion; I can picture him presently seeking to return with pious and infallible remedies against that trouble, and the infinite dismay with which he must have faced the tumbled vastness where the gorge had once come out. But the rest of his story of mischances is lost to me, save that I know of his evil death after several years. Poor stray from that remoteness! The stream that had once made the gorge now bursts from the mouth of a rocky cave, and the legend his poor, ill-told story set going developed into the legend of a race of blind men somewhere "over there" one may still hear to-day.

And amidst the little population of that now isolated and forgotten valley the disease ran its course. The old became groping and purblind, the young saw but dimly, and the children that were born to them saw never at all. But life was very easy in that snow-rimmed basin, lost to all the world, with neither thorns nor briars, with no evil insects nor any beasts save the gentle breed of llamas they had lugged and thrust and followed up the beds of the shrunken rivers in the gorges up which they had come. The seeing had become purblind so gradually that they scarcely noted their loss. They guided the sightless youngsters hither and thither until they knew the whole Valley marvelously, and when at last sight died out among them the race lived on. They had even time to adapt themselves to the blind control of fire, which they made care-

fully in stoves of stone. They were a simple strain of people at the first, un-
lettered, only slightly touched with the Spanish civilization, but with something of a tradition of the arts of old Peru and of its lost philosophy. Generation followed generation. They forgot many things; they devised many things.
Their tradition of the greater world they came from became mythical in color
and uncertain. In all things save sight they were strong and able, and presently
the chance of birth and heredity sent one who had an original mind and who
could talk and persuade among them, and then afterwards another. These two
passed, leaving their effects, and the little community grew in numbers and
in understanding, and met and settled social and economic problems that
arose. Generation followed generation. Generation followed generation. There
came a time when a child was born who was fifteen generations from that an-
cestor who went out of the valley with a bar of silver to seek God's aid, and
who never returned. Thereabouts it chanced that a man came into this community from the outer world. And this is the story of that man.

He was a mountaineer from the country near Quito, a man who had been
down to the sea and had seen the world, a reader of books in an original way,
an acute and enterprising man, and he was taken on by a party of Englishmen
who had come out to Ecuador to climb mountains, to replace one of their three
Swiss guides who had fallen ill. He climbed here and he climbed there, and
then came the attempt on Parascotopetl, the Matterhorn of the Andes, in
which he was lost to the outer world. The story of the accident has been written a dozen times. Pointer's narrative is the best. He tells how the little party
worked their difficult and almost vertical way up to the very foot of the last
and greatest precipice, and how they built a night shelter amidst the snow upon
a little shelf of rock, and, with a touch of real dramatic power, how presently
they found Nunez had gone from them. They shouted, and there was no reply;
shouted and whistled, and for the rest of that night they slept no more.

As the morning broke they saw the traces of his fall. It seems impossible he
could have not uttered a sound. He had slipped eastward towards the unknown
side of the mountain; far below he had struck a steep slope of snow, and
ploughed his way down it in the midst of a snow avalanche. His track went
straight to the edge of a frightful precipice, and beyond that everything was
hidden. Far, far below, and hazy with distance, they could see trees rising out
of a narrow, shut-in valley—the lost Country of the Blind. But they did not
know it was the lost Country of the Blind, nor distinguish it in any way from
any other narrow streak of upland valley. Unnerved by this disaster, they abandoned their attempt in the afternoon, and Pointer was called away to the war
before he could make another attack. To this day Parascotopetl lifts an uncon-
quered crest, and Pointer's shelter crumbles unvisited amidst the snows.

And the man who fell survived.

At the end of the slope he fell a thousand feet, and came down in the midst of a cloud of snow upon a snow slope even steeper than the one above. Down this he was whirled, stunned and insensible, but without a bone broken in his body; and then at last came to gentler slopes, and at last rolled out and lay still, buried amidst a softening heap of the white masses that had accompanied and saved him. He came to himself with a dim fancy that he was ill in bed; then realized his position with a mountaineer's intelligence, and worked himself loose and, after a rest or so, out until he saw the stars. He rested flat upon his chest for a space, wondering where he was and what had happened to him. He explored his limbs, and discovered that several of his buttons were gone and his coat turned over his head. His knife had gone from his pocket and his hat was lost, though he had tied it under his chin. He recalled that he had been looking for loose stones to raise his piece of the shelter wall. His ice-axe had disappeared.

He decided he must have fallen, and looked up to see, exaggerated by the ghastly light of the rising moon, the tremendous flight he had taken. For a while he lay, gazing blankly at that vast pale cliff towering above, rising moment by moment out of a subsiding tide of darkness. Its phantasmal, mysterious beauty held him for a space, and then he was seized with a paroxysm of sobbing laughter ...

After a great interval of time he became aware that he was near the lower edge of the snow. Below, down what was now a moonlit and practicable slope, he saw the dark and broken appearance of rock-strewn turf. He struggled to his feet, aching in every joint and limb, got down painfully from the heaped loose snow about him, went downward until he was on the turf, and there dropped rather than lay beside a boulder, drank deep from the flask in his inner pocket, and instantly fell asleep ...

He was awakened by the singing of birds in the trees far below.

He sat up and perceived he was on a little alp at the foot of a vast precipice, that was grooved by the gully down which he and his snow had come. Over against him another wall of rock reared itself against the sky. The gorge between these precipices ran east and west and was full of the morning sunlight, which lit to the westward the mass of fallen mountain that closed the descending gorge. Below him it seemed there was a precipice equally steep, but behind the snow in the gully he found a sort of chimney-cleft dripping with snow-water down which a desperate man might venture. He found it easier than it seemed, and came at last to another desolate alp, and then after a rock climb of no particular difficulty to a steep slope of trees. He took his bearings and turned his face up the gorge, for he saw it opened out above upon green meadows, among which he now glimpsed quite distinctly a cluster of stone huts of unfamiliar fashion. At times his progress was like clambering along the face of a wall, and after a time the rising sun ceased to strike along the gorge, the voices of the singing birds died away, and the air grew cold and dark about him. But the distant valley with its houses was all the brighter for that. He came presently to talus, and among the rocks he noted—for he was an observant man—an unfamiliar fern that seemed to clutch out of the crevices with intense green hands. He picked a frond or so and gnawed its stalk and found it helpful.

About midday he came at last out of the throat of the gorge into the plain and the sunlight. He was stiff and weary; he sat down in the shadow of a rock, filled up his flask with water from a spring and drank it down, and remained for a time resting before he went on to the houses.

They were very strange to his eyes, and indeed the whole aspect of that valley became, as he regarded it, queerer and more unfamiliar. The greater part of its surface was lush green meadow, starred with many beautiful flowers, irrigated with extraordinary care, and bearing evidence of systematic cropping piece by piece. High up and ringing the valley about was a wall, and what appeared to be a circumferential water-channel, from which the little trickles of water that fed the meadow plants came, and on the higher slopes above this flocks of llamas cropped the scanty herbage. Sheds, apparently shelters or feeding-places for the llamas, stood against the boundary wall here and there. The irrigation streams ran together into a main channel down the centre of the valley, and this was enclosed on either side by a wall breast high. This gave a singularly urban quality to this secluded place, a quality that was greatly enhanced by the fact that a number of paths paved with black and white stones, and each with a curious little curb at the side, ran hither and thither in an orderly manner. The houses of the central village were quite unlike the casual and higgledy-piggledy agglomeration of the mountain villages he knew; they stood in a continuous row on either side of a central street of astonishing cleanness; here and there their parti-colored facade was pierced by a door, and not a solitary window broke their even frontage. They were parti-colored with extraordinary irregularity, smeared with a sort of plaster that was sometimes gray, sometimes drab, sometimes slate-colored or dark brown; and it was the sight of this wild plastering that first brought the word "blind" into the thoughts of the explorer. "The good man who did that," he thought, "must have been as blind as a bat."

He descended a steep place, and so came to the wall and channel that ran about the valley, near where the latter spouted out its surplus contents into the deeps of the gorge in a thin and wavering thread of cascade. He could now see a number of men and women resting on piled heaps of grass, as if taking a siesta, in the remoter part of the meadow, and nearer the village a number of recumbent children, and then nearer at hand three men carrying pails on yokes along a little path that ran from the encircling wall towards the houses. These latter were clad in garments of llama cloth and boots and belts of leather, and they wore caps of cloth with back and ear flaps. They followed one another in single file, walking slowly and yawning as they walked, like men who have been up all night. There was something so reassuringly prosperous and respectable in their bearing that after a moment's hesitation Nunez stood forward as conspicuously as possible upon his rock, and gave vent to a mighty shout that echoed round the valley.

The three men stopped, and moved their heads as though they were looking about them. They turned their faces this way and that, and Nunez gesticulated with freedom. But they did not appear to see him for all his gestures, and after a time, directing themselves towards the mountains far away to the right, they shouted as if in answer. Nunez bawled again, and then once more, and as he gestured ineffectually the word "blind" came up to the top of his thoughts. "The fools must be blind," he said.

When at last, after much shouting and wrath, Nunez crossed the stream by a little bridge, came through a gate in the wall, and approached them, he was sure that they were blind. He was sure that this was the Country of the Blind of which the legends told. Conviction had sprung upon him, and a sense of great and rather enviable adventure. The three stood side by side, not looking at him, but with their ears directed towards him, judging him by his unfamiliar steps. They stood close together like men a little afraid, and he could see their eyelids closed and sunken, as though the very balls beneath had shrunk away. There was an expression near awe on their faces.

"A man," one said, in hardly recognizable Spanish—"a man it is—a man or a spirit—coming down from the rocks."

But Nunez advanced with the confident steps of a youth who enters upon life. All the old stories of the lost valley and the Country of the Blind had come back to his mind, and through his thoughts ran this old proverb, as if it were a refrain—

"In the Country of the Blind the One-eyed Man is King."

And very civilly he gave them greeting. He talked to them and used his eyes.

"Where does he come from, brother Pedro?" asked one.

"Down out of the rocks."

"Over the mountains I come," said Nunez, "out of the country beyond there —where men can see. From near Bogotá, where there are a hundred thousands of people, and where the city passes out of sight."

"Sight?" muttered Pedro. "Sight?"

"He comes," said the second blind man, "out of the rocks."

The cloth of their coats Nunez saw was curiously fashioned, each with a different sort of stitching.

They startled him by a simultaneous movement towards him, each with a hand outstretched. He stepped back from the advance of these spread fingers.

"Come hither," said the third blind man, following his motion and clutching him neatly.

And they held Nunez and felt him over, saying no word further until they had done so.

"Carefully," he cried, with a finger in his eye, and found they thought that organ, with its fluttering lids, a queer thing in him. They went over it again.

"A strange creature, Correa," said the one called Pedro. "Feel the coarseness of his hair. Like a llama's hair."

"Rough he is as the rocks that begot him," said Correa, investigating Nunez's unshaven chin with a soft and slightly moist hand. "Perhaps he will grow finer." Nunez struggled a little under their examination, but they gripped him firm.

"Carefully," he said again.

"He speaks," said the third man. "Certainly he is a man."

"Ugh!" said Pedro, at the roughness of his coat.

"And you have come into the world?" asked Pedro.

"*Out* of the world. Over mountains and glaciers; right over above there, half-way to the sun. Out of the great big world that goes down, twelve days' journey to the sea."

They scarcely seemed to heed him. "Our fathers have told us men may be made by the forces of Nature," said Correa. "It is the warmth of things and moisture, and rottenness—rottenness."

"Let us lead him to the elders," said Pedro.

"Shout first," said Correa, "lest the children be afraid.... This is a marvelous occasion."

So they shouted, and Pedro went first and took Nunez by the hand to lead him to the houses.

He drew his hand away. "I can see," he said.

"See?" said Correa.

"Yes, see," said Nunez, turning towards him, and stumbled against Pedro's pail.

"His senses are still imperfect," said the third blind man. "He stumbles, and talks unmeaning words. Lead him by the hand."

"As you will," said Nunez, and was led along, laughing.

It seemed they knew nothing of sight.

Well, all in good time he would teach them.

He heard people shouting, and saw a number of figures gathering together in the middle roadway of the village.

He found it taxed his nerve and patience more than he had anticipated, that first encounter with the population of the Country of the Blind. The place seemed larger as he drew near to it, and the smeared plasterings queerer, and a crowd of children and men and women (the women and girls, he was pleased to note, had some of them quite sweet faces, for all that their eyes were shut and sunken) came about him, holding on to him, touching him with soft, sensitive hands, smelling at him, and listening at every word he spoke. Some of the maidens and children, however, kept aloof as if afraid, and indeed his voice seemed coarse and rude beside their softer notes. They mobbed him. His three guides kept close to him with an effect of proprietorship, and said again and again, "A wild man out of the rock."

"Bogotá," he said. "Bogotá. Over the mountain crests."

"A wild man—using wild words," said Pedro. "Did you hear that—*Bogotá*? His mind is hardly formed yet. He has only the beginnings of speech."

A little boy nipped his hand. "Bogotá!" he said mockingly.

"Ay! A city to your village. I come from the great world—where men have eyes and see."

"His name's Bogotá," they said.

"He stumbled," said Correa, "stumbled twice as we came hither."

"Bring him to the elders."

And they thrust him suddenly through a doorway into a room as black as pitch, save at the end there faintly glowed a fire. The crowd closed in behind him and shut out all but the faintest glimmer of day, and before he could arrest himself he had fallen headlong over the feet of a seated man. His arm, outflung, struck the face of someone else as he went down; he felt the soft impact of features and heard a cry of anger, and for a moment he struggled against a number of hands that clutched him. It was a one-sided fight. An inkling of the situation came to him, and he lay quiet.

"I fell down," he said; "I couldn't see in this pitchy darkness."

There was a pause as if the unseen persons about him tried to understand his words. Then the voice of Correa said: "He is but newly formed. He stumbles as he walks and mingles words that mean nothing with his speech."

Others also said things about him that he heard or understood imperfectly.

"May I sit up?" he asked, in a pause. "I will not struggle against you again."

They consulted and let him rise.

The voice of an older man began to question him, and Nunez found himself trying to explain the great world out of which he had fallen, and the sky and mountains and sight and such-like marvels, to these elders who sat in darkness in the Country of the Blind. And they would believe and understand nothing whatever he told them, a thing quite outside his expectation. They would not even understand many of his words. For fourteen generations these people had been blind and cut off from all the seeing world; the names for all the things of sight had faded and changed; the story of the outer world was faded and changed to a child's story; and they had ceased to concern themselves with anything beyond the rocky slopes above their circling wall. Blind men of genius had arisen among them and questioned the shreds of belief and tradition they had brought with them from their seeing days, and had dismissed all these things as idle fancies, and replaced them with new and saner explanations. Much of their imagination had shriveled with their eyes, and they had made for themselves new imaginations with their ever more sensitive ears and fingertips. Slowly Nunez realized this; that his expectation of wonder and reverence at his origin and his gifts was not to be borne out; and after his poor attempt to explain sight to them had been set aside as the confused version of a new-made being describing the marvels of his incoherent sensations, he subsided, a little dashed, into listening to their instruction. And the eldest of the blind men explained to him life and philosophy and religion, how that the world (meaning their valley) had been first an empty hollow in the rocks, and then had come, first, inanimate things without the gift of touch, and llamas and a few other creatures that had little sense, and then men, and at last angels, whom one could hear singing and making fluttering sounds, but whom no one could touch at all, which puzzled Nunez greatly until he thought of the birds.

He went on to tell Nunez how this time had been divided into the warm and the cold, which are the blind equivalents of day and night, and how it was good to sleep in the warm and work during the cold, so that now, but for his advent, the whole town of the blind would have been asleep. He said Nunez must have been specially created to learn and serve the wisdom they had acquired, and that for all his mental incoherency and stumbling behavior he must have courage, and do his best to learn, and at that all the people in the doorway murmured encouragingly. He said the night—for the blind call their day night—was now far gone, and it behooved everyone to go back to sleep. He asked Nunez if he knew how to sleep, and Nunez said he did, but that before sleep he wanted food.

They brought him food—llama's milk in a bowl, and rough salted bread— and led him into a lonely place, to eat out of their hearing, and afterwards to slumber until the chill of the mountain evening roused them to begin their day again. But Nunez slumbered not at all.

Instead, he sat up in the place where they had left him, resting his limbs and turning the unanticipated circumstances of his arrival over and over in his mind.

Every now and then he laughed, sometimes with amusement, and sometimes with indignation.

"Unformed mind!" he said. "Got no senses yet! They little know they've been insulting their heaven-sent king and master. I see I must bring them to reason. Let me think—let me think."

He was still thinking when the sun set.

Nunez had an eye for all beautiful things, and it seemed to him that the glow upon the snowfields and glaciers that rose about the valley on every side was the most beautiful thing he had ever seen. His eyes went from that inaccessible glory to the village and irrigated fields, fast sinking into the twilight, and suddenly a wave of emotion took him, and he thanked God from the bottom of his heart that the power of sight had been given him.

He heard a voice calling to him from out of the village. "Ya ho there, Bogotá! Come hither!"

At that he stood up smiling. He would show these people once and for all what sight would do for a man. They would seek him, but not find him.

"You move not, Bogotá," said the voice.

He laughed noiselessly, and made two stealthy steps aside from the path.

"Trample not on the grass, Bogotá; that is not allowed."

Nunez had scarcely heard the sound he made himself. He stopped amazed.

The owner of the voice came running up the piebald path towards him.

He stepped back into the pathway. "Here I am," he said.

"Why did you not come when I called you?" said the blind man. "Must you be led like a child? Cannot you hear the path as you walk?"

Nunez laughed. "I can see it," he said.

"There is no such word as *see*," said the blind man, after a pause. "Cease this folly, and follow the sound of my feet."

Nunez followed, a little annoyed.

"My time will come," he said.

"You'll learn," the blind man answered. "There is much to learn in the world."

"Has no one told you, 'In the Country of the Blind the One-eyed Man is King'?"

"What is blind?" asked the blind man carelessly over his shoulder.

Four days passed, and the fifth found the King of the Blind still incognito, as a clumsy and useless stranger among his subjects.

It was, he found, much more difficult to proclaim himself than he had supposed, and in the meantime, while he meditated his *coup d'état*, he did what he was told and learnt the manners and customs of the Country of the Blind.

He found working and going about at night a particularly irksome thing, and he decided that that should be the first thing he would change.

They led a simple, laborious life, these people, with all the elements of virtue and happiness, as these things can be understood by men. They toiled, but not oppressively; they had food and clothing sufficient for their needs; they had days and seasons of rest; they made much of music and singing, and there was love among them, and little children.

It was marvelous with what confidence and precision they went about their ordered world. Everything, you see, had been made to fit their needs; each of the radiating paths of the valley area had a constant angle to the others, and was distinguished by a special notch upon its kerbing; all obstacles and irregularities of path or meadow had long since been cleared away; all their methods and procedure arose naturally from their special needs. Their senses had become marvelously acute; they could hear and judge the slightest gesture of a man a dozen paces away—could hear the very beating of his heart. Intonation had long replaced expression with them, and touches gesture, and their work with hoe and spade and fork was as free and confident as garden work can be. Their sense of smell was extraordinarily fine; they could distinguish individual differences as readily as a dog can, and they went about the tending of the llamas, who lived among the rocks above and came to the wall for food and shelter, with ease and confidence. It was only when at last Nunez sought to assert himself that he found how easy and confident their movements could be.

He rebelled only after he had tried persuasion.

He tried at first on several occasions to tell them of sight. "Look you here, you people," he said. "There are things you do not understand in me."

Once or twice one or two of them attended to him; they sat with faces downcast and ears turned intelligently towards him, and he did his best to tell them what it was to see. Among his hearers was a girl, with eyelids less red and sunken than the others, so that one could almost fancy she was hiding eyes, whom especially he hoped to persuade. He spoke of the beauties of sight, of watching the mountains, of the sky and the sunrise, and they heard him with amused incredulity that presently became condemnatory. They told him there were indeed no mountains at all, but that the end of the rocks where the llamas grazed was indeed the end of the world; thence sprang a cavernous roof of the universe, from which the dew and the avalanches fell; and when he maintained stoutly the world had neither end nor roof such as they supposed, they said his thoughts were wicked. So far as he could describe sky and clouds and stars to them it seemed to them a hideous void, a terrible blankness in the place of the smooth roof to things in which they believed—it was an article of faith with them that the cavern roof was exquisitely smooth to the touch. He saw that in some manner he shocked them, and gave up that aspect of the matter altogether, and tried to show them the practical value of sight. One morning he saw Pedro in the path called Seventeen and coming towards the central houses, but still too far off for hearing or scent, and he told them as much. "In a little while," he prophesied, "Pedro will be here." An old man remarked that Pedro had no business on path Seventeen, and then, as if in confirmation, that individual as he drew near turned and went transversely into path Ten, and so back with nimble paces towards the outer wall. They mocked Nunez when Pedro did not arrive, and afterwards, when he asked Pedro questions to clear his character, Pedro denied and outfaced him, and was afterwards hostile to him.

Then he induced them to let him go a long way up the sloping meadows towards the wall with one complacent individual, and to him he promised to describe all that happened among the houses. He noted certain goings and comings, but the things that really seemed to signify to these people happened inside of or behind the windowless houses—the only things they took note of to test him by—and of these he could see or tell nothing; and it was after the failure of this attempt, and the ridicule they could not repress, that he resorted to force. He thought of seizing a spade and suddenly smiting one or two of them to earth, and so in fair combat showing the advantage of eyes. He went so far with that resolution as to seize his spade, and then he discovered a new thing about himself, and that was that it was impossible for him to hit a blind man in cold blood.

He hesitated, and found them all aware that he had snatched up the spade. They stood alert, with their heads on one side, and bent ears towards him for what he would do next.

"Put that spade down," said one, and he felt a sort of helpless horror. He came near obedience.

Then he thrust one backwards against a house wall, and fled past him and out of the village.

He went athwart one of their meadows, leaving a track of trampled grass behind his feet, and presently sat down by the side of one of their ways.

He felt something of the buoyancy that comes to all men in the beginning of a fight, but more perplexity. He began to realize that you cannot even fight happily with creatures who stand upon a different mental basis to yourself. Far away he saw a number of men carrying spades and sticks come out of the street of houses, and advance in a spreading line along the several paths towards him. They advanced slowly, speaking frequently to one another, and ever and again the whole cordon would halt and sniff the air and listen.

The first time they did this Nunez laughed. But afterwards he did not laugh.

One struck his trail in the meadow grass, and came stooping and feeling his way along it.

For five minutes he watched the slow extension of the cordon, and then his vague disposition to do something forthwith became frantic. He stood up, went a pace or so towards the circumferential wall, turned, and went back a little way. There they all stood in a crescent, still and listening.

He also stood still, gripping his spade very tightly in both hands. Should he charge them?

The pulse in his ears ran into the rhythm of "In the Country of the Blind the One-eyed Man is King!"

Should he charge them?

He looked back at the high and unclimbable wall behind—unclimbable because of its smooth plastering, but withal pierced with many little doors, and at the approaching line of seekers. Behind these others were now coming out of the street of houses.

Should he charge them?

"Bogotá!" called one. "Bogotá! where are you?"

He gripped his spade still tighter, and advanced down the meadows towards the place of habitations, and directly as he moved they converged upon him.

"I'll hit them if they touch me," he swore; "by Heaven, I will. I'll hit."

He called aloud, "Look here, I'm going to do what I like in this valley. Do you hear? I'm going to do what I like and go where I like!"

They were moving in upon him quickly, groping, yet moving rapidly. It was like playing blind man's bluff, with everyone blindfolded except one. "Get hold of him!" cried one. He found himself in the arc of a loose curve of pursuers. He felt suddenly he must be active and resolute.

"You don't understand," he cried in a voice that was meant to be great and resolute, and which broke. "You are blind, and I can see. Leave me alone!"

"Bogotá! Put down that spade, and come off the grass!"

The last order, grotesque in its urban familiarity, produced a gust of anger.

"I'll hurt you," he said, sobbing with emotion. "By Heaven, I'll hurt you. Leave me alone!"

He began to run, not knowing clearly where to run. He ran from the nearest blind man, because it was a horror to hit him. He stopped, and then made a dash to escape from their closing ranks. He made for where a gap was wide, and the men on either side, with a quick perception of the approach of his paces, rushed in on one another. He sprang forward, and then saw he must be caught, and *swish*! the spade had struck. He felt the soft thud of hand and arm, and the man was down with a yell of pain, and he was through.

Through! And then he was close to the street of houses again, and blind men, whirling spades and stakes, were running with a sort of reasoned swiftness hither and thither.

He heard steps behind him just in time, and found a tall man rushing forward and swiping at the sound of him. He lost his nerve, hurled his spade a yard wide at his antagonist, and whirled about and fled, fairly yelling as he dodged another.

He was panic-stricken. He ran furiously to and fro, dodging when there was no need to dodge, and in his anxiety to see on every side of him at once, stumbling. For a moment he was down and they heard his fall. Far away in the circumferential wall a little doorway looked like heaven, and he set off in a wild rush for it. He did not even look round at his pursuers until it was gained, and he had stumbled across the bridge, clambered a little way among the rocks, to the surprise and dismay of a young llama, who went leaping out of sight, and lay down sobbing for breath.

And so his *coup d'état* came to an end.

He stayed outside the wall of the valley of the Blind for two nights and days without food or shelter, and meditated upon the unexpected. During these meditations he repeated very frequently and always with a profounder note of derision the exploded proverb: "In the Country of the Blind the One-Eyed Man is King." He thought chiefly of ways of fighting and conquering these people, and it grew clear that for him no practicable way was possible. He had no weapons, and now it would be hard to get one.

The canker of civilization had got to him even in Bogotá, and he could not find it in himself to go down and assassinate a blind man. Of course, if he did that, he might then dictate terms on the threat of assassinating them all. But— sooner or later he must sleep!

He tried also to find food among the pine trees, to be comfortable under pine boughs while the frost fell at night, and—with less confidence—to catch a llama by artifice in order to try to kill it—perhaps by hammering it with a stone—and so finally, perhaps, to eat some of it. But the llamas had a doubt of him and regarded him with distrustful brown eyes, and spat when he drew near. Fear came on him the second day and fits of shivering. Finally he crawled down to the wall of the Country of the Blind and tried to make terms. He crawled along by the stream, shouting, until two blind men came out to the gate and talked to him.

"I was mad," he said. "But I was only newly made."

They said that was better.

He told them he was wiser now, and repented of all he had done.

Then he wept without intention, for he was very weak and ill now, and they took that as a favorable sign.

They asked him if he still thought he could "*see.*"

"No," he said. "That was folly. The word means nothing—less than nothing!"

They asked him what was overhead.

"About ten times ten the height of a man there is a roof above the world—of rock—and very, very smooth." He burst again into hysterical tears. "Before you ask me anymore, give me some food or I shall die."

He expected dire punishments, but these blind people were capable of toleration. They regarded his rebellion as but one more proof of his general idiocy and inferiority; and after they had whipped him they appointed him to do the simplest and heaviest work they had for anyone to do, and he, seeing no other way of living, did submissively what he was told.

He was ill for some days, and they nursed him kindly. That refined his submission. But they insisted on his lying in the dark, and that was a great misery. And blind philosophers came and talked to him of the wicked levity of his mind, and reproved him so impressively for his doubts about the lid of rock that covered their cosmic casserole that he almost doubted whether indeed he was not the victim of hallucination in not seeing it overhead.

So Nunez became a citizen of the Country of the Blind, and these people ceased to be a generalized people and became individualities and familiar to him, while the world beyond the mountains became more and more remote and unreal. There was Yacob, his master, a kindly man when not annoyed; there was Pedro, Yacob's nephew; and there was Medina-saroté, who was the youngest daughter of Yacob. She was little esteemed in the world of the blind, because she had a clear-cut face, and lacked that satisfying, glossy smoothness that is the blind man's ideal of feminine beauty; but Nunez thought her beautiful at first, and presently the most beautiful thing in the whole creation. Her closed eyelids were not sunken and red after the common way of the valley, but lay as though they might open again at any moment; and she had long eyelashes, which were considered a grave disfigurement. And her voice was strong, and did not satisfy the acute hearing of the valley swains, so that she had no lover.

There came a time when Nunez thought that, could he win her, he would be resigned to live in the valley for all the rest of his days.

He watched her; he sought opportunities of doing her little services, and presently he found that she observed him. Once at a rest-day gathering they sat side by side in the dim starlight, and the music was sweet. His hand came upon hers and he dared to clasp it. Then very tenderly she returned his pressure. And one day, as they were at their meal in the darkness, he felt her hand very softly seeking him, and as it chanced the fire leapt then and he saw the tenderness of her face.

He sought to speak to her.

He went to her one day when she was sitting in the summer moonlight spinning. The light made her a thing of silver and mystery. He sat down at her feet and told her he loved her, and told her how beautiful she seemed to him. He had a lover's voice, he spoke with a tender reverence that came near to awe, and she had never before been touched by adoration. She made him no definite answer, but it was clear his words pleased her.

After that he talked to her whenever he could take an opportunity. The valley became the world for him, and the world beyond the mountains where men lived in sunlight seemed no more than a fairy tale he would someday pour into her ears. Very tentatively and timidly he spoke to her of sight.

Sight seemed to her the most poetical of fancies, and she listened to his description of the stars and the mountains and her own sweet white-lit beauty as though it was a guilty indulgence. She did not believe, she could only half understand, but she was mysteriously delighted, and it seemed to him that she completely understood.

His love lost its awe and took courage. Presently he was for demanding her of Yacob and the elders in marriage, but she became fearful and delayed. And it was one of her elder sisters who first told Yacob that Medina-saroté and Nunez were in love.

There was from the first very great opposition to the marriage of Nunez and Medina-saroté; not so much because they valued her as because they held him as a being apart, an idiot, incompetent thing below the permissible level of a man. Her sisters opposed it bitterly as bringing discredit on them all; and old Yacob, though he had formed a sort of liking for his clumsy, obedient serf, shook his head and said the thing could not be. The young men were all angry at the idea of corrupting the race, and one went so far as to revile and strike Nunez. He struck back. Then for the first time he found an advantage in seeing, even by twilight, and after that fight was over no one was disposed to raise a hand against him. But they still found his marriage impossible.

Old Yacob had a tenderness for his last little daughter, and was grieved to have her weep upon his shoulder.

"You see, my dear, he's an idiot. He has delusions; he can't do anything right."

"I know," wept Medina-saroté. "But he's better than he was. He's getting better. And he's strong, dear father, and kind—stronger and kinder than any other man in the world. And he loves me—and, father, I love him."

Old Yacob was greatly distressed to find her inconsolable, and, besides— what made it more distressing—he liked Nunez for many things. So he went and sat in the windowless council-chamber with the other elders and watched the trend of the talk, and said, at the proper time, "He's better than he was. Very likely, some day, we shall find him as sane as ourselves."

Then afterwards one of the elders, who thought deeply, had an idea. He was the great doctor among these people, their medicine-man, and he had a very philosophical and inventive mind, and the idea of curing Nunez of his peculiarities appealed to him. One day when Yacob was present he returned to the topic of Nunez.

"I have examined Bogotá," he said, "and the case is clearer to me. I think very probably he might be cured."

"That is what I have always hoped," said old Yacob.

"His brain is affected," said the blind doctor.

The elders murmured assent.

"Now, what affects it?"

"Ah!" said old Yacob.

"*This*," said the doctor, answering his own question. "Those queer things that are called the eyes, and which exist to make an agreeable soft depression in the face, are diseased, in the case of Bogotá, in such a way as to affect his brain. They are greatly distended, he has eyelashes, and his eyelids move, and consequently his brain is in a state of constant irritation and distraction."

"Yes?" said old Yacob. "Yes?"

"And I think I may say with reasonable certainty that, in order to cure him completely, all that we need do is a simple and easy surgical operation—namely, to remove these irritant bodies."

"And then he will be sane?"

"Then he will be perfectly sane, and a quite admirable citizen."

"Thank Heaven for science!" said old Yacob, and went forth at once to tell Nunez of his happy hopes.

But Nunez's manner of receiving the good news struck him as being cold and disappointing.

"One might think," he said, "from the tone you take, that you did not care for my daughter."

It was Medina-saroté who persuaded Nunez to face the blind surgeons.

"*You* do not want me," he said, "to lose my gift of sight?"

She shook her head.

"My world is sight."

Her head drooped lower.

"There are the beautiful things, the beautiful little things—the flowers, the lichens among the rocks, the lightness and softness on a piece of fur, the far sky with its drifting down of clouds, the sunsets and the stars. And there is *you*. For you alone it is good to have sight, to see your sweet, serene face, your kindly lips, your dear, beautiful hands folded together ... It is these eyes of mine you won, these eyes that hold me to you, that these idiots seek. Instead, I must touch you, hear you, and never see you again. I must come under that roof of rock and stone and darkness, that horrible roof under which your imagination stoops ... No; you would not have me do that?"

A disagreeable doubt had arisen in him. He stopped, and left the thing a question.

"I wish," she said, "sometimes—." She paused.

"Yes," said he, a little apprehensively.

"I wish sometimes—you would not talk like that."

"Like what?"

"I know it's pretty—it's your imagination. I love it, but *now*—"

He felt cold. "*Now?*" he said faintly.

She sat quite still.

"You mean—you think—I should be better, better perhaps—"

He was realizing things very swiftly. He felt anger, indeed, anger at the dull course of fate, but also sympathy for her lack of understanding—a sympathy near akin to pity.

"*Dear,*" he said, and he could see by her whiteness how intensely her spirit pressed against the things she could not say. He put his arms about her, he kissed her ear, and they sat for a time in silence.

"If I were to consent to this?" he said at last, in a voice that was very gentle.

She flung her arms about him, weeping wildly. "Oh, if you would," she sobbed, "if only you would!"

For a week before the operation that was to raise him from his servitude and inferiority to the level of a blind citizen, Nunez knew nothing of sleep, and all through the warm sunlit hours, while the others slumbered happily, he sat brooding or wandered aimlessly, trying to bring his mind to bear on his dilemma. He had given his answer, he had given his consent, and still he was not sure. And at last work-time was over, the sun rose in splendor over the golden crests, and his last day of vision began for him. He had a few minutes with Medina-saroté before she went apart to sleep.

"Tomorrow," he said, "I shall see no more."

"Dear heart!" she answered, and pressed his hands with all her strength.

"They will hurt you but little," she said; "and you are going through this pain—you are going through it, dear lover, for *me* ... Dear, if a woman's heart and life can do it, I will repay you. My dearest one, my dearest with the tender voice, I will repay."

He was drenched in pity for himself and her.

He held her in his arms, and pressed his lips to hers, and looked on her sweet face for the last time. "Good-bye!" he whispered at that dear sight, "good-bye!"

And then in silence he turned away from her.

She could hear his slow retreating footsteps, and something in the rhythm of them threw her into a passion of weeping.

He had fully meant to go to a lonely place where the meadows were beautiful with white narcissus, and there remain until the hour of his sacrifice should come, but as he went he lifted up his eyes and saw the morning, the morning like an angel in golden armor, marching down the steeps ...

It seemed to him that before this splendor he, and this blind world in the valley, and his love, and all, were no more than a pit of sin.

He did not turn aside as he had meant to do, but went on, and passed through the wall of the circumference and out upon the rocks, and his eyes were always upon the sunlit ice and snow.

He saw their infinite beauty, and his imagination soared over them to the things beyond he was now to resign forever.

He thought of that great free world he was parted from, the world that was his own, and he had a vision of those further slopes, distance beyond distance, with Bogotá, a place of multitudinous stirring beauty, a glory by day, a luminous mystery by night, a place of palaces and fountains and statues and white houses, lying beautifully in the middle distance. He thought how for a day or so one might come down through passes, drawing ever nearer and nearer to its busy streets and ways. He thought of the river journey, day by day, from great Bogotá to the still vaster world beyond, through towns and villages, forest and desert places, the rushing river day by day, until its banks receded and the big steamers came splashing by, and one had reached the sea—the limitless sea, with its thousand islands, its thousands of islands, and its ships seen dimly far away in their incessant journeyings round and about that greater world. And there, unpent by mountains, one saw the sky—the sky, not such a disc as one saw it here, but an arch of immeasurable blue, a deep of deeps in which the circling stars were floating ...

His eyes scrutinized the great curtain of the mountains with a keener inquiry.

For example, if one went so, up that gully and to that chimney there, then one might come out high among those stunted pines that ran round in a sort of shelf and rose still higher and higher as it passed above the gorge. And then? That talus might be managed. Thence perhaps a climb might be found to take him up to the precipice that came below the snow; and if that chimney failed, then another farther to the east might serve his purpose better. And then? Then one would be out upon the amber-lit snow there, and half-way up to the crest of those beautiful desolations.

He glanced back at the village, then turned right round and regarded it steadfastly.

He thought of Medina-saroté, and she had become small and remote.

He turned again towards the mountain wall, down which the day had come to him.

Then very circumspectly he began to climb.

When sunset came he was no longer climbing, but he was far and high. He had been higher, but he was still very high. His clothes were torn, his limbs were blood-stained, he was bruised in many places, but he lay as if he were at his ease, and there was a smile on his face.

From where he rested the valley seemed as if it were in a pit and nearly a mile below. Already it was dim with haze and shadow, though the mountain summits around him were things of light and fire. The mountain summits around him were things of light and fire, and the little details of the rocks near at hand were drenched with subtle beauty—a vein of green mineral piercing the grey, the flash of crystal faces here and there, a minute, minutely-beautiful orange lichen close beside his face. There were deep mysterious shadows in the gorge, blue deepening into purple, and purple into a luminous darkness, and overhead was the illimitable vastness of the sky. But he heeded these things no longer, but lay quite inactive there, smiling as if he were satisfied merely to have escaped from the valley of the Blind in which he had thought to be King.

The glow of the sunset passed, and the night came, and still he lay peacefully contented under the cold clear stars.

Country of the Blind

Questions for discussion

1. Was the ending what you expected? Why or why not? (This story was also written with an alternate ending. You can find it anthologized in *The Complete Short Stories of H.G. Wells*.)

2. What was the villagers' attitude toward the narrator's sight? Why?

3. How did the narrator's perceptions change over time? What was his attitude towards the villagers' blindness? Did his fiancee try to require too much of him?

4. A number of authors have written stories or books about societies that are sealed off from the rest of the world and have various features (all-female, all-

blind, etc). Why do you think the author chose to have this society sealed off from the rest of the world?

5. What do you think a disability rights advocate might say about this story? Do some elements of it seem outdated?

6. Design your own discussion questions for this story.

For Further Reading

About fictional societies with disability themes

Moon, Elizabeth. *The Speed of Dark*. A futuristic novel about a possible cure for autism and the narrator's dilemma: to cure or not to cure?

Le Guin, Ursula. "The Ones Who Walk Away from Omelas." An almost-Utopian society guards a disturbing secret.

Arthur Bradford was born in Boothbay Harbor, Maine. An O. Henry Award winner, he has published fiction and nonfiction in *Esquire*, *McSweeney's*, *Men's Journal*, and the *New York Times*. He is also the creator and director of "How's Your News," a documentary film series which has been broadcast on HBO, PBS and MTV. He directs a summer camp and lives in Portland, Oregon.

The Texas School for the Blind

I was given charge of an eleven-year-old boy named Marvin who was both blind and deaf. He would walk around with his head down and both his arms waving about in front of him so that he could feel if he was going to bump into anything. Sometimes he would just take off and run, zigzagging around the room until he got tripped up or smacked into some object which his outstretched hands did not detect.

I had no idea how to communicate with Marvin. During the day he attended classes with trained professionals who tried to teach him words by drawing letters onto his palm with their fingers. No one explained to me how this worked. My job was to get him some exercise, feed him dinner, and put him to bed.

I would often talk to Marvin, though I understood, obviously, that he could not hear me. I'd say things like, "Look out, Marvin!" or "Come here."

An interesting thing about Marvin was that he could identify people by the way they smelled. Each afternoon, when I picked him up at the school building, he would take my arm and sniff it. When we walked together, with Marvin holding my arm lightly at the elbow like we'd been taught, he'd keep his head pointed down, like a hunchback. I tried to get him to hold his head up, but he didn't like that. It was understandable, I guess, why he would see no reason to hold his head up while he walked.

Marvin and I never really became good friends. He bit me the first time I tried to give him a shower. He didn't like water touching his skin. He would often grab my arms and squeeze very tightly and it was for this reason I made sure to keep his fingernails cut short. The residential staff had a set of fingernail clippers which we were supposed to use for such tasks, but Marvin had unusually thick fingernails and I couldn't get the clippers to fit around them.

So I used a set of scissors from the office. They were very sharp scissors designed for cutting paper and they performed the job well.

One evening I was getting Marvin ready for bed and he grabbed my hair and wouldn't let go. When I finally pried his fingers loose I noticed that his nails needed to be cut. I got the scissors from the office and began to clip away. Then Marvin grabbed my hair again with his other hand. I put down the scissors and tried to pry him off. He was pretty strong. I sat there trying to break free for quite a while. I was thinking about picking up Marvin and dunking him into a tub of water so he'd be forced to either drown or let me go. Then I noticed that there were streaks of red blood on the bedsheets and suddenly there was a warm damp spot underneath where I was sitting. I thought, "Marvin has cut me."

But what had actually happened was he had grabbed the scissors with his other hand, the hand which wasn't holding my hair, and stabbed himself in the leg. This was a real mess. I'm not even sure if Marvin knew what he had done. I picked him up and wrapped him in the sheet. I ran down the hallway with Marvin in my arms. He was still holding on to my hair. When we reached the front desk I got on the phone and dialed for an ambulance. As we waited, I tried again to pry my hair from his fingers. Eventually I saw that he would never release me so I just tugged it hard and he took a whole fistful of my hair with him. Then I sat him on a plastic chair and used towels to soak up the blood, which was dark and copious, from his leg. Then the ambulance arrived.

I expected Marvin to wrestle with the paramedics, but he was very calm. Perhaps he'd been through this before. Maybe he recognized them by the way that they smelled. The paramedics wrapped his leg up tight and off we went to the hospital. Marvin had punctured a large vein in his inner thigh. It wasn't an artery, they said, but close. They gave him fourteen stitches and a pint of new blood. When we got back from the hospital the supervisor at the school made me fill out several pages of "incident report" forms and then I had to clean up the bed. The mattress was coated with plastic to protect it from bed wetting, so I just rinsed it off in the shower. After I was through I met with the residential staff supervisor who explained that I should never have brought those scissors into his room. I should have filled out a request form for a more hefty pair of clippers.

I was suspended from work for two weeks while they reviewed my conduct. When I returned to the school I was no longer working with Marvin. I was transferred to another dormitory altogether. There I was given charge of two brothers from Mexico, Santos and Miguel. Their parents were farmworkers who had been exposed to some strong pesticides in South Texas. As a result Santos and Miguel had been born without eyes. Where their eyes should have been, they had these little flesh-colored balls of skin.

But Santos and Miguel could hear everything. Their ears worked well. They knew how to communicate. Everything with them would be fine.

Texas School for the Blind

Questions for discussion

1. What is the point of this story?

2. What does the story say about the narrator's attitudes? How does the narrator perceive disability?

3. What does this story say about institutionalization? Do you think the narrator is a good fit for this job? Why or why not? Do you think the scissor incident was his fault? What allusions does he make to the training he has or has not received? Do you think his next assignment with the two brothers will go better? Why or why not?

4. Many states have eliminated such "schools" in favor of community living. What is the history of such institutions in your state?

5. Design your own discussion questions for this story.

For Further Reading

About institutionalization

Porter, Katherine Anne. "He." Short story about a family who decides to institutionalize their child.

Shapiro, Joseph. *No Pity*, chapter 10: "Crossing the Luck Line." The author's autobiographical account of befriending someone with developmental disabilities who lives in an institution, and the advocacy efforts required to get his friend moved to a community setting.

Plath, Sylvia. *The Bell Jar*. Semi-autobiographical novel that includes harrowing episodes of electric shock "therapy" and institutionalization.

About Arthur Bradford's work

http://www.randomhouse.com/knopf/authors/bradford/desktop.html

The Man That Was Used Up

I cannot just now remember when or where I first made the acquaintance of that truly fine-looking fellow, Brevet Brigadier General John A. B. C. Smith. Someone *did* introduce me to the gentleman, I am sure—at some public meeting, I know very well—held about something of great importance, no doubt—at some place or other, I feel convinced—whose name I have unaccountably forgotten. The truth is—that the introduction was attended, upon my part, with a degree of anxious embarrassment which operated to prevent any definite impressions of either time or place. I am constitutionally nervous—this, with me, is a family failing, and I can't help it. In especial, the slightest appearance of mystery—of any point I cannot exactly comprehend— puts me at once into a pitiable state of agitation.

There was something, as it were, remarkable—yes, *remarkable*, although this is but a feeble term to express my full meaning—about the entire individuality of the personage in question. He was, perhaps, six feet in height, and of a presence singularly commanding. There was an *air distingué* pervading the whole man, which spoke of high breeding, and hinted at high birth. Upon this topic—the topic of Smith's personal appearance—I have a kind of melancholy satisfaction in being minute. His head of hair would have done honor to a Brutus;—nothing could be more richly flowing, or possess a brighter gloss. It was of a jetty black;—which was also the color, or more properly the no color of his unimaginable whiskers. You perceive I cannot speak of these latter without enthusiasm; it is not too much to say that they were the handsomest pair of whiskers under the sun. At all events, they encircled, and at times partially overshadowed, a mouth utterly unequalled. Here were the most entirely even, and the most brilliantly white of all conceivable teeth. From between them, upon every proper occasion, issued a voice of surpassing clearness, melody, and strength. In the matter of eyes, also, my acquaintance was pre-eminently endowed. Either one of such a pair was worth a couple of the ordinary ocular organs. They were of a deep hazel, exceedingly large and lustrous; and there was perceptible about them, ever and anon, just that amount of interesting obliquity which gives pregnancy to expression.

The bust of the General was unquestionably the finest bust I ever saw. For your life you could not have found a fault with its wonderful proportion. This rare peculiarity set off to great advantage a pair of shoulders which would have called up a blush of conscious inferiority into the countenance of the marble Apollo. I have a passion for fine shoulders, and may say that I never beheld them in perfection before. The arms altogether were admirably modeled. Nor were the lower limbs less superb. These were, indeed, the *ne plus ultra* of good legs. Every connoisseur in such matters admitted the legs to be good. There was neither too much flesh, nor too little,—neither rudeness nor fragility. I could not imagine a more graceful curve than that of the *os femoris*, and there was just that due gentle prominence in the rear of the fibula which goes to the conformation of a properly proportioned calf. I wish to God my young and talented friend Chiponchipino, the sculptor, had but seen the legs of Brevet Brigadier General John A. B. C. Smith.

But although men so absolutely fine-looking are neither as plenty as reasons or blackberries, still I could not bring myself to believe that the remarkable something to which I alluded just now,—that the odd air of *je ne sais quoi* which hung about my new acquaintance,—lay altogether, or indeed at all, in the supreme excellence of his bodily endowments. Perhaps it might be traced to the manner;—yet here again I could not pretend to be positive. There was a primness, not to say stiffness, in his carriage—a degree of measured, and, if I may so express it, of rectangular precision, attending his every movement, which, observed in a more diminutive figure, would have had the least little savor in the world, of affectation, pomposity or constraint, but which noticed in a gentleman of his undoubted dimensions, was readily placed to the account of reserve, hauteur—of a commendable sense, in short, of what is due to the dignity of colossal proportion.

The kind friend who presented me to General Smith whispered in my ear some few words of comment upon the man. He was a *remarkable* man—a *very remarkable* man—indeed one of the *most remarkable men* of the age. He was an especial favorite, too, with the ladies—chiefly on account of his high reputation for courage.

"In that point he is unrivaled—indeed he is a perfect desperado—a downright fire-eater, and no mistake," said my friend, here dropping his voice excessively low, and thrilling me with the mystery of his tone.

"A downright fire-eater, and *no* mistake. Showed *that*, I should say, to some purpose, in the late tremendous swamp-fight away down South, with the Bugaboo and Kickapoo Indians." (Here my friend opened his eyes to some extent.) "Bless my soul!—blood and thunder, and all that!—prodigies of valor!—heard of him of course?—you know he's the man—"

"Man alive, how do you do? Why, how are ye? Very glad to see ye, indeed!" here interrupted the General himself, seizing my companion by the hand as he drew near, and bowing stiffly, but profoundly, as I was presented. I then thought, (and I think so still,) that I never heard a clearer nor a stronger voice, nor beheld a finer set of teeth: but I must say that I was sorry for the interruption just at that moment, as, owing to the whispers and insinuations aforesaid, my interest had been greatly excited in the hero of the Bugaboo and Kickapoo campaign.

However, the delightfully luminous conversation of Brevet Brigadier General John A. B. C. Smith soon completely dissipated this chagrin. My friend leaving us immediately, we had quite a long *tête-à-tête*, and I was not only pleased but really instructed. I never heard a more fluent talker, or a man of greater general information. With becoming modesty, he forbore, nevertheless, to touch upon the theme I had just then most at heart—I mean the mysterious circumstances attending the Bugaboo war—and, on my own part, what I conceive to be a proper sense of delicacy forbade me to broach the subject; although, in truth, I was exceedingly tempted to do so. I perceived, too, that the gallant soldier preferred topics of philosophical interest, and that he delighted, especially, in commenting upon the rapid march of mechanical invention. Indeed, lead him where I would, this was a point to which he invariably came back.

"There is nothing at all like it," he would say; "we are a wonderful people, and live in a wonderful age. Parachutes and railroads—man-traps and spring-guns! Our steam-boats are upon every sea, and the Nassau balloon packet is about to run regular trips (fare either way only twenty pounds sterling) between London and Timbuktu. And who shall calculate the immense influence upon social life—upon arts—upon commerce—upon literature—which will be the immediate result of the great principles of electromagnetics! Nor is this all, let me assure you! There is really no end to the march of invention. The most wonderful—the most ingenious—and let me add, Mr.—Mr.— Thompson, I believe, is your name—let me add, I say, the most *useful*—the most truly useful mechanical contrivances, are daily springing up like mushrooms, if I may so express myself, or, more figuratively, like—ah—grasshoppers—like grasshoppers, Mr. Thompson—about us and ah—ah—ah—around us!"

Thompson, to be sure, is not my name; but it is needless to say that I left General Smith with a heightened interest in the man, with an exalted opinion of his conversational powers, and a deep sense of the valuable privileges we enjoy in living in this age of mechanical invention. My curiosity, however, had not been altogether satisfied, and I resolved to prosecute immediate inquiry among my acquaintances touching the Brevet Brigadier General himself, and particularly respecting the tremendous events during the Bugaboo and Kickapoo campaign.

The first opportunity which presented itself, and which I did not in the least scruple to seize, occurred at the Church of the Reverend Doctor Drummummupp, where I found myself established, one Sunday, just at sermon time, not only in the pew, but by the side, of that worthy and communicative little friend of mine, Miss Tabitha T. Thus seated, I congratulated myself, and with much reason, upon the very flattering state of affairs. If any person knew anything about Brevet Brigadier General John A. B. C. Smith, that person, it was clear to me, was Miss Tabitha T. We telegraphed a few signals, and then commenced, *sotto voce*, a brisk *tête-à-tête*.

"Smith!" said she, in reply to my very earnest inquiry; "Smith!—why, not General John A. B. C.? Bless me, I thought you *knew* all about him! This is a wonderfully inventive age! Horrid affair that!—a bloody set of wretches, those Kickapoos!—fought like a hero—prodigies of valor—immortal renown. Smith! —Brevet Brigadier General John A. B. C.! Why, you know he's the man"—

"Man," here broke in Doctor Drummummupp, at the top of his voice, and with a thump that came near knocking the pulpit about our ears; "man that is born of a woman hath but a short time to live; he cometh up and is cut down like a flower!" I started to the extremity of the pew, and perceived by the animated looks of the divine, that the wrath which had nearly proved fatal to the pulpit had been excited by the whispers of the lady and myself. There was no help for it; so I submitted with a good grace, and listened, in all the martyrdom of dignified silence, to the balance of that very capital discourse.

Next evening found me a somewhat late visitor at the Rantipole theatre, where I felt sure of satisfying my curiosity at once, by merely stepping into the box of those exquisite specimens of affability and omniscience, the Misses Arabella and Miranda Cognoscenti. That fine tragedian, Climax, was doing Iago to a very crowded house, and I experienced some little difficulty in making my wishes understood; especially, as our box was next to the slips, and completely overlooked the stage.

"Smith?" said Miss Arabella, as she at length comprehended the purport of my query; "Smith?—why, not General John A. B. C.?"

"Smith?" inquired Miranda, musingly. "God bless me, did you ever behold a finer figure?"

"Never, madam, but *do* tell me—"

"Or so inimitable grace?"

"Never, upon my word!—But pray inform me—"

"Or so just an appreciation of stage effect?"

"Madam!"

"Or a more delicate sense of the true beauties of Shakespeare? Be so good as to look at that leg!"

"The devil!" and I turned again to her sister.

"Smith?" said she, "why, not General John A. B. C.? Horrid affair that, wasn't it?—great wretches, those Bugaboos—savage and so on—but we live in a wonderfully inventive age!—Smith!—O yes! great man!—perfect desperado—immortal renown—prodigies of valor! Never heard!" (This was given in a scream.) "Bless my soul! why, he's the man—"

Here roared our Climax just in my ear, and shaking his fist in my face all the time, in a way that I *couldn't* stand, and I *wouldn't.* I left the Misses Cognoscenti immediately, went behind the scenes forthwith, and gave the beggarly scoundrel such a thrashing as I trust he will remember to the day of his death.

At the *soirée* of the lovely widow, Mrs. Kathleen O'Trump, I was confident that I should meet with no similar disappointment. Accordingly, I was no sooner seated at the card-table, with my pretty hostess for a *vis-à-vis*, than I propounded those questions the solution of which had become a matter so essential to my peace.

"Smith?" said my partner, "why, not General John A. B. C.? Horrid affair that, wasn't it?—diamonds, did you say?—terrible wretches those Kickapoos!—we are playing whist, if you please, Mr. Tattle—however, this is the age of invention, most certainly *the* age, one may say—the age *par excellence*—speak French?—oh, quite a hero—perfect desperado!—*no hearts*, Mr. Tattle? I don't believe it!—immortal renown and all that!—prodigies of valor! Never heard!!—why, bless me, he's the man—"

"Mann?—Captain Mann?" here screamed some little feminine interloper from the farthest corner of the room. "Are you talking about Captain Mann and the duel?—oh, I *must* hear—do tell—go on, Mrs. O'Trump!—do now go on!" And go on Mrs. O'Trump did—all about a certain Captain Mann, who was either shot or hung, or should have been both shot and hung. Yes! Mrs. O'Trump, she went on, and I—I went off. There was no chance of hearing anything farther that evening in regard to Brevet Brigadier General John A. B. C. Smith.

Still I consoled myself with the reflection that the tide of ill luck would not run against me forever, and so determined to make a bold push for information at the rout of that bewitching little angel, the graceful Mrs. Pirouette.

"Smith?" said Mrs. P., as we twirled about together in a *pas de zephyr,* "Smith?—why, not General John A. B. C.? Dreadful business that of the Bugaboos, wasn't it?—*Do* turn out your toes! I really am ashamed of you—man of great courage, poor fellow!—but this is a wonderful age for invention—O dear me, I'm out of breath—quite a desperado—prodigies of valor—never heard!!—can't believe it—I shall have to sit down and enlighten you—Smith! why, he's the man—"

"Man-Fred, I tell you!" here bawled out Miss Bas-Bleu, as I led Mrs. Pirouette to a seat. "Did ever anybody hear the like? It's Man-Fred, I say, and not at all by any means Man-Friday." Here Miss Bas-Bleu beckoned to me in a very peremptory manner; and I was obliged, willy-nilly, to leave Mrs. P. for the purpose of deciding a dispute touching the title of a certain poetical drama of Lord Byron's. Although I pronounced, with great promptness, that the true title was Man-Friday, and not by any means Man-Fred, yet when I returned to seek Mrs. Pirouette she was not to be discovered, and I made my retreat from the house in a very bitter spirit of animosity against the whole race of the Bas-Bleus.

There was one resource left me yet. I would go to the fountain-head. I would call forthwith upon the General himself, and demand, in explicit terms, a solution of this abominable piece of mystery. Here, at least, there should be no chance for equivocation. I would be plain, positive, peremptory—as short as pie-crust—as concise as Tacitus or Montesquieu.

It was early when I called, and the General was dressing; but I pleaded urgent business, and was shown at once into his bed-room by an old valet, who remained in attendance during my visit. As I entered the chamber, I looked about, of course, for the occupant, but did not immediately perceive him. There was a large and exceedingly odd-looking bundle of something which lay close by my feet on the floor, and, as I was not in the best humor in the world, I gave it a kick out of the way.

"Hem! Ahem! Rather civil that, I should say!" said the bundle, in one of the smallest, and altogether the funniest little voices, between a squeak and a whistle, that I ever heard in all the days of my existence.

I fairly shouted with terror, and made off, at a tangent, into the farthest extremity of the room.

"God bless me! my dear fellow," here again whistled the bundle, "what—what —what—why, what *is* the matter? I really believe you don't know me at all."

What *could* I say to all this—what *could* I? I staggered into an arm-chair, and, with staring eyes and open mouth, awaited the solution of the wonder.

"Strange you shouldn't know me though, isn't it?" presently re-squeaked the nondescript, which I now perceived was performing, upon the floor, some inexplicable evolution, very analogous to the drawing on of a stocking. There was only a single leg, however, apparent.

"Strange you shouldn't know me, though, isn't it? Pompey, bring me that leg!" Here Pompey handed the bundle a very capital cork leg, already dressed, which it screwed on in a trice; and then it stood up before my eyes.

"And a bloody action it *was*," continued the thing, as if in a soliloquy; "but then one mustn't fight with the Bugaboos and Kickapoos, and think of coming off with a mere scratch. Pompey, I'll thank you now for that arm. Thomas," (turning to me), "is decidedly the best hand at a cork leg; but if you should ever want an arm, my dear fellow, you must really let me recommend you to Bishop." Here Pompey screwed on an arm.

"We had rather hot work of it, that you may say. Now, you dog, slip on my shoulders and bosom! Pettitt makes the best shoulders, but for a bosom you will have to go to Ducrow."

"Bosom!" said I.

"Pompey, will you *never* be ready with that wig? Scalping is a rough process after all; but then you can procure such a capital scratch at DeL'Orme's."

"Scratch!"

"Now, my teeth! For a *good* set of these you had better go to Parmly's at once; high prices, but excellent work. I swallowed some very capital articles, though, when the big Bugaboo rammed me down with the butt end of his rifle."

"Butt end! Ram down!! My eye!!"

"O yes, by-the-by, my eye—here, Pompey, you scamp, screw it in! Those Kickapoos are not so very slow at a gouge; but he's a belied man, that Dr. Williams, after all; you can't imagine how well I see with the eyes of his make."

I now began very clearly to perceive that the object before me was nothing more nor less than my new acquaintance, Brevet Brigadier General John A. B. C. Smith. The manipulations of Pompey had made, I must confess, a very striking difference in the appearance of the personal man. The voice, however, still puzzled me no little; but even this apparent mystery was speedily cleared up.

"Pompey, you rascal," squeaked the General, "I really do believe you would let me go out without my palate."

Hereupon, the servant, grumbling out an apology, went up to his master, opened his mouth with the knowing air of a horse-jockey, and adjusted therein a somewhat singular-looking machine, in a very dexterous manner, that I could not altogether comprehend. The alteration, however, in the entire expression of the General's countenance was instantaneous and surprising. When he again spoke, his voice had resumed all that rich melody and strength which I had noticed upon our original introduction.

"Damn the vagabonds!" said he, in so clear a tone that I positively started at the change, "Damn the vagabonds! They not only knocked in the roof of my mouth, but took the trouble to cut off at least seven-eighths of my tongue. There isn't Bonfanti's equal, however, in America, for really good articles of this description. I can recommend you to him with confidence," (here the General bowed,) "and assure you that I have the greatest pleasure in so doing."

I acknowledged his kindness in my best manner, and took leave of him at once, with a perfect understanding of the true state of affairs — with a full comprehension of the mystery which had troubled me so long. It was evident. It was a clear case. Brevet Brigadier General John A. B. C. Smith was the man — was *the man that was used up.*

The Man That Was Used Up

Questions for discussion

1. What did you think of this story? What did you think the secret about the general was going to be?

2. This story raises the issue of hidden disabilities. Have you ever known someone a while before becoming aware of a disability they had? How did the issue arise?

3. Can you think of other characters in fiction that have prosthetics? Who are they, and how are their prosthetics treated in the story?

4. Design your own discussion questions for this story.

For Further Reading

About hidden disabilities

Kleege, Georgina. "Disabled Students Come Out." A professor's discussion about students' disclosures about their disabilities.

About prosthetics

http://www.cbsnews.com/stories/2008/01/14/sports/main3707924.shtml. A story about a sprinter who is disqualified from the Olympics because his two prosthetic legs "give him a clear competitive advantage."

Alexander McCall Smith (1948–) was born in Zimbabwe and educated there and in Scotland. He is a Professor of Medical Law at the University of Edinburgh. He has written several texts on medical law, criminal law, and philosophy, as well as several best-selling series of books, including the No. 1 Ladies Detective Agency Series, from which the following excerpt derives.

from Tears of the Giraffe

[Editor's note: Mr. J. L. B. Matekoni lives in Botswana and owns a mechanic shop, Tlokweng Road Speedy Motors. He is engaged to marry Mma Ramotswe, who runs her own detective agency. Mr. J. L. B. Matekoni often goes out to a local orphan farm to help with any mechanical issues they have. One day, while at the farm, he meets a young girl in a wheelchair, and is impressed with her manners and demeanor. Mma Potokwane, who is in charge of the orphans, later tells him how this young girl, after being orphaned, cared for herself and her brother before being brought to the farm. Mr. J. L. B. Matekoni is moved by her story, and Mma Potokwane, realizing this, tries to persuade him to care for the girl and her brother at his home.]

"They will be here in a few moments," [Mma Potokwane] said. "Do you want me to say that you might be prepared to take them?"

Mr. J. L. B. Matekoni closed his eyes. He had not spoken to Mma Ramotswe about it and it seemed quite wrong to land her with something like this without consulting her first. Was this the way to start a marriage? To take a decision of such momentum without consulting one's spouse? Surely not.

And yet here were the children. The girl in her wheelchair, smiling up at him and the boy standing there so gravely, eyes lowered out of respect.

He drew in his breath. There were times in life when one had to act, and this, he suspected, was one of them.

"Would you children like to come and stay with me?" he said.

. . . .

[Editor's note: the children gladly come to stay with Mr. J. L. B. Matekoni, and he quickly becomes attached to them. However, he has not yet had the courage to tell his fiancee that he has assumed care of two children without asking her! He takes the children to town to go shopping and have their photographs taken, and while there, they run into his fiancee Mma Ramotswe.]

Mr. J. L. B. Matekoni was aware of the fact that he was standing directly under the branch of an acacia tree. He looked up, and saw for a moment, in utter clarity, the details of the leaves against the emptiness of the sky. Drawn in upon themselves for the midday heat, the leaves were like tiny hands clasped in prayer; a bird, a common butcher bird, scruffy and undistinguished, was perched farther up the branch, claws clasped tight, black eyes darting. It was the sheer enormity of Mr. J. L. B. Matekoni's plight that made this perception so vivid; as a condemned man might peep out of his cell on his last morning and see the familiar, fading world.

He looked down, and saw that Mma Ramotswe was still there, standing some ten feet away, her expression one of bemused puzzlement. She knew that he worked for the orphan farm, and she was aware of Mma Silvia Potokwane's persuasive ways. She would be imagining, he thought, that here was Mr. J. L. B. Matekoni taking two of the orphans out for the day and arranging for them to have their photographs taken. She would not be imagining that here was Mr. J. L. B. Matekoni with his two new foster children, soon to be her foster children too.

Mma Ramotswe broke the silence. "What are you doing?" she said simply. It was an entirely reasonable question—the sort of question that any friend or indeed fiancee may ask of another. Mr. J. L. B. Matekoni looked down at the children. The girl had placed her photograph in a plastic carrier bag that was attached to the side of her wheelchair; the boy was clutching his photograph to his chest, as if Mma Ramotswe might wish to take it from him.

"These are two children from the orphan farm," stuttered Mr. J. L. B. Matekoni. "This one is the girl and this one is the boy."

Mma Ramotswe laughed. "Well!" she said. "So that is it. That is very helpful."

The girl smiled and greeted Mma Ramotswe politely.

"I am called Motholeli," she said. "My brother is called Puso. These are the names that we have been given at the orphan farm."

Mma Ramotswe nodded. "I hope that they are looking after you well, there. Mma Potokwane is a kind lady."

"She is kind," said the girl. "Very kind."

She looked as if she was about to say something else, and Mr. J. L. B. Matekoni broke in rapidly.

"I have had the children's photographs taken," he explained, and turning to the girl, he said: "Show them to Mma Ramotswe, Motholeli."

The girl propelled her chair forward and passed the photograph to Mma Ramotswe, who admired it.

"That is a very nice photograph to have," she said. "I have only one or two photographs of myself when I was your age. If ever I am feeling old, I go and take a look at them and I think that maybe I am not so old after all."

"You are still young," said Mr. J. L. B. Matekoni. "We are not old these days until we are seventy—maybe more. It has all changed."

"That's what we like to think," chuckled Mma Ramotswe, passing the photograph back to the girl. "Is Mr. J. L. B. Matekoni taking you back now, or are you going to eat in town?"

"We have been shopping," Mr. J. L. B. Matekoni blurted out. "We may have one or two other things to do."

"We will go back to his house soon," the girl said. "We are living with Mr. J. L. B. Matekoni now. We are staying in his house."

Mr. J. L. B. Matekoni felt his heart thump wildly against his chest. I am going to have a heart attack, he thought. I am going to die now. And for a moment he felt immense regret that he would never marry Mma Ramotswe, that he would go to his grave a bachelor, that the children would be twice orphaned, that Tlokweng Road Speedy Motors would close. But his heart did not stop, but continued to beat, and Mma Ramotswe and all the physical world remained stubbornly there.

Mma Ramotswe looked quizzically at Mr. J. L. B. Matekoni.

"They are staying in your house?" she said. "This is a new development. Have they just come?"

He nodded bleakly. "Yesterday," he said.

Mma Ramotswe looked down at the children and then back at Mr. J. L. B. Matekoni.

"I think that we should have a talk," she said. "You children stay here for a moment. Mr. J. L. B. Matekoni and I are going to the post office."

There was no escape. Head hanging, like a schoolboy caught in delinquency, he followed Mma Ramotswe to the corner of the post office, where before the stacked rows of private postal boxes, he faced the judgment and sentence that he knew were his lot. She would divorce him—if that was the correct term for the breakup of an engagement. He had lost her because of his dishonesty and stupidity—and it was all Mma Silvia Potokwane's fault. Women like that were always interfering in the lives of others, forcing them to do things; and then matters went badly astray and lives were ruined in the process.

Mma Ramotswe put down her basket of letters.

"Why did you not tell me about these children?" she asked. "What have you done?"

He hardly dared meet her gaze. "I was going to tell you," he said. "I was out at the orphan farm yesterday. The pump was playing up. It's so old. Then their minibus needs new brakes. I have tried to fix those brakes, but they are always giving problems. We shall have to try and find new parts, I have told them that, but ..."

"Yes, yes," pressed Mma Ramotswe. "You have told me about those brakes before. But what about these children?"

Mr. J. L. B. Matekoni sighed. "Mma Potokwane is a very strong woman. She told me that I should take some foster children. I did not mean to do it without talking to you, but she would not listen to me. She brought in the children and I really had no alternative. It was very hard for me."

He stopped. A man passed on his way to his postal box, fumbling in his pocket for his key, muttering something to himself. Mma Ramotswe glanced at the man and then looked back at Mr. J. L. B. Matekoni.

"So," she said, "you agreed to take these children. And now they think that they are going to stay."

"Yes, I suppose so," he mumbled.

"And how long for?" asked Mma Ramotswe.

Mr. J. L. B. Matekoni took a deep breath. "For as long as they need a home," he said. "Yes, I offered them that."

Unexpectedly he felt a new confidence. He had done nothing wrong. He had not stolen anything, or killed anybody, or committed adultery. He had just offered to change the lives of two poor children who had nothing and who would now be loved and looked after. If Mma Ramotswe did not like that, well, there was nothing he could do about it now. He had been impetuous, but his impetuosity had been in a good cause.

Mma Ramotswe suddenly laughed. "Well, Mr. J. L. B. Matekoni," she said. "Nobody could say of you that you are not a kind man. You are, I think, the kindest man in Botswana. What other man would do that? I do not know of one, not one single one. Nobody else would do that. Nobody."

He stared at her. "You are not cross?"

"I was," she said. "But only for a little while. One minute maybe. But then I thought: Do I want to marry the kindest man in the country? I do. Can I be a mother for them? I can."

❦

from Tears of the Giraffe

Questions for discussion

1. Mr. J. L. B. Matekoni says there are times in life when one has to act. Can you think of such instances?

2. Throughout this book and its sequels, Motholeli is consistently shown as just a good person, with her disability rarely mentioned as having any importance to the plot. Can you think of other instances in literature or film where characters with disabilities are seen just as themselves, without special focus on the disability?

3. What do you know about the prevalence of children with disabilities in the foster care system? What could be done to alleviate this problem?

4. Design your own discussion questions for this selection.

For Further Reading

About becoming disabled

Smith, Alexander McCall. *The Double Comfort Safari Club.* Another installment in the No. 1 Ladies' Detective Agency, in which a friend of Mma Ramotswe becomes injured and disabled.

About the plight of orphans with disabilities

Bratt, Kay. *Silent Tears: A Journey of Hope in a Chinese Orphanage.* An American spends time volunteering in a Chinese orphanage, and meets and befriends many children with disabilities.

The Metamorphosis

I

One morning, when Gregor Samsa woke from troubled dreams, he found himself transformed in his bed into a horrible vermin. He lay on his armor-like back, and if he lifted his head a little he could see his brown belly, slightly domed and divided by arches into stiff sections. The bedding was hardly able to cover it and seemed ready to slide off any moment. His many legs, pitifully thin compared with the size of the rest of him, waved about helplessly as he looked.

"What's happened to me?" he thought. It wasn't a dream. His room, a proper human room although a little too small, lay peacefully between its four familiar walls. A collection of textile samples lay spread out on the table—Samsa was a travelling salesman—and above it there hung a picture that he had recently cut out of an illustrated magazine and housed in a nice, gilded frame. It showed a lady fitted out with a fur hat and fur boa who sat upright, raising a heavy fur muff that covered the whole of her lower arm towards the viewer.

Gregor then turned to look out the window at the dull weather. Drops of rain could be heard hitting the pane, which made him feel quite sad. "How about if I sleep a little bit longer and forget all this nonsense," he thought, but that was something he was unable to do because he was used to sleeping on his right, and in his present state couldn't get into that position. However hard he threw himself onto his right, he always rolled back to where he was. He must have tried it a hundred times, shut his eyes so that he wouldn't have to look at the floundering legs, and only stopped when he began to feel a mild, dull pain there that he had never felt before.

"Oh, God," he thought, "what a strenuous career it is that I've chosen! Traveling day in and day out. Doing business like this takes much more effort than doing your own business at home, and on top of that there's the curse of trav-eling, worries about making train connections, bad and irregular food, con-tact with different people all the time so that you can never get to know any-one or become friendly with them. It can all go to Hell!" He felt a slight itch up on his belly; pushed himself slowly up on his back towards the headboard so that he could lift his head better; found where the itch was, and saw that it was covered with lots of little white spots which he didn't know what to make of; and when he tried to feel the place with one of his legs he drew it quickly back because as soon as he touched it he was overcome by a cold shudder.

He slid back into his former position. "Getting up early all the time," he thought, "it makes you stupid. You've got to get enough sleep. Other travel-ling salesmen live a life of luxury. For instance, whenever I go back to the guest house during the morning to copy out the contract, these gentlemen are al-ways still sitting there eating their breakfasts. I ought to just try that with my boss; I'd get kicked out on the spot. But who knows, maybe that would be the best thing for me. If I didn't have my parents to think about I'd have given in my notice a long time ago, I'd have gone up to the boss and told him just what I think, tell him everything I would, let him know just what I feel. He'd fall right off his desk! And it's a funny sort of business to be sitting up there at your desk, talking down at your subordinates from up there, especially when you have to go right up close because the boss is hard of hearing. Well, there's still some hope; once I've got the money together to pay off my parents' debt to him—another five or six years I suppose—that's definitely what I'll do. That's when I'll make the big change. First of all though, I've got to get up, my train leaves at five."

And he looked over at the alarm clock, ticking on the chest of drawers. "God in Heaven!" he thought. It was half past six and the hands were quietly moving forwards, it was even later than half past, more like quarter to seven. Had the alarm clock not rung? He could see from the bed that it had been set for four o'clock as it should have been; it certainly must have rung. Yes, but was it possible to quietly sleep through that furniture-rattling noise? True, he had not slept peacefully, but probably all the more deeply because of that. What should he do now? The next train went at seven; if he were to catch that he would have to rush like mad and the collection of samples was still not packed, and he did not at all feel particularly fresh and lively. And even if he did catch the train he would not avoid his boss's anger as the office assistant would have been there to see the five o'clock train go, he would have put in his report about Gregor's not being there a long time ago. The office assistant was the boss's man, spineless, and with no understanding. What about if he reported sick? But that would be extremely strained and suspicious as in fif-

teen years of service Gregor had never once yet been ill. His boss would certainly come round with the doctor from the medical insurance company, accuse his parents of having a lazy son, and accept the doctor's recommendation not to make any claim as the doctor believed that no-one was ever ill but
that many were workshy. And what's more, would he have been entirely wrong
in this case? Gregor did in fact, apart from excessive sleepiness after sleeping
for so long, feel completely well and even felt much hungrier than usual.

He was still hurriedly thinking all this through, unable to decide to get out
of the bed, when the clock struck quarter to seven. There was a cautious knock
at the door near his head.

"Gregor," somebody called—it was his mother—"it's quarter to seven.
Didn't you want to go somewhere?"

That gentle voice! Gregor was shocked when he heard his own voice an
swering, it could hardly be recognized as the voice he had had before. As if
from deep inside him, there was a painful and uncontrollable squeaking mixed
in with it, the words could be made out at first but then there was a sort of
echo which made them unclear, leaving the hearer unsure whether he had
heard properly or not. Gregor had wanted to give a full answer and explain
everything, but in the circumstances contented himself with saying: "Yes,
mother, yes, thank you, I'm getting up now." The change in Gregor's voice
probably could not be noticed outside through the wooden door, as his
mother was satisfied with this explanation and shuffled away. But this short
conversation made the other members of the family aware that Gregor, against
their expectations, was still at home, and soon his father came knocking at
one of the side doors, gently, but with his fist.

"Gregor, Gregor," he called, "what's wrong?" And after a short while he
called again with a warning deepness in his voice: "Gregor! Gregor!"

At the other side door his sister came plaintively: "Gregor? Aren't you well?
Do you need anything?"

Gregor answered to both sides: "I'm ready, now," making an effort to remove all the strangeness from his voice by enunciating very carefully and putting long pauses between each, individual word.

His father went back to his breakfast, but his sister whispered: "Gregor,
open the door, I beg of you." Gregor, however, had no thought of opening the
door, and instead congratulated himself for his cautious habit, acquired from
his traveling, of locking all doors at night even when he was at home.

The first thing he wanted to do was to get up in peace without being disturbed, to get dressed, and most of all to have his breakfast. Only then would
he consider what to do next, as he was well aware that he would not bring his
thoughts to any sensible conclusions by lying in bed. He remembered that he

had often felt a slight pain in bed, perhaps caused by lying awkwardly, but that had always turned out to be pure imagination and he wondered how his imaginings would slowly resolve themselves today. He did not have the slightest doubt that the change in his voice was nothing more than the first sign of a serious cold, which was an occupational hazard for traveling salesmen.

It was a simple matter to throw off the covers; he only had to blow himself up a little and they fell off by themselves. But it became difficult after that, especially as he was so exceptionally broad. He would have used his arms and his hands to push himself up; but instead of them he only had all those little legs continuously moving in different directions, and which he was moreover unable to control. If he wanted to bend one of them, then that was the first one that would stretch itself out; and if he finally managed to do what he wanted with that leg, all the others seemed to be set free and would move about painfully. "This is something that can't be done in bed," Gregor said to himself, "so don't keep trying to do it."

The first thing he wanted to do was get the lower part of his body out of the bed, but he had never seen this lower part, and could not imagine what it looked like; it turned out to be too hard to move; it went so slowly; and finally, almost in a frenzy, when he carelessly shoved himself forwards with all the force he could gather, he chose the wrong direction, hit hard against the lower bedpost, and learned from the burning pain he felt that the lower part of his body might well, at present, be the most sensitive.

So then he tried to get the top part of his body out of the bed first, carefully turning his head to the side. This he managed quite easily, and despite its breadth and its weight, the bulk of his body eventually followed slowly in the direction of the head. But when he had at last got his head out of the bed and into the fresh air it occurred to him that if he let himself fall it would be a miracle if his head were not injured, so he became afraid to carry on pushing himself forward the same way. And he could not knock himself out now at any price; better to stay in bed than lose consciousness.

It took just as much effort to get back to where he had been earlier, but when he lay there sighing, and was once more watching his legs as they struggled against each other even harder than before, if that was possible, he could think of no way of bringing peace and order to this chaos. He told himself once more that it was not possible for him to stay in bed and that the most sensible thing to do would be to get free of it in whatever way he could at whatever sacrifice. At the same time, though, he did not forget to remind himself that calm consideration was much better than rushing to desperate conclusions. At times like this he would direct his eyes to the window and look out as clearly as he could, but unfortunately, even the other side of the narrow street was enveloped in morning fog and the view had little confidence or cheer to offer him. "Seven o'clock, already," he said to himself when the clock struck again, "seven o'clock, and there's still a fog like this." And he lay there quietly a while longer, breathing lightly as if he perhaps expected the total stillness to bring things back to their real and natural state.

But then he said to himself: "Before it strikes quarter past seven I'll definitely have to have got properly out of bed. And by then somebody will have come round from work to ask what's happened to me as well, as they open up at work before seven o'clock." And so he set himself to the task of swinging the entire length of his body out of the bed all at the same time. If he succeeded in falling out of bed in this way and kept his head raised as he did so he could probably avoid injuring it. His back seemed to be quite hard, and probably nothing would happen to it falling onto the carpet. His main concern was for the loud noise he was bound to make, and which even through all the doors would probably raise concern if not alarm. But it was something that had to be risked.

When Gregor was already sticking half way out of the bed—the new method was more of a game than an effort, all he had to do was rock back and forth—it occurred to him how simple everything would be if somebody came to help him. Two strong people—he had his father and the maid in mind—would have been more than enough; they would only have to push their arms under the dome of his back, peel him away from the bed, bend down with the load and then be patient and careful as he swung over onto the floor, where, hopefully, the little legs would find a use. Should he really call for help though, even apart from the fact that all the doors were locked? Despite all the difficulty he was in, he could not suppress a smile at this thought.

After a while he had already moved so far across that it would have been hard for him to keep his balance if he rocked too hard. The time was now ten past seven and he would have to make a final decision very soon. Then there was a ring at the door of the flat. "That'll be someone from work," he said to himself, and froze very still, although his little legs only became all the more lively as they danced around. For a moment everything remained quiet. "They're not opening the door," Gregor said to himself, caught in some nonsensical hope. But then of course, the maid's firm steps went to the door as ever and opened it. Gregor only needed to hear the visitor's first words of greeting and he knew who it was—the chief clerk himself. Why did Gregor have to be the only one condemned to work for a company where they immediately became highly suspicious at the slightest shortcoming? Were all employees, every one of them, louts, was there not one of them who was faithful and devoted who would go so mad with pangs of conscience that he couldn't get out of bed if he didn't spend at least a couple of hours in the morning on company business? Was it really not enough to let one of the trainees make inquiries—assuming inquiries were even necessary—did the chief clerk have to come himself, and did they have to show the whole, innocent family that this was so suspicious that only the chief clerk could be trusted to have the wisdom to investigate it? And more because these thoughts had made him upset than through any proper decision, he swung himself with all his force out of the bed. There was a loud thump, but it wasn't really a loud noise. His fall was softened a little by the carpet, and Gregor's back was also more elastic than he had thought, which made the sound muffled and not too noticeable. He had not held his head carefully enough, though, and hit it as he fell; annoyed and in pain, he turned it and rubbed it against the carpet.

"Something's fallen down in there," said the chief clerk in the room on the left. Gregor tried to imagine whether something of the sort that had happened to him today could ever happen to the chief clerk too; you had to concede that it was possible. But as if in gruff reply to this question, the chief clerk's firm footsteps in his highly polished boots could now be heard in the adjoining room. From the room on his right, Gregor's sister whispered to him to let him know: "Gregor, the chief clerk is here." "Yes, I know," said Gregor to himself; but without daring to raise his voice loud enough for his sister to hear him.

"Gregor," said his father now from the room to his left, "the chief clerk has come round and wants to know why you didn't leave on the early train. We don't know what to say to him. And anyway, he wants to speak to you personally. So please open up this door. I'm sure he'll be good enough to forgive the untidiness of your room."

Then the chief clerk called, "Good morning, Mr. Samsa."

"He isn't well," said his mother to the chief clerk, while his father continued to speak through the door. "He isn't well, please believe me. Why else would Gregor have missed a train! The lad only ever thinks about the business. It nearly makes me cross the way he never goes out in the evenings; he's been in town for a week now but stayed home every evening. He sits with us in the kitchen and just reads the paper or studies train timetables. His idea of relaxation is working with his fretsaw. He's made a little frame, for instance, it only took him two or three evenings, you'll be amazed how nice it is; it's hanging up in his room; you'll see it as soon as Gregor opens the door. Anyway, I'm glad you're here; we wouldn't have been able to get Gregor to open the door by ourselves; he's so stubborn; and I'm sure he isn't well, he said this morning that he is, but he isn't."

"I'll be there in a moment," said Gregor slowly and thoughtfully, but without moving so that he would not miss any word of the conversation.

"Well, I can't think of any other way of explaining it, Mrs. Samsa," said the chief clerk, "I hope it's nothing serious. But on the other hand, I must say that if we people in commerce ever become slightly unwell then, fortunately or unfortunately as you like, we simply have to overcome it because of business considerations."

"Can the chief clerk come in to see you now, then?" asked his father impatiently, knocking at the door again.

"No," said Gregor. In the room on his right there followed a painful silence; in the room on his left his sister began to cry.

So why did his sister not go and join the others? She had probably only just got up and had not even begun to get dressed. And why was she crying? Was it because he had not got up, and had not let the chief clerk in, because he was in danger of losing his job and if that happened his boss would once more pursue their parents with the same demands as before? There was no need to worry about things like that yet. Gregor was still there and had not the slightest intention of abandoning his family. For the time being he just lay there on the carpet, and no one who knew the condition he was in would seriously have expected him to let the chief clerk in. It was only a minor discourtesy, and a suitable excuse could easily be found for it later on, it was not something for which Gregor could be sacked on the spot. And it seemed to Gregor much more sensible to leave him now in peace instead of disturbing him with talking at him and crying. But the others didn't know what was happening, they were worried, that would excuse their behavior.

The chief clerk now raised his voice. "Mr. Samsa," he called to him, "what is wrong? You barricade yourself in your room, give us no more than yes or no for an answer, you are causing serious and unnecessary concern to your parents and you fail—and I mention this just by the way—you fail to carry out your business duties in a way that is quite unheard of. I'm speaking here on behalf of your parents and of your employer, and really must request a clear and immediate explanation. I am astonished, quite astonished. I thought I knew you as a calm and sensible person, and now you suddenly seem to be showing off with peculiar whims. This morning, your employer did suggest a possible reason for your failure to appear, it's true—it had to do with the money that was recently entrusted to you—but I came near to giving him my word of honor that that could not be the right explanation. But now that I see your incomprehensible stubbornness I no longer feel any wish whatsoever to intercede on your behalf. And nor is your position all that secure. I had originally intended to say all this to you in private, but since you cause me to waste my time here for no good reason I don't see why your parents should not also learn of it. Your turnover has been very unsatisfactory of late; I grant you that it's not the time of year to do especially good business, we recognize that; but there simply is no time of year to do no business at all, Mr. Samsa, we cannot allow there to be."

"But Sir," called Gregor, beside himself and forgetting all else in the excitement, "I'll open up immediately, just a moment. I'm slightly unwell, an attack of dizziness, I haven't been able to get up. I'm still in bed now. I'm quite fresh again now, though. I'm just getting out of bed. Just a moment. Be patient! It's not quite as easy as I'd thought. I'm quite all right now, though. It's shocking, what can suddenly happen to a person! I was quite all right last night, my parents know about it, perhaps better than me, I had a small symptom of it last night already. They must have noticed it. I don't know why I didn't let you know at work! But you always think you can get over an illness without staying at home. Please, don't make my parents suffer! There's no basis for any of the accusations you're making; nobody's ever said a word to me about any of these things. Maybe you haven't read the latest contracts I sent in. I'll set off with the eight o'clock train, as well, these few hours of rest have given me strength. You don't need to wait, sir; I'll be in the office soon after you, and please be so good as to tell that to the boss and recommend me to him!"

And while Gregor gushed out these words, hardly knowing what he was saying, he made his way over to the chest of drawers—this was easily done, probably because of the practice he had already had in bed—where he now tried to get himself upright. He really did want to open the door, really did want to let them see him and to speak with the chief clerk; the others were being so insistent, and he was curious to learn what they would say when they caught sight of him. If they were shocked then it would no longer be Gregor's responsibility and he could rest. If, however, they took everything calmly he would still have no reason to be upset, and if he hurried he really could be at the station for eight o'clock. The first few times he tried to climb up on the smooth chest of drawers he just slid down again, but he finally gave himself one last swing and stood there upright; the lower part of his body was in serious pain but he no longer gave any attention to it. Now he let himself fall against the back of a nearby chair and held tightly to the edges of it with his little legs. By now he had also calmed down, and kept quiet so that he could listen to what the chief clerk was saying.

"Did you understand a word of all that?" the chief clerk asked his parents, "surely he's not trying to make fools of us."

"Oh, God!" called his mother, who was already in tears, "he could be seriously ill and we're making him suffer. Grete! Grete!" she then cried.

"Mother?" his sister called from the other side. They communicated across Gregor's room. "You'll have to go for the doctor straight away. Gregor is ill. Quick, get the doctor. Did you hear the way Gregor spoke just now?"

"That was the voice of an animal," said the chief clerk, with a calmness that was in contrast with his mother's screams.

"Anna! Anna!" his father called into the kitchen through the entrance hall, clapping his hands, "get a locksmith here, now!" And the two girls, their skirts swishing, immediately ran out through the hall, wrenching open the front door of the flat as they went. How had his sister managed to get dressed so quickly? There was no sound of the door banging shut again; they must have left it open; people often do in homes where something awful has happened.

Gregor, in contrast, had become much calmer. So they couldn't understand his words any more, although they seemed clear enough to him, clearer than before—perhaps his ears had become used to the sound. They had realized, though, that there was something wrong with him, and were ready to help. The first response to his situation had been confident and wise, and that made him feel better. He felt that he had been drawn back in among people, and from the doctor and the locksmith he expected great and surprising achievements—although he did not really distinguish one from the other. Whatever was said next would be crucial, so, in order to make his voice as clear as possible, he coughed a little, but taking care to do this not too loudly as even this might well sound different from the way that a human coughs and he was no longer sure he could judge this for himself. Meanwhile, it had become very quiet in the next room. Perhaps his parents were sat at the table whispering with the chief clerk, or perhaps they were all pressed against the door and listening.

Gregor slowly pushed his way over to the door with the chair. Once there he let go of it and threw himself onto the door, holding himself upright against it using the adhesive on the tips of his legs. He rested there a little while to recover from the effort involved and then set himself to the task of turning the key in the lock with his mouth. He seemed, unfortunately, to have no proper teeth—how was he, then, to grasp the key?—but the lack of teeth was, of course, made up for with a very strong jaw; using the jaw, he really was able to start the key turning, ignoring the fact that he must have been causing some kind of damage as a brown fluid came from his mouth, flowed over the key and dripped onto the floor.

"Listen," said the chief clerk in the next room, "he's turning the key." Gregor was greatly encouraged by this; but they all should have been calling to him, his father and his mother too: "Well done, Gregor," they should have cried, "keep at it, keep hold of the lock!" And with the idea that they were all excitedly following his efforts, he bit on the key with all his strength, paying no attention to the pain he was causing himself. As the key turned round he turned around the lock with it, only holding himself upright with his mouth, and hung onto the key or pushed it down again with the whole weight of his body as needed. The clear sound of the lock as it snapped back was Gregor's sign that he could break his concentration, and as he regained his breath he said to himself: "So, I didn't need the locksmith after all." Then he lay his head on the handle of the door to open it completely.

Because he had to open the door in this way, it was already wide open before he could be seen. He had first to slowly turn himself around one of the double doors, and he had to do it very carefully if he did not want to fall flat on his back before entering the room. He was still occupied with this difficult movement, unable to pay attention to anything else, when he heard the chief clerk exclaim a loud "Oh!", which sounded like the soughing of the wind. Now he also saw him—he was the nearest to the door—his hand pressed against his open mouth and slowly retreating as if driven by a steady and invisible force. Gregor's mother, her hair still disheveled from bed despite the chief clerk's being there, looked at his father. Then she unfolded her arms, took two steps forward towards Gregor and sank down onto the floor into her skirts that spread themselves out around her as her head disappeared down onto her breast. His father looked hostile, and clenched his fists as if wanting to knock Gregor back into his room. Then he looked uncertainly round the living room, covered his eyes with his hands and wept so that his powerful chest shook.

So Gregor did not go into the room, but leant against the inside of the other door which was still held bolted in place. In this way only half of his body could be seen, along with his head above it which he leant over to one side as he peered out at the others. Meanwhile the day had become much lighter; part of the endless, grey-black building on the other side of the street—which was a hospital—could be seen quite clearly with the austere and regular line of windows piercing its facade; the rain was still falling, now throwing down large, individual droplets which hit the ground one at a time. The washing up from breakfast lay on the table; there was so much of it because, for Gregor's father, breakfast was the most important meal of the day and he would stretch it out for several hours as he sat reading a number of different newspapers. On the wall exactly opposite there was photograph of Gregor when he was a lieutenant in the army, his sword in his hand and a carefree smile on his face as he called forth respect for his uniform and bearing. The door to the entrance hall was open and as the front door of the flat was also open he could see onto the landing and the stairs where they began their way down below.

"Now, then," said Gregor, well aware that he was the only one to have kept calm, "I'll get dressed straight away now, pack up my samples and set off. Will you please just let me leave? You can see," he said to the chief clerk, "that I'm not stubborn and I like to do my job; being a commercial traveler is arduous but without traveling I couldn't earn my living. So where are you going, in to the office? Yes? Will you report everything accurately, then? It's quite possible for someone to be temporarily unable to work, but that's just the right time to remember what's been achieved in the past and consider that later on, once the difficulty has been removed, he will certainly work with all the more diligence and concentration. You're well aware that I'm seriously in debt to our employer as well as having to look after my parents and my sister, so that I'm trapped in a difficult situation, but I will work my way out of it again. Please don't make things any harder for me than they are already, and don't take sides against me at the office. I know that nobody likes the travelers. They think we earn an enormous wage as well as having a soft time of it. That's just prejudice but they have no particular reason to think better of it. But you, sir, you have a better overview than the rest of the staff, in fact, if I can say this in confidence, a better overview than the boss himself—it's very easy for a businessman like him to make mistakes about his employees and judge them more harshly than he should. And you're also well aware that we travelers spend almost the whole year away from the office, so that we can very easily fall victim to gossip and chance and groundless complaints, and it's almost impossible to defend yourself from that sort of thing, we don't usually even hear about them, or if at all it's when we arrive back home exhausted from a trip, and that's when we feel the harmful effects of what's been going on without even knowing what caused them. Please, don't go away, at least first say something to show that you grant that I'm at least partly right!"

But the chief clerk had turned away as soon as Gregor had started to speak, and, with protruding lips, only stared back at him over his trembling shoulders as he left. He did not keep still for a moment while Gregor was speaking, but moved steadily towards the door without taking his eyes off him. He moved very gradually, as if there had been some secret prohibition on leaving the room. It was only when he had reached the entrance hall that he made a sudden movement, drew his foot from the living room, and rushed forward in a panic. In the hall, he stretched his right hand far out towards the stairway as if out there, there were some supernatural force waiting to save him.

Gregor realized that it was out of the question to let the chief clerk go away in this mood if his position in the firm was not to be put into extreme danger. That was something his parents did not understand very well; over the years, they had become convinced that this job would provide for Gregor for his entire life, and besides, they had so much to worry about at present that they had lost sight of any thought for the future. Gregor, though, did think about the future. The chief clerk had to be held back, calmed down, convinced and finally won over; the future of Gregor and his family depended on it! If only his sister were here! She was clever; she was already in tears while Gregor was still lying peacefully on his back. And the chief clerk was a lover of women, surely she could persuade him; she would close the front door in the entrance hall and talk him out of his shocked state. But his sister was not there, Gregor would have to do the job himself. And without considering that he still was not familiar with how well he could move about in his present state, or that his speech still might not—or probably would not—be understood, he let go of the door; pushed himself through the opening; tried to reach the chief clerk on the landing who, ridiculously, was holding on to the banister with both hands; but Gregor fell immediately over and, with a little scream as he sought something to hold onto, landed on his numerous little legs.

Hardly had that happened than, for the first time that day, he began to feel all right with his body; the little legs had the solid ground under them; to his pleasure, they did exactly as he told them; they were even making the effort to carry him where he wanted to go; and he was soon believing that all his sorrows would soon be finally at an end. He held back the urge to move but swayed from side to side as he crouched there on the floor. His mother was not far away in front of him and seemed, at first, quite engrossed in herself, but then she suddenly jumped up with her arms outstretched and her fingers spread shouting: "Help, for pity's sake, Help!" The way she held her head suggested she wanted to see Gregor better, but the unthinking way she was hurrying backwards showed that she did not; she had forgotten that the table was behind her with all the breakfast things on it; when she reached the table she sat quickly down on it without knowing what she was doing; without even seeming to notice that the coffee pot had been knocked over and a gush of coffee was pouring down onto the carpet.

"Mother, mother," said Gregor gently, looking up at her. He had completely forgotten the chief clerk for the moment, but could not help himself snapping in the air with his jaws at the sight of the flow of coffee. That set his mother screaming anew; she fled from the table and into the arms of his father as he rushed towards her. Gregor, though, had no time to spare for his parents now; the chief clerk had already reached the stairs; with his chin on the banister, he looked back for the last time. Gregor made a run for him; he wanted to be sure of reaching him. The chief clerk must have expected something, as he leapt down several steps at once and disappeared, his shouts resounding all around the staircase. The flight of the chief clerk seemed, unfortunately, to put Gregor's father into a panic as well. Until then he had been relatively self controlled, but now, instead of running after the chief clerk himself, or at least not impeding Gregor as he ran after him, Gregor's father seized the chief clerk's stick in his right hand (the chief clerk had left it behind on a chair, along with his hat and overcoat), picked up a large newspaper from the table with his left, and used them to drive Gregor back into his room, stamping his foot at him as he went. Gregor's appeals to his father were of no help, his appeals were simply not understood, however much he humbly turned his head his father merely stamped his foot all the harder.

Across the room, despite the chilly weather, Gregor's mother had pulled open a window, leant far out of it and pressed her hands to her face. A strong draught of air flew in from the street towards the stairway, the curtains flew up, the newspapers on the table fluttered and some of them were blown onto the floor. Nothing would stop Gregor's father as he drove him back, making hissing noises at him like a wild man. Gregor had never had any practice in moving backwards and was only able to go very slowly. If Gregor had only been allowed to turn round he would have been back in his room straight away, but he was afraid that if he took the time to do that his father would become impatient, and there was the threat of a lethal blow to his back or head from the stick in his father's hand any moment. Eventually, though, Gregor realized that he had no choice as he saw, to his disgust, that he was quite incapable of going backwards in a straight line; so he began, as quickly as possible and with frequent anxious glances at his father, to turn himself round. It went very slowly, but perhaps his father was able to see his good intentions as he did nothing to hinder him, in fact now and then he used the tip of his stick to give directions from a distance as to which way to turn. If only his father would stop that unbearable hissing! It was making Gregor quite confused. When he had nearly finished turning round, still listening to that hissing, he made a mistake and turned himself back a little the way he had just come. He was pleased when he finally had his head in front of the doorway, but then saw that it was too narrow, and his body was too broad to get through it without further difficulty. In his present mood, it obviously did not occur to his father to open the other of the double doors so that Gregor would have enough space to get through. He was merely fixed on the idea that Gregor should be got back into his room as quickly as possible. Nor would he ever have allowed Gregor the time to get himself upright as preparation for getting through the doorway. What he did, making more noise than ever, was to drive Gregor forwards all the harder as if there had been nothing in the way; it sounded to Gregor as if there was now more than one father behind him; it was not a pleasant experience, and Gregor pushed himself into the doorway without regard for what might happen. One side of his body lifted itself, he lay at an angle in the doorway, one flank scraped on the white door and was painfully injured, leaving vile brown flecks on it. Soon he was stuck fast and would not have been able to move at all by himself, the little legs along one side hung quivering in the air while those on the other side were pressed painfully against the ground. Then his father gave him a hefty shove from behind which released him from where he was held and sent him flying, and heavily bleeding, deep into his room. The door was slammed shut with the stick, then, finally, all was quiet.

II

It was not until it was getting dark that evening that Gregor awoke from his deep and coma-like sleep. He would have woken soon afterwards anyway even if he hadn't been disturbed, as he had had enough sleep and felt fully rested. But he had the impression that some hurried steps and the sound of the door leading into the front room being carefully shut had woken him. The light from the electric street lamps shone palely here and there onto the ceiling and tops of the furniture, but down below, where Gregor was, it was dark. He pushed himself over to the door, feeling his way clumsily with his antennae—of which he was now beginning to learn the value—in order to see what had been happening there. The whole of his left side seemed like one, painfully stretched scar, and he limped badly on his two rows of legs. One of the legs had been badly injured in the events of that morning—it was nearly a miracle that only one of them had been—and dragged along lifelessly.

It was only when he had reached the door that he realized what it actually was that had drawn him over to it; it was the smell of something to eat. By the door there was a dish filled with sweetened milk with little pieces of white bread floating in it. He was so pleased he almost laughed, as he was even hungrier than he had been that morning, and immediately dipped his head into the milk, nearly covering his eyes with it. But he soon drew his head back again in disappointment; not only did the pain in his tender left side make it difficult to eat the food—he was only able to eat if his whole body worked together as a snuffling whole—but the milk did not taste at all nice. Milk like this was normally his favorite drink, and his sister had certainly left it there for him because of that, but he turned, almost against his own will, away from the dish and crawled back into the center of the room.

Through the crack in the door, Gregor could see that the gas had been lit in the living room. His father at this time would normally be sitting with his evening paper, reading it out in a loud voice to Gregor's mother, and sometimes to his sister, but there was now not a sound to be heard. Gregor's sister would often write and tell him about this reading, but maybe his father had lost the habit in recent times. It was so quiet all around too, even though there must have been somebody in the flat. "What a quiet life it is the family lead," said Gregor to himself, and, gazing into the darkness, felt a great pride that he was able to provide a life like that in such a nice home for his sister and parents. But what now, if all this peace and wealth and comfort should come to a horrible and frightening end? That was something that Gregor did not want to think about too much, so he started to move about, crawling up and down the room.

Once during that long evening, the door on one side of the room was opened very slightly and hurriedly closed again; later on the door on the other side did the same; it seemed that someone needed to enter the room but thought better of it. Gregor went and waited immediately by the door, resolved either to bring the timorous visitor into the room in some way or at least to find out who it was, but the door was opened no more that night and Gregor waited in vain. The previous morning while the doors were locked everyone had wanted to get in there to him, but now, now that he had opened up one of the doors and the other had clearly been unlocked some time during the day, no one came, and the keys were in the other side.

It was not until late at night that the gaslight in the living room was put out, and now it was easy to see that his parents and sister had stayed awake all that time, as they all could be distinctly heard as they went away together on tiptoe. It was clear that no one would come into Gregor's room anymore until morning; that gave him plenty of time to think undisturbed about how he would have to re-arrange his life. For some reason, the tall, empty room where he was forced to remain made him feel uneasy as he lay there flat on the floor, even though he had been living in it for five years. Hardly aware of what he was doing other than a slight feeling of shame, he hurried under the couch. It pressed down on his back a little, and he was no longer able to lift his head, but he nonetheless felt immediately at ease and his only regret was that his body was too broad to get it all underneath.

He spent the whole night there. Some of the time he passed in a light sleep, although he frequently woke from it in alarm because of his hunger, and some of the time was spent in worries and vague hopes which, however, always led to the same conclusion: for the time being he must remain calm, he must show patience and the greatest consideration so that his family could bear the unpleasantness that he, in his present condition, was forced to impose on them.

Gregor soon had the opportunity to test the strength of his decisions, as early the next morning, almost before the night had ended, his sister, nearly fully dressed, opened the door from the front room and looked anxiously in.

She did not see him straight away, but when she did notice him under the couch—he had to be somewhere, for God's sake, he couldn't have flown away—she was so shocked that she lost control of herself and slammed the door shut again from outside. But she seemed to regret her behavior, as she opened the door again straight away and came in on tiptoe as if entering the room of someone seriously ill or even of a stranger. Gregor had pushed his head forward, right to the edge of the couch, and watched her. Would she notice that he had left the milk as it was, realize that it was not from any lack of hunger and bring him in some other food that was more suitable? If he didn't do it herself he would rather go hungry than draw her attention to it, although he did feel a terrible urge to rush forward from under the couch, throw himself at his sister's feet and beg her for something good to eat. However, his sister noticed the full dish immediately and looked at it and the few drops of milk splashed around it with some surprise. She immediately picked it up—using a rag, not her bare hands—and carried it out.

Gregor was extremely curious as to what she would bring in its place, imagining the wildest possibilities, but he never could have guessed what his sister, in her goodness, actually did bring. In order to test his taste, she brought him a whole selection of things, all spread out on an old newspaper. There were old, half-rotten vegetables; bones from the evening meal, covered in white sauce that had gone hard; a few raisins and almonds; some cheese that Gregor had declared inedible two days before; a dry roll and some bread spread with butter and salt. As well as all that, she had poured some water into the dish, which had probably been permanently set aside for Gregor's use, and placed it beside them. Then, out of consideration for Gregor's feelings, as she knew that he would not eat in front of her, she hurried out again and even turned the key in the lock so that Gregor would know he could make things as comfortable for himself as he liked. Gregor's little legs whirred; at last he could eat. What's more, his injuries must already have completely healed as he found no difficulty in moving. This amazed him, as more than a month earlier he had cut his finger slightly with a knife, and he thought of how his finger had still hurt the day before yesterday. "Am I less sensitive than I used to be, then?" he thought, and was already sucking greedily at the cheese which had immediately, almost compellingly, attracted him much more than the other foods on the newspaper. Quickly one after another, his eyes watering with pleasure, he consumed the cheese, the vegetables and the sauce; the fresh foods, on the other hand, he didn't like at all, and he even dragged the things he did want to eat a little way away from them because he couldn't stand the smell.

Long after he had finished eating and lay lethargic in the same place, his sister slowly turned the key in the lock as a sign to him that he should withdraw. He was immediately startled, although he had been half asleep, and he hurried back under the couch. But he needed great self control to stay there even for the short time that his sister was in the room, as eating so much food had rounded out his body a little and he could hardly breathe in that narrow space. Half suffocating, he watched with bulging eyes as his sister unselfconsciously took a broom and swept up the leftovers, mixing them in with the food he had not even touched at all as if it could not be used any more. She quickly dropped it all into a bin, closed it with its wooden lid, and carried everything out. She had hardly turned her back before Gregor came out again from under the couch and stretched himself.

This was how Gregor received his food each day now, once in the morning while his parents and the maid were still asleep, and the second time after everyone had eaten their meal at midday as his parents would sleep for a little while then as well, and Gregor's sister would send the maid away on some errand. Gregor's father and mother certainly did not want him to starve either, but perhaps it would have been more than they could stand to have any more experience of his feeding than being told about it, and perhaps his sister wanted to spare them what distress she could as they were indeed suffering enough.

It was impossible for Gregor to find out what they had told the doctor and the locksmith that first morning to get them out of the flat. As nobody could understand him, nobody, not even his sister, thought that he could understand them, so he had to be content to hear his sister's sighs and appeals to the saints as she moved about his room. It was only later, when she had become a little more used to everything—there was, of course, no question of her ever becoming fully used to the situation—that Gregor would sometimes catch a friendly comment, or at least a comment that could be construed as friendly. "He's enjoyed his dinner today," she might say when he had diligently cleared away all the food left for him, or if he left most of it, which slowly became more and more frequent, she would often say, sadly, "now everything's just been left there again."

Although Gregor wasn't able to hear any news directly he did listen to much of what was said in the next rooms, and whenever he heard anyone speaking he would scurry straight to the appropriate door and press his whole body against it. There was seldom any conversation, especially at first, that was not about him in some way, even if only in secret. For two whole days, all the talk at every mealtime was about what they should do now, but even between meals they spoke about the same subject as there were always at least two members of the family at home—nobody wanted to be at home by themselves and it was out of the question to leave the flat entirely empty. And on the very first day the maid had fallen to her knees and begged Gregor's mother to let her go without delay. It was not very clear how much she knew of what had happened but she left within a quarter of an hour, tearfully thanking Gregor's mother for her dismissal as if she had done her an enormous service. She even swore emphatically not to tell anyone the slightest about what had happened, even though no one had asked that of her.

Now Gregor's sister also had to help his mother with the cooking, although that was not so much bother as no one ate very much. Gregor often heard how one of them would unsuccessfully urge another to eat, and receive no more answer than "no thanks, I've had enough," or something similar. No one drank very much either. His sister would sometimes ask his father whether he would like a beer, hoping for the chance to go and fetch it herself. When his father then said nothing she would add, so that he would not feel selfish, that she could send the housekeeper for it, but then his father would close the matter with a big, loud "No," and no more would be said.

Even before the first day had come to an end, his father had explained to Gregor's mother and sister what their finances and prospects were. Now and then he stood up from the table and took some receipt or document from the little cash box he had saved from his business when it had collapsed five years earlier. Gregor heard how he opened the complicated lock and then closed it again after he had taken the item he wanted. What he heard his father say was some of the first good news that Gregor heard since he had first been incarcerated in his room. He had thought that nothing at all remained from his father's business, at least he had never told him anything different, and Gregor had never asked him about it anyway. Their business misfortune had reduced the family to a state of total despair, and Gregor's only concern at that time had been to arrange things so that they could all forget about it as quickly as possible. So then he started working especially hard, with a fiery vigor that raised him from a junior salesman to a traveling representative almost overnight, bringing with it the chance to earn money in quite different ways. Gregor converted his success at work straight into cash that he could lay on the table at home for the benefit of his astonished and delighted family. They had been good times and they had never come again, at least not with the same splendor, even though Gregor had later earned so much that he was in a position to bear the costs of the whole family, and did bear them. They had even got used to it, both Gregor and the family. They took the money with gratitude and he was glad to provide it, although there was no longer much warm affection given in return. Gregor only remained close to his sister now. Unlike him, she was very fond of music and a gifted and expressive violinist; it was his secret plan to send her to the conservatory next year even though it would cause great expense that would have to be made up for in some other way. During Gregor's short periods in town, conversation with his sister would often turn to the conservatory but it was only ever mentioned as a lovely dream that could never be realized. Their parents did not like to hear this innocent talk, but Gregor thought about it quite hard and decided he would let them know what he planned with a grand announcement of it on Christmas day.

That was the sort of totally pointless thing that went through his mind in his present state, pressed up right against the door and listening. There were times when he simply became too tired to continue listening, when his head would fall wearily against the door and he would pull it up again with a start, as even the slightest noise he caused would be heard next door and they would all go silent. "What's that he's doing now?" his father would say after a while, clearly having gone over to the door, and only then would the interrupted conversation slowly be taken up again.

When explaining things, his father repeated himself several times, partly because it was a long time since he had been occupied with these matters himself and partly because Gregor's mother did not understand everything the first time. From these repeated explanations Gregor learned, to his pleasure, that despite all their misfortunes there was still some money available from the old days. It was not a lot, but it had not been touched in the meantime and some interest had accumulated. Besides that, they had not been using up all the money that Gregor had been bringing home every month, keeping only a little for himself, so that that, too, had been accumulating. Behind the door, Gregor nodded with enthusiasm in his pleasure at this unexpected thrift and caution. He could actually have used this surplus money to reduce his father's debt to his boss, and the day when he could have freed himself from that job would have come much closer, but now it was certainly better the way his father had done things.

This money, however, was certainly not enough to enable the family to live off the interest; it was enough to maintain them for, perhaps, one or two years, no more. That's to say, it was money that should not really be touched but set aside for emergencies; money to live on had to be earned. His father was healthy but old, and lacking in self confidence. During the five years that he had not been working—the first holiday in a life that had been full of strain and no success—he had put on a lot of weight and become very slow and clumsy. Would Gregor's elderly mother now have to go and earn money? She suffered from asthma and it was a strain for her just to move about the home, every other day would be spent struggling for breath on the sofa by the open window. Would his sister have to go and earn money? She was still a child of seventeen, her life up till then had been very enviable, consisting of wearing nice clothes, sleeping late, helping out in the business, joining in with a few modest pleasures and most of all playing the violin. Whenever they began to talk of the need to earn money, Gregor would always first let go of the door and then throw himself onto the cool, leather sofa next to it, as he became quite hot with shame and regret.

He would often lie there the whole night through, not sleeping a wink but scratching at the leather for hours on end. Or he might go to all the effort of pushing a chair to the window, climbing up onto the sill and, propped up in the chair, leaning on the window to stare out of it. He had used to feel a great sense of freedom from doing this, but doing it now was obviously something more remembered than experienced, as what he actually saw in this way was becoming less distinct every day, even things that were quite near; he had used to curse the ever-present view of the hospital across the street, but now he could not see it at all, and if he had not known that he lived in Charlotten-strasse, which was a quiet street despite being in the middle of the city, he could have thought that he was looking out the window at a barren waste where the gray sky and the gray earth mingled inseparably. His observant sister only needed to notice the chair twice before she would always push it back to its exact position by the window after she had tidied up the room, and even left the inner pane of the window open from then on.

If Gregor had only been able to speak to his sister and thank her for all that she had to do for him it would have been easier for him to bear it; but as it was it caused him pain. His sister, naturally, tried as far as possible to pretend there was nothing burdensome about it, and the longer it went on, of course, the better she was able to do so, but as time went by Gregor was also able to see through it all so much better. It had even become very unpleasant for him, now, whenever she entered the room. No sooner had she come in than she would quickly close the door as a precaution so that no one would have to suf-fer the view into Gregor's room, then she would go straight to the window and pull it hurriedly open almost as if she were suffocating. Even if it was cold, she would stay at the window breathing deeply for a little while. She would alarm Gregor twice a day with this running about and noise making; he would stay under the couch shivering the whole while, knowing full well that she would certainly have liked to spare him this ordeal, but it was impossible for her to be in the same room with him with the windows closed.

One day, about a month after Gregor's transformation when his sister no longer had any particular reason to be shocked at his appearance, she came into the room a little earlier than usual and found him still staring out the window, motionless, and just where he would be most horrible. In itself, his sister's not coming into the room would have been no surprise for Gregor as it would have been difficult for her to immediately open the window while he was still there, but not only did she not come in, she went straight back and closed the door behind her; a stranger would have thought he had threatened her and tried to bite her. Gregor went straight to hide himself under the couch, of course, but he had to wait until midday before his sister came back and she seemed much more uneasy than usual. It made him realize that she still found his appearance unbearable and would continue to do so; she probably even had to overcome the urge to flee when she saw the little bit of him that protruded from under the couch. One day, in order to spare her even this sight, he spent four hours carrying the bedsheet over to the couch on his back and arranged it so that he was completely covered and his sister would not be able to see him even if she bent down. If she did not think this sheet was necessary then all she had to do was take it off again, as it was clear enough that it was no pleasure for Gregor to cut himself off so completely. She left the sheet where it was. Gregor even thought he glimpsed a look of gratitude one time when he carefully looked out from under the sheet to see how his sister liked the new arrangement.

For the first fourteen days, Gregor's parents could not bring themselves to come into the room to see him. He would often hear them say how they appreciated all the new work his sister was doing even though, before, they had seen her as a girl who was somewhat useless and frequently been annoyed with her. But now the two of them, father and mother, would often both wait outside the door of Gregor's room while his sister tidied up in there, and as soon as she went out again she would have to tell them exactly how everything looked, what Gregor had eaten, how he had behaved this time and whether, perhaps, any slight improvement could be seen. His mother also wanted to go in and visit Gregor relatively soon but his father and sister at first persuaded her against it. Gregor listened very closely to all this, and approved fully. Later, though, she had to be held back by force, which made her call out: "Let me go and see Gregor, he is my unfortunate son! Can't you understand I have to see him?" and Gregor would think to himself that maybe it would be better if his mother came in, not every day of course, but one day a week, perhaps; she could understand everything much better than his sister who, for all her courage, was still just a child after all, and really might not have had an adult's appreciation of the burdensome job she had taken on.

Gregor's wish to see his mother was soon realized. Out of consideration for his parents, Gregor wanted to avoid being seen at the window during the day. The few square meters of the floor did not give him much room to crawl about, it was hard to just lie quietly through the night, his food soon stopped giving him any pleasure at all, and so, to entertain himself, he got into the habit of crawling up and down the walls and ceiling. He was especially fond of hanging from the ceiling; it was quite different from lying on the floor; he could breathe more freely; his body had a light swing to it; and up there, relaxed and almost happy, it might happen that he would surprise even himself by letting go of the ceiling and landing on the floor with a crash. But now, of course, he had far better control of his body than before and, even with a fall as great as that, caused himself no damage.

Very soon his sister noticed Gregor's new way of entertaining himself—he had, after all, left traces of the adhesive from his feet as he crawled about—and got it into her head to make it as easy as possible for him by removing the furniture that got in his way, especially the chest of drawers and the desk. Now, this was not something that she would be able to do by herself; she did not dare to ask for help from her father; the sixteen-year-old maid had carried on bravely since the cook had left but she certainly would not have helped in this, she had even asked to be allowed to keep the kitchen locked at all times and never to have to open the door unless it was especially important; so his sister had no choice but to choose sometime when Gregor's father was not there and fetch his mother to help her. As she approached the room, Gregor could hear his mother express her joy, but once at the door she went silent.

First, of course, his sister came in and looked round to see that everything in the room was all right, and only then did she let her mother enter. Gregor had hurriedly pulled the sheet down lower over the couch and put more folds into it so that everything really looked as if it had just been thrown down by chance. Gregor also refrained, this time, from spying out from under the sheet; he gave up the chance to see his mother until later and was simply glad that she had come.

"You can come in, he can't be seen," said his sister, obviously leading her in by the hand. The old chest of drawers was too heavy for a pair of feeble women to be heaving about, but Gregor listened as they pushed it from its place, his sister always taking on the heaviest part of the work for herself and ignoring her mother's warnings that she would strain herself. This lasted a very long time. After laboring at it for fifteen minutes or more his mother said it would be better to leave the chest where it was; for one thing it was too heavy for them to get the job finished before Gregor's father got home and leaving it in the middle of the room it would be in his way even more, and for another thing it wasn't even sure that taking the furniture away would really be any help to him. She thought just the opposite; the sight of the bare walls saddened her right to her heart; and why wouldn't Gregor feel the same way about it, he'd been used to this furniture in his room for a long time and it would make him feel abandoned to be in an empty room like that. Then, quietly, almost whispering as if wanting Gregor (whose whereabouts she did not know) to hear not even the tone of her voice, as she was convinced that he did not understand her words, she added "and by taking the furniture away, won't it seem like we're showing that we've given up all hope of improvement and we're abandoning him to cope for himself? I think it'd be best to leave the room exactly the way it was before so that when Gregor comes back to us again he'll find everything unchanged and he'll be able to forget the time in between all the easier."

Hearing these words from his mother made Gregor realize that the lack of any direct human communication, along with the monotonous life led by the family during these two months, must have made him confused—he could think of no other way of explaining to himself why he had seriously wanted his room emptied out. Had he really wanted to transform his room into a cave, a warm room fitted out with the nice furniture he had inherited? That would have let him crawl around unimpeded in any direction, but it would also have let him quickly forget his past when he had still been human. He had come very close to forgetting, and it had only been the voice of his mother, unheard for so long, that had shaken him out of it. Nothing should be removed; everything had to stay; he could not do without the good influence the furniture had on his condition; and if the furniture made it difficult for him to crawl about mindlessly that was not a loss but a great advantage.

His sister, unfortunately, did not agree; she had become used to the idea, not without reason, that she was Gregor's spokesman to his parents about the things that concerned him. This meant that his mother's advice now was sufficient reason for her to insist on removing not only the chest of drawers and the desk, as she had thought at first, but all the furniture apart from the all-important couch. It was more than childish perversity, of course, or the unexpected confidence she had recently acquired, that made her insist; she had indeed noticed that Gregor needed a lot of room to crawl about in, whereas the furniture, as far as anyone could see, was of no use to him at all. Girls of that age, though, do become enthusiastic about things and feel they must get their way whenever they can. Perhaps this was what tempted Grete to make Gregor's situation seem even more shocking than it was so that she could do even more for him. Grete would probably be the only one who would dare enter a room dominated by Gregor crawling about the bare walls by himself.

So she refused to let her mother dissuade her. Gregor's mother already looked uneasy in his room; she soon stopped speaking and helped Gregor's sister to get the chest of drawers out with what strength she had. The chest of drawers was something that Gregor could do without if he had to, but the writing desk had to stay. Hardly had the two women pushed the chest of drawers, groaning, out of the room than Gregor poked his head out from under the couch to see what he could do about it. He meant to be as careful and considerate as he could, but, unfortunately, it was his mother who came back first while Grete in the next room had her arms round the chest, pushing and pulling at it from side to side by herself without, of course, moving it an inch. His mother was not used to the sight of Gregor, he might have made her ill, so Gregor hurried backwards to the far end of the couch. In his startlement, though, he was not able to prevent the sheet at its front from moving a little. It was enough to attract his mother's attention. She stood very still, remained there a moment, and then went back out to Grete.

Gregor kept trying to assure himself that nothing unusual was happening, it was just a few pieces of furniture being moved after all, but he soon had to admit that the women going to and fro, their little calls to each other, the scraping of the furniture on the floor, all these things made him feel as if he were being assailed from all sides. With his head and legs pulled in against him and his body pressed to the floor, he was forced to admit to himself that he could not stand all of this much longer. They were emptying his room out; taking away everything that was dear to him; they had already taken out the chest containing his fretsaw and other tools; now they threatened to remove the writing desk with its place clearly worn into the floor, the desk where he had done his homework as a business trainee, at high school, even while he had been at infant school—he really could not wait any longer to see whether the two women's intentions were good. He had nearly forgotten they were there anyway, as they were now too tired to say anything while they worked and he could only hear their feet as they stepped heavily on the floor.

So, while the women were leant against the desk in the other room catching their breath, he sallied out, changed direction four times not knowing what he should save first before his attention was suddenly caught by the picture on the wall—which was already denuded of everything else that had been on it—of the lady dressed in copious fur. He hurried up onto the picture and pressed himself against its glass; it held him firmly and felt good on his hot belly. This picture at least, now totally covered by Gregor, would certainly be taken away by no one. He turned his head to face the door into the living room so that he could watch the women when they came back.

They had not allowed themselves a long rest and came back quite soon; Grete had put her arm around her mother and was nearly carrying her. "What shall we take now, then?" said Grete and looked around. Her eyes met those of Gregor on the wall. Perhaps only because her mother was there, she remained calm, bent her face to her so that she would not look round and said, albeit hurriedly and with a tremor in her voice: "Come on, let's go back in the living room for a while?" Gregor could see what Grete had in mind, she wanted to take her mother somewhere safe and then chase him down from the wall. Well, she could certainly try it! He sat unyielding on his picture. He would rather jump at Grete's face.

But Grete's words had made her mother quite worried. She stepped to one side, saw the enormous brown patch against the flowers of the wallpaper, and before she even realized it was Gregor that she saw, screamed: "Oh God, oh God!" Arms outstretched, she fell onto the couch as if she had given up everything and stayed there immobile. "Gregor!" shouted his sister, glowering at him and shaking her fist. That was the first word she had spoken to him directly since his transformation. She ran into the other room to fetch some kind of smelling salts to bring her mother out of her faint; Gregor wanted to help too—he could save his picture later, although he stuck fast to the glass and had to pull himself off by force; then he, too, ran into the next room as if he could advise his sister like in the old days; but he had to just stand behind her doing nothing; she was looking into various bottles, and he startled her when she turned round; a bottle fell to the ground and broke; a splinter cut Gregor's face, some kind of caustic medicine splashed all over him; now, without delaying any longer, Grete took hold of all the bottles she could and ran with them in to her mother; she slammed the door shut with her foot. So now Gregor was shut out from his mother, who, because of him, might be near to death; he could not open the door if he did not want to chase his sister away, and she had to stay with his mother; there was nothing for him to do but wait; and, oppressed with anxiety and self-reproach, he began to crawl about. He crawled over everything, walls, furniture, ceiling, and finally in his confusion as the whole room began to spin around him he fell down into the middle of the dinner table.

He lay there for a while, numb and immobile. All around him it was quiet; maybe that was a good sign. Then there was someone at the door. The maid, of course, had locked herself in her kitchen so that Grete would have to go and answer it. His father had arrived home. "What's happened?" were his first words; Grete's appearance must have made everything clear to him. She answered him with subdued voice, and openly pressed her face into his chest: "Mother's fainted, but she's better now. Gregor got out."

"Just as I expected," said his father, "just as I always said, but you women wouldn't listen, would you." It was clear to Gregor that Grete had not said enough and that his father took it to mean that something bad had happened, that he was responsible for some act of violence. That meant Gregor would now have to try to calm his father, as he did not have the time to explain things to him even if that had been possible. So he fled to the door of his room and pressed himself against it so that his father, when he came in from the hall, could see straight away that Gregor had the best intentions and would go back into his room without delay, that it would not be necessary to drive him back but that they had only to open the door and he would disappear.

His father, though, was not in the mood to notice subtleties like that; "Ah!" he shouted as he came in, sounding as if he were both angry and glad at the same time. Gregor drew his head back from the door and lifted it towards his father. He really had not imagined his father the way he stood there now; of late, with his new habit of crawling about, he had neglected to pay attention to what was going on the rest of the flat the way he had done before. He really ought to have expected things to have changed, but still, still, was that really his father? The same tired man as used to be laying there entombed in his bed when Gregor came back from his business trips, who would receive him sitting in the armchair in his nightgown when he came back in the evenings; who was hardly even able to stand up but, as a sign of his pleasure, would just raise his arms and who, on the couple of times a year when they went for a walk together on a Sunday or public holiday wrapped up tightly in his overcoat between Gregor and his mother, would always labor his way forward a little more slowly than them, who were already walking slowly for his sake; who would place his stick down carefully and, if he wanted to say something would invariably stop and gather his companions around him? He was standing up straight enough now; dressed in a smart blue uniform with gold buttons, the sort worn by the employees at the banking institute; above the high, stiff collar of the coat his strong double-chin emerged; under the bushy eyebrows, his piercing, dark eyes looked out fresh and alert; his normally unkempt white hair was combed down painfully close to his scalp. He took his cap, with its gold monogram from, probably, some bank, and threw it in an arc right across the room onto the sofa, put his hands in his trouser pockets, pushing back the bottom of his long uniform coat, and, with look of determination, walked towards Gregor. He probably did not even know himself what he had in mind, but nonetheless lifted his feet unusually high. Gregor was amazed at the enormous size of the soles of his boots, but wasted no time with that—he knew full well, right from the first day of his new life, that his father thought it necessary to always be extremely strict with him.

And so he ran up to his father, stopped when his father stopped, scurried forwards again when he moved, even slightly. In this way they went round the room several times without anything decisive happening, without even giving the impression of a chase as everything went so slowly. Gregor remained all this time on the floor, largely because he feared his father might see it as especially provoking if he fled onto the wall or ceiling. Whatever he did, Gregor had to admit that he certainly would not be able to keep up this running about for long, as for each step his father took he had to carry out countless movements. He became noticeably short of breath; even in his earlier life his lungs had not been very reliable. Now, as he lurched about in his efforts to muster all the strength he could for running he could hardly keep his eyes open; his thoughts became too slow for him to think of any other way of saving himself than running; he almost forgot that the walls were there for him to use although, here, they were concealed behind carefully carved furniture full of notches and protrusions—then, right beside him, lightly tossed, something flew down and rolled in front of him. It was an apple; then another one immediately flew at him; Gregor froze in shock; there was no longer any point in running as his father had decided to bombard him. He had filled his pockets with fruit from the bowl on the sideboard and now, without even taking the time for careful aim, threw one apple after another. These little, red apples rolled about on the floor, knocking into each other as if they had electric motors. An apple thrown without much force glanced against Gregor's back and slid off without doing any harm. Another one however, immediately following it, hit squarely and lodged in his back; Gregor wanted to drag himself away, as if he could remove the surprising, the incredible pain by changing his position; but he felt as if nailed to the spot and spread himself out, all his senses in confusion. The last thing he saw was the door of his room being pulled open, his sister was screaming, his mother ran out in front of her in her blouse (as his sister had taken off some of her clothes after she had fainted to make it easier for her to breathe), she ran to his father, her skirts unfastened and sliding one after another to the ground, stumbling over the skirts she pushed herself to his father, her arms around him, uniting herself with him totally—now Gregor lost his ability to see anything—her hands behind his father's head begging him to spare Gregor's life.

III

No one dared to remove the apple lodged in Gregor's flesh, so it remained there as a visible reminder of his injury. He had suffered it there for more than a month, and his condition seemed serious enough to remind even his father that Gregor, despite his current sad and revolting form, was a family member who could not be treated as an enemy. On the contrary, as a family there was a duty to swallow any revulsion for him and to be patient, just to be patient.

Because of his injuries, Gregor had lost much of his mobility—probably permanently. He had been reduced to the condition of an ancient invalid and it took him long, long minutes to crawl across his room—crawling over the ceiling was out of the question—but this deterioration in his condition was fully (in his opinion) made up for by the door to the living room being left open every evening. He got into the habit of closely watching it for one or two hours before it was opened and then, lying in the darkness of his room where he could not be seen from the living room, he could watch the family in the light of the dinner table and listen to their conversation—with everyone's permission, in a way, and thus quite differently from before.

They no longer held the lively conversations of earlier times, of course, the ones that Gregor always thought about with longing when he was tired and getting into the damp bed in some small hotel room. All of them were usually very quiet nowadays. Soon after dinner, his father would go to sleep in his chair; his mother and sister would urge each other to be quiet; his mother, bent deeply under the lamp, would sew fancy underwear for a fashion shop; his sister, who had taken a sales job, learned shorthand and French in the evenings so that she might be able to get a better position later on. Sometimes his father would wake up and say to Gregor's mother, "you're doing so much sewing again today!" as if he did not know that he had been dozing—and then he would go back to sleep again while mother and sister would exchange a tired grin.

With a kind of stubbornness, Gregor's father refused to take his uniform off even at home; while his nightgown hung unused on its peg Gregor's father would slumber where he was, fully dressed, as if always ready to serve and expecting to hear the voice of his superior even here. The uniform had not been new to start with, but as a result of this it slowly became even shabbier despite the efforts of Gregor's mother and sister to look after it. Gregor would often spend the whole evening looking at all the stains on this coat, with its gold buttons always kept polished and shiny, while the old man in it would sleep, highly uncomfortable but peaceful.

As soon as it struck ten, Gregor's mother would speak gently to his father to wake him and try to persuade him to go to bed, as he couldn't sleep properly where he was and he really had to get his sleep if he was to be up at six to get to work. But since he had been in work he had become more obstinate and would always insist on staying longer at the table, even though he regularly fell asleep and it was then harder than ever to persuade him to exchange the chair for his bed. Then, however much mother and sister would importune him with little reproaches and warnings he would keep slowly shaking his head for a quarter of an hour with his eyes closed and refusing to get up. Gregor's mother would tug at his sleeve, whisper endearments into his ear; Gregor's sister would leave her work to help her mother, but nothing would have any effect on him. He would just sink deeper into his chair. Only when the two women took him under the arms he would abruptly open his eyes, look at them one after the other and say: "What a life! This is what peace I get in my old age!" And supported by the two women he would lift himself up carefully as if he were carrying the greatest load himself, let the women take him to the door, send them off and carry on by himself while Gregor's mother would throw down her needle and his sister her pen so that they could run after his father and continue being of help to him.

Who, in this tired and overworked family, would have had time to give more attention to Gregor than was absolutely necessary? The household budget became even smaller; so now the maid was dismissed; an enormous, thick-boned charwoman with white hair that flapped around her head came every morning and evening to do the heaviest work; everything else was looked after by Gregor's mother on top of the large amount of sewing work she did. Gregor even learned, listening to the evening conversation about what price they had hoped for, that several items of jewelry belonging to the family had been sold, even though both mother and sister had been very fond of wearing them at functions and celebrations. But the loudest complaint was that although the flat was much too big for their present circumstances, they could not move out of it; there was no imaginable way of transferring Gregor to the new address. He could see quite well, though, that there were more reasons than consideration for him that made it difficult for them to move. It would have been quite easy to transport him in any suitable crate with a few air holes in it; the main thing holding the family back from their decision to move was much more to do with their total despair, and the thought that they had been struck with a misfortune unlike anything experienced by anyone else they knew or were related to. They carried out absolutely everything that the world expects from poor people: Gregor's father brought bank employees their breakfast, his mother sacrificed herself by washing clothes for strangers, his sister ran back and forth behind her desk at the behest of the customers, but they just did not have the strength to do any more. And the injury in Gregor's back began to hurt as much as when it was new. After they had come back from taking his father to bed Gregor's mother and sister would now leave their work where it was and sit close together, cheek to cheek; his mother would point to Gregor's room and say "close that door, Grete," and then, when he was in the dark again, they would sit in the next room and their tears would mingle, or they would simply sit there staring dry-eyed at the table.

Gregor hardly slept at all, either night or day. Sometimes he would think of taking over the family's affairs, just like before, the next time the door was opened; he had long forgotten about his boss and the chief clerk, but they would appear again in his thoughts, the salesmen and the apprentices, that stupid teaboy, two or three friends from other businesses, one of the chambermaids from a provincial hotel, a tender memory that appeared and disappeared again, a cashier from a hat shop for whom his attention had been serious but too slow—all of them appeared to him, mixed together with strangers and others he had forgotten, but instead of helping him and his family they were all of them inaccessible, and he was glad when they disappeared. Other times he was not at all in the mood to look after his family; he was filled with simple rage about the lack of attention he was shown, and although he could think of nothing he would have wanted, he made plans of how he could get into the pantry where he could take all the things he was entitled to, even if he was not hungry. Gregor's sister no longer thought about how she could please him but would hurriedly push some food or other into his room with her foot before she rushed out to work in the morning and at midday, and in the evening she would sweep it away again with the broom, indifferent as to whether it had been eaten or—more often than not—had been left totally untouched. She still cleared up the room in the evening, but now she could not have been any quicker about it. Smears of dirt were left on the walls, here and there were little balls of dust and filth. At first, Gregor went into one of the worst of these places when his sister arrived as a reproach to her, but he could have stayed there for weeks without his sister doing anything about it; she could see the dirt as well as he could but she had simply decided to leave him to it. At the same time she became touchy in a way that was quite new for her and which everyone in the family understood—cleaning up Gregor's room was for her and her alone. Gregor's mother did once thoroughly clean his room, and needed to use several bucketfuls of water to do it—although that much dampness also made Gregor ill and he lay flat on the couch, bitter and immobile. But his mother was to be punished still more for what she had done, as hardly had his sister arrived home in the evening than she noticed the change in Gregor's room and, highly aggrieved, ran back into the living room where, despite her mother's raised and imploring hands, she broke into convulsive tears. Her father, of course, was startled out of his chair and the two parents looked on astonished and helpless; then they, too, became agitated; Gregor's father, standing to the right of his mother, accused her of not leaving the cleaning of Gregor's room to his sister; from her left, Gregor's sister screamed at her that she was never to clean Gregor's room again; while his mother tried to draw his father, who was beside himself with anger, into the bedroom; his sister, quaking with tears, thumped on the table with her small fists; and Gregor hissed in anger that no one had even thought of closing the door to save him the sight of this and all its noise.

Gregor's sister was exhausted from going out to work, and looking after Gregor as she had done before was even more work for her, but even so his mother ought certainly not to have taken her place. Gregor, on the other hand, ought not to be neglected. Now, though, the charwoman was here. This elderly widow, with a robust bone structure that made her able to withstand the hardest of things in her long life, wasn't really repelled by Gregor. Just by chance one day, rather than by any real curiosity, she opened the door to Gregor's room and found herself face to face with him. He was taken totally by surprise, no one was chasing him but he began to rush to and fro while she just stood there in amazement with her hands crossed in front of her. From then on she never failed to open the door slightly every evening and morning and look briefly in on him. At first she would call to him as she did so with words that she probably considered friendly, such as "come on then, you old dung-beetle!" or "look at the old dung-beetle there!" Gregor never responded to being spoken to in that way, but just remained where he was without moving as if the door had never even been opened. If only they had told this charwoman to clean up his room every day instead of letting her disturb him for no reason whenever she felt like it! One day, early in the morning while a heavy rain struck the windowpanes, perhaps indicating that spring was coming, she began to speak to him in that way once again. Gregor was so resentful of it that he started to move toward her, he was slow and infirm, but it was like a kind of attack. Instead of being afraid, the charwoman just lifted up one of the chairs from near the door and stood there with her mouth open, clearly intending not to close her mouth until the chair in her hand had been slammed down into Gregor's back. "Aren't you coming any closer, then?" she asked when Gregor turned round again, and she calmly put the chair back in the corner.

Gregor had almost entirely stopped eating. Only if he happened to find himself next to the food that had been prepared for him he might take some of it into his mouth to play with it, leave it there a few hours and then, more often than not, spit it out again. At first he thought it was distress at the state of his room that stopped him eating, but he had soon got used to the changes made there. They had got into the habit of putting things into this room that they had no room for anywhere else, and there were now many such things as one of the rooms in the flat had been rented out to three gentlemen. These earnest gentlemen—all three of them had full beards, as Gregor learned peering through the crack in the door one day—were painfully insistent on things being tidy. This meant not only in their own room, but, since they had taken a room in this establishment, in the entire flat and especially in the kitchen. Unnecessary clutter was something they could not tolerate, especially if it was dirty. They had moreover brought most of their own furnishings and equipment with them. For this reason, many things had become superfluous which, although they could not be sold, the family did not wish to discard. All these things found their way into Gregor's room. The dustbins from the kitchen found their way in there too. The charwoman was always in a hurry, and anything she couldn't use for the time being she would just chuck in there. He, fortunately, would usually see no more than the object and the hand that held it. The woman most likely meant to fetch the things back out again when she had time and the opportunity, or to throw everything out in one go, but what actually happened was that they were left where they landed when they had first been thrown unless Gregor made his way through the junk and moved it somewhere else. At first he moved it because, with no other room free where he could crawl about, he was forced to, but later on he came to enjoy it, although moving about in the way left him sad and tired to death and he would remain immobile for hours afterwards.

The gentlemen who rented the room would sometimes take their evening meal at home in the living room that was used by everyone, and so the door to this room was often kept closed in the evening. But Gregor found it easy to give up having the door open; he had, after all, often failed to make use of it when it was open and, without the family having noticed it, lain in his room in its darkest corner. One time, though, the charwoman left the door to the living room slightly open, and it remained open when the gentlemen who rented the room came in in the evening and the light was put on. They sat up at the table where, formerly, Gregor had taken his meals with his father and mother, they unfolded the serviettes and picked up their knives and forks. Gregor's mother immediately appeared in the doorway with a dish of meat and soon behind her came his sister with a dish piled high with potatoes. The food was steaming, and filled the room with its smell. The gentlemen bent over the dishes set in front of them as if they wanted to test the food before eating it, and the gentleman in the middle, who seemed to count as an authority for the other two, did indeed cut off a piece of meat while it was still in its dish, clearly wishing to establish whether it was sufficiently cooked or whether it should be sent back to the kitchen. It was to his satisfaction, and Gregor's mother and sister, who had been looking on anxiously, began to breathe again and smiled.

The family themselves ate in the kitchen. Nonetheless, Gregor's father came into the living room before he went into the kitchen, bowed once with his cap in his hand and did his round of the table. The gentlemen stood as one, and mumbled something into their beards. Then, once they were alone, they ate in near perfect silence. It seemed remarkable to Gregor that above all the various noises of eating their chewing teeth could still be heard, as if they had wanted to show Gregor that you need teeth in order to eat and it was not possible to perform anything with jaws that are toothless however nice they might be. "I'd like to eat something," said Gregor anxiously, "but not anything like they're eating. They do feed themselves. And here I am, dying!"

Throughout all this time, Gregor could not remember having heard the violin being played, but this evening it began to be heard from the kitchen. The three gentlemen had already finished their meal, the one in the middle had produced a newspaper, given a page to each of the others, and now they leant back in their chairs reading them and smoking. When the violin began playing they became attentive, stood up and went on tiptoe over to the door of the hallway where they stood pressed against each other. Someone must have heard them in the kitchen, as Gregor's father called out: "is the playing perhaps unpleasant for the gentlemen? We can stop it straight away."

"On the contrary," said the middle gentleman, "would the young lady not like to come in and play for us here in the room, where it is, after all, much more cozy and comfortable?"

"Oh yes, we'd love to," called back Gregor's father, as if he had been the violin player himself. The gentlemen stepped back into the room and waited. Gregor's father soon appeared with the music stand, his mother with the music and his sister with the violin. She calmly prepared everything for her to begin playing; his parents, who had never rented a room out before and therefore showed an exaggerated courtesy towards the three gentlemen, did not even dare to sit on their own chairs; his father leant against the door with his right hand pushed in between two buttons on his uniform coat; his mother, though, was offered a seat by one of the gentlemen and sat—leaving the chair where the gentleman happened to have placed it—out of the way in a corner.

His sister began to play; father and mother paid close attention, one on each side, to the movements of her hands. Drawn in by the playing, Gregor had dared to come forward a little and already had his head in the living room. Before, he had taken great pride in how considerate he was but now it hardly occurred to him that he had become so thoughtless about the others. What's more, there was now all the more reason to keep himself hidden as he was covered in the dust that lay everywhere in his room and flew up at the slightest movement; he carried threads, hairs, and remains of food about on his back and sides; he was much too indifferent to everything now to lay on his back and wipe himself on the carpet like he had used to do several times a day. And despite this condition, he was not too shy to move forward a little onto the immaculate floor of the living room.

No one noticed him, though. The family was totally preoccupied with the violin playing; at first, the three gentlemen had put their hands in their pockets and come up far too close behind the music stand to look at all the notes being played, and they must have disturbed Gregor's sister, but soon, in contrast with the family, they withdrew back to the window with their heads sunk and talking to each other at half volume, and they stayed by the window while Gregor's father observed them anxiously. It really now seemed very obvious that they had expected to hear some beautiful or entertaining violin playing but had been disappointed, that they had had enough of the whole performance and it was only now out of politeness that they allowed their peace to be disturbed. It was especially unnerving, the way they all blew the smoke from their cigarettes upwards from their mouth and noses. Yet Gregor's sister was playing so beautifully. Her face was leant to one side, following the lines of music with a careful and melancholy expression. Gregor crawled a little further forward, keeping his head close to the ground so that he could meet her eyes if the chance came. Was he an animal if music could captivate him so? It seemed to him that he was being shown the way to the unknown nourishment he had been yearning for. He was determined to make his way forward to his sister and tug at her skirt to show her she might come into his room with her violin, as no one appreciated her playing here as much as he would. He never wanted to let her out of his room, not while he lived, anyway; his shocking appearance should, for once, be of some use to him; he wanted to be at every door of his room at once to hiss and spit at the attackers; his sister should not be forced to stay with him, though, but stay of her own free will; she would sit beside him on the couch with her ear bent down to him while he told her how he had always intended to send her to the conservatory, how he would have told everyone about it last Christmas—had Christmas really come and gone already?—if this misfortune hadn't got in the way, and refuse to let anyone dissuade him from it. On hearing all this, his sister would break out in tears of emotion, and Gregor would climb up to her shoulder and kiss her neck, which, since she had been going out to work, she had kept free without any necklace or collar.

"Mr. Samsa!" shouted the middle gentleman to Gregor's father, pointing, without wasting any more words, with his forefinger at Gregor as he slowly moved forward. The violin went silent, the middle of the three gentlemen first smiled at his two friends, shaking his head, and then looked back at Gregor. His father seemed to think it more important to calm the three gentlemen before driving Gregor out, even though they were not at all upset and seemed to think Gregor was more entertaining that the violin playing had been. He rushed up to them with his arms spread out and attempted to drive them back into their room at the same time as trying to block their view of Gregor with his body. Now they did become a little annoyed, and it was not clear whether it was his father's behavior that annoyed them or the dawning realization that they had had a neighbor like Gregor in the next room without knowing it. They asked Gregor's father for explanations, raised their arms like he had, tugged excitedly at their beards and moved back towards their room only very slowly. Meanwhile Gregor's sister had overcome the despair she had fallen into when her playing was suddenly interrupted. She had let her hands drop and let violin and bow hang limply for a while but continued to look at the music as if still playing, but then she suddenly pulled herself together, lay the instrument on her mother's lap who still sat laboriously struggling for breath where she was, and ran into the next room which, under pressure from her father, the three gentlemen were more quickly moving toward. Under his sister's experienced hand, the pillows and covers on the beds flew up and were put into order and she had already finished making the beds and slipped out again before the three gentlemen had reached the room.

Gregor's father seemed so obsessed with what he was doing that he forgot all the respect he owed to his tenants. He urged them and pressed them until, when he was already at the door of the room, the middle of the three gentlemen shouted like thunder and stamped his foot and thereby brought Gregor's father to a halt. "I declare here and now," he said, raising his hand and glancing at Gregor's mother and sister to gain their attention too, "that with regard to the repugnant conditions that prevail in this flat and with this family"— here he looked briefly but decisively at the floor—"I give immediate notice on my room. For the days that I have been living here I will, of course, pay nothing at all; on the contrary I will consider whether to proceed with some kind of action for damages from you, and believe me it would be very easy to set out the grounds for such an action." He was silent and looked straight ahead as if waiting for something. And indeed, his two friends joined in with the words: "And we also give immediate notice." With that, he took hold of the door handle and slammed the door.

Gregor's father staggered back to his seat, feeling his way with his hands, and fell into it; it looked as if he was stretching himself out for his usual evening nap but from the uncontrolled way his head kept nodding it could be seen that he was not sleeping at all. Throughout all this, Gregor had lain still where the three gentlemen had first seen him. His disappointment at the failure of his plan, and perhaps also because he was weak from hunger, made it impossible for him to move. He was sure that everyone would turn on him any moment, and he waited. He was not even startled out of this state when the violin on his mother's lap fell from her trembling fingers and landed loudly on the floor.

"Father, Mother," said his sister, hitting the table with her hand as introduction, "we can't carry on like this. Maybe you can't see it, but I can. I don't want to call this monster my brother, all I can say is: we have to try and get rid of it. We've done all that's humanly possible to look after it and be patient; I don't think anyone could accuse us of doing anything wrong."

"She's absolutely right," said Gregor's father to himself. His mother, who still had not had time to catch her breath, began to cough dully, her hand held out in front of her and a deranged expression in her eyes.

Gregor's sister rushed to his mother and put her hand on her forehead. Her words seemed to give Gregor's father some more definite ideas. He sat upright, played with his uniform cap between the plates left by the three gentlemen after their meal, and occasionally looked down at Gregor as he lay there immobile.

"We have to try and get rid of it," said Gregor's sister, now speaking only to her father, as her mother was too occupied with coughing to listen, "it'll be the death of both of you, I can see it coming. We can't all work as hard as we have to and then come home to be tortured like this, we can't endure it. I can't endure it any more." And she broke out so heavily in tears that they flowed down the face of her mother, and she wiped them away with mechanical hand movements.

"My child," said her father with sympathy and obvious understanding, "what are we to do?"

His sister just shrugged her shoulders as a sign of the helplessness and tears that had taken hold of her, displacing her earlier certainty.

"If he could just understand us," said his father almost as a question; his sister shook her hand vigorously through her tears as a sign that of that there was no question.

"If he could just understand us," repeated Gregor's father, closing his eyes in acceptance of his sister's certainty that that was quite impossible, "then perhaps we could come to some kind of arrangement with him. But as it is …"

"It's got to go," shouted his sister, "that's the only way, Father. You've got to get rid of the idea that that's Gregor. We've only harmed ourselves by believing it for so long. How can that be Gregor? If it were Gregor he would have seen long ago that it's not possible for human beings to live with an animal like that and he would have gone of his own free will. We wouldn't have a brother any more, then, but we could carry on with our lives and remember him with respect. As it is this animal is persecuting us, it's driven out our tenants, it obviously wants to take over the whole flat and force us to sleep on the streets. Father, look, just look," she suddenly screamed, "he's starting again!" In her alarm, which was totally beyond Gregor's comprehension, his sister even abandoned his mother as she pushed herself vigorously out of her chair as if more willing to sacrifice her own mother than stay anywhere near Gregor. She rushed over to behind her father, who had become excited merely because she was and stood up half raising his hands in front of Gregor's sister as if to protect her.

But Gregor had had no intention of frightening anyone, least of all his sister. All he had done was begin to turn round so that he could go back into his room, although that was in itself quite startling as his pain-wracked condition meant that turning round required a great deal of effort and he was using his head to help himself do it, repeatedly raising it and striking it against the floor. He stopped and looked round. They seemed to have realized his good intention and had only been alarmed briefly. Now they all looked at him in unhappy silence. His mother lay in her chair with her legs stretched out and pressed against each other, her eyes nearly closed with exhaustion; his sister sat next to his father with her arms around his neck.

"Maybe now they'll let me turn round," thought Gregor and went back to work. He could not help panting loudly with the effort and had sometimes to stop and take a rest. No one was making him rush any more; everything was left up to him. As soon as he had finally finished turning round he began to move straight ahead. He was amazed at the great distance that separated him from his room, and could not understand how he had covered that distance in his weak state a little while before and almost without noticing it. He concentrated on crawling as fast as he could and hardly noticed that there was not a word, not any cry, from his family to distract him. He did not turn his head until he had reached the doorway. He did not turn it all the way round as he felt his neck becoming stiff, but it was nonetheless enough to see that nothing behind him had changed, only his sister had stood up. With his last glance he saw that his mother had now fallen completely asleep.

He was hardly inside his room before the door was hurriedly shut, bolted and locked. The sudden noise behind Gregor so startled him that his little legs collapsed under him. It was his sister who had been in so much of a rush. She had been standing there waiting and sprung forward lightly: Gregor had not heard her coming at all, and as she turned the key in the lock she said loudly to her parents "at last!"

"What now, then?" Gregor asked himself as he looked round in the darkness. He soon made the discovery that he could no longer move at all. This was no surprise to him, it seemed rather that being able to actually move around on those spindly little legs until then was unnatural. He also felt relatively comfortable. It is true that his entire body was aching, but the pain seemed to be slowly getting weaker and weaker and would finally disappear altogether. He could already hardly feel the decayed apple in his back or the inflamed area around it, which was entirely covered in white dust. He thought back on his family with emotion and love. If it was possible, he felt that he must go away even more strongly than his sister. He remained in this state of empty and peaceful rumination until he heard the clock tower strike three in the morning. He watched as it slowly began to get light everywhere outside the window too. Then, without his willing it, his head sank down completely, and his last breath flowed weakly from his nostrils.

When the cleaner came in early in the morning—they'd often asked her not to keep slamming the doors but with her strength and in her hurry she still did, so that everyone in the flat knew when she'd arrived and from then on it was impossible to sleep in peace—she made her usual brief look in on Gregor and at first found nothing special. She thought he was laying there so still on purpose, playing the martyr; she attributed all possible understanding to him. She happened to be holding the long broom in her hand, so she tried to tickle Gregor with it from the doorway. When she had no success with that she tried to make a nuisance of herself and poked at him a little, and only when she found she could shove him across the floor with no resistance at all did she start to pay attention. She soon realized what had really happened, opened her eyes wide, whistled to herself, but did not waste time to yank open the bedroom doors and shout loudly into the darkness of the bedrooms: "Come and 'ave a look at this, it's dead, just lying there, stone dead!"

Mr. and Mrs. Samsa sat upright there in their marriage bed and had to make an effort to get over the shock caused by the cleaner before they could grasp what she was saying. But then, each from his own side, they hurried out of bed. Mr. Samsa threw the blanket over his shoulders, Mrs. Samsa just came out in her nightdress; and that is how they went into Gregor's room. On the way they opened the door to the living room where Grete had been sleeping since the three gentlemen had moved in; she was fully dressed as if she had never been asleep, and the paleness of her face seemed to confirm this. "Dead?" asked Mrs. Samsa, looking at the charwoman inquiringly, even though she could have checked for herself and could have known it even without checking. "That's what I said," replied the cleaner, and to prove it she gave Gregor's body another shove with the broom, sending it sideways across the floor. Mrs. Samsa made a movement as if she wanted to hold back the broom, but did not complete it.

"Now then," said Mr. Samsa, "let's give thanks to God for that." He crossed himself, and the three women followed his example. Grete, who had not taken her eyes from the corpse, said: "Just look how thin he was. He didn't eat anything for so long. The food came out again just the same as when it went in." Gregor's body was indeed completely dried up and flat, they had not seen it until then, but now he was not lifted up on his little legs, nor did he do anything to make them look away.

"Grete, come with us in here for a little while," said Mrs. Samsa with a pained smile, and Grete followed her parents into the bedroom but not without looking back at the body. The cleaner shut the door and opened the window wide. Although it was still early in the morning the fresh air had something of warmth mixed in with it. It was already the end of March, after all.

The three gentlemen stepped out of their room and looked round in amazement for their breakfasts; they had been forgotten about. "Where is our breakfast?" the middle gentleman asked the cleaner irritably. She just put her finger on her lips and made a quick and silent sign to the men that they might like to come into Gregor's room. They did so, and stood around Gregor's corpse with their hands in the pockets of their well-worn coats. It was now quite light in the room.

Then the door of the bedroom opened and Mr. Samsa appeared in his uniform with his wife on one arm and his daughter on the other. All of them had been crying a little; Grete now and then pressed her face against her father's arm.

"Leave my home. Now!" said Mr. Samsa, indicating the door and without letting the women from him.

"What do you mean?" asked the middle of the three gentlemen somewhat disconcerted, and he smiled sweetly. The other two held their hands behind their backs and continually rubbed them together in gleeful anticipation of a loud quarrel which could only end in their favor.

"I mean just what I said," answered Mr. Samsa, and, with his two companions, went in a straight line towards the man. At first, he stood there still, looking at the ground as if the contents of his head were rearranging themselves into new positions. "All right, we'll go then," he said, and looked up at Mr. Samsa as if he had been suddenly overcome with humility and wanted permission again from Mr. Samsa for his decision. Mr. Samsa merely opened his eyes wide and briefly nodded to him several times. At that, and without delay, the man actually did take long strides into the front hallway; his two friends had stopped rubbing their hands some time before and had been listening to what was being said. Now they jumped off after their friend as if taken with a sudden fear that Mr. Samsa might go into the hallway in front of them and break the connection with their leader. Once there, all three took their hats from the stand, took their sticks from the holder, bowed without a word and left the premises.

Mr. Samsa and the two women followed them out onto the landing; but they had had no reason to mistrust the men's intentions and as they leaned over the landing they saw how the three gentlemen made slow but steady progress down the many steps. As they turned the corner on each floor they disappeared and would reappear a few moments later; the further down they went, the more that the Samsa family lost interest in them; when a butcher's boy, proud of posture with his tray on his head, passed them on his way up and came nearer than they were, Mr. Samsa and the women came away from the landing and went, as if relieved, back into the flat.

They decided the best way to make use of that day was for relaxation and to go for a walk; not only had they earned a break from work but they were in serious need of it. So they sat at the table and wrote three letters of excusal, Mr. Samsa to his employers, Mrs. Samsa to her contractor and Grete to her principal. The cleaner came in while they were writing to tell them she was going: she'd finished her work for that morning. The three of them at first just nodded without looking up from what they were writing, and it was only when the cleaner still did not seem to want to leave that they looked up in ir-ritation. "Well?"asked Mr. Samsa. The charwoman stood in the doorway with a smile on her face as if she had some tremendous good news to report, but would only do it if she was clearly asked to. The almost vertical little ostrich feather on her hat, which had been source of irritation to Mr. Samsa all the time she had been working for them, swayed gently in all directions.

"What is it you want then?" asked Mrs. Samsa, whom the cleaner had the most respect for. "Yes," she answered, and broke into a friendly laugh that made her unable to speak straight away, "well then, that thing in there, you needn't worry about how you're going to get rid of it. That's all been sorted out."

Mrs. Samsa and Grete bent down over their letters as if intent on contin-uing with what they were writing; Mr. Samsa saw that the cleaner wanted to start describing everything in detail but, with outstretched hand, he made it quite clear that she was not to. So, as she was prevented from telling them all about it, she suddenly remembered what a hurry she was in and, clearly peeved, called out "Cheerio then, everyone," turned round sharply and left, slamming the door terribly as she went.

"Tonight she gets sacked," said Mr. Samsa, but he received no reply from either his wife or his daughter as the charwoman seemed to have destroyed the peace they had only just gained. They got up and went over to the win-dow where they remained with their arms around each other. Mr. Samsa twisted round in his chair to look at them and sat there watching for a while. Then he called out: "Come here, then. Let's forget about all that old stuff, shall we. Come and give me a bit of attention." The two women immediately did as he said, hurrying over to him where they kissed him and hugged him and then they quickly finished their letters.

After that, the three of them left the flat together, which was something they had not done for months, and took the tram out to the open country outside the town. They had the tram, filled with warm sunshine, all to themselves. Leant back comfortably on their seats, they discussed their prospects and found that on closer examination they were not at all bad—until then they had never asked each other about their work but all three had jobs which were very good and held particularly good promise for the future. The greatest improvement for the time being, of course, would be achieved quite easily by moving house; what they needed now was a flat that was smaller and cheaper than the current one which had been chosen by Gregor, one that was in a better location and, most of all, more practical. All the time, Grete was becoming livelier. With all the worry they had been having of late her cheeks had become pale, but, while they were talking, Mr. and Mrs. Samsa were struck, almost simultaneously, with the thought of how their daughter was blossoming into a well built and beautiful young lady. They became quieter. Just from each other's glance and almost without knowing it they agreed that it would soon be time to find a good man for her. And, as if in confirmation of their new dreams and good intentions, as soon as they reached their destination Grete was the first to get up and stretch out her young body.

The Metamorphosis

Questions for discussion

1. How did Gregor feel about no longer being able to provide for his family? How does disability affect those who have been providers? What did you think of the chief clerk, and what do you think he is supposed to represent?

2. How did Gregor's family react to his inability to work, and to his changed state? How did his sister "step up" in the beginning, and why do you think she changed? How did his parents react? How did they handle the financial issues that arose? How do you think your family would react if you were suddenly disabled?

3. Everyone assumed that Gregor could not understand them, when, in fact, he could. In what other contexts might people assume a lower level of functioning for someone with a disability?

4. Gregor hid himself so that others would not have to look at him, saying that he did so for their benefit. What benefits did Gregor gain from this behavior? Why is it sometimes uncomfortable to look at someone with a dis-

ability, and why is it sometimes hard to be looked at if we have something different about us?

5. What else do you think this story says about disability?

6. Design your own discussion questions for this story.

For Further Reading

About appearance and disability

Hathaway, Katharine Butler. *The Little Locksmith.* Autobiography about a
woman with a disability (perhaps polio) who, in the early 1900s, meets a
man, the local locksmith, who also has a bent back. As she stares at him,
she develops both a sense of kinship and a fear of him.

Thomson-Garland, Rosemarie. "Staring at the Other," Disability Studies Quarterly, Fall 2005, Volume 25, No. 4.

About family and friends' reaction to a disability

Hockenberry, John. *Moving Violations.*

Montalambert, Hugues de. *Invisible.* An assault leaves a man blind and his
friends react in different ways.

Tolstoy, Leo. *The Death of Ivan Ilych.* A powerful judge becomes disabled and
ill; he is surprised by the reactions of his family and colleagues.

Rubio, Gwyn Hyman. *Icy Sparks.* A young girl with Tourette's syndrome con-
ceals her symptoms as much as possible; her family knows of her tics but
is slow to seek a diagnosis.

from The Maytrees

[Editor's note: In this novel, a couple, Lou and her husband Maytree, are married for a number of years and have a child, Pete, together. Maytree then runs off with a friend of the family, Deary, and they are gone for twenty years. Deary begins to have problems with her heart, and Maytree begins caring for her. Then, one day, Maytree is carrying Deary to a doctor's appointment. He slips on the ice and drops Deary.]

One morning after a December snowstorm he slipped on the ice and dropped her. Rather, he threw her—just a lob.

He was carrying her down to Dr. Cobo, the sight of whose Castilian face soothed them. It was voodoo after all.

The day he dropped her, he was bearing forward like a tray. She weighed ninety pounds. He felt his foot slip on iced stone. In that instant he tossed her in the fresh snowbank by the steps. At the toss he recoiled, and his slip became a wreck.

. . . .

Much later he learned that he had broken his left humerus just above the elbow. He broke his left clavicle. He broke his right radius twice. He broke his right wrist and thumb; he snapped his right ulna in two at the elbow. One lumbar vertebra cracked—the crucial one, he felt, that every twitch cracked anew. Without puncturing his lungs, his fourth and fifth ribs sustained greenstick fractures dorsally. Far from "sustaining" anything, he thought, his bones broke. The orthopedist reduced Maytree's four arm fractures in memorable jerks, and unrolled wet plaster casts over both his arms, one high, one low.

. . . .

Mrs. Smither, driving them home, wore a green felt hat. He addressed her from the backseat as loudly as he could.

121

—Mrs. Smither. I know you both work hard. I wonder. His ribs broke again every time he breathed. His vertebra halves ground like floes. His two broken arms. His head lay on his coat folded on Deary's lap. All day since he fell, or since he pitched her on the show, she seemed dumbstruck. No choices for them or even chances presented, if he could not carry her and wait on her. She knew it, too.

He had no one to turn to. Under tires dry snow yelped. His bones jolted as if the car had triangular wheels. Moving to Provincetown for now would content Deary and keep his word. Since he botched life with Lou twenty years ago, he honored his every word sometimes to absurdity, like skating with friends after his viral pneumonia had turned to lobar pneumonia.

—If you, or if Sarah … If we offer you twice whatever you earn … Could you help us out for a few months while I mend? In Provincetown on Cape Cod, some nice house? Or (this in a rush) do you think Sarah would help us now and postpone graduation? Has she ever seen Cape Cod? She would have her own room and no other duties. Whether he could use his arms or not, Deary was still dying. Why had they not moved to Provincetown yesterday?

Sarah, Mrs. Smither said, was starting in June as a counselor for the county. Nor could Mrs. Smither herself leave her squash doughnut supervisor post.

....

He reminded himself that perhaps a billion people like him worldwide were lying awake in pain now and at their wits' end. In Provincetown he could rent a place off-season, for Deary and him and a live-in helper or two, if Deary could stand strangers whose accents and clothes betrayed sloppy families. For what purpose had he amassed so much money if it was useless? Well, for three private nurses in eight-hour shifts, if there were any nurses. And again, if Deary would permit as witnesses strangers who would misplace everything in a twinkling, and pat her head.

....

Now what to hope? For he had known all day he would appeal to Lou. He knew it as he fell.

....

To Lou he appeared in the doorway as a watch cap and orange-white eyebrows. It was in-the-flesh Maytree. Lord love a duck. Empty sleeves hung from his bulged jacket, as if behind his buttons he held a new baby he happened across. The kerosene lamp blinded him and paled his irises.

—Well, come on in. He nodded without moving. You'll let the heat out.

Tall thin fellow, neck a bit forward. His skin had shrunk over his temples, nose, and cheekbones, revealing a round skull.—Take off your hat, she said, and plucked it up for him, handless as he was. His hair was thin, but there. He stood at a loss in the room. She started tea.

Then she saw Maytree could not shed his jacket. She unbuttoned it and bared two plaster casts from which his blue fingers dangled like squid arms. She found herself amused for no reason. She drew for him his usual chair. She stuck a quarter-round and another in the stove. You would think plucking a man's hat from his personal head and so naturally unbuttoning his jacket would relax him, and it seemed to. He sat and shrugged the jacket halfway off, and sat in his damp socks. He had a short red beard. Pete had mentioned a beard, she recalled. She herself was easy as ever. She could see his creased face had a smiling habit it cost him to sober. He rose, opened the door, and looked around.

—What?

—There was a dog. He stepped outside. Without bumping him, she too looked into the living night for a moment.

From where they sat, the windowpane made of one lantern two. The weaker one trembled like a moth outside. He turned. What big ears you have! Aging had thinned his mouth as it thinned hers; they were drying up. Only stubby rows of white lashes propped his eyelids. The lines at his eyes' edges splayed like the comet's tail in the Bayeux tapestry.

—Pray, what brings you out here? She stopped herself. There was no reason to kid him. She was pretty sure she knew: if he had hurt his arms he could not take care of Deary whose heart was failing.

—Maytree, she started again, and smiled. Good to see you. He was the one who used to overdo things.

He bent to his tea mug and looked worried into it.

—You used to do the talking, she said. How are you both?

Had they no close friends after twenty years in Maine? Had Deary no mother? She used to possess quite a well-tailored, competent-looking mother who fled Provincetown eons ago when she saw a topless sunbather on the beach, then two men holding hands. Had Deary a brother or sister? No. No hospitals in Maine? Nursing homes? Visiting nurses? She knew Deary thought medical science killed its victims. Lou's only sincere question was this: should she break into Maytree's travails now, and put him out of his misery, or let him dangle a bit for the sake of the long-lost jilted Lou? Of course she would take them in. Anyone would.

—Deary's dying real soon. He looked up at her like the gentleman he was. Maybe you've heard. She nodded.—Actually, she doesn't know she is dying. I always promised to bring her to Provincetown to die and here we are. I can't take care of her anymore. I broke my arms. I can't take care of myself for now.

—I will take care of her, of course, she said.

. . . .

What would ease Deary? Lou would have to learn. She bade her solitude good-bye. Good-bye no schedule but whim; good-bye her life among no things but her own and each always in place; good-bye no real meals, good-bye free thought. The whole fat flock of them flapped away. But what was solitude for if not to foster decency?

from The Maytrees

Questions for discussion

1. How does it feel to have to ask for help? How does it feel to be asked to give help? Who would you ask to help you if you had broken both of your arms? Who might ask such a request of you, and what would you say? Is it beyond the call of duty for Lou, who was jilted by Maytree, to then care for him and his lover?

2. This piece draws a distinction between paid medical help and being helped by friends or family. Why do you think so many older people want to remain in their own homes? What issues are faced by people with disabilities who require paid care?

3. When Lou accepts the job of caring for Deary and Maytree, she bids her solitude and her unscheduled life good-bye. What other sacrifices are required by those who care for friends and family?

4. Design your own discussion questions for this story.

For Further Reading

About caretaking

Simon, Rachel. "It Takes a Village to Help A Sister."

Gloss, Molly. *Hearts of Horses.* A young woman tames horses in a small town and gets to know the residents, including one that needs extensive caretaking due to cancer.

Taylor, Jill Bolte. *My Stroke of Insight.* A 37-year-old neuroanatomist suffers a stroke and details her recovery.

Grisham, John. "Quiet Haven." A harrowing short story about a nursing-home worker who travels the country scamming patients, anthologized in Grisham's short story collection entitled *Ford County.*

Leo Tolstoy (1828–1910) was a Russian writer, the author of the realist masterpieces *Anna Karenina* and *War and Peace*. He was a social reformer, advocating for social equities and non-violent resistance. He is known as one of the world's most influential novelists and philosophers.

from The Death of Ivan Ilych

Ivan Ilych's life had been most simple and most ordinary and therefore most terrible.

He had been a member of the Court of Justice, and died at the age of forty-five. His father had been an official who after serving in various ministries and departments in Petersburg had made the sort of career which brings men to positions from which by reason of their long service they cannot be dismissed, though they are obviously unfit to hold any responsible position, and for whom therefore posts are specially created, which though fictitious carry salaries of from six to ten thousand rubles that are not fictitious, and in receipt of which they live on to a great age.

Such was the Privy Councillor and superfluous member of various superfluous institutions, Ilya Epimovich Golovin.

He had three sons, of whom Ivan Ilych was the second. The eldest son was following in his father's footsteps only in another department, and was already approaching that stage in the service at which a similar sinecure would be reached. The third son was a failure. He had ruined his prospects in a number of positions and was now serving in the railway department. His father and brothers, and still more their wives, not merely disliked meeting him, but avoided remembering his existence unless compelled to do so. His sister had married Baron Greff, a Petersburg official of her father's type. Ivan Ilych was *le phenix de la famille*, as people said. He was neither as cold and formal as his elder brother nor as wild as the younger, but was a happy mean between them—an intelligent, polished, lively and agreeable man. He had studied with his younger brother at the School of Law, but the latter had failed to complete the course and was expelled when he was in the fifth class. Ivan Ilych finished the course well. Even when he was at the School of Law he was just what he remained for the rest of his life: a capable, cheerful, good-natured, and sociable man, though strict in the fulfillment of what he considered to be his duty: and he considered his duty to be what was so considered by those in authority. Neither as a boy nor as a man was he a toady, but from early youth was by nature attracted to people of high station as a fly is drawn to the light, assimilating their ways and views of life and establishing friendly relations with them. All the enthusiasms of childhood and youth passed without leaving much trace on him; he succumbed to sensuality, to vanity, and latterly among the highest classes to liberalism, but always within limits which his instinct unfailingly indicated to him as correct.

At school he had done things which had formerly seemed to him very horrid and made him feel disgusted with himself when he did them; but when later on he saw that such actions were done by people of good position and that they did not regard them as wrong, he was able not exactly to regard them as right, but to forget about them entirely or not be at all troubled at remembering them.

Having graduated from the School of Law and qualified for the tenth rank of the civil service, and having received money from his father for his equipment, Ivan Ilych ordered himself clothes at Scharmer's, the fashionable tailor, hung a medallion inscribed *respice finem* on his watch-chain, took leave of his professor and the prince who was patron of the school, had a farewell dinner with his comrades at Donon's first-class restaurant, and with his new and fashionable portmanteau, linen, clothes, shaving and other toilet appliances, and a travelling rug, all purchased at the best shops, he set off for one of the provinces where through his father's influence, he had been attached to the governor as an official for special service.

In the province Ivan Ilych soon arranged as easy and agreeable a position for himself as he had had at the School of Law. He performed his official task, made his career, and at the same time amused himself pleasantly and decorously. Occasionally he paid official visits to country districts where he behaved with dignity both to his superiors and inferiors, and performed the duties entrusted to him, which related chiefly to the sectarians, with an exactness and incorruptible honesty of which he could not but feel proud.

In official matters, despite his youth and taste for frivolous gaiety, he was exceedingly reserved, punctilious, and even severe; but in society he was often amusing and witty, and always good-natured, correct in his manner, and *bon enfant*, as the governor and his wife—with whom he was like one of the family—used to say of him.

In the province he had an affair with a lady who made advances to the elegant young lawyer, and there was also a milliner; and there were carousals with aides-de-camp who visited the district, and after-supper visits to a cer-

tain outlying street of doubtful reputation; and there was too some obse-
quiousness to his chief and even to his chief's wife, but all this was done with
such a tone of good breeding that no hard names could be applied to it. It all
came under the heading of the French saying: *"Il faut que jeunesse se passe."* It
was all done with clean hands, in clean linen, with French phrases, and above
all among people of the best society and consequently with the approval of
people of rank.

So Ivan Ilych served for five years and then came a change in his official life.
The new and reformed judicial institutions were introduced, and new men
were needed. Ivan Ilych became such a new man. He was offered the post of
examining magistrate, and he accepted it though the post was in another
province and obliged him to give up the connections he had formed and to
make new ones. His friends met to give him a send-off; they had a group photograph taken and presented him with a silver cigarette-case, and he set off to
his new post.

As examining magistrate Ivan Ilych was just as *comme il faut* and decorous
a man, inspiring general respect and capable of separating his official duties
from his private life, as he had been when acting as an official on special service. His duties now as examining magistrate were far more interesting and attractive than before. In his former position it had been pleasant to wear an
undress uniform made by Scharmer, and to pass through the crowd of petitioners and officials who were timorously awaiting an audience with the governor, and who envied him as with free and easy gait he went straight into his
chief's private room to have a cup of tea and a cigarette with him. But not
many people had then been directly dependent on him—only police officials
and the sectarians when he went on special missions—and he liked to treat
them politely, almost as comrades, as if he were letting them feel that he who
had the power to crush them was treating them in this simple, friendly way.
There were then but few such people.

But now, as an examining magistrate, Ivan Ilych felt that everyone without
exception, even the most important and self-satisfied, was in his power, and
that he need only write a few words on a sheet of paper with a certain heading, and this or that important, self-satisfied person would be brought before
him in the role of an accused person or a witness, and if he did not choose to
allow him to sit down, would have to stand before him and answer his questions. Ivan Ilych never abused his power; he tried on the contrary to soften its
expression, but the consciousness of it and the possibility of softening its effect, supplied the chief interest and attraction of his office. In his work itself,
especially in his examinations, he very soon acquired a method of eliminat-
ing all considerations irrelevant to the legal aspect of the case, and reducing

even the most complicated case to a form in which it would be presented on paper only in its externals, completely excluding his personal opinion of the matter, while above all observing every prescribed formality. The work was new and Ivan Ilych was one of the first men to apply the new Code of 1864.

On taking up the post of examining magistrate in a new town, he made new acquaintances and connections, placed himself on a new footing and assumed a somewhat different tone. He took up an attitude of rather dignified aloofness towards the provincial authorities, but picked out the best circle of legal gentlemen and wealthy gentry living in the town and assumed a tone of slight dissatisfaction with the government, of moderate liberalism, and of enlightened citizenship. At the same time, without at all altering the elegance of his toilet, he ceased shaving his chin and allowed his beard to grow as it pleased.

Ivan Ilych settled down very pleasantly in this new town. The society there, which inclined towards opposition to the governor, was friendly, his salary was larger, and he began to play vint [a form of bridge], which he found added not a little to the pleasure of life, for he had a capacity for cards, played good-humouredly, and calculated rapidly and astutely, so that he usually won.

After living there for two years he met his future wife, Praskovya Fedorovna Mikhel, who was the most attractive, clever, and brilliant girl of the set in which he moved, and among other amusements and relaxations from his labours as examining magistrate, Ivan Ilych established light and playful relations with her.

While he had been an official on special service he had been accustomed to dance, but now as an examining magistrate it was exceptional for him to do so. If he danced now, he did it as if to show that though he served under the reformed order of things, and had reached the fifth official rank, yet when it came to dancing he could do it better than most people. So at the end of an evening he sometimes danced with Praskovya Fedorovna, and it was chiefly during these dances that he captivated her. She fell in love with him. Ivan Ilych had at first no definite intention of marrying, but when the girl fell in love with him he said to himself: "Really, why shouldn't I marry?"

Praskovya Fedorovna came of a good family, was not bad looking, and had some little property. Ivan Ilych might have aspired to a more brilliant match, but even this was good. He had his salary, and she, he hoped, would have an equal income. She was well connected, and was a sweet, pretty, and thoroughly correct young woman. To say that Ivan Ilych married because he fell in love with Praskovya Fedorovna and found that she sympathized with his views of life would be as incorrect as to say that he married because his social circle approved of the match. He was swayed by both these considerations: the marriage gave him personal satisfaction, and at the same time it was considered the right thing by the most highly placed of his associates.

So Ivan Ilych got married.

The preparations for marriage and the beginning of married life, with its conjugal caresses, the new furniture, new crockery, and new linen, were very pleasant until his wife became pregnant—so that Ivan Ilych had begun to think that marriage would not impair the easy, agreeable, gay and always decorous character of his life, approved of by society and regarded by himself as natural, but would even improve it. But from the first months of his wife's pregnancy, something new, unpleasant, depressing, and unseemly, and from which there was no way of escape, unexpectedly showed itself.

His wife, without any reason—*de gaiete de coeur* as Ivan Ilych expressed it to himself—began to disturb the pleasure and propriety of their life. She began to be jealous without any cause, expected him to devote his whole attention to her, found fault with everything, and made coarse and ill-mannered scenes.

At first Ivan Ilych hoped to escape from the unpleasantness of this state of affairs by the same easy and decorous relation to life that had served him heretofore: he tried to ignore his wife's disagreeable moods, continued to live in his usual easy and pleasant way, invited friends to his house for a game of cards, and also tried going out to his club or spending his evenings with friends. But one day his wife began upbraiding him so vigorously, using such coarse words, and continued to abuse him every time he did not fulfill her demands, so resolutely and with such evident determination not to give way till he submitted—that is, till he stayed at home and was bored just as she was—that he became alarmed. He now realized that matrimony—at any rate with Praskovya Fedorovna—was not always conducive to the pleasures and amenities of life, but on the contrary often infringed both comfort and propriety, and that he must therefore entrench himself against such infringement. And Ivan Ilych began to seek for means of doing so. His official duties were the one thing that imposed upon Praskovya Fedorovna, and by means of his official work and the duties attached to it he began struggling with his wife to secure his own independence.

With the birth of their child, the attempts to feed it and the various failures in doing so, and with the real and imaginary illnesses of mother and child, in which Ivan Ilych's sympathy was demanded but about which he understood nothing, the need of securing for himself an existence outside his family life became still more imperative.

As his wife grew more irritable and exacting and Ivan Ilych transferred the center of gravity of his life more and more to his official work, so did he grow to like his work better and became more ambitious than before.

Very soon, within a year of his wedding, Ivan Ilych had realized that marriage, though it may add some comforts to life, is in fact a very intricate and difficult affair towards which in order to perform one's duty, that is, to lead a decorous life approved of by society, one must adopt a definite attitude just as towards one's official duties.

And Ivan Ilych evolved such an attitude towards married life. He only required of it those conveniences—dinner at home, housewife, and bed—which it could give him, and above all that propriety of external forms required by public opinion. For the rest he looked for lighthearted pleasure and propriety, and was very thankful when he found them, but if he met with antagonism and querulousness he at once retired into his separate fenced-off world of official duties, where he found satisfaction.

Ivan Ilych was esteemed a good official, and after three years was made Assistant Public Prosecutor. His new duties, their importance, the possibility of indicting and imprisoning anyone he chose, the publicity his speeches received, and the success he had in all these things, made his work still more attractive.

More children came. His wife became more and more querulous and ill-tempered, but the attitude Ivan Ilych had adopted towards his home life rendered him almost impervious to her grumbling.

After seven years' service in that town he was transferred to another province as Public Prosecutor. They moved, but were short of money and his wife did not like the place they moved to. Though the salary was higher the cost of living was greater, besides which two of their children died and family life became still more unpleasant for him.

Praskovya Fedorovna blamed her husband for every inconvenience they encountered in their new home. Most of the conversations between husband and wife, especially as to the children's education, led to topics which recalled former disputes, and these disputes were apt to flare up again at any moment. There remained only those rare periods of amorousness which still came to them at times but did not last long. These were islets at which they anchored for a while and then again set out upon that ocean of veiled hostility which showed itself in their aloofness from one another. This aloofness might have grieved Ivan Ilych had he considered that it ought not to exist, but he now regarded the position as normal, and even made it the goal at which he aimed in family life. His aim was to free himself more and more from those unpleasantries and to give them a semblance of harmlessness and propriety. He attained this by spending less and less time with his family, and when obliged to be at home he tried to safeguard his position by the presence of outsiders. The chief thing however was that he had his official duties. The whole interest of his life now centered in the official world and that interest absorbed him. The consciousness of his power, being able to ruin anybody he wished to ruin, the importance, even the external dignity of his entry into court, or meetings with his subordinates, his success with superiors and inferiors, and above all his masterly handling of cases, of which he was conscious—all this gave him pleasure and filled his life, together with chats with his colleagues, dinners, and bridge. So that on the whole Ivan Ilych's life continued to flow as he considered it should do—pleasantly and properly.

So things continued for another seven years. His eldest daughter was already sixteen, another child had died, and only one son was left, a schoolboy and a subject of dissension. Ivan Ilych wanted to put him in the School of Law, but to spite him Praskovya Fedorovna entered him at the High School. The daughter had been educated at home and had turned out well: the boy did not learn badly either.

So Ivan Ilych lived for seventeen years after his marriage. He was already a Public Prosecutor of long standing, and had declined several proposed transfers while awaiting a more desirable post, when an unanticipated and unpleasant occurrence quite upset the peaceful course of his life. He was expecting to be offered the post of presiding judge in a University town, but Happe somehow came to the front and obtained the appointment instead. Ivan Ilych became irritable, reproached Happe, and quarreled both with him and with his immediate superiors—who became colder to him and again passed him over when other appointments were made.

This was in 1880, the hardest year of Ivan Ilych's life. It was then that it became evident on the one hand that his salary was insufficient for them to live on, and on the other that he had been forgotten, and not only this, but that what was for him the greatest and most cruel injustice appeared to others a quite ordinary occurrence. Even his father did not consider it his duty to help him. Ivan Ilych felt himself abandoned by everyone, and that they regarded his position with a salary of 3,500 rubles as quite normal and even fortunate. He alone knew that with the consciousness of the injustices done him, with his wife's incessant nagging, and with the debts he had contracted by living beyond his means, his position was far from normal.

In order to save money that summer he obtained leave of absence and went with his wife to live in the country at her brother's place.

In the country, without his work, he experienced ennui for the first time in his life, and not only ennui but intolerable depression, and he decided that it was impossible to go on living like that, and that it was necessary to take energetic measures.

Having passed a sleepless night pacing up and down the veranda, he decided to go to Petersburg and bestir himself, in order to punish those who had failed to appreciate him and to get transferred to another ministry.

Next day, despite many protests from his wife and her brother, he started for Petersburg with the sole object of obtaining a post with a salary of five thousand rubles a year. He was no longer bent on any particular department, or tendency, or kind of activity. All he now wanted was an appointment to another post with a salary of five thousand rubles, either in the administration, in the banks, with the railways in one of the Empress Marya's Institutions, or even in the customs—but it had to carry with it a salary of five thousand rubles and be in a ministry other than that in which they had failed to appreciate him.

And this quest of Ivan Ilych's was crowned with remarkable and unexpected success. At Kursk an acquaintance of his, F. I. Ilyin, got into the first-class carriage, sat down beside Ivan Ilych, and told him of a telegram just received by the governor of Kursk announcing that a change was about to take place in the ministry: Peter Ivanovich was to be superseded by Ivan Semonovich.

The proposed change, apart from its significance for Russia, had a special significance for Ivan Ilych, because by bringing forward a new man, Peter Petrovich, and consequently his friend Zachar Ivanovich, it was highly favourable for Ivan Ilych, since Zachar Ivanovich was a friend and colleague of his.

In Moscow this news was confirmed, and on reaching Petersburg Ivan Ilych found Zachar Ivanovich and received a definite promise of an appointment in his former Department of Justice.

A week later he telegraphed to his wife: "Zachar in Miller's place. I shall receive appointment on presentation of report."

Thanks to this change of personnel, Ivan Ilych had unexpectedly obtained an appointment in his former ministry which placed him two states above his former colleagues besides giving him five thousand rubles salary and three thousand five hundred rubles for expenses connected with his removal. All his ill humour towards his former enemies and the whole department vanished, and Ivan Ilych was completely happy.

He returned to the country more cheerful and contented than he had been for a long time. Praskovya Fedorovna also cheered up and a truce was arranged between them. Ivan Ilych told of how he had been feted by everybody in Petersburg, how all those who had been his enemies were put to shame and now fawned on him, how envious they were of his appointment, and how much everybody in Petersburg had liked him.

Praskovya Fedorovna listened to all this and appeared to believe it. She did not contradict anything, but only made plans for their life in the town to which they were going. Ivan Ilych saw with delight that these plans were his plans, that he and his wife agreed, and that, after a stumble, his life was regaining its due and natural character of pleasant lightheartedness and decorum.

Ivan Ilych had come back for a short time only, for he had to take up his new duties on the 10th of September. Moreover, he needed time to settle into the new place, to move all his belongings from the province, and to buy and order many additional things: in a word, to make such arrangements as he had resolved on, which were almost exactly what Praskovya Fedorovna too had decided on.

Now that everything had happened so fortunately, and that he and his wife were at one in their aims and moreover saw so little of one another, they got on together better than they had done since the first years of marriage. Ivan Ilych had thought of taking his family away with him at once, but the insistence of his wife's brother and her sister-in-law, who had suddenly become particularly amiable and friendly to him and his family, induced him to depart alone.

So he departed, and the cheerful state of mind induced by his success and by the harmony between his wife and himself, the one intensifying the other, did not leave him. He found a delightful house, just the thing both he and his wife had dreamt of. Spacious, lofty reception rooms in the old style, a convenient and dignified study, rooms for his wife and daughter, a study for his son—it might have been specially built for them. Ivan Ilych himself superintended the arrangements, chose the wallpapers, supplemented the furniture (preferably with antiques which he considered particularly *comme il faut*), and supervised the upholstering. Everything progressed and progressed and approached the ideal he had set himself: even when things were only half completed they exceeded his expectations. He saw what a refined and elegant character, free from vulgarity, it would all have when it was ready. On falling asleep he pictured to himself how the reception room would look. Looking at the yet unfinished drawing room he could see the fireplace, the screen, the whatnot, the little chairs dotted here and there, the dishes and plates on the walls, and the bronzes, as they would be when everything was in place. He was pleased by the thought of how his wife and daughter, who shared his taste in this matter, would be impressed by it. They were certainly not expecting as much. He had been particularly successful in finding, and buying cheaply, antiques which gave a particularly aristocratic character to the whole place. But in his letters he intentionally understated everything in order to be able to surprise them. All this so absorbed him that his new duties—though he liked his official work—interested him less than he had expected. Sometimes he even had moments of absent-mindedness during the court sessions and would consider whether he should have straight or curved cornices for his curtains. He was so interested in it all that he often did things himself, rearranging the furniture, or re-hanging the curtains. Once when mounting a step-ladder to show the upholsterer, who did not understand, how he wanted the hangings draped, he made a false step and slipped, but being a strong and agile man he clung on and only knocked his side against the knob of the window frame. The bruised place was painful but the pain soon passed, and he felt particularly bright and well just then. He wrote: "I feel fifteen years younger." He thought he would have everything ready by September, but it dragged on till mid-October. But the result was charming not only in his eyes but to everyone who saw it.

In reality it was just what is usually seen in the houses of people of moderate means who want to appear rich, and therefore succeed only in resembling others like themselves: there are damasks, dark wood, plants, rugs, and dull and polished bronzes—all the things people of a certain class have in order to resemble other people of that class. His house was so like the others that it would never have been noticed, but to him it all seemed to be quite exceptional. He was very happy when he met his family at the station and brought them to the newly furnished house all lit up, where a footman in a white tie opened the door into the hall decorated with plants, and when they went on into the drawing-room and the study uttering exclamations of delight. He conducted them everywhere, drank in their praises eagerly, and beamed with pleasure. At tea that evening, when Praskovya Fedorovna among other things asked him about his fall, he laughed, and showed them how he had gone flying and had frightened the upholsterer.

"It's a good thing I'm a bit of an athlete. Another man might have been killed, but I merely knocked myself, just here; it hurts when it's touched, but it's passing off already—it's only a bruise."

So they began living in their new home—in which, as always happens, when they got thoroughly settled in they found they were just one room short—and with the increased income, which as always was just a little (some five hundred rubles) too little, but it was all very nice.

Things went particularly well at first, before everything was finally arranged and while something had still to be done: this thing bought, that thing ordered, another thing moved, and something else adjusted. Though there were some disputes between husband and wife, they were both so well satisfied and had so much to do that it all passed off without any serious quarrels. When nothing was left to arrange it became rather dull and something seemed to be lacking, but they were then making acquaintances, forming habits, and life was growing fuller.

Ivan Ilych spent his mornings at the law court and came home to dinner, and at first he was generally in a good humor, though he occasionally became irritable just on account of his house. (Every spot on the tablecloth or the upholstery, and every broken window-blind string, irritated him. He had devoted so much trouble to arranging it all that every disturbance of it distressed him.) But on the whole his life ran its course as he believed life should do: easily, pleasantly, and decorously.

He got up at nine, drank his coffee, read the paper, and then put on his undress uniform and went to the law courts. There the harness in which he worked had already been stretched to fit him and he donned it without a hitch: petitioners, inquiries at the chancery, the chancery itself, and the sittings public and administrative. In all this the thing was to exclude everything fresh and vital, which always disturbs the regular course of official business, and to admit only official relations with people, and then only on official grounds. A man would come, for instance, wanting some information. Ivan Ilych, as one in whose sphere the matter did not lie, would have nothing to do with him: but if the man had some business with him in his official capacity, something that could be expressed on officially stamped paper, he would do everything, positively everything he could within the limits of such relations, and in doing so would maintain the semblance of friendly human relations, that is, would observe the courtesies of life. As soon as the official relations ended, so did everything else. Ivan Ilych possessed this capacity to separate his real life from the official side of affairs and not mix the two, in the highest degree, and by long practice and natural aptitude had brought it to such a pitch that sometimes, in the manner of a virtuoso, he would even allow himself to let the human and official relations mingle. He let himself do this just because he felt that he could at any time he chose resume the strictly official attitude again and drop the human relation. and he did it all easily, pleasantly, correctly, and even artistically. In the intervals between the sessions he smoked, drank tea, chatted a little about politics, a little about general topics, a little about cards, but most of all about official appointments. Tired, but with the feelings of a virtuoso—one of the first violins who has played his part in an orchestra with precision—he would return home to find that his wife and daughter had been out paying calls, or had a visitor, and that his son had been to school, had done his homework with his tutor, and was surely learning what is taught at High Schools. Everything was as it should be. After dinner, if they had no visitors, Ivan Ilych sometimes read a book that was being much discussed at the time, and in the evening settled down to work, that is, read official papers, compared the depositions of witnesses, and noted paragraphs of the Code applying to them. This was neither dull nor amusing. It was dull when he might have been playing bridge, but if no bridge was available it was at any rate better than doing nothing or sitting with his wife. Ivan Ilych's chief pleasure was giving little dinners to which he invited men and women of good social position, and just as his drawing-room resembled all other drawing-rooms so did his enjoyable little parties resemble all other such parties.

Once they even gave a dance. Ivan Ilych enjoyed it and everything went off well, except that it led to a violent quarrel with his wife about the cakes and sweets. Praskovya Fedorovna had made her own plans, but Ivan Ilych insisted on getting everything from an expensive confectioner and ordered too many cakes, and the quarrel occurred because some of those cakes were left over and the confectioner's bill came to forty-five rubles. It was a great and disagreeable quarrel. Praskovya Fedorovna called him "a fool and an imbecile," and he clutched at his head and made angry allusions to divorce.

But the dance itself had been enjoyable. The best people were there, and Ivan Ilych had danced with Princess Trufonova, a sister of the distinguished founder of the Society "Bear My Burden."

The pleasures connected with his work were pleasures of ambition; his social pleasures were those of vanity; but Ivan Ilych's greatest pleasure was playing bridge. He acknowledged that whatever disagreeable incident happened in his life, the pleasure that beamed like a ray of light above everything else was to sit down to bridge with good players, not noisy partners, and of course to four-handed bridge (with five players it was annoying to have to stand out, though one pretended not to mind), to play a clever and serious game (when the cards allowed it) and then to have supper and drink a glass of wine. After a game of bridge, especially if he had won a little (to win a large sum was unpleasant), Ivan Ilych went to bed in a specially good humor.

So they lived. They formed a circle of acquaintances among the best people and were visited by people of importance and by young folk. In their views as to their acquaintances, husband, wife and daughter were entirely agreed, and tacitly and unanimously kept at arm's length and shook off the various shabby friends and relations who, with much show of affection, gushed into the drawing-room with its Japanese plates on the walls. Soon these shabby friends ceased to obtrude themselves and only the best people remained in the Golovins' set.

Young men made up to Lisa, and Petrishchev, an examining magistrate and Dmitri Ivanovich Petrishchev's son and sole heir, began to be so attentive to her that Ivan Ilych had already spoken to Praskovya Fedorovna about it, and considered whether they should not arrange a party for them, or get up some private theatricals.

So they lived, and all went well, without change, and life flowed pleasantly.

They were all in good health. It could not be called ill health if Ivan Ilych sometimes said that he had a queer taste in his mouth and felt some discomfort in his left side.

But this discomfort increased and, though not exactly painful, grew into a sense of pressure in his side accompanied by ill humor. And his irritability became worse and worse and began to mar the agreeable, easy, and correct life that had established itself in the Golovin family. Quarrels between husband and wife became more and more frequent, and soon the ease and amenity disappeared and even the decorum was barely maintained. Scenes again became frequent, and very few of those islets remained on which husband and wife could meet without an explosion. Praskovya Fedorovna now had good reason to say that her husband's temper was trying. With characteristic exaggeration she said he had always had a dreadful temper, and that it had needed all her good nature to put up with it for twenty years. It was true that now the quarrels were started by him. His bursts of temper always came just before dinner, often just as he began to eat his soup. Sometimes he noticed that a plate or dish was chipped, or the food was not right, or his son put his elbow on the table, or his daughter's hair was not done as he liked it, and for all this he blamed Praskovya Fedorovna. At first she retorted and said disagreeable things to him, but once or twice he fell into such a rage at the beginning of dinner that she realized it was due to some physical derangement brought on by taking food, and so she restrained herself and did not answer, but only hurried to get the dinner over. She regarded this self-restraint as highly praiseworthy. Having come to the conclusion that her husband had a dreadful temper and made her life miserable, she began to feel sorry for herself, and the more she pitied herself the more she hated her husband. She began to wish he would die; yet she did not want him to die because then his salary would cease. And this irritated her against him still more. She considered herself dreadfully unhappy just because not even his death could save her, and though she concealed her exasperation, that hidden exasperation of hers increased his irritation also.

After one scene in which Ivan Ilych had been particularly unfair and after which he had said in explanation that he certainly was irritable but that it was due to his not being well, she said that if he was ill it should be attended to, and insisted on his going to see a celebrated doctor.

He went. Everything took place as he had expected and as it always does. There was the usual waiting and the important air assumed by the doctor, with which he was so familiar (resembling that which he himself assumed in court), and the sounding and listening, and the questions which called for answers that were foregone conclusions and were evidently unnecessary, and the look of importance which implied that "if only you put yourself in our hands we will arrange everything—we know indubitably how it has to be done, always in the same way for everybody alike." It was all just as it was in the law courts. The doctor put on just the same air towards him as he himself put on towards an accused person.

The doctor said that so-and-so indicated that there was so-and-so inside the patient, but if the investigation of so-and-so did not confirm this, then he must assume that and that. If he assumed that and that, then ... and so on. To Ivan Ilych only one question was important: was his case serious or not? But the doctor ignored that inappropriate question. From his point of view it was not the one under consideration, the real question was to decide between a floating kidney, chronic catarrh, or appendicitis. It was not a question the doctor solved brilliantly, as it seemed to Ivan Ilych, in favor of the appendix, with the reservation that should an examination of the urine give fresh indications the matter would be reconsidered. All this was just what Ivan Ilych had himself brilliantly accomplished a thousand times in dealing with men on trial. The doctor summed up just as brilliantly, looking over his spectacles triumphantly and even gaily at the accused. From the doctor's summing up Ivan Ilych concluded that things were bad, but that for the doctor, and perhaps for everybody else, it was a matter of indifference, though for him it was bad. And this conclusion struck him painfully, arousing in him a great feeling of pity for himself and of bitterness towards the doctor's indifference to a matter of such importance.

He said nothing of this, but rose, placed the doctor's fee on the table, and remarked with a sigh: "We sick people probably often put inappropriate questions. But tell me, in general, is this complaint dangerous, or not? ..."

The doctor looked at him sternly over his spectacles with one eye, as if to say: "Prisoner, if you will not keep to the questions put to you, I shall be obliged to have you removed from the court."

"I have already told you what I consider necessary and proper. The analysis may show something more." And the doctor bowed.

Ivan Ilych went out slowly, seated himself disconsolately in his sledge, and drove home. All the way home he was going over what the doctor had said, trying to translate those complicated, obscure, scientific phrases into plain language and find in them an answer to the question: "Is my condition bad? Is it very bad? Or is there as yet nothing much wrong?" And it seemed to him that the meaning of what the doctor had said was that it was very bad. Everything in the streets seemed depressing. The cabmen, the houses, the passersby, and the shops, were dismal. His ache, this dull gnawing ache that never ceased for a moment, seemed to have acquired a new and more serious significance from the doctor's dubious remarks. Ivan Ilych now watched it with a new and oppressive feeling.

He reached home and began to tell his wife about it. She listened, but in the middle of his account his daughter came in with her hat on, ready to go out with her mother. She sat down reluctantly to listen to this tedious story, but could not stand it long, and her mother too did not hear him to the end.

"Well, I am very glad," she said. "Mind now to take your medicine regularly. Give me the prescription and I'll send Gerasim to the chemist's." And she went to get ready to go out.

While she was in the room Ivan Ilych had hardly taken time to breathe, but he sighed deeply when she left it.

"Well," he thought, "perhaps it isn't so bad after all."

He began taking his medicine and following the doctor's directions, which had been altered after the examination of the urine. But then it happened that there was a contradiction between the indications drawn from the examination of the urine and the symptoms that showed themselves. It turned out that what was happening differed from what the doctor had told him, and that he had either forgotten or blundered, or hidden something from him. He could not, however, be blamed for that, and Ivan Ilych still obeyed his orders implicitly and at first derived some comfort from doing so.

From the time of his visit to the doctor, Ivan Ilych's chief occupation was the exact fulfillment of the doctor's instructions regarding hygiene and the taking of medicine, and the observation of his pain and his excretions. His chief interest came to be people's ailments and people's health. When sickness, deaths, or recoveries were mentioned in his presence, especially when the illness resembled his own, he listened with agitation which he tried to hide, asked questions, and applied what he heard to his own case.

The pain did not grow less, but Ivan Ilych made efforts to force himself to think that he was better. And he could do this so long as nothing agitated him. But as soon as he had any unpleasantness with his wife, any lack of success in his official work, or held bad cards at bridge, he was at once acutely sensible of his disease. He had formerly borne such mischances, hoping soon to adjust what was wrong, to master it and attain success, or make a grand slam. But now every mischance upset him and plunged him into despair. He would say to himself: "there now, just as I was beginning to get better and the medicine had begun to take effect, comes this accursed misfortune, or unpleasantness ..." And he was furious with the mishap, or with the people who were causing the unpleasantness and killing him, for he felt that this fury was killing him but he could not restrain it. One would have thought that it should have been clear to him that this exasperation with circumstances and people aggravated his illness, and that he ought therefore to ignore unpleasant occurrences. But he drew the very opposite conclusion: he said that he needed peace, and he watched for everything that might disturb it and became irritable at the slightest infringement of it. His condition was rendered worse by the fact that he read medical books and consulted doctors. The progress of his disease was so gradual that he could deceive himself when comparing one day with another—the difference was so slight. But when he consulted the doctors it seemed to him that he was getting worse, and even very rapidly. Yet despite this he was continually consulting them.

That month he went to see another celebrity, who told him almost the same as the first had done but put his questions rather differently, and the interview with this celebrity only increased Ivan Ilych's doubts and fears. A friend of a friend of his, a very good doctor, diagnosed his illness again quite differently from the others, and though he predicted recovery, his questions and suppositions bewildered Ivan Ilych still more and increased his doubts. A homeopathist diagnosed the disease in yet another way, and prescribed medicine which Ivan Ilych took secretly for a week. But after a week, not feeling any improvement and having lost confidence both in the former doctor's treatment and in this one's, he became still more despondent. One day a lady acquaintance mentioned a cure effected by a wonder-working icon. Ivan Ilych caught himself listening attentively and beginning to believe that it had occurred. This incident alarmed him. "Has my mind really weakened to such an extent?" he asked himself. "Nonsense! It's all rubbish. I mustn't give way to nervous fears but having chosen a doctor must keep strictly to his treatment. That is what I will do. Now it's all settled. I won't think about it, but will follow the treatment seriously till summer, and then we shall see. From now there must be no more of this wavering!" This was easy to say but impossible to carry out. The pain in his side oppressed him and seemed to grow worse and more incessant, while the taste in his mouth grew stranger and stranger. It seemed to him that his breath had a disgusting smell, and he was conscious of a loss of appetite and strength. There was no deceiving himself: something terrible, new, and more important than anything before in his life, was taking place within him of which he alone was aware. Those about him did not understand or would not understand it, but thought everything in the world was going on as usual. That tormented Ivan Ilych more than anything. He saw that his household, especially his wife and daughter who were in a perfect whirl of visiting, did not understand anything of it and were annoyed that he was so depressed and so exacting, as if he were to blame for it. Though they tried to disguise it he saw that he was an obstacle in their path, and that his wife had adopted a definite line in regard to his illness and kept to it regardless of anything he said or did. Her attitude was this: "You know," she would say to her friends, "Ivan Ilych can't do as other people do, and keep to the treatment prescribed for him. One day he'll take his drops and keep strictly to his diet and go to bed in good time, but the next day unless I watch him he'll suddenly forget his medicine, eat sturgeon—which is forbidden—and sit up playing cards till one o'clock in the morning."

"Oh, come, when was that?" Ivan Ilych would ask in vexation. "Only once at Peter Ivanovich's."

"And yesterday with Shebek."

"Well, even if I hadn't stayed up, this pain would have kept me awake."

"Be that as it may you'll never get well like that, but will always make us wretched."

Praskovya Fedorovna's attitude to Ivan Ilych's illness, as she expressed it both to others and to him, was that it was his own fault and was another of the annoyances he caused her. Ivan Ilych felt that this opinion escaped her involuntarily—but that did not make it easier for him.

At the law courts too, Ivan Ilych noticed, or thought he noticed, a strange attitude towards himself. It sometimes seemed to him that people were watching him inquisitively as a man whose place might soon be vacant. Then again, his friends would suddenly begin to chaff him in a friendly way about his low spirits, as if the awful, horrible, and unheard-of thing that was going on within him, incessantly gnawing at him and irresistibly drawing him away, was a very agreeable subject for jests. Schwartz in particular irritated him by his jocularity, vivacity, and *savoir-faire*, which reminded him of what he himself had been ten years ago.

Friends came to make up a set and they sat down to cards. They dealt, bending the new cards to soften them, and he sorted the diamonds in his hand and found he had seven. His partner said "No trumps" and supported him with two diamonds. What more could be wished for? It ought to be jolly and lively. They would make a grand slam. But suddenly Ivan Ilych was conscious of that gnawing pain, that taste in his mouth, and it seemed ridiculous that in such circumstances he should be pleased to make a grand slam.

He looked at his partner Mikhail Mikhaylovich, who rapped the table with his strong hand and instead of snatching up the tricks pushed the cards courteously and indulgently towards Ivan Ilych that he might have the pleasure of gathering them up without the trouble of stretching out his hand for them. "Does he think I am too weak to stretch out my arm?" thought Ivan Ilych, and forgetting what he was doing he over-trumped his partner, missing the grand slam by three tricks. And what was most awful of all was that he saw how upset Mikhail Mikhaylovich was about it but did not himself care. And it was dreadful to realize why he did not care.

They all saw that he was suffering, and said: "We can stop if you are tired. Take a rest." Lie down? No, he was not at all tired, and he finished the rubber. All were gloomy and silent. Ivan Ilych felt that he had diffused this gloom over them and could not dispel it. They had supper and went away, and Ivan Ilych was left alone with the consciousness that his life was poisoned and was poisoning the lives of others, and that this poison did not weaken but penetrated more and more deeply into his whole being.

With this consciousness, and with physical pain besides the terror, he must go to bed, often to lie awake the greater part of the night. Next morning he had to get up again, dress, go to the law courts, speak, and write; or if he did not go out, spend at home those twenty-four hours a day each of which was a torture. And he had to live thus all alone on the brink of an abyss, with no one who understood or pitied him.

So one month passed and then another. Just before the New Year his brother-in-law came to town and stayed at their house. Ivan Ilych was at the law courts and Praskovya Fedorovna had gone shopping. When Ivan Ilych came home and entered his study he found his brother-in-law there—a healthy, florid man—unpacking his portmanteau himself. He raised his head on hearing Ivan Ilych's footsteps and looked up at him for a moment without a word. That stare told Ivan Ilych everything. His brother-in-law opened his mouth to utter an exclamation of surprise but checked himself, and that action confirmed it all. "I have changed, eh?" "Yes, there is a change." And after that, try as he would to get his brother-in-law to return to the subject of his looks, the latter would say nothing about it. Praskovya Fedorovna came home and her brother went out to her. Ivan Ilych locked the door and began to examine himself in the glass, first full face, then in profile. He took up a portrait of himself taken with his wife, and compared it with what he saw in the glass. The change in him was immense. Then he bared his arms to the elbow, looked at them, drew the sleeves down again, sat down on an ottoman, and grew blacker than night.

"No, no, this won't do!" he said to himself, and jumped up, went to the table, took up some law papers and began to read them, but could not continue. He unlocked the door and went into the reception-room. The door leading to the drawing-room was shut. He approached it on tiptoe and listened.

"No, you are exaggerating!" Praskovya Fedorovna was saying.

"Exaggerating! Don't you see it? Why, he's a dead man! Look at his eyes—there's no life in them. But what is it that is wrong with him?"

"No one knows. Nikolaevich (that was another doctor) said something, but I don't know what. And Seshchetitsky (this was the celebrated specialist) said quite the contrary ..."

Ivan Ilych walked away, went to his own room, lay down, and began musing: "The kidney, a floating kidney." He recalled all the doctors had told him of how it detached itself and swayed about. And by an effort of imagination he tried to catch that kidney and arrest it and support it. So little was needed for this, it seemed to him. "No, I'll go to see Peter Ivanovich again." (That was the friend whose friend was a doctor.) He rang, ordered the carriage, and got ready to go.

"Where are you going, Jean?" asked his wife with a specially sad and exceptionally kind look.

This exceptionally kind look irritated him. He looked morosely at her.

"I must go to see Peter Ivanovich."

He went to see Peter Ivanovich, and together they went to see his friend, the doctor. He was in, and Ivan Ilych had a long talk with him.

Reviewing the anatomical and physiological details of what in the doctor's opinion was going on inside him, he understood it all.

There was something, a small thing, in the vermiform appendix. It might all come right. Only stimulate the energy of one organ and check the activity of another, then absorption would take place and everything would come right. He got home rather late for dinner, ate his dinner, and conversed cheerfully, but could not for a long time bring himself to go back to work in his room. At last, however, he went to his study and did what was necessary, but the consciousness that he had put something aside—an important, intimate matter which he would revert to when his work was done—never left him. When he had finished his work he remembered that this intimate matter was the thought of his vermiform appendix. But he did not give himself up to it, and went to the drawing-room for tea. There were callers there, including the examining magistrate who was a desirable match for his daughter, and they were conversing, playing the piano, and singing. Ivan Ilych, as Praskovya Fedorovna remarked, spent that evening more cheerfully than usual, but he never for a moment forgot that he had postponed the important matter of the appendix. At eleven o'clock he said goodnight and went to his bedroom. Since his illness he had slept alone in a small room next to his study. He undressed and took up a novel by Zola, but instead of reading it he fell into thought, and in his imagination that desired improvement in the vermiform appendix occurred. There was the absorption and evacuation and the re-establishment of normal activity. "Yes, that's it!" he said to himself. "One need only assist nature, that's all."

He remembered his medicine, rose, took it, and lay down on his back watching for the beneficent action of the medicine and for it to lessen the pain.

"I need only take it regularly and avoid all injurious influences. I am already feeling better, much better." He began touching his side: it was not painful to the touch. "There, I really don't feel it. It's much better already." He put out the light and turned on his side. "The appendix is getting better, absorption is occurring." Suddenly he felt the old, familiar, dull, gnawing pain, stubborn and serious. There was the same familiar loathsome taste in his mouth. His heart sank and he felt dazed. "My God! My God!" he muttered. "Again, again! And it will never cease." And suddenly the matter presented itself in a quite different aspect. "Vermiform appendix! Kidney!" he said to himself. "It's not a question of appendix or kidney, but of life and … death. Yes, life was there and now it is going, going and I cannot stop it. Yes. Why deceive myself? Isn't it obvious to everyone but me that I'm dying, and that it's only a question of weeks, days … it may happen this moment. There was light and now there is darkness. I was here and now I'm going there! Where?" A chill came over him, his breathing ceased, and he felt only the throbbing of his heart.

"When I am not, what will there be? There will be nothing. Then where shall I be when I am no more? Can this be dying? No, I don't want to!" He jumped up and tried to light the candle, felt for it with trembling hands, dropped candle and candlestick on the floor, and fell back on his pillow.

"What's the use? It makes no difference," he said to himself, staring with wide-open eyes into the darkness. "Death. Yes, death. And none of them knows or wishes to know it, and they have no pity for me. Now they are playing." (He heard through the door the distant sound of a song and its accompaniment.) "It's all the same to them, but they will die too! Fools! I first, and they later, but it will be the same for them. And now they are merry … the beasts!"

Anger choked him and he was agonizingly, unbearably miserable. "It is impossible that all men have been doomed to suffer this awful horror!" He raised himself.

"Something must be wrong. I must calm myself—must think it all over from the beginning." And he again began thinking. "Yes, the beginning of my illness: I knocked my side, but I was still quite well that day and the next. It hurt a little, then rather more. I saw the doctors, then followed despondency and anguish, more doctors, and I drew nearer to the abyss. My strength grew less and I kept coming nearer and nearer, and now I have wasted away and there is no light in my eyes. I think of the appendix—but this is death! I think of mending the appendix, and all the while here is death! Can it really be death?" Again terror seized him and he gasped for breath. He leant down and began feeling for the matches, pressing with his elbow on the stand beside the bed. It was in his way and hurt him, he grew furious with it, pressed on it still harder, and upset it. Breathless and in despair he fell on his back, expecting death to come immediately.

Meanwhile the visitors were leaving. Praskovya Fedorovna was seeing them off. She heard something fall and came in.

"What has happened?"

"Nothing. I knocked it over accidentally."

She went out and returned with a candle. He lay there panting heavily, like a man who has run a thousand yards, and stared upwards at her with a fixed look.

"What is it, Jean?"

"No ... o ... thing. I upset it." ("Why speak of it? She won't understand," he thought.)

And in truth she did not understand. She picked up the stand, lit his candle, and hurried away to see another visitor off. When she came back he still lay on his back, looking upwards.

"What is it? Do you feel worse?"

"Yes."

She shook her head and sat down.

"Do you know, Jean, I think we must ask Leshchetitsky to come and see you here."

This meant calling in the famous specialist, regardless of expense. He smiled malignantly and said "No." She remained a little longer and then went up to him and kissed his forehead.

While she was kissing him he hated her from the bottom of his soul and with difficulty refrained from pushing her away.

"Good night. Please God you'll sleep."

"Yes."

Ivan Ilych saw that he was dying, and he was in continual despair.

And to replace that thought he called up a succession of others, hoping to find in them some support. He tried to get back into the former current of thoughts that had once screened the thought of death from him. But strange to say, all that had formerly shut off, hidden, and destroyed his consciousness of death, no longer had that effect. Ivan Ilych now spent most of his time in attempting to re-establish that old current. He would say to himself: "I will take up my duties again—after all I used to live by them." And banishing all doubts he would go to the law courts, enter into conversation with his colleagues, and sit carelessly as was his wont, scanning the crowd with a thoughtful look and leaning both his emaciated arms on the arms of his oak chair; bending over as usual to a colleague and drawing his papers nearer he would interchange whispers with him, and then suddenly raising his eyes and sitting erect would pronounce certain words and open the proceedings. But suddenly in the midst of those proceedings the pain in his side, regardless of the stage the proceedings had reached, would begin its own gnawing work. Ivan Ilych would turn his attention to it and try to drive the thought of it away, but without success. "It" would come and stand before him and look at him, and he would be petrified and the light would die out of his eyes, and he would again begin asking himself whether "It" alone was true. And his colleagues and subordinates would see with surprise and distress that he, the brilliant and subtle judge, was becoming confused and making mistakes. He would shake himself, try to pull himself together, manage somehow to bring the sitting to a close, and return home with the sorrowful consciousness that his judicial labors could not as formerly hide from him what he wanted them to hide, and could not deliver him from "It." And what was worst of all was that "It" drew his attention to itself not in order to make him take some action but only that he should look at "It," look it straight in the face: look at it and without doing anything, suffer inexpressibly.

In these latter days he would go into the drawing-room he had arranged—that drawing-room where he had fallen and for the sake of which (how bitterly ridiculous it seemed) he had sacrificed his life—for he knew that his illness originated with that knock. He would enter and see that something had scratched the polished table. He would look for the cause of this and find that it was the bronze ornamentation of an album, that had got bent. He would take up the expensive album which he had lovingly arranged, and feel vexed with his daughter and her friends for their untidiness—for the album was torn here and there and some of the photographs turned upside down. He would put it carefully in order and bend the ornamentation back into position. Then it would occur to him to place all those things in another corner of the room, near the plants. He would call the footman, but his daughter or wife would come to help him. They would not agree, and his wife would contradict him, and he would dispute and grow angry. But that was all right, for then he did not think about "It." "It" was invisible.

But then, when he was moving something himself, his wife would say: "Let the servants do it. You will hurt yourself again." And suddenly "It" would flash through the screen and he would see it. It was just a flash, and he hoped it would disappear, but he would involuntarily pay attention to his side. "It sits there as before, gnawing just the same!" And he could no longer forget "It," but could distinctly see it looking at him from behind the flowers. "What is it all for?"

"It really is so! I lost my life over that curtain as I might have done when storming a fort. Is that possible? How terrible and how stupid. It can't be true! It can't, but it is."

How it happened it is impossible to say because it came about step by step, unnoticed, but in the third month of Ivan Ilych's illness, his wife, his daughter, his son, his acquaintances, the doctors, the servants, and above all he himself, were aware that the whole interest he had for other people was whether he would soon vacate his place, and at last release the living from the discomfort caused by his presence and be himself released from his sufferings.

He slept less and less. He was given opium and hypodermic injections of morphine, but this did not relieve him. The dull depression he experienced in a somnolent condition at first gave him a little relief, but only as something new, afterwards it became as distressing as the pain itself or even more so.

Special foods were prepared for him by the doctors' orders, but all those foods became increasingly distasteful and disgusting to him.

For his excretions also special arrangements had to be made, and this was a torment to him every time—a torment from the uncleanliness, the unseemliness, and the smell, and from knowing that another person had to take part in it.

But just through his most unpleasant matter, Ivan Ilych obtained comfort. Gerasim, the butler's young assistant, always came in to carry the things out. Gerasim was a clean, fresh peasant lad, grown stout on town food and always cheerful and bright. At first the sight of him, in his clean Russian peasant costume, engaged on that disgusting task embarrassed Ivan Ilych.

Once when he got up from the commode too weak to draw up his trousers, he dropped into a soft armchair and looked with horror at his bare, enfeebled thighs with the muscles so sharply marked on them.

Gerasim with a firm light tread, his heavy boots emitting a pleasant smell of tar and fresh winter air, came in wearing a clean Hessian apron, the sleeves of his print shirt tucked up over his strong bare young arms; and refraining from looking at his sick master out of consideration for his feelings, and restraining the joy of life that beamed from his face, he went up to the commode.

"Gerasim!" said Ivan Ilych in a weak voice.

Gerasim started, evidently afraid he might have committed some blunder, and with a rapid movement turned his fresh, kind, simple young face which just showed the first downy signs of a beard.

"Yes, sir?"

"That must be very unpleasant for you. You must forgive me. I am helpless."

"Oh, why, sir," and Gerasim's eyes beamed and he showed his glistening white teeth, "what's a little trouble? It's a case of illness with you, sir." And his deft strong hands did their accustomed task, and he went out of the room stepping lightly. Five minutes later he as lightly returned.

Ivan Ilych was still sitting in the same position in the armchair.

"Gerasim," he said when the latter had replaced the freshly-washed utensil. "Please come here and help me." Gerasim went up to him. "Lift me up. It is hard for me to get up, and I have sent Dmitri away."

Gerasim went up to him, grasped his master with his strong arms deftly but gently, in the same way that he stepped—lifted him, supported him with one hand, and with the other drew up his trousers and would have set him down again, but Ivan Ilych asked to be led to the sofa. Gerasim, without an effort and without apparent pressure, led him, almost lifting him, to the sofa and placed him on it.

"Thank you. How easily and well you do it all!"

Gerasim smiled again and turned to leave the room. But Ivan Ilych felt his presence such a comfort that he did not want to let him go.

"One thing more, please move up that chair. No, the other one—under my feet. It is easier for me when my feet are raised."

Gerasim brought the chair, set it down gently in place, and raised Ivan Ilych's legs on it. It seemed to Ivan Ilych that he felt better while Gerasim was holding up his legs.

"It's better when my legs are higher," he said. "Place that cushion under them."

Gerasim did so. He again lifted the legs and placed them, and again Ivan Ilych felt better while Gerasim held his legs. When he set them down Ivan Ilych fancied he felt worse.

"Gerasim," he said. "Are you busy now?"

"Not at all, sir," said Gerasim, who had learnt from the townsfolk how to speak to gentlefolk.

"What have you still to do?"

"What have I to do? I've done everything except chopping the logs for to-morrow."

"Then hold my legs up a bit higher, can you?"

"Of course I can. Why not?" and Gerasim raised his master's legs higher and Ivan Ilych thought that in that position he did not feel any pain at all.

"And how about the logs?"

"Don't trouble about that, sir. There's plenty of time."

Ivan Ilych told Gerasim to sit down and hold his legs, and began to talk to him. And strange to say it seemed to him that he felt better while Gerasim held his legs up.

After that Ivan Ilych would sometimes call Gerasim and get him to hold his legs on his shoulders, and he liked talking to him. Gerasim did it all easily, willingly, simply, and with a good nature that touched Ivan Ilych. Health, strength, and vitality in other people were offensive to him, but Gerasim's strength and vitality did not mortify but soothed him.

What tormented Ivan Ilych most was the deception, the lie, which for some reason they all accepted, that he was not dying but was simply ill, and he only need keep quiet and undergo a treatment and then something very good would result. He however knew that do what they would nothing would come of it, only still more agonizing suffering and death. This deception tortured him—their not wishing to admit what they all knew and what he knew, but wanting to lie to him concerning his terrible condition, and wishing and forcing him to participate in that lie. Those lies—lies enacted over him on the eve of his death and destined to degrade this awful, solemn act to the level of their visitings, their curtains, their sturgeon for dinner—were a terrible agony for Ivan Ilych. And strangely enough, many times when they were going through their antics over him he had been within a hairbreadth of calling out to them: "Stop lying! You know and I know that I am dying. Then at least stop lying about it!" But he had never had the spirit to do it. The awful, terrible act of his dying was, he could see, reduced by those about him to the level of a casual, unpleasant, and almost indecorous incident (as if someone entered a drawing room defusing an unpleasant odor) and this was done by that very decorum which he had served all his life long. He saw that no one felt for him, because no one even wished to grasp his position. Only Gerasim recognized it and pitied him. And so Ivan Ilych felt at ease only with him. He felt comforted when Gerasim supported his legs (sometimes all night long) and refused to go to bed, saying: "Don't you worry, Ivan Ilych. I'll get sleep enough later on," or when he suddenly became familiar and exclaimed: "If you weren't sick it would be another matter, but as it is, why should I grudge a little trouble?" Gerasim alone did not lie; everything showed that he alone understood the facts of the case and did not consider it necessary to disguise them, but simply felt sorry for his emaciated and enfeebled master. Once when Ivan Ilych was sending him away he even said straight out: "We shall all of us die, so why should I grudge a little trouble?"—expressing the fact that he did not think his work burdensome, because he was doing it for a dying man and hoped someone would do the same for him when his time came.

Apart from this lying, or because of it, what most tormented Ivan Ilych was that no one pitied him as he wished to be pitied. At certain moments after prolonged suffering he wished most of all (though he would have been ashamed to confess it) for someone to pity him as a sick child is pitied. He longed to be petted and comforted. He knew he was an important functionary, that he had a beard turning grey, and that therefore what he longed for was impossible, but still he longed for it. And in Gerasim's attitude towards him there was something akin to what he wished for, and so that attitude comforted him. Ivan Ilych wanted to weep, wanted to be petted and cried over, and then his colleague Shebek would come, and instead of weeping and being petted, Ivan Ilych would assume a serious, severe, and profound air, and by force of habit would express his opinion on a decision of the Court of Cassation and would stubbornly insist on that view. This falsity around him and within him did more than anything else to poison his last days.

It was morning. He knew it was morning because Gerasim had gone, and Peter the footman had come and put out the candles, drawn back one of the curtains, and begun quietly to tidy up. Whether it was morning or evening, Friday or Sunday, made no difference, it was all just the same: the gnawing, unmitigated, agonizing pain, never ceasing for an instant, the consciousness of life inexorably waning but not yet extinguished, the approach of that ever dreaded and hateful Death which was the only reality, and always the same falsity. What were days, weeks, hours, in such a case?

"Will you have some tea, sir?"

"He wants things to be regular, and wishes the gentlefolk to drink tea in the morning," thought Ivan Ilych, and only said "No."

"Wouldn't you like to move onto the sofa, sir?"

"He wants to tidy up the room, and I'm in the way. I am uncleanliness and disorder," he thought, and said only: "No, leave me alone."

The man went on bustling about. Ivan Ilych stretched out his hand. Peter came up, ready to help.

"What is it, sir?"

"My watch."

Peter took the watch which was close at hand and gave it to his master.

"Half-past eight. Are they up?"

"No sir, except Vladimir Ivanovich" (the son) "who has gone to school. Praskovya Fedorovna ordered me to wake her if you asked for her. Shall I do so?"

"No, there's no need to."

"Perhaps I'd better have some tea," he thought, and added aloud: "Yes, bring me some tea."

Peter went to the door, but Ivan Ilych dreaded being left alone. "How can I keep him here? Oh yes, my medicine."

"Peter, give me my medicine. Why not? Perhaps it may still do some good." He took a spoonful and swallowed it. "No, it won't help. It's all tomfoolery, all deception," he decided as soon as he became aware of the familiar, sickly, hopeless taste. "No, I can't believe in it any longer. But the pain, why this pain? If it would only cease just for a moment!" And he moaned. Peter turned towards him. "It's all right. Go and fetch me some tea."

Peter went out. Left alone Ivan Ilych groaned not so much with pain, terrible thought that was, as from mental anguish. Always and forever the same, always these endless days and nights. If only it would come quicker! If only what would come quicker? Death, darkness? … No, no! anything rather than death!

When Peter returned with the tea on a tray, Ivan Ilych stared at him for a time in perplexity, not realizing who and what he was. Peter was disconcerted by that look and his embarrassment brought Ivan Ilych to himself.

"Oh, tea! All right, put it down. Only help me to wash and put on a clean shirt."

And Ivan Ilych began to wash. With pauses for rest, he washed his hands and then his face, cleaned his teeth, brushed his hair, looked in the glass. He was terrified by what he saw, especially by the limp way in which his hair clung to his pallid forehead.

While his shirt was being changed he knew that he would be still more frightened at the sight of his body, so he avoided looking at it. Finally he was ready. He drew on a dressing-gown, wrapped himself in a plaid, and sat down in the armchair to take his tea. For a moment he felt refreshed, but as soon as he began to drink the tea he was again aware of the same taste, and the pain also returned. He finished it with an effort, and then lay down stretching out his legs, and dismissed Peter.

Always the same. Now a spark of hope flashes up, then a sea of despair rages, and always pain; always pain, always despair, and always the same. When alone he had a dreadful and distressing desire to call someone, but he knew beforehand that with others present it would be still worse. "Another dose of morphine — to lose consciousness. I will tell him, the doctor, that he must think of something else. It's impossible, impossible, to go on like this."

An hour and another pass like that. But now there is a ring at the door bell. Perhaps it's the doctor? It is. He comes in fresh, hearty, plump, and cheerful, with that look on his face that seems to say: "There now, you're in a panic about something, but we'll arrange it all for you directly!" The doctor knows this expression is out of place here, but he has put it on once for all and can't take it off—like a man who has put on a frock-coat in the morning to pay a round of calls.

The doctor rubs his hands vigorously and reassuringly.

"Brr! How cold it is! There's such a sharp frost; just let me warm myself!" he says, as if it were only a matter of waiting till he was warm, and then he would put everything right.

"Well now, how are you?"

Ivan Ilych feels that the doctor would like to say: "Well, how are our affairs?" but that even he feels that this would not do, and says instead: "What sort of a night have you had?"

Ivan Ilych looks at him as much as to say: "Are you really never ashamed of lying?" But the doctor does not wish to understand this question, and Ivan Ilych says: "Just as terrible as ever. The pain never leaves me and never subsides. If only something ..."

"Yes, you sick people are always like that.... There, now I think I am warm enough. Even Praskovya Fedorovna, who is so particular, could find no fault with my temperature. Well, now I can say good-morning," and the doctor presses his patient's hand.

Then dropping his former playfulness, he begins with a most serious face to examine the patient, feeling his pulse and taking his temperature, and then begins the sounding and auscultation.

Ivan Ilych knows quite well and definitely that all this is nonsense and pure deception, but when the doctor, getting down on his knee, leans over him, putting his ear first higher then lower, and performs various gymnastic movements over him with a significant expression on his face, Ivan Ilych submits to it all as he used to submit to the speeches of the lawyers, though he knew very well that they were all lying and why they were lying.

The doctor, kneeling on the sofa, is still sounding him when Praskovya Fedorovna's silk dress rustles at the door and she is heard scolding Peter for not having let her know of the doctor's arrival.

She comes in, kisses her husband, and at once proceeds to prove that she has been up a long time already, and only owing to a misunderstanding failed to be there when the doctor arrived.

Ivan Ilych looks at her, scans her all over, sets against her the whiteness and plumpness and cleanness of her hands and neck, the gloss of her hair, and the sparkle of her vivacious eyes. He hates her with his whole soul. And the thrill of hatred he feels for her makes him suffer from her touch.

Her attitude towards him and his diseases is still the same. Just as the doctor had adopted a certain relation to his patient which he could not abandon, so had she formed one towards him—that he was not doing something he ought to do and was himself to blame, and that she reproached him lovingly for this—and she could not now change that attitude.

"You see he doesn't listen to me and doesn't take his medicine at the proper time. And above all he lies in a position that is no doubt bad for him—with his legs up."

She described how he made Gerasim hold his legs up.

The doctor smiled with a contemptuous affability that said: "What's to be done? These sick people do have foolish fancies of that kind, but we must forgive them."

When the examination was over the doctor looked at his watch, and then

Praskovya Fedorovna announced to Ivan Ilych that it was of course as he pleased, but she had sent today for a celebrated specialist who would examine him and have a consultation with Michael Danilovich (their regular doctor).

"Please don't raise any objections. I am doing this for my own sake," she said ironically, letting it be felt that she was doing it all for his sake and only said this to leave him no right to refuse. He remained silent, knitting his brows. He felt that he was surrounded and involved in such a mesh of falsity that it was hard to unravel anything.

Everything she did for him was entirely for her own sake, and she told him she was doing for herself what she actually was doing for herself, as if that was so incredible that he must understand the opposite.

At half-past eleven the celebrated specialist arrived. Again the sounding began and the significant conversations in his presence and in another room, about the kidneys and the appendix, and the questions and answers, with such an air of importance that again, instead of the real question of life and death which now alone confronted him, the question arose of the kidney and appendix which were not behaving as they ought to and would now be attached by Michael Danilovich and the specialist and forced to amend their ways.

The celebrated specialist took leave of him with a serious though not hopeless look, and in reply to the timid question Ivan Ilych, with eyes glistening with fear and hope, put to him as to whether there was a chance of recovery, said that he could not vouch for it but there was a possibility. The look of hope with which Ivan Ilych watched the doctor out was so pathetic that Praskovya Fedorovna, seeing it, even wept as she left the room to hand the doctor his fee.

The gleam of hope kindled by the doctor's encouragement did not last long. The same room, the same pictures, curtains, wall-paper, medicine bottles, were all there, and the same aching suffering body, and Ivan Ilych began to moan. They gave him a subcutaneous injection and he sank into oblivion.

It was twilight when he came to. They brought him his dinner and he swallowed some beef tea with difficulty, and then everything was the same again and night was coming on.

After dinner, at seven o'clock, Praskovya Fedorovna came into the room in evening dress, her full bosom pushed up by her corset, and with traces of powder on her face. She had reminded him in the morning that they were going to the theatre. Sarah Bernhardt was visiting the town and they had a box, which he had insisted on their taking. Now he had forgotten about it and her toilet offended him, but he concealed his vexation when he remembered that he had himself insisted on their securing a box and going because it would be an instructive and aesthetic pleasure for the children.

Praskovya Fedorovna came in, self-satisfied but yet with a rather guilty air. She sat down and asked how he was, but, as he saw, only for the sake of asking and not in order to learn about it, knowing that there was nothing to learn—and then went on to what she really wanted to say: that she would not on any account have gone but that the box had been taken and Helen and their daughter were going, as well as Petrishchev (the examining magistrate, their daughter's fiancée) and that it was out of the question to let them go alone; but that she would have much preferred to sit with him for a while; and he must be sure to follow the doctor's orders while she was away.

"Oh, and Fedor Petrovich" (the fiancée) "would like to come in. May he? And Lisa?"

"All right."

Their daughter came in in full evening dress, her fresh young flesh exposed (making a show of that very flesh which in his own case caused so much suffering), strong, healthy, evidently in love, and impatient with illness, suffering, and death, because they interfered with her happiness.

Fedor Petrovich came in too, in evening dress, his hair curled, a tight stiff collar round his long sinewy neck, an enormous white shirt-front and narrow black trousers tightly stretched over his strong thighs. He had one white glove tightly drawn on, and was holding his opera hat in his hand.

Following him the schoolboy crept in unnoticed, in a new uniform, poor little fellow, and wearing gloves. Terribly dark shadows showed under his eyes, the meaning of which Ivan Ilych knew well. His son had always seemed pathetic to him, and now it was dreadful to see the boy's frightened look of pity. It seemed to Ivan Ilych that Vasya was the only one besides Gerasim who understood and pitied him.

They all sat down and again asked how he was. A silence followed. Lisa asked her mother about the opera glasses, and there was an altercation between mother and daughter as to who had taken them and where they had been put. This occasioned some unpleasantness.

Fedor Petrovich inquired of Ivan Ilych whether he had ever seen Sarah Bernhardt. Ivan Ilych did not at first catch the question, but then replied: "No, have you seen her before?"

"Yes, in *Adrienne Lecouvreur*."

Praskovya Fedorovna mentioned some roles in which Sarah Bernhardt was particularly good. Her daughter disagreed. Conversation sprang up as to the elegance and realism of her acting—the sort of conversation that is always repeated and is always the same.

In the midst of the conversation Fedor Petrovich glanced at Ivan Ilych and became silent. The others also looked at him and grew silent. Ivan Ilych was staring with glittering eyes straight before him, evidently indignant with them. This had to be rectified, but it was impossible to do so. The silence had to be broken, but for a time no one dared to break it and they all became afraid that the conventional deception would suddenly become obvious and the truth become plain to all. Lisa was the first to pluck up courage and break that silence, but by trying to hide what everybody was feeling, she betrayed it.

"Well, if we are going it's time to start," she said, looking at her watch, a present from her father, and with a faint and significant smile at Fedor Petrovich relating to something known only to them. She got up with a rustle of her dress.

They all rose, said good-night, and went away.

When they had gone it seemed to Ivan Ilych that he felt better; the falsity had gone with them. But the pain remained—that same pain and that same fear that made everything monotonously alike, nothing harder and nothing easier. Everything was worse.

Again minute followed minute and hour followed hour. Everything remained the same and there was no cessation. And the inevitable end of it all became more and more terrible.

"Yes, send Gerasim here," he replied to a question Peter asked.

His wife returned late at night. She came in on tiptoe, but he heard her, opened his eyes, and made haste to close them again. She wished to send Gerasim away and to sit with him herself, but he opened his eyes and said: "No, go away."

"Are you in great pain?"

"Always the same."

"Take some opium."

He agreed and took some. She went away.

Till about three in the morning he was in a state of stupefied misery. It seemed to him that he and his pain were being thrust into a narrow, deep black sack, but though they were pushed further and further in they could not be pushed to the bottom. And this, terrible enough in itself, was accompanied by suffering. He was frightened yet wanted to fall through the sack, he struggled but yet co-operated. And suddenly he broke through, fell, and regained consciousness. Gerasim was sitting at the foot of the bed dozing quietly and patiently, while he himself lay with his emaciated stockinged legs resting on Gerasim's shoulders; the same shaded candle was there and the same unceasing pain.

"Go away, Gerasim," he whispered.

"It's all right, sir. I'll stay a while."

"No. Go away."

He removed his legs from Gerasim's shoulders, turned sideways onto his arm, and felt sorry for himself. He only waited till Gerasim had gone into the next room and then restrained himself no longer but wept like a child. He wept on account of his helplessness, his terrible loneliness, the cruelty of man, the cruelty of God, and the absence of God.

"Why hast Thou done all this? Why hast Thou brought me here? Why, why dost Thou torment me so terribly?"

He did not expect an answer and yet wept because there was no answer and could be none. The pain again grew more acute, but he did not stir and did not call. He said to himself: "Go on! Strike me! But what is it for? What have I done to Thee? What is it for?"

Then he grew quiet and not only ceased weeping but even held his breath and became all attention. It was as though he were listening not to an audible voice but to the voice of his soul, to the current of thoughts arising within him.

"What is it you want?" was the first clear conception capable of expression in words, that he heard.

"What do you want? What do you want?" he repeated to himself.

"What do I want? To live and not to suffer," he answered.

And again he listened with such concentrated attention that even his pain did not distract him.

"To live? How?" asked his inner voice.

"Why, to live as I used to—well and pleasantly."

"As you lived before, well and pleasantly?" the voice repeated.

And in imagination he began to recall the best moments of his pleasant life. But strange to say none of those best moments of his pleasant life now seemed at all what they had then seemed—none of them except the first recollections of childhood. There, in childhood, there had been something really pleasant with which it would be possible to live if it could return. But the child who had experienced that happiness existed no longer, it was like a reminiscence of somebody else.

As soon as the period began which had produced the present Ivan Ilych, all that had then seemed joys now melted before his sight and turned into something trivial and often nasty.

And the further he departed from childhood and the nearer he came to the present the more worthless and doubtful were the joys. This began with the School of Law. A little that was really good was still found there—there was light-heartedness, friendship, and hope. But in the upper classes there had already been fewer of such good moments. Then during the first years of his official career, when he was in the service of the governor, some pleasant moments again occurred: they were the memories of love for a woman.

Then all became confused and there was still less of what was good; later on again there was still less that was good, and the further he went the less there was. His marriage, a mere accident, then the disenchantment that followed it, his wife's bad breath and the sensuality and hypocrisy: then that deadly official life and those preoccupations about money, a year of it, and two, and ten, and twenty, and always the same thing. And the longer it lasted the more deadly it became. "It is as if I had been going downhill while I imagined I was going up. And that is really what it was. I was going up in public opinion, but to the same extent life was ebbing away from me. And now it is all done and there is only death.

"Then what does it mean? Why? It can't be that life is so senseless and horrible. But if it really has been so horrible and senseless, why must I die and die in agony? There is something wrong!

"Maybe I did not live as I ought to have done," it suddenly occurred to him. "But how could that be, when I did everything properly?" he replied, and immediately dismissed from his mind this, the sole solution of all the riddles of life and death, as something quite impossible.

"Then what do you want now? To live? Live how? Live as you lived in the law courts when the usher proclaimed 'The judge is coming! The judge is coming, the judge!'" he repeated to himself. "Here he is, the judge. But I am not guilty!" he exclaimed angrily. "What is it for?" And he ceased crying, but turning his face to the wall continued to ponder on the same question: Why, and for what purpose, is there all this horror? But however much he pondered he found no answer. And whenever the thought occurred to him, as it often did, that it all resulted from his not having lived as he ought to have done, he at once recalled the correctness of his whole life and dismissed so strange an idea.

Another fortnight passed. Ivan Ilych now no longer left his sofa. He would not lie in bed but lay on the sofa, facing the wall nearly all the time. He suffered ever the same unceasing agonies and in his loneliness pondered always on the same insoluble question: "What is this? Can it be that it is Death?" And the inner voice answered: "Yes, it is Death."

"Why these sufferings?" And the voice answered, "For no reason—they just are so." Beyond and besides this there was nothing.

From the very beginning of his illness, ever since he had first been to see the doctor, Ivan Ilych's life had been divided between two contrary and alternating moods: now it was despair and the expectation of this uncomprehended and terrible death, and now hope and an intently interested observation of the functioning of his organs. Now before his eyes there was only a kidney or an intestine that temporarily evaded its duty, and now only that incomprehensible and dreadful death from which it was impossible to escape.

These two states of mind had alternated from the very beginning of his illness, but the further it progressed the more doubtful and fantastic became the conception of the kidney, and the more real the sense of impending death.

He had but to call to mind what he had been three months before and what he was now, to call to mind with what regularity he had been going downhill, for every possibility of hope to be shattered.

Latterly during the loneliness in which he found himself as he lay facing the back of the sofa, a loneliness in the midst of a populous town and surrounded by numerous acquaintances and relations but that yet could not have been more complete anywhere—either at the bottom of the sea or under the earth—during that terrible loneliness Ivan Ilych had lived only in memories of the past. Pictures of his past rose before him one after another. They always began with what was nearest in time and then went back to what was most remote—to his childhood—and rested there. If he thought of the stewed prunes that had been offered him that day, his mind went back to the raw shriveled French plums of his childhood, their peculiar flavor and the flow of saliva when he sucked their stones, and along with the memory of that taste came a whole series of memories of those days: his nurse, his brother, and their toys. "No, I mustn't think of that…. It is too painful," Ivan Ilych said to himself, and brought himself back to the present—to the button on the back of the sofa and the creases in its morocco. "Morocco is expensive, but it does not wear well: there had been a quarrel about it. It was a different kind of quarrel and a different kind of morocco that time when we tore father's portfolio and were punished, and mamma brought us some tarts…." And again his thoughts dwelt on his childhood, and again it was painful and he tried to banish them and fix his mind on something else.

Then again together with that chain of memories another series passed through his mind—of how his illness had progressed and grown worse. There also the further back he looked the more life there had been. There had been more of what was good in life and more of life itself. The two merged together. "Just as the pain went on getting worse and worse, so my life grew worse and worse," he thought. "There is one bright spot there at the back, at the beginning of life, and afterwards all becomes blacker and blacker and proceeds more and more rapidly—in inverse ration to the square of the distance from death," thought Ivan Ilych. And the example of a stone falling downwards with increasing velocity entered his mind. Life, a series of increasing sufferings, flies further and further towards its end—the most terrible suffering. "I am flying…." He shuddered, shifted himself, and tried to resist, but was already aware that resistance was impossible, and again with eyes weary of gazing but unable to cease seeing what was before them, he stared at the back of the sofa and waited—awaiting that dreadful fall and shock and destruction.

"Resistance is impossible!" he said to himself. "If I could only understand what it is all for! But that too is impossible. An explanation would be possible if it could be said that I have not lived as I ought to. But it is impossible to say that," and he remembered all the legality, correctitude, and propriety of his life. "That at any rate can certainly not be admitted," he thought, and his lips smiled ironically as if someone could see that smile and be taken in by it. "There is no explanation! Agony, death.... What for?"

Another two weeks went by in this way and during that fortnight an event occurred that Ivan Ilych and his wife had desired. Petrishchev formally proposed. It happened in the evening. The next day Praskovya Fedorovna came into her husband's room considering how best to inform him of it, but that very night there had been a fresh change for the worse in his condition. She found him still lying on the sofa but in a different position. He lay on his back, groaning and staring fixedly straight in front of him.

She began to remind him of his medicines, but he turned his eyes towards her with such a look that she did not finish what she was saying; so great an animosity, to her in particular, did that look express.

"Let me die in peace!" he said.

She would have gone away, but just then their daughter came in and went up to say good morning. He looked at her as he had done at his wife, and in reply to her inquiry about his health said dryly that he would soon free them all of himself. They were both silent and after sitting with him for a while went away.

"Is it our fault?" Lisa said to her mother. "It's as if we were to blame! I am sorry for papa, but why should we be tortured?"

The doctor came at his usual time. Ivan Ilych answered "Yes" and "No," never taking his angry eyes from him, and at last said: "You know you can do nothing for me, so leave me alone."

"We can ease your sufferings."

"You can't even do that. Let me be."

The doctor went into the drawing room and told Praskovya Fedorovna that the case was very serious and that the only resource left was opium to allay her husband's sufferings, which must be terrible.

It was true, as the doctor said, that Ivan Ilych's physical sufferings were terrible, but worse than the physical sufferings were his mental sufferings which were his chief torture. His mental sufferings were due to the fact that that night, as he looked at Gerasim's sleepy, good-natured face with its prominent cheek-bones, the question suddenly occurred to him: "What if my whole life has been wrong?"

It occurred to him that what had appeared perfectly impossible before, namely that he had not spent his life as he should have done, might after all be true. It occurred to him that his scarcely perceptible attempts to struggle against

what was considered good by the most highly placed people, those scarcely noticeable impulses which he had immediately suppressed, might have been the
real thing, and all the rest false. And his professional duties and the whole
arrangement of his life and of his family, and all his social and official interests,
might all have been false. He tried to defend all those things to himself and suddenly felt the weakness of what he was defending. There was nothing to defend.

"But if that is so," he said to himself, "and I am leaving this life with the
consciousness that I have lost all that was given me and it is impossible to rec-
tify it—what then?"

He lay on his back and began to pass his life in review in quite a new way.
In the morning when he saw first his footman, then his wife, then his daughter, and then the doctor, their every word and movement confirmed to him
the awful truth that had been revealed to him during the night. In them he
saw himself—all that for which he had lived—and saw clearly that it was not
real at all, but a terrible and huge deception which had hidden both life and
death. This consciousness intensified his physical suffering tenfold. He
groaned and tossed about, and pulled at his clothing which choked and sti-
fled him. And he hated them on that account.

He was given a large dose of opium and became unconscious, but at noon his
sufferings began again. He drove everybody away and tossed from side to side.

His wife came to him and said: "Jean, my dear, do this for me. It can't do
any harm and often helps. Healthy people often do it."

He opened his eyes wide.

"What? Take communion? Why? It's unnecessary! However …"

She began to cry.

"Yes, do, my dear. I'll send for our priest. He is such a nice man."

"All right. Very well," he muttered.

When the priest came and heard his confession, Ivan Ilych was softened
and seemed to feel a relief from his doubts and consequently from his sufferings, and for a moment there came a ray of hope. He again began to think of
the vermiform appendix and the possibility of correcting it. He received the
sacrament with tears in his eyes.

When they laid him down again afterwards he felt a moment's ease, and the
hope that he might live awoke in him again. He began to think of the operation
that had been suggested to him. "To live! I want to live!" he said to himself.

His wife came in to congratulate him after his communion, and when uttering the usual conventional words she added: "You feel better, don't you?"

Without looking at her he said "Yes."

Her dress, her figure, the expression of her face, the tone of her voice, all
revealed the same thing. "This is wrong, it is not as it should be. All you have

lived for and still live for is falsehood and deception, hiding life and death from you." And as soon as he admitted that thought, his hatred and his agonizing physical suffering again sprang up, and with that suffering a consciousness of the unavoidable, approaching end. And to this was added a new sensation of grinding shooting pain and a feeling of suffocation.

The expression of his face when he uttered that "Yes" was dreadful. Having uttered it, he looked her straight in the eyes, turned on his face with a rapidity extraordinary in his weak state and shouted:

"Go away! Go away and leave me alone!"

From that moment the screaming began that continued for three days, and was so terrible that one could not hear it through two closed doors without horror. At the moment he answered his wife he realized that he was lost, that there was no return, that the end had come, the very end, and his doubts were still unsolved and remained doubts.

"Oh! Oh! Oh!" he cried in various intonations. He had begun by screaming "I won't!" and continued screaming on the letter "O."

For three whole days, during which time did not exist for him, he struggled in that black sack into which he was being thrust by an invisible, resistless force. He struggled as a man condemned to death struggles in the hands of the executioner, knowing that he cannot save himself. And every moment he felt that despite all his efforts he was drawing nearer and nearer to what terrified him. He felt that his agony was due to his being thrust into that black hole and still more to his not being able to get right into it. He was hindered from getting into it by his conviction that his life had been a good one. That very justification of his life held him fast and prevented his moving forward, and it caused him most torment of all.

Suddenly some force struck him in the chest and side, making it still harder to breathe, and he fell through the hole and there at the bottom was a light. What had happened to him was like the sensation one sometimes experiences in a railway carriage when one thinks one is going backwards while one is really going forwards and suddenly becomes aware of the real direction.

"Yes, it was not the right thing," he said to himself, "but that's no matter. It can be done. But what *is* the right thing?" he asked himself, and suddenly grew quiet.

This occurred at the end of the third day, two hours before his death. Just then his schoolboy son had crept softly in and gone up to the bedside. The dying man was still screaming desperately and waving his arms. His hand fell on the boy's head, and the boy caught it, pressed it to his lips, and began to cry.

At that very moment Ivan Ilych fell through and caught sight of the light, and it was revealed to him that though his life had not been what it should have been, this could still be rectified. He asked himself, "What *is* the right thing?" and grew still, listening. Then he felt that someone was kissing his hand. He opened his eyes, looked at his son, and felt sorry for him. His wife came up to him and he glanced at her. She was gazing at him open-mouthed, with undried tears on her nose and cheek and a despairing look on her face. He felt sorry for her too.

"Yes, I am making them wretched," he thought. "They are sorry, but it will be better for them when I die." He wished to say this but had not the strength to utter it. "Besides, why speak? I must act," he thought. With a look at his wife he indicated his son and said: "Take him away … sorry for him … sorry for you too.…" He tried to add, "Forgive me," but said "Forego," and waved his hand, knowing that He whose understanding mattered would understand.

And suddenly it grew clear to him that what had been oppressing him and would not leave him was all dropping away at once from two sides, from ten sides, and from all sides. He was sorry for them, he must act so as not to hurt them: release them and free himself from these sufferings. "How good and how simple!" he thought. "And the pain?" he asked himself. "What has become of it? Where are you, pain?"

He turned his attention to it.

"Yes, here it is. Well, what of it? Let the pain be."

"And death … where is it?"

He sought his former accustomed fear of death and did not find it. "Where is it? What death?" There was no fear because there was no death.

In place of death there was light.

"So that's what it is!" he suddenly exclaimed aloud. "What joy!"

To him all this happened in a single instant, and the meaning of that instant did not change. For those present his agony continued for another two hours. Something rattled in his throat, his emaciated body twitched, then the gasping and rattle became less and less frequent.

"It is finished!" said someone near him.

He heard these words and repeated them in his soul.

"Death is finished," he said to himself. "It is no more!"

He drew in a breath, stopped in the midst of a sigh, stretched out, and died.

from The Death of Ivan Ilych

Questions for discussion

1. It has been said that disability is the one minority status that anyone can become a member of at any time. Whether Ivan Ilych became disabled by his fall or by a gradual illness, how does he react to his new status as someone who must be cared for?

2. How do Ivan Ilych's family and friends react to his illness and death? Why can it be difficult to know how to respond to another person's discomfort or illness?

3. Why does Ivan Ilych derive comfort from Gerasim? What makes a good caretaker?

4. What role do the doctors play in this story? Have you ever dealt with a professional that you did not feel you could communicate well with? What happened, and why?

5. Design your own discussion questions for this piece.

For Further Reading

About caretaking

Dillard, Annie. *The Maytrees.* Two broken arms cause an ex-husband to seek the help of his ex-wife.

Gloss, Molly. *Hearts of Horses.* A young woman tames horses in a small town and gets to know the residents, including one that needs extensive caretaking due to cancer.

About interacting with professionals

Park, Clara Claiborne. *The Siege*, especially chapter 9, "The Professionals."

Plath, Sylvia. *The Bell Jar*, especially chapter 11, about the main character's psychiatrist.

Walker, Cami. *29 Gifts.* A woman learns that she has MS after a decade of chronic pain.

Tan, Amy. *The Opposite of Fate.* The best-selling author tells how she contracted Lyme disease.

from The Bell Jar

Doctor Gordon's waiting room was hushed and beige.

The walls were beige, and the carpets were beige, and the upholstered chairs and sofas were beige. There were no mirrors or pictures, only certificates from different medical schools, with Doctor Gordon's name in Latin, hung about the walls. Pale green loopy ferns and spiked leaves of a much darker green filled the ceramic pots on the end table and the coffee table and the magazine table.

At first I wondered why the room felt so safe. Then I realized it was because there were no windows.

The air-conditioning made me shiver.

I was still wearing Betsy's white blouse and dirndl skirt. They drooped a bit now, as I hadn't washed them in my three weeks at home. The sweaty cotton gave off a sour but friendly smell.

I hadn't washed my hair for three weeks, either.

I hadn't slept for seven nights.

My mother told me I must have slept, it was impossible not to sleep in all that time, but if I slept, it was with my eyes open, for I had followed the green, luminous course of the second hand and the minute hand and the hour hand of the bedside clock through their circles and semicircles, every night for seven nights, without missing a second, or a minute, or an hour.

The reason I hadn't washed my clothes or my hair was because it seemed so silly.

I saw the days of the year stretching ahead like a series of bright, white boxes, and separating one box from another was sleep, like a black shade. Only for me, the long perspective of shades that set off one box from the next had suddenly snapped up, and I could see day after day after day glaring ahead of me like a white, broad, infinitely desolate avenue.

It seemed silly to wash one day when I would only have to wash again the next.

It made me tired just to think of it.

I wanted to do everything once and for all and be through with it.

Dr. Gordon twiddled a silver pencil.

"Your mother tells me you are upset."

I curled in the cavernous leather chair and faced Doctor Gordon across an acre of highly polished desk.

Doctor Gordon waited. He tapped his pencil—tap, tap, tap—across the neat green field of his blotter.

His eyelashes were so long and thick they looked artificial. Black plastic reeds fringing two green, glacial pools.

Doctor Gordon's features were so perfect he was almost pretty.

I hated him the minute I walked through the door.

I had imagined a kind, ugly, intuitive man looking up and saying "Ah!" in an encouraging way, as if he could see something I couldn't, and then I would find words to tell him how I was so scared, as if I were being stuffed farther and farther into a black, airless sack with no way out.

Then he would lean back in his chair and match the tips of his fingers together in a little steeple and tell me why I couldn't sleep and why I couldn't read and why I couldn't eat and why everything people did seemed so silly, because they only died in the end.

And then, I thought, he would help me, step by step, to be myself again.

But Doctor Gordon wasn't like that at all. He was young and good-looking, and I could see right away he was conceited.

Doctor Gordon had a photograph on his desk, in a silver frame, that half faced him and half faced my leather chair. It was a family photograph, and it showed a beautiful dark-haired woman, who could have been Doctor Gordon's sister, smiling out over the heads of two blond children.

I think one child was a boy and one was a girl, but it may have been that both children were boys or that both were girls, it is hard to tell when children are so small. I think there was also a dog in the picture, toward the bottom—a kind of airedale or a golden retriever—but it may have only been the pattern in the woman's skirt.

For some reason the photograph made me furious.

I didn't see why it should be turned half toward me unless Doctor Gordon was trying to show me right away that he was married to some glamorous woman and I'd better not get any funny ideas.

Then I thought, how could this Doctor Gordon help me anyway, with a beautiful wife and beautiful children and a beautiful dog haloing him like the angels on a Christmas card?

"Suppose you try and tell me what you think is wrong."

I turned the words over suspiciously, like round, sea-polished pebbles that might suddenly put out a claw and change into something else.

What did I *think* was wrong?

That made it sound as if nothing was *really* wrong, I only *thought* it was wrong.

In a dull, flat voice—to show I was not beguiled by his good looks or his family photograph—I told Doctor Gordon about not sleeping and not eating and not reading. I didn't tell him about the handwriting, which bothered me most of all.

That morning I had tried to write a letter to Doreen, down in West Virginia, asking whether I could come and live with her and maybe get a job at her college waiting on tables or something.

But when I took up my pen, my hand made big, jerky letters like those of a child, and the lines sloped down the page from left to right almost diagonally, as if they were loops of string lying on the paper, and someone had come along and blown them askew.

I knew I couldn't send a letter like that, so I tore it up in little pieces and put them in my pocketbook, next to my all-purpose compact, in case the psychiatrist asked to see them.

But of course Doctor Gordon didn't ask to see them, as I hadn't mentioned them, and I began to feel pleased at my cleverness. I thought I only need tell him what I wanted to, and that I could control the picture he had of me by hiding this and revealing that, all the while he thought he was so smart.

The whole time I was talking, Doctor Gordon bent his head as if he were praying, and the only noise apart from the dull, flat voice was the tap, tap, tap of Doctor Gordon's pencil at the same point on the green blotter, like a stalled walking stick.

When I had finished, Doctor Gordon lifted his head.

"Where did you say you went to college?"

Baffled, I told him. I didn't see where college fitted in.

"Ah!" Doctor Gordon leaned back in his chair, staring into the air over my shoulder with a reminiscent smile.

I thought he was going to tell me his diagnosis, and that perhaps I had judged him too hastily and too unkindly. But he only said, "I remember your college well. I was up there, during the war. They had a WAC station, didn't they? Or was it WAVES?"

I said I didn't know.

"Yes, a WAC station, I remember now. I was doctor for the lot, before I was sent overseas. My, they were a pretty bunch of girls."

Doctor Gordon laughed.

Then, in one smooth move, he rose to his feet and strolled toward me round the corner of his desk. I wasn't sure what he meant to do, so I stood up as well.

Doctor Gordon reached for the hand that hung at my right side and shook it.

"See you next week, then."

The full, bosomy elms made a tunnel of shade over the yellow and red brick fronts along Commonwealth Avenue, and a trolley car was threading itself toward Boston down its slim, silver track. I waited for the trolley to pass, then crossed to the gray Chevrolet at the opposite curb.

I could see my mother's face, anxious and sallow as a slice of lemon, peering up at me through the windshield.

"Well, what did he say?"

I pulled the car door shut. It didn't catch. I pushed it out and drew it in again with a dull slam.

"He said he'll see me next week."

My mother sighed.

Doctor Gordon cost twenty-five dollars an hour.

from The Bell Jar

Questions for discussion

1. Why do you think the narrator chooses to hide some of her symptoms from the doctor? Why do you think he does not ask her any relevant questions?

2. What experiences do you have with interacting with professionals? How did those professionals meet or not meet your expectations?

3. What are your feelings or beliefs about mental health treatment? When do you believe people should seek mental health treatment? Do you think insurance should cover it?

4. Design your own questions for this piece.

For Further Reading

About interacting with professionals

Park, Clara Claiborne. *The Siege*, especially chapter 9, "The Professionals."

Tolstoy, Leo. *The Death of Ivan Ilych*.

About mental illness

Gilman, Charlotte Perkins. "The Yellow Wallpaper."

Kaysen, Susanna. *Girl, Interrupted*. An edgy, semi-autobiographical book about a teenage girl who is institutionalized for mental illness.

Packer, Ann. *Songs Without Words*. Two childhood friends, now adults, try to maintain their friendship throughout various obstacles, including one of the friend's anxiety issues.

Gwyn Human Rubio (1949–   ) was born in Georgia. She holds a B.A. in English from Florida State University and an MFA in Creative Writing from Warren Wilson College. She has written a number of short stories and two novels.

from Icy Sparks

On June tenth, I turned ten. The Saturday after my birthday, the eye blinking and popping began. We were eating breakfast. Matanni was sitting across from me; Patanni was at the head of the table. To this day, I can remember my first urge—so intense it was, like an itch needing to be scratched. I could feel little invisible rubber bands fastened to my eyelids, pulled tight through my brain, and attached to the back of my head. Every few seconds, a crank behind my skull turned slowly. With each turn, the rubber bands yanked harder, and the space inside my head grew smaller. My grandmother was studying me, making sure my face had been washed, my hair combed and fastened on each side with the blue barrettes she had bought me for my birthday. While Matanni studied me, I stared straight ahead and glued my eyes, growing tighter with each second, on the brown fuzz above her lip.

"Icy," she said, sipping her coffee, "what are you staring at?"

"Them hairs above your lip," I blurted, extending my arm and pointing at her face. "They're turning gray," I said, jiggling my arm at her nose, "right there."

Patanni, spooning sugar over his oatmeal, snatched up his head and turned toward me. "Calling attention to a person's weakness ain't nice," he said.

"B-but Patanni ..." I stammered, aware only of the pressure squeezing my head and the space inside it constricting.

My grandfather laid his spoon beside his bowl. "Apologize, Icy," he demanded. "Tell Matanni you're sorry."

"But Virgil ..." My grandmother reached out and caught his hand in hers. "What the child said ain't so bad. If them hairs turn gray, they won't stand out. Gray is almost white, Virgil, and white matches my skin." She smiled, caressing the top of his hand with her index finger. "It even feels white," she said, releasing his hand, stroking her upper lip.

Patanni pushed back his chair; the legs scraped against the blue-checked linoleum rug. "That ain't the point, Tillie," he said. "Icy, here, made mention of your weakness like it weren't nothing."

"She's just a child," my grandmother said.

"But it ain't respectful," he said.

"She meant no harm," Matanni assured him.

"Icy, what do you say?" Patanni insisted, leaning toward me.

"'Tain't necessary," my grandmother said, sitting on the edge of her chair, her large breasts weaving over her bowl.

"Icy!" Patanni ordered.

"Icy!" Matanni shot back, looking straight into my eyes.

"Icy!" he began again.

"Icy!" she repeated.

I jumped up. "There ain't no fuzz on you!" I hollered, feeling the rubber bands tug tighter and tighter, sensing the blood in my body pooling behind my eyes, pushing them forward, so far forward that I could stand it no longer, not a moment longer, and, hopping up and down, I bellowed again, "Fuzz is on my eyeballs! It itches my eyes!" Frantically, I wiggled my fingers in front of my face. "They itch!" I screamed, fluttering my fingertips. "They itch!"

Then, unable to close my eyelids or scratch my eyes, I covered my face with my palms and inhaled deeply, hoping that the itchiness and tightness would go away; but instead I felt my eyelids, rolling up further like shades snapping open, and my eyeballs, rolling back like two turtles ducking inside their shells, and the space inside my head, shrinking smaller and smaller until only a few thoughts could fit inside; and, terrified of the contraction, of each thought's strangulation, I threw back my head and cried, "Baby Jesus! Sweet Jesus!"; and, not knowing what to do or how to stop it, I gave in completely to the urge.

Out popped my eyes, like ice cubes leaping from a tray.

Patanni and Matanni just sat there and watched my eyes spring from my head, but a minute later both pretended that everything had passed like it always did each morning. Matanni drank four cups of her mud-black coffee with a squirt of Essie's cream. Patanni finished his one cup, black with six tablespoons of sugar, and I drank my milk. All of us ate our oatmeal. I ladled honey on mine. Patanni preferred sugar. Matanni ate hers unadorned. No one resurrected Matanni's mustache. That one big pop had unleashed all of the tension, and the space inside my head grew large again, plumped up with thoughts. We ate in silence, and I sat calmly, as though nothing had happened.

Still, after that Saturday morning, during the summer of 1956, the urges claimed me. I was no longer Icy Sparks from Poplar Holler. I was no longer that little girl from Icy Creek Farm—our sixty-acre homestead, replete with two milk cows, a dozen chickens, and Big Fat, the five-hundred-pound sow. I was now a little girl who had to keep all of her compulsions inside. Whenever it became too much, after hours of hoarding blinkings and poppings that threatened to burst out in a thousand grotesque movements, I'd offer to get Matanni a jar of green beans from the root cellar, a pantry-sized room dug from a hill not twenty feet from the back door; and, once inside, I'd close the wooden planked door and let loose. Every blink that had been stored up spilled forth. Every jerk that had been contained leaped out. For ten minutes, I'd contort until the anxiety was all spent. Then I'd climb up on the footstool and grab the Mason jar.

With canned beans in hand, heading toward the house, I thought, secrets are evil, and wondered what secrets my grandparents kept hidden. I listened to the crickets sing. Covered in shadows, their legs contorted deep in the woods; chirping, they gave their secrets away. A wildcat cried, mourning over something forbidden. Down a dirt road cradled between two gnarled, unfriendly mountains, Poplar Holler guarded its mysteries. So far, mine were hidden in a root cellar.

If I could catch a ride into town, I went to the movies whenever I could. Immersed in celluloid fantasies, I became a rugged, square-jawed pioneer with a rifle, protecting my land, shooting bloodthirsty Comanches, or I was Running Deer, a Navajo Indian maiden, sitting cross-legged in front of a fire, cradling a baby in my arms. I became Shirley Temple, dancing across the floor, or Joan Crawford, mysterious and dark, scheming for money, plotting out murder. As I sat in the second row of the Darley theater in Ginseng, I longed to be anyone else. Even Ginseng's Jeanette Owens in her wheelchair seemed luckier than I was. At least the townsfolk pitied her. They thought her brave, rolling through life, a sour grin plastered over her face. Lonnie spikes, a 20-year-old simpleton, elicited clucking sounds and slow pendulous swings of the head. The poor thing," the townsfolk said. "He ain't got no idea. 'Tis a blessing." Each citizen slackened his pace to let Lonnie stumble by. He'd amble toward the Ginseng Post Office, where he'd sit for hours on the outside steps, his tongue lolling from his mouth, his eyes enameled over like those of a corpse.

Clutching a Coke in one hand and a box of Milk Duds in the other, I scrunched back into the brown leather seat, my feet nervously rapping the floor, and waited for *Coyote Sunrise* to begin. The lights blinked three times. Joel McRoy, slouched in the chair behind me, kicked back my seat and said, "Icy Sparks ain't nobody's girlfriend."

"Who cares?" I answered, swallowing some Coke and munching ice.

"Peavy Lawson does," Joel said. "He likes you."

I twisted around and glared at him. "I'm only ten," I snarled. "I don't like boys."

"You ought to like him," Joel said.

"How come?" I snapped, tossing back my head, flicking a Milk Dud in my mouth.

"'Cause he has frog eyes like you." Joel held on to a Chilly Dilly, a long green dill pickle sold at the candy counter.

I slammed the Coke and Milk Duds down on the armrests, one on each side, and jumped up. "You polecat of a dog!" I didn't know if those words meant anything nasty, but I liked the sound of them. "You big fat liar!"

"Your eyes pop out like a frog's," Joel said, waving the pickle around like a baton.

"They don't," I said.

"They do, too," Joel said, thrusting the Chilly Dilly in my direction.

"Liar, liar, pants on fire!" I screamed, losing all composure, pointing my fist at his pickle.

"Shush!" came a voice from a few rows back.

"I seen you, Icy Sparks. I seen you behind Old Man Potter's barn."

"You seen what?" I demanded. "Polecats stink. They ain't able to see."

Joel McRoy rose to his feet, swung his hand upward, and angrily crunched. One-half of the Chilly Dilly disappeared into his mouth. "I ... seen you ..." he said between bites, chomping down dill pickle like it was an ear of sweet corn, "jer ... king, pop ... ping them frog ... eyes of yours ... behind Old Man Pot ... ter's barn."

"You slimy ole pickle!" I bellowed. "You ain't seen nothing."

"Frog eyes! Frog eyes! Frog eyes!" Joel screamed back.

"Be quiet, you two!" someone warned.

"Liar! Liar! Liar!" I yelled, ignoring the warning, then grabbed my cup of Coke, rocked up on my toes, leaned over, and poured the whole drink, ice and all, over Joel's head. Stunned, he just stood there, a green chunk of Chilly Dilly inside his mouth, swelling out his cheek, a half-eaten pickle gripped in his hand.

"You ain't seen nothing! You just tell lies!" And with these final words, I marched out—knowing full well that Joel McRoy was telling the truth, that the week before when I was out playing tag with him and his cousin, Janie Lou, the urges had gotten really bad, and I had stolen away behind Old Man Potter's barn and let loose such a string of jerks and eye pops that the ground behind the barn seemed to shake.

Not only was I a hoarder of secrets, but—in the space of ten minutes—I had also become a full-fledged liar.

❧

from Icy Sparks

Questions for discussion

1. Why do you think Icy's grandparents ignored her tics? Do you think it is helpful or harmful to ignore differences? Do you think that family members tend to accept each other's differences more easily than outsiders might? Why or why not? Is ignoring a difference acceptance, or is it denial?

2. Why do some children seem so tolerant and others so intolerant of differences? What can we, as adults, do to help children learn tolerance?

3. Is it healthy to keep one's disability a secret? What are the pros and cons of talking with others about one's disability?

4. Icy is diagnosed later in the book with Tourette's Syndrome. What do you know about Tourette's, and how have you learned it?

5. Although Icy herself could be labeled "different," she is not kind when describing the differences of others. Have you seen this happen with people you have known?

6. Design your own questions for discussion.

For Further Reading

About Tourette's Syndrome

http://www.tsa-usa.org/

http://www.mayoclinic.com/health/tourette-syndrome/DS00541

Sacks, Oliver. *An Anthropologist on Mars.* Book by an acclaimed neurologist, containing profiles of seven individuals, one of them a surgeon with Tourette's.

Cohen, Brad. *Front of the Class: How Tourette Syndrome Made Me the Teacher I Never Had.* Autobiography of a man with Tourette's who becomes a teacher.

About disclosing disability

Kleege, Georgina. "Disabled Students Come Out."

http://www.nami.org/template.cfm?section=fight_stigma

Elizabeth Moon is a native Texan who grew up two hundred and fifty miles south of San Antonio. After earning a degree in history from Rice University, she spent three years in the Marine Corps, then earned a degree in biology from the University of Texas, Austin. She is intimately acquainted with autism, through the raising of an autistic son. The author of a number of previous novels, including the Hugo Award finalist *Remnant Population*, she lives in Florence, Texas.

from The Speed of Dark

[Editor's note: The narrator of this sci-fi novel is Lou, a young adult with autism. He lives independently and works in an office with many other people with autism. One day, he and his friend Lars, and his co-workers Cameron, Chuy, Dale, and Linda, learn of an experimental treatment that may reverse autism, and soon their boss, Mr. Crenshaw, approaches them about it.]

My messager light is blinking when I get home. It's Lars's code; he wants me to come on-line. It's late. I don't want to oversleep and be late tomorrow. But Lars knows I fence on Wednesdays, and he doesn't usually try to contact me then. It must be important.

I sign on and find his message. He has clipped a journal article for me, research on reversal of autistic-like symptoms in adult primates. I skim it, my heart thudding....

As I read, other icons pop up on my screen. The logo of our local autistic society. Cameron's logo and Dale's. So they've heard about it, too. I ignore them for the time being and go on reading. Even though it is about brains like mine, this is not my field and I cannot quite understand how the treatment is supposed to work. The authors keep referring to other articles in which the procedures were spelled out. Those articles aren't accessible—not to me, not tonight. I don't know what "Ho and Delgracia's method" is. I don't know what all the words mean, either, and my dictionary doesn't have them.

When I look at the clock, it is long after midnight. Bed. I must sleep. I turn everything off, set the alarm, and go to bed.

....

I wonder what it would be like to be normal. I made myself quit thinking about that when I left school. When it comes up, I push the thought away. But now ... what would it be like to not be worried that people think I'm crazy when I stutter or when I can't answer at all and have to write on my little pad? What would it be like to not carry that card in my pocket? To be able to see and hear everywhere? To know what people are thinking just by looking at their faces?

....

Eventually I am ready to think and feel again. I am sad. I am not supposed to be sad ... I am sad anyway. I try so hard, and it is still not working. I wear the same clothes as the others. I say the same words at the same times: good morning, hi, how are you, I'm fine, good night, please, thank you, you're welcome, no thank you, not right now. I obey the traffic laws; I obey the rules. I have ordinary furniture in my apartment, and I play my unusual music very softly or use headphones. But it is not enough. Even as hard as I try, the real people still want me to change, to be like them. They do not know how hard it is. They do not care. They want me to change. They want to put things in my head, to change my brain. They would say they don't, but they do.

....

Friday morning at 8:53 Mr. Crenshaw calls us together and says he has an announcement to make. My stomach knots.

"You are all very lucky," he says. "In today's tough economic climate I am, frankly, very surprised that this is even remotely possible, but in fact ... you have the chance to receive a brand-new treatment at no cost to yourselves." His mouth is stretched in a big false grin; his face is shiny with the effort he is making.

He must think we are really stupid. I glance at Cameron, then Dale, then Chuy, the only ones I can see without turning my head. Their eyes are moving, too.

Cameron says, in a flat voice, "You mean the experimental treatment developed in Cambridge and reported in *Nature Neuroscience* a few weeks ago?"

Crenshaw pales and swallows. "Who told you about that?"

"It was on the Internet," Chuy says.

"It—it—" Crenshaw stops, and glares at all of us. Then he twists his mouth into a smile again. "Be that as it may, there is a new treatment, which you have the opportunity to receive at no cost to you."

"I don't want it," Linda says. "I do not need a treatment; I am fine the way I am." I turn and look at her.

Crenshaw turns red. "You are *not* fine," he says, his voice getting louder and harsher. "And you are not normal. You are autistics, you are disabled, you were hired under a special provision—"

"'Normal' is a dryer setting," Chuy and Linda say together. They grin briefly.

"You have to adapt," Crenshaw says. "You can't expect to get special privileges forever, not when there's a treatment that will make you normal. That gym, and private offices, and all that music, and all those ridiculous decorations—you can be normal and there's no need for that. It's uneconomic. It's ridiculous." He turns as if to leave and then whirls back. "It has to stop," he says. Then he does leave.

We all look at one another. Nobody says anything for several minutes. Then Chuy says, "Well, it's happened."

"I won't do it," Linda says. "They can't make me."

"Maybe they can," Chuy says. "We don't know for sure."

In the afternoon, we each get a letter by interoffice mail, a letter on paper. The letter says that due to economic pressure and the need to diversify and remain competitive, each department must reduce staff. Individuals actively taking part in research protocols are exempt from consideration for termination, the letter says. Others will be offered attractive separation allowances for voluntary separation. The letter does not specifically say that we must agree to treatment or lose our jobs, but I think that is what it means …

from **The Speed of Dark**

Questions for discussion

1. What does it mean to be "normal"? Who decides what "normal" is?

2. Do you think that people with disabilities should want to "cure" them? Why or why not? Which things about yourself might you "cure" if you could? Would you be willing to risk undergoing treatment?

3. What ethical issues are raised by research on humans? By forced treatment?

4. Lou complains that he tries to be like everyone else, but it never seems to be enough. What do you think he means? Why is society not more tolerant of differences? How could this change?

5. What depictions of autism have you seen in the media or in literature?

6. Design your own discussion questions for this piece.

For Further Reading

About autism

www.autismspeaks.org

Park, Clara Claiborne. *The Siege.* A mother's memoir recounting her young daughter's autism.

Tammet, Daniel. *Born on a Blue Day.* A man with autism's memoir, including a fantastic chapter about his fascination with the mathematical constant Pi.

Grandin, Temple. *Thinking in Pictures.* Memoir written by a woman with autism who has built an enormously successful career as a livestock-handling facility designer.

About curing disabilities

Huxley, Aldous. "Jacob's Hands." A screenplay about a man with the power to heal. After he heals people's physical ailments, are they better off?

About fictional societies with disability issues

Le Guin, Ursula. "The Ones Who Walk Away from Omelas."

Wells, H.G. "The Country of the Blind."

from Jane Eyre

The month of courtship had wasted: its very last hours were being numbered. There was no putting off the day that advanced—the bridal day; and all preparations for its arrival were complete. I, at least, had nothing more to do: there were my trunks, packed, locked, corded, ranged in a row along the wall of my little chamber; tomorrow, at this time, they would be far on their road to London: and so should I.

It was not only the hurry of preparation that made me feverish; not only the anticipation of the great change—the new life which was to commence tomorrow: both these circumstances had their share, doubtless, in producing that restless, excited mood which hurried me forth at this late hour into the darkening grounds: but a third cause influenced my mind more than they.

I had at heart a strange and anxious thought. Something had happened which I could not comprehend; no one knew of or had seen the event but myself: it had taken place the preceding night. Mr. Rochester that night was absent from home; nor was he yet returned: business had called him to a small estate of two or three farms he possessed thirty miles off—business it was requisite he should settle in person, previous to his meditated departure from England. I waited now his return; eager to disburden my mind, and to seek of him the solution of the enigma that perplexed me. Stay till he comes, reader; and, when I disclose my secret to him, you shall share the confidence.

I sought the orchard, driven to its shelter by the wind, which all day had blown strong and full from the south, without, however, bringing a speck of rain. Instead of subsiding as night drew on, it seemed to augment its rush and deepen its roar: the trees blew steadfastly one way, never writhing round, and scarcely tossing back their boughs once in an hour; so continuous was the strain bending their branchy heads northward—the clouds drifted from pole to pole, fast following, mass on mass: no glimpse of blue sky had been visible that July day.

It was not without a certain wild pleasure I ran before the wind, delivering my trouble of mind to the measureless air-torrent thundering through space. Descending the laurel walk, I faced the wreck of the chestnut-tree; it stood up black and riven: the trunk, split down the centre, gasped ghastly. The cloven halves were not broken from each other, for the firm base and strong roots kept them unsundered below; though community of vitality was destroyed—the sap could flow no more: their great boughs on each side were dead, and next winter's tempests would be sure to fell one or both to earth: as yet, however, they might be said to form one tree—a ruin, but an entire ruin.

"You did right to hold fast to each other," I said: as if the monster-splinters were living things, and could hear me. "I think, scathed as you look, and charred and scorched, there must be a little sense of life in you yet, rising out of that adhesion at the faithful, honest roots: you will never have green leaves more—never more see birds making nests and singing idylls in your boughs; the time of pleasure and love is over with you: but you are not desolate: each of you has a comrade to sympathize with him in his decay." As I looked up at them, the moon appeared momentarily in that part of the sky which filled their fissure; her disk was blood-red and half overcast; she seemed to throw on me one bewildered, dreary glance, and buried herself again instantly in the deep drift of cloud. The wind fell, for a second, round Thornfield; but far away over wood and water, poured a wild, melancholy wail: it was sad to listen to, and I ran off again.

"How late it grows!" I said. "I will run down to the gates: it is moonlight at intervals; I can see a good way on the road. He may be coming now, and to meet him will save some minutes of suspense."

The wind roared high in the great trees which embowered the gates; but the road as far as I could see, to the right hand and the left, was all still and solitary: save for the shadows of clouds crossing it at intervals as the moon looked out, it was but a long pale line, unvaried by one moving speck.

A puerile tear dimmed my eye while I looked—a tear of disappointment and impatience; ashamed of it, I wiped it away. I lingered; the moon shut herself wholly within her chamber, and drew close her curtain of dense cloud: the night grew dark; rain came driving fast on the gale.

"I wish he would come! I wish he would come!" I exclaimed, seized with hypochondriac foreboding. I had expected his arrival before tea; now it was dark: what could keep him? Had an accident happened? The event of last night again recurred to me. I interpreted it as a warning of disaster. I feared my hopes were too bright to be realized; and I had enjoyed so much bliss lately that I imagined my fortune had passed its meridian, and must now decline.

"Well, I cannot return to the house," I thought; "I cannot sit by the fireside, while he is abroad in inclement weather: better tire my limbs than strain my heart; I will go forward and meet him."

I set out; I walked fast, but not far: ere I had measured a quarter of a mile, I heard the tramp of hoofs; a horseman came on, full gallop; a dog ran by his side. Away with evil presentiment! It was he: here he was, mounted on [his horse] Mesrour, followed by [his dog] Pilot. He saw me; for the moon had opened a blue field in the sky, and rode in it watery bright: he took his hat off, and waved it round his head. I now ran to meet him.

"There!" he exclaimed, as he stretched out his hand and bent from the saddle: "You can't do without me, that is evident. Step on my boot-toe; give me both hands: mount!"

I obeyed: joy made me agile: I sprang up before him. A hearty kissing I got for a welcome, and some boastful triumph, which I swallowed as well as I could. He checked himself in his exultation to demand, "But is there anything the matter, Janet, that you come to meet me at such an hour? Is there anything wrong?"

"No, but I thought you would never come. I could not bear to wait in the house for you, especially with this rain and wind."

"Rain and wind, indeed! Yes, you are dripping like a mermaid; pull my cloak round you: but I think you are feverish, Jane: both your cheek and hand are burning hot. I ask again, is there anything the matter?"

"Nothing now; I am neither afraid nor unhappy."

"Then you have been both?"

"Rather: but I'll tell you all about it by-and-bye, sir; and I daresay you will only laugh at me for my pains."

"I'll laugh at you heartily when tomorrow is past; till then I dare not: my prize is not certain. This is you, who have been as slippery as an eel this last month, and as thorny as a briar-rose? I could not lay a finger anywhere but I was pricked; and now I seem to have gathered up a stray lamb in my arms. You wandered out of the fold to seek your shepherd, did you, Jane?"

"I wanted you: but don't boast. Here we are at Thornfield: now let me get down."

He landed me on the pavement. As John took his horse, and he followed me into the hall, he told me to make haste and put something dry on, and then return to him in the library; and he stopped me, as I made for the staircase, to extort a promise that I would not be long: nor was I long; in five minutes I rejoined him. I found him at supper.

"It is near midnight," I said.

"Yes: but remember, Jane, you promised to wake with me the night before my wedding."

"I did; and I will keep my promise, for an hour or two at least: I have no wish to go to bed."

"Are all your arrangements complete?"

"All, sir."

"And on my part likewise," he returned, "I have settled everything; and we shall leave Thornfield tomorrow, within half an hour after our return from church."

"Very well, sir."

"With what an extraordinary smile you uttered that word—'very well,' Jane! What a bright spot of color you have on each cheek! And how strangely your eyes glitter! Are you well?"

"I believe I am."

"Believe! What is the matter? Tell me what you feel."

"I could not, sir: no words could tell you what I feel. I wish this present hour would never end: who knows with what fate the next may come charged?"

"This is hypochondria, Jane. You have been over-excited, or over-fatigued."

"Do you, sir, feel calm and happy?"

"Calm?—no: but happy—to the heart's core."

I looked up at him to read the signs of bliss in his face: it was ardent and flushed.

"Give me your confidence, Jane," he said: "relieve your mind of any weight that oppresses it, by imparting it to me. What do you fear?—that I shall not prove a good husband?"

"It is the idea farthest from my thoughts."

"Are you apprehensive of the new sphere you are about to enter?—of the new life into which you are passing?"

"No."

"You puzzle me, Jane: your look and tone of sorrowful audacity perplex and pain me. I want an explanation."

"Then, sir, listen. You were from home last night?"

"I was: I know that; and you hinted a while ago at something which had happened in my absence:—nothing, probably, of consequence; but, in short, it has disturbed you. Let me hear it. Mrs. Fairfax has said something, perhaps? Or you have overheard the servants talk? Your sensitive self-respect has been wounded?"

"No, sir." It struck twelve—I waited till the time-piece had concluded its silver chime, and the clock its hoarse, vibrating stroke, and then I proceeded.

"All day yesterday I was very busy, and very happy in my ceaseless bustle; for I am not, as you seem to think, troubled by any haunting fears about the new sphere, et cetera: I think it a glorious thing to have the hope of living with you, because I love you. No, sir, don't caress me now—let me talk undisturbed. Yesterday I trusted well in Providence, and believed that events were working together for your good and mine: it was a fine day, if you recollect— the calmness of the air and sky forbade apprehensions respecting your safety or comfort on your journey. I walked a little while on the pavement after tea, thinking of you; and I beheld you in imagination so near me, I scarcely missed your actual presence. I thought of the life that lay before me—*your* life, sir— an existence more expansive and stirring than my own: as much more so as the depths of the sea to which the brook runs are than the shallows of its own strait channel. I wondered why moralists call this world a dreary wilderness: for me it blossomed like a rose. Just at sunset, the air turned cold and the sky cloudy: I went in, Sophie called me upstairs to look at my wedding-dress, which they had just brought; and under it in the box I found your present— the veil which, in your princely extravagance, you sent for from London: resolved, I suppose, since I would not have jewels, to cheat me into accepting something as costly. I smiled as I unfolded it, and devised how I would tease you about your aristocratic tastes, and your efforts to masque your plebeian bride in the attributes of a peeress. I thought how I would carry down to you the square of unembroidered blond I had myself prepared as a covering for my low-born head, and ask if that was not good enough for a woman who could bring her husband neither fortune, beauty, nor connections. I saw plainly how you would look; and heard your impetuous republican answers, and your haughty disavowal of any necessity on your part to augment your wealth, or elevate your standing, by marrying either a purse or a coronet."

"How well you read me, you witch!" interposed Mr. Rochester: "but what did you find in the veil besides its embroidery? Did you find poison, or a dagger, that you look so mournful now?"

"No, no, sir; besides the delicacy and richness of the fabric, I found nothing save Edward Fairfax Rochester's pride; and that did not scare me, because I am used to the sight of the demon. But, sir, as it grew dark, the wind rose: it blew yesterday evening, not as it blows now—wild and high—but with a sullen, moaning sound far more eerie. I wished you were at home. I came into this room, and the sight of the empty chair and fireless hearth chilled me. For some time after I went to bed, I could not sleep—a sense of anxious excitement distressed me. The gale still rising, seemed to my ear to muffle a mournful under-sound; whether in the house or abroad I could not at first tell, but it recurred, doubtful yet doleful at every lull; at last I made out it must be some dog howling at a distance. I was glad when it ceased. On sleeping, I continued in dreams the idea of a dark and gusty night. I continued also the wish to be with you, and experienced a strange, regretful consciousness of some barrier dividing us. During all my first sleep, I was following the windings of an unknown road; total obscurity environed me; rain pelted me; I was burdened with the charge of a little child: a very small creature, too young and feeble to walk, and which shivered in my cold arms, and wailed piteously in my ear. I thought, sir, that you were on the road a long way before me; and I strained every nerve to overtake you, and made effort on effort to utter your name and entreat you to stop—but my movements were fettered, and my voice still died away inarticulate; while you, I felt, withdrew farther and farther every moment."

"And these dreams weigh on your spirits now, Jane, when I am close to you? Little nervous subject! Forget visionary woe, and think only of real happiness! You say you love me, Janet: yes—I will not forget that; and you cannot deny it. Those words did not die inarticulate on your lips. I heard them clear and soft: a thought too solemn perhaps, but sweet as music—'I think it is a glorious thing to have the hope of living with you, Edward, because I love you.' Do you love me, Jane?—repeat it."

"I do, sir—I do, with my whole heart."

"Well," he said, after some minutes' silence, "it is strange; but that sentence has penetrated my breast painfully. Why? I think because you said it with such an earnest, religious energy, and because your upward gaze at me now is the very sublime of faith, truth, and devotion: it is too much as if some spirit were near me. Look wicked, Jane: as you know well how to look: coin one of your wild, shy, provoking smiles; tell me you hate me—tease me, vex me; do anything but move me: I would rather be incensed than saddened."

"I will tease you and vex you to your heart's content, when I have finished my tale: but hear me to the end."

"I thought, Jane, you had told me all. I thought I had found the source of your melancholy in a dream."

I shook my head.

"What! Is there more? But I will not believe it to be anything important. I warn you of incredulity beforehand. Go on."

The disquietude of his air, the somewhat apprehensive impatience of his manner, surprised me: but I proceeded.

"I dreamt another dream, sir: that Thornfield Hall was a dreary ruin, the retreat of bats and owls. I thought that of all the stately front nothing remained but a shell-like wall, very high and very fragile-looking. I wandered, on a moonlight night, through the grass-grown enclosure within: here I stumbled over a marble hearth, and there over a fallen fragment of cornice. Wrapped up in a shawl, I still carried the unknown little child: I might not lay it down anywhere, however tired were my arms—however much its weight impeded my progress, I must retain it. I heard the gallop of a horse at a distance on the road; I was sure it was you; and you were departing for many years and for a distant country. I climbed the thin wall with frantic perilous haste, eager to catch one glimpse of you from the top: the stones rolled from under my feet, the ivy branches I grasped gave way, the child clung round my neck in terror, and almost strangled me; at last I gained the summit. I saw you like a speck on a white track, lessening every moment. The blast blew so strong I could not stand. I sat down on the narrow ledge; I hushed the scared infant in my lap: you turned an angle of the road: I bent forward to take a last look; the wall crumbled; I was shaken; the child rolled from my knee, I lost my balance, fell, and woke."

"Now, Jane, that is all."

"All the preface, sir; the tale is yet to come. On waking, a gleam dazzled my eyes; I thought—oh, it is daylight! But I was mistaken; it was only candle-light. Sophie, I supposed, had come in. There was a light in the dressing-table, and the door of the closet, where, before going to bed, I had hung my wedding-dress and veil, stood open; I heard a rustling there. I asked, 'Sophie, what are you doing?' No one answered; but a form emerged from the closet; it took the light, held it aloft, and surveyed the garments pendent from the portmanteau. 'Sophie! Sophie!' I again cried: and still it was silent. I had risen up in bed, I bent forward: first surprise, then bewilderment, came over me; and then my blood crept cold through my veins. Mr. Rochester, this was not Sophie, it was not Leah, it was not Mrs. Fairfax: it was not—no, I was sure of it, and am still—it was not even that strange woman, Grace Poole."

"It must have been one of them," interrupted my master.

"No, sir, I solemnly assure you to the contrary. The shape standing before me had never crossed my eyes within the precincts of Thornfield Hall before; the height, the contour were new to me."

"Describe it, Jane."

"It seemed, sir, a woman, tall and large, with thick and dark hair hanging long down her back. I know not what dress she had on: it was white and straight; but whether gown, sheet, or shroud, I cannot tell."

"Did you see her face?"

"Not at first. But presently she took my veil from its place; she held it up, gazed at it long, and then she threw it over her own head, and turned to the mirror. At that moment I saw the reflection of the visage and features quite distinctly in the dark oblong glass."

"And how were they?"

"Fearful and ghastly to me—oh, sir, I never saw a face like it! It was a discolored face—it was a savage face. I wish I could forget the roll of the red eyes and the fearful blackened inflation of the lineaments!"

"Ghosts are usually pale, Jane."

"This, sir, was purple: the lips were swelled and dark; the brow furrowed: the black eyebrows widely raised over the bloodshot eyes. Shall I tell you of what it reminded me?"

"You may."

"Of the foul German specter—the Vampyre."

"Ah!—what did it do?"

"Sir, it removed my veil from its gaunt head, rent it in two parts, and flinging both on the floor, trampled on them."

"Afterwards?"

"It drew aside the window-curtain and looked out; perhaps it saw dawn approaching, for, taking the candle, it retreated to the door. Just at my bedside, the figure stopped: the fiery eyes glared upon me—she thrust up her candle close to my face, and extinguished it under my eyes. I was aware her lurid visage flamed over mine, and I lost consciousness: for the second time in my life—only the second time—I became insensible from terror."

"Who was with you when you revived?"

"No one, sir, but the broad day. I rose, bathed my head and face in water, drank a long draught; felt that though enfeebled I was not ill, and determined that to none but you would I impart this vision. Now, sir, tell me who and what that woman was?"

"The creature of an over-stimulated brain; that is certain. I must be careful of you, my treasure: nerves like yours were not made for rough handling."

"Sir, depend on it, my nerves were not in fault; the thing was real: the transaction actually took place."

"And your previous dreams, were they real too? Is Thornfield Hall a ruin? Am I severed from you by insuperable obstacles? Am I leaving you without a tear—without a kiss—without a word?"

"Not yet."

"Am I about to do it? Why, the day is already commenced which is to bind us indissolubly; and when we are once united, there shall be no recurrence of these mental terrors: I guarantee that."

"Mental terrors, sir! I wish I could believe them to be only such: I wish it more now than ever; since even you cannot explain to me the mystery of that awful visitant."

"And since I cannot do it, Jane, it must have been unreal."

"But, sir, when I said so to myself on rising this morning, and when I looked round the room to gather courage and comfort from the cheerful aspect of each familiar object in full daylight, there—on the carpet—I saw what gave the distinct lie to my hypothesis,—the veil, torn from top to bottom in two halves!"

I felt Mr. Rochester start and shudder; he hastily flung his arms round me. "Thank God!" he exclaimed, "that if anything malignant did come near you last night, it was only the veil that was harmed. Oh, to think what might have happened!"

He drew his breath short, and strained me so close to him, I could scarcely pant. After some minutes' silence, he continued, cheerily—

"Now, Janet, I'll explain to you all about it. It was half dream, half reality. A woman did, I doubt not, enter your room: and that woman was—must have been—Grace Poole. You call her a strange being yourself: from all you know, you have reason so to call her—what did she do to me? In a state between sleeping and waking, you noticed her entrance and her actions; but feverish, almost delirious as you were, you ascribed to her a goblin appearance different from her own: the long disheveled hair, the swelled black face, the exaggerated stature, were figments of imagination; results of nightmare: the spiteful tearing of the veil was real: and it is like her. I see you would ask why I keep such a woman in my house: when we have been married a year and a day, I will tell you; but not now. Are you satisfied, Jane? Do you accept my solution of the mystery?"

I reflected, and in truth it appeared to me the only possible one: satisfied I was not, but to please him I endeavored to appear so—relieved, I certainly did feel; so I answered him with a contented smile. And now, as it was long past one, I prepared to leave him.

"Does not Sophie sleep with Adele [Mr. Rochester's niece] in the nursery?" he asked, as I lit my candle.

"Yes, sir."

"And there is room enough in Adele's little bed for you. You must share it with her to-night, Jane: it is no wonder that the incident you have related should make you nervous, and I would rather you did not sleep alone: promise me to go to the nursery."

"I shall be very glad to do so, sir."

"And fasten the door securely on the inside. Wake Sophie when you go upstairs, under pretence of requesting her to rouse you in good time to-morrow; for you must be dressed and have finished breakfast before eight. And now, no more somber thoughts: chase dull care away, Janet. Don't you hear to what soft whispers the wind has fallen? And there is no more beating of rain against the window-panes: look here" (he lifted up the curtain)—"it is a lovely night!"

It was. Half heaven was pure and stainless: the clouds, now trooping before the wind, which had shifted to the west, were filing off eastward in long, silvered columns. The moon shone peacefully.

"Well," said Mr. Rochester, gazing inquiringly into my eyes, "how is my Janet now?"

"The night is serene, sir; and so am I."

"And you will not dream of separation and sorrow tonight; but of happy love and blissful union."

This prediction was but half fulfilled: I did not indeed dream of sorrow, but as little did I dream of joy; for I never slept at all. With little Adele in my arms, I watched the slumber of childhood—so tranquil, so passionless, so innocent—and waited for the coming day: all my life was awake and astir in my frame: and as soon as the sun rose I rose too. I remember Adele clung to me as I left her: I remember I kissed her as I loosened her little hands from my neck; and I cried over her with strange emotion, and quitted her because I feared my sobs would break her still sound repose. She seemed the emblem of my past life; and here I was now to array myself to meet, the dread, but adored, type of my unknown future day.

Sophie came at seven to dress me: she was very long indeed in accomplishing her task; so long that Mr. Rochester, grown, I suppose, impatient of my delay, sent up to ask why I did not come. She was just fastening my veil (the plain square of blond after all) to my hair with a brooch; I hurried from under her hands as soon as I could.

"Stop!" she cried in French. "Look at yourself in the mirror: you have not taken one peep."

So I turned at the door: I saw a robed and veiled figure, so unlike my usual self that it seemed almost the image of a stranger. "Jane!" called a voice, and I hastened down. I was received at the foot of the stairs by Mr. Rochester.

"Lingerer!" he said, "my brain is on fire with impatience, and you tarry so long!"

He took me into the dining-room, surveyed me keenly all over, pronounced me "fair as a lily, and not only the pride of his life, but the desire of his eyes," and then telling me he would give me but ten minutes to eat some breakfast, he rang the bell. One of his lately hired servants, a footman, answered it.

"Is John getting the carriage ready?"

"Yes, sir."

"Is the luggage brought down?"

"They are bringing it down, sir."

"Go you to the church: see if Mr. Wood [the clergyman] and the clerk are there: return and tell me."

The church, as the reader knows, was but just beyond the gates; the footman soon returned.

"Mr. Wood is in the vestry, sir, putting on his surplice."

"And the carriage?"

"The horses are harnessing."

"We shall not want it to go to church; but it must be ready the moment we return: all the boxes and luggage arranged and strapped on, and the coachman in his seat."

"Yes, sir."

"Jane, are you ready?"

I rose. There were no groomsmen, no bridesmaids, no relatives to wait for or marshal: none but Mr. Rochester and I. Mrs. Fairfax stood in the hall as we passed. I would fain have spoken to her, but my hand was held by a grasp of iron: I was hurried along by a stride I could hardly follow; and to look at Mr. Rochester's face was to feel that not a second of delay would be tolerated for any purpose. I wonder what other bridegroom ever looked as he did—so bent up to a purpose, so grimly resolute: or who, under such steadfast brows, ever revealed such flaming and flashing eyes.

I know not whether the day was fair or foul; in descending the drive, I gazed neither on sky nor earth: my heart was with my eyes; and both seemed migrated into Mr. Rochester's frame. I wanted to see the invisible thing on which, as we went along, he appeared to fasten a glance fierce and fell. I wanted to feel the thoughts whose force he seemed breasting and resisting.

At the churchyard wicket he stopped: he discovered I was quite out of breath. "Am I cruel in my love?" he said. "Delay an instant: lean on me, Jane."

And now I can recall the picture of the gray old house of God rising calm before me, of a rook wheeling round the steeple, of a ruddy morning sky beyond. I remember something, too, of the green grave-mounds; and I have not forgotten, either, two figures of strangers straying amongst the low hillocks and reading the mementoes graven on the few mossy headstones. I noticed them, because, as they saw us, they passed round to the back of the church; and I doubted not they were going to enter by the side-aisle door and witness the ceremony. By Mr. Rochester they were not observed; he was earnestly looking at my face from which the blood had, I daresay, momentarily fled: for I felt my forehead dewy, and my cheeks and lips cold. When I rallied, which I soon did, he walked gently with me up the path to the porch.

We entered the quiet and humble temple; the priest waited in his white surplice at the lowly altar, the clerk beside him. All was still: two shadows only moved in a remote corner. My conjecture had been correct: the strangers had slipped in before us, and they now stood by the vault of the Rochesters, their backs towards us, viewing through the rails the old time-stained marble tomb, where a kneeling angel guarded the remains of Damer de Rochester, slain at Marston Moor in the time of the civil wars, and of Elizabeth, his wife.

Our place was taken at the communion rails. Hearing a cautious step behind me, I glanced over my shoulder: one of the strangers—a gentleman, evidently—was advancing up the chancel. The service began. The explanation of the intent of matrimony was gone through; and then the clergyman came a step further forward, and, bending slightly towards Mr. Rochester, went on.

"I require and charge you both (as ye will answer at the dreadful day of judgment, when the secrets of all hearts shall be disclosed), that if either of you know any impediment why ye may not lawfully be joined together in matrimony, ye do now confess it; for be ye well assured that so many as are coupled together otherwise than God's Word doth allow, are not joined together by God, neither is their matrimony lawful."

He paused, as the custom is. When is the pause after that sentence ever broken by reply? Not, perhaps, once in a hundred years. And the clergyman, who had not lifted his eyes from his book, and had held his breath but for a moment, was proceeding: his hand was already stretched towards Mr. Rochester, as his lips unclosed to ask, "Wilt thou have this woman for thy wedded wife?"—when a distinct and near voice said—

"The marriage cannot go on: I declare the existence of an impediment."

The clergyman looked up at the speaker and stood mute; the clerk did the same; Mr. Rochester moved slightly, as if an earthquake had rolled under his feet: taking a firmer footing, and not turning his head or eyes, he said, "Proceed."

Profound silence fell when he had uttered that word, with deep but low intonation. Presently Mr. Wood said—

"I cannot proceed without some investigation into what has been asserted, and evidence of its truth or falsehood."

"The ceremony is quite broken off," subjoined the voice behind us. "I am in a condition to prove my allegation: an insuperable impediment to this marriage exists."

Mr. Rochester heard, but heeded not: he stood stubborn and rigid, making no movement but to possess himself of my hand. What a hot and strong grasp he had! And how like quarried marble was his pale, firm, massive front at this moment! How his eye shone, still watchful, and yet wild beneath!

Mr. Wood seemed at a loss. "What is the nature of the impediment?" he asked. "Perhaps it may be got over—explained away?"

"Hardly," was the answer. "I have called it insuperable, and I speak advisedly."

The speaker came forward and leaned on the rails. He continued, uttering each word distinctly, calmly, steadily, but not loudly—

"It simply consists in the existence of a previous marriage. Mr. Rochester has a wife now living."

My nerves vibrated to those low-spoken words as they had never vibrated to thunder—my blood felt their subtle violence as it had never felt frost or fire; but I was collected, and in no danger of swooning. I looked at Mr. Rochester: I made him look at me. His whole face was colorless rock: his eye was both spark and flint. He disavowed nothing: he seemed as if he would defy all things. Without speaking, without smiling, without seeming to recognize in me a human being, he only twined my waist with his arm and riveted me to his side.

"Who are you?" he asked of the intruder.

"My name is Briggs, a solicitor of—Street, London."

"And you would thrust on me a wife?"

"I would remind you of your lady's existence, sir, which the law recognizes, if you do not."

"Favor me with an account of her—with her name, her parentage, her place of abode."

"Certainly." Mr. Briggs calmly took a paper from his pocket, and read out in a sort of official, nasal voice:—

"'I affirm and can prove that on the 20th of October A.D.—(a date of fifteen years back), Edward Fairfax Rochester, of Thornfield Hall, in the county of—, and of Ferndean Manor, in—shire, England, was married to my sister, Bertha Antoinetta Mason, daughter of Jonas Mason, merchant, and of Antoinetta his wife, a Creole, at—church, Spanish Town, Jamaica. The record of the marriage will be found in the register of that church—a copy of it is now in my possession. Signed, Richard Mason.'"

"That—if a genuine document—may prove I have been married, but it does not prove that the woman mentioned therein as my wife is still living."

"She was living three months ago," returned the lawyer.

"How do you know?"

"I have a witness to the fact, whose testimony even you, sir, will scarcely controvert."

"Produce him—or go to hell."

"I will produce him first—he is on the spot. Mr. Mason, have the goodness to step forward."

Mr. Rochester, on hearing the name, set his teeth; he experienced, too, a sort of strong convulsive quiver; near to him as I was, I felt the spasmodic

movement of fury or despair run through his frame. The second stranger, who
had hitherto lingered in the background, now drew near; a pale face looked
over the solicitor's shoulder—yes, it was Mason himself. Mr. Rochester turned
and glared at him. His eye, as I have often said, was a black eye: it had now a
tawny, nay, a bloody light in its gloom; and his face flushed—olive cheek and
hueless forehead received a glow as from spreading, ascending heart-fire: and
he stirred, lifted his strong arm—he could have struck Mason, dashed him
on the church-floor, shocked by ruthless blow the breath from his body—but
Mason shrank away, and cried faintly, "Good God!" Contempt fell cool on Mr.
Rochester—his passion died as if a blight had shriveled it up: he only asked—
"What have *you* to say?"

An inaudible reply escaped Mason's white lips.

"The devil is in it if you cannot answer distinctly. I again demand, what
have you to say?"

"Sir—sir," interrupted the clergyman, "do not forget you are in a sacred
place." Then addressing Mason, he inquired gently, "Are you aware, sir,
whether or not this gentleman's wife is still living?"

"Courage," urged the lawyer,—"speak out."

"She is now living at Thornfield Hall," said Mason, in more articulate tones:
"I saw her there last April. I am her brother."

"At Thornfield Hall!" ejaculated the clergyman. "Impossible! I am an old
resident in this neighborhood, sir, and I never heard of a Mrs. Rochester at
Thornfield Hall."

I saw a grim smile contort Mr. Rochester's lips, and he muttered—

"No, by God! I took care that none should hear of it—or of her under that
name." He mused—for ten minutes he held counsel with himself: he formed
his resolve, and announced it—

"Enough! All shall bolt out at once, like the bullet from the barrel. Wood,
close your book and take off your surplice; John Green (to the clerk), leave
the church: there will be no wedding today." The man obeyed.

Mr. Rochester continued, hardily and recklessly: "Bigamy is an ugly word!
—I meant, however, to be a bigamist; but fate has out-maneuvered me, or
Providence has checked me,—perhaps the last. I am little better than a devil
at this moment; and, as my pastor there would tell me, deserve no doubt the
sternest judgments of God, even to the quenchless fire and deathless worm.
Gentlemen, my plan is broken up:—what this lawyer and his client say is true:
I have been married, and the woman to whom I was married lives! You say
you never heard of a Mrs. Rochester at the house up yonder, Wood; but I
daresay you have many a time inclined your ear to gossip about the mysterious lunatic kept there under watch and ward. Some have whispered to you

that she is my bastard half-sister: some, my cast-off mistress. I now inform you that she is my wife, whom I married fifteen years ago,—Bertha Mason by name; sister of this resolute personage, who is now, with his quivering limbs and white cheeks, showing you what a stout heart men may bear. Cheer up, Dick!—never fear me!—I'd almost as soon strike a woman as you. Bertha Mason is mad; and she came of a mad family; idiots and maniacs through three generations! Her mother, the Creole, was both a madwoman and a drunkard!—as I found out after I had wed the daughter: for they were silent on family secrets before. Bertha, like a dutiful child, copied her parent in both points. I had a charming partner—pure, wise, modest: you can fancy I was a happy man. I went through rich scenes! Oh! My experience has been heavenly, if you only knew it! But I owe you no further explanation. Briggs, Wood, Mason, I invite you all to come up to the house and visit Mrs. Poole's patient, and *my wife*! You shall see what sort of a being I was cheated into espousing, and judge whether or not I had a right to break the compact, and seek sympathy with something at least human. This girl," he continued, looking at me, "knew no more than you, Wood, of the disgusting secret: she thought all was fair and legal and never dreamt she was going to be entrapped into a feigned union with a defrauded wretch, already bound to a bad, mad, and embruted partner! Come all of you—follow!"

Still holding me fast, he left the church: the three gentlemen came after. At the front door of the hall we found the carriage.

"Take it back to the coach-house, John," said Mr. Rochester coolly; "it will not be wanted today."

At our entrance, Mrs. Fairfax, Adele, Sophie, Leah, advanced to meet and greet us.

"To the right-about—every soul!" cried the master; "away with your congratulations! Who wants them? Not I!—they are fifteen years too late!"

He passed on and ascended the stairs, still holding my hand, and still beckoning the gentlemen to follow him, which they did. We mounted the first staircase, passed up the gallery, proceeded to the third story: the low, black door, opened by Mr. Rochester's master-key, admitted us to the tapestried room, with its great bed and its pictorial cabinet.

"You know this place, Mason," said our guide; "she bit and stabbed you here."

He lifted the hangings from the wall, uncovering the second door: this, too, he opened. In a room without a window, there burnt a fire guarded by a high and strong fender, and a lamp suspended from the ceiling by a chain. Grace Poole bent over the fire, apparently cooking something in a saucepan. In the deep shade, at the farther end of the room, a figure ran backwards and forwards. What it was, whether beast or human being, one could not, at first sight, tell: it groveled, seemingly, on all fours; it snatched and growled like some strange wild animal: but it was covered with clothing, and a quantity of dark, grizzled hair, wild as a mane, hid its head and face.

"Good-morrow, Mrs. Poole!" said Mr. Rochester. "How are you? and how is your charge today?"

"We're tolerable, sir, I thank you," replied Grace, lifting the boiling mess carefully on to the hob: "rather snappish, but not 'rageous."

A fierce cry seemed to give the lie to her favorable report: the clothed hyena rose up, and stood tall on its hind feet.

"Ah! sir, she sees you!" exclaimed Grace: "you'd better not stay."

"Only a few moments, Grace: you must allow me a few moments."

"Take care then, sir!—for God's sake, take care!"

The maniac bellowed: she parted her shaggy locks from her visage, and gazed wildly at her visitors. I recognized well that purple face,—those bloated features. Mrs. Poole advanced.

"Keep out of the way," said Mr. Rochester, thrusting her aside: "she has no knife now, I suppose, and I'm on my guard."

"One never knows what she has, sir: she is so cunning: it is not in mortal discretion to fathom her craft."

"We had better leave her," whispered Mason.

"Go to the devil!" was his brother-in-law's recommendation.

"'Ware!" cried Grace. The three gentlemen retreated simultaneously. Mr. Rochester flung me behind him: the lunatic sprang and grappled his throat viciously, and laid her teeth to his cheek: they struggled. She was a big woman, in stature almost equaling her husband, and corpulent besides: she showed virile force in the contest—more than once she almost throttled him, athletic as he was. He could have settled her with a well-planted blow; but he would not strike: he would only wrestle. At last he mastered her arms; Grace Poole gave him a cord, and he pinioned them behind her: with more rope, which was at hand, he bound her to a chair. The operation was performed amidst the fiercest yells and the most convulsive plunges. Mr. Rochester then turned to the spectators: he looked at them with a smile both acrid and desolate.

"That is *my wife*," said he. "Such is the sole conjugal embrace I am ever to know—such are the endearments which are to solace my leisure hours! And *this* is what I wished to have" (laying his hand on my shoulder): "this young girl, who stands so grave and quiet at the mouth of hell, looking collectedly at the gambols of a demon, I wanted her just as a change after that fierce ragout. Wood and Briggs, look at the difference! Compare these clear eyes with the red balls yonder—this face with that mask—this form with that bulk;

then judge me, priest of the gospel and man of the law, and remember with what judgment ye judge ye shall be judged! Off with you now. I must shut up my prize."

We all withdrew.

I then sat down: I felt weak and tired. I leaned my arms on a table, and my head dropped on them. And now I thought: till now I had only heard, seen, moved—followed up and down where I was led or dragged—watched event rush on event, disclosure open beyond disclosure: but now, I *thought*.

Sometime in the afternoon I raised my head, and looking round and seeing the western sun gilding the sign of its decline on the wall, I asked, "What am I to do?"

But the answer my mind gave—"Leave Thornfield at once"—was so prompt, so dread, that I stopped my ears. I said I could not bear such words now. "That I am not Edward Rochester's bride is the least part of my woe," I alleged: "that I have wakened out of most glorious dreams, and found them all void and vain, is a horror I could bear and master; but that I must leave him decidedly, instantly, entirely, is intolerable. I cannot do it."

But, then, a voice within me averred that I could do it and foretold that I should do it. I wrestled with my own resolution: I wanted to be weak that I might avoid the awful passage of further suffering I saw laid out for me; and Conscience, turned tyrant, held Passion by the throat, told her tauntingly, she had yet but dipped her dainty foot in the slough, and swore that with that arm of iron he would thrust her down to unsounded depths of agony.

. . . .

[Editor's note: Jane leaves for a year and builds a new life for herself with some friends, Diana and Mary. Their brother wants to become a missionary in India and wants Jane to accompany him as his wife. Jane refuses because he and she have no feelings for each other. After the proposal, Jane hears Mr. Rochester's voice calling her name in the wind, and longs to return to see what has become of him.]

"Ere many days," I said, as I terminated my musings, "I will know something of him whose voice seemed last night to summon me. Letters have proved of no avail—personal inquiry shall replace them."

At breakfast I announced to Diana and Mary that I was going a journey, and should be absent at least four days.

"Alone, Jane?" they asked.

"Yes; it was to see or hear news of a friend about whom I had for some time been uneasy."

They might have said, as I have no doubt they thought, that they had believed me to be without any friends save them: for, indeed, I had often said so; but, with their true natural delicacy, they abstained from comment, except that Diana asked me if I was sure I was well enough to travel. I looked very pale, she observed. I replied, that nothing ailed me save anxiety of mind, which I hoped soon to alleviate.

It was a journey of six-and-thirty hours. I had set out from Whitcross on a Tuesday afternoon, and early on the succeeding Thursday morning the coach stopped to water the horses at a wayside inn, situated in the midst of scenery whose green hedges and large fields and low pastoral hills met my eye like the lineaments of a once familiar face. Yes, I knew the character of this landscape: I was sure we were near my bourne.

"How far is Thornfield Hall from here?" I asked of the ostler.

"Just two miles, ma'am, across the fields."

"My journey is closed," I thought to myself. I got out of the coach, gave a box I had into the ostler's charge, to be kept till I called for it; paid my fare; satisfied the coachman, and was going: the brightening day gleamed on the sign of the inn, and I read in gilt letters, "The Rochester Arms." My heart leapt up: I was already on my master's very lands. It fell again: the thought struck it:—

"Your master himself may be beyond the British Channel, for aught you know: and then, if he is at Thornfield Hall, towards which you hasten, who besides him is there? His lunatic wife: and you have nothing to do with him: you dare not speak to him or seek his presence. You have lost your labor—you had better go no farther," urged the monitor. "Ask information of the people at the inn; they can give you all you seek: they can solve your doubts at once. Go up to that man, and inquire if Mr. Rochester be at home."

The suggestion was sensible, and yet I could not force myself to act on it. I so dreaded a reply that would crush me with despair. To prolong doubt was to prolong hope. I might yet once more see the Hall under the ray of her star. There was the stile before me—the very fields through which I had hurried, blind, deaf, distracted with a revengeful fury tracking and scourging me, on the morning I fled from Thornfield: ere I well knew what course I had resolved to take, I was in the midst of them. How fast I walked! How I ran sometimes! How I looked forward to catch the first view of the well-known woods! With what feelings I welcomed single trees I knew, and familiar glimpses of meadow and hill between them!

At last the woods rose; the rookery clustered dark; a loud cawing broke the morning stillness. Strange delight inspired me: on I hastened. Another field crossed—a lane threaded—and there were the courtyard walls—the back offices: the house itself, the rookery still hid. "My first view of it shall be in front," I determined, "where its bold battlements will strike the eye nobly at once, and where I can single out my master's very window: perhaps he will be standing at it—he rises early: perhaps he is now walking in the orchard, or on the pavement in front. Could I but see him!—but a moment! Surely, in that case, I should not be so mad as to run to him? I cannot tell—I am not certain. And if I did—what then? God bless him! What then? Who would be hurt by my once more tasting the life his glance can give me? I rave: perhaps at this moment he is watching the sun rise over the Pyrenees, or on the tide-less sea of the south."

I had coasted along the lower wall of the orchard—turned its angle: there was a gate just there, opening into the meadow, between two stone pillars crowned by stone balls. From behind one pillar I could peep round quietly at the full front of the mansion. I advanced my head with precaution, desirous to ascertain if any bedroom window-blinds were yet drawn up: battlements, windows, long front—all from this sheltered station were at my command.

I looked with timorous joy towards a stately house: I saw a blackened ruin.

No need to cower behind a gate-post, indeed!—to peep up at chamber lattices, fearing life was astir behind them! No need to listen for doors opening—to fancy steps on the pavement or the gravel-walk! The lawn, the grounds were trodden and waste: the portal yawned void. The front was, as I had once seen it in a dream, but a well-like wall, very high and very fragile-looking, perforated with paneless windows: no roof, no battlements, no chimneys—all had crashed in.

And there was the silence of death about it: the solitude of a lonesome wild. No wonder that letters addressed to people here had never received an answer: as well dispatch epistles to a vault in a church aisle. The grim blackness of the stones told by what fate the Hall had fallen—by conflagration: but how kindled? What story belonged to this disaster? What loss, besides mortar and marble and wood-work had followed upon it? Had life been wrecked as well as property? If so, whose? Dreadful question: there was no one here to answer it—not even dumb sign, mute token.

In wandering round the shattered walls and through the devastated interior, I gathered evidence that the calamity was not of late occurrence. Winter snows, I thought, had drifted through that void arch, winter rains beaten in at those hollow casements; for, amidst the drenched piles of rubbish, spring had cherished vegetation: grass and weed grew here and there between the stones and fallen rafters. And oh! where meantime was the hapless owner of this wreck? In what land? Under what auspices? My eye involuntarily wandered to the grey church tower near the gates, and I asked, "Is he with Damer de Rochester, sharing the shelter of his narrow marble house?"

Some answer must be had to these questions. I could find it nowhere but at the inn, and thither, ere long, I returned. The host himself brought my breakfast into the parlor. I requested him to shut the door and sit down: I had some questions to ask him. But when he complied, I scarcely knew how to begin; such horror had I of the possible answers. And yet the spectacle of desolation I had just left prepared me in a measure for a tale of misery. The host was a respectable-looking, middle-aged man.

"You know Thornfield Hall, of course?" I managed to say at last.

"Yes, ma'am; I lived there once."

"Did you?" Not in my time, I thought: you are a stranger to me.

"I was the late Mr. Rochester's butler," he added.

The late! I seem to have received, with full force, the blow I had been trying to evade.

"The late!" I gasped. "Is he dead?"

"I mean the present gentleman, Mr. Edward's father," he explained. I breathed again: my blood resumed its flow. Fully assured by these words that Mr. Edward—*my* Mr. Rochester (God bless him, wherever he was!)—was at least alive: was, in short, "the present gentleman." Gladdening words! It seemed I could hear all that was to come—whatever the disclosures might be—with comparative tranquility. Since he was not in the grave, I could bear, I thought, to learn that he was at the Antipodes.

"Is Mr. Rochester living at Thornfield Hall now?" I asked, knowing, of course, what the answer would be, but yet desirous of deferring the direct question as to where he really was.

"No, ma'am—oh, no! No one is living there. I suppose you are a stranger in these parts, or you would have heard what happened last autumn,—Thornfield Hall is quite a ruin: it was burnt down just about harvest-time. A dreadful calamity! Such an immense quantity of valuable property destroyed: hardly any of the furniture could be saved. The fire broke out at dead of night, and before the engines arrived from Millcote, the building was one mass of flame. It was a terrible spectacle: I witnessed it myself."

"At dead of night!" I muttered. Yes, that was ever the hour of fatality at Thornfield. "Was it known how it originated?" I demanded.

"They guessed, ma'am: they guessed. Indeed, I should say it was ascertained beyond a doubt. You are not perhaps aware," he continued, edging his chair a little nearer the table, and speaking low, "that there was a lady—a—a lunatic, kept in the house?"

"I have heard something of it."

"She was kept in very close confinement, ma'am: people even for some years were not absolutely certain of her existence. No one saw her: they only knew by rumor that such a person was at the Hall; and who or what she was it was difficult to conjecture. They said Mr. Edward had brought her from abroad, and some believed she had been his mistress. But a queer thing happened a year since—a very queer thing."

I feared now to hear my own story. I endeavored to recall him to the main fact.

"And this lady?"

"This lady, ma'am," he answered, "turned out to be Mr. Rochester's wife! The discovery was brought about in the strangest way. There was a young lady, a governess at the Hall, that Mr. Rochester fell in—"

"But the fire," I suggested.

"I'm coming to that, ma'am—that Mr. Edward fell in love with. The servants say they never saw anybody so much in love as he was: he was after her continually. They used to watch him—servants will, you know, ma'am—and he set store on her past everything: for all, nobody but him thought her so very handsome. She was a little small thing, they say, almost like a child. I never saw her myself; but I've heard Leah, the house-maid, tell of her. Leah liked her well enough. Mr. Rochester was about forty, and this governess not twenty; and you see, when gentlemen of his age fall in love with girls, they are often like as if they were bewitched. Well, he would marry her."

"You shall tell me this part of the story another time," I said; "but now I have a particular reason for wishing to hear all about the fire. Was it suspected that this lunatic, Mrs. Rochester, had any hand in it?"

"You've hit it, ma'am: it's quite certain that it was her, and nobody but her, that set it going. She had a woman to take care of her called Mrs. Poole—an able woman in her line, and very trustworthy, but for one fault—a fault common to a deal of them nurses and matrons—she kept a private bottle of gin by her, and now and then took a drop over-much. It is excusable, for she had a hard life of it: but still it was dangerous; for when Mrs. Poole was fast asleep after the gin and water, the mad lady, who was as cunning as a witch, would take the keys out of her pocket, let herself out of her chamber, and go roaming about the house, doing any wild mischief that came into her head. They say she had nearly burnt her husband in his bed once: but I don't know about that. However, on this night, she set fire first to the hangings of the room next her own, and then she got down to a lower story, and made her way to the chamber that had been the governess's—(she was like as if she knew somehow how matters had gone on, and had a spite at her)—and she kindled the bed there; but there was nobody sleeping in it, fortunately. The governess had run away two months before; and for all Mr. Rochester sought her as if she had been the most precious thing he had in the world, he never could hear a word of her; and he grew savage—quite savage on his disappointment: he never was a wild man, but he got dangerous after he lost her. He would be alone, too. He sent Mrs. Fairfax, the housekeeper, away to her friends at a distance; but he did it handsomely, for he settled an annuity on her for life: and she deserved it—she was a very good woman. Miss Adele, a ward he had, was put to school. He broke off acquaintance with all the gentry, and shut himself up like a hermit at the Hall."

"What! Did he not leave England?"

"Leave England? Bless you, no! He would not cross the door-stones of the house, except at night, when he walked just like a ghost about the grounds and in the orchard as if he had lost his senses—which it is my opinion he had; for a more spirited, bolder, keener gentleman than he was before that midge of a governess crossed him, you never saw, ma'am. He was not a man given to wine, or cards, or racing, as some are, and he was not so very handsome; but he had a courage and a will of his own, if ever man had. I knew him from a boy, you see: and for my part, I have often wished that Miss Eyre had been sunk in the sea before she came to Thornfield Hall."

"Then Mr. Rochester was at home when the fire broke out?"

"Yes, indeed was he; and he went up to the attics when all was burning above and below, and got the servants out of their beds and helped them down himself, and went back to get his mad wife out of her cell. And then they called out to him that she was on the roof, where she was standing, waving her arms, above the battlements, and shouting out till they could hear her a mile off: I saw her and heard her with my own eyes. She was a big woman, and had long black hair: we could see it streaming against the flames as she stood. I witnessed, and several more witnessed, Mr. Rochester ascend through the sky-light on to the roof; we heard him call 'Bertha!' We saw him approach her; and then, ma'am, she yelled and gave a spring, and the next minute she lay smashed on the pavement."

"Dead?"

"Dead! Ay, dead as the stones on which her brains and blood were scattered."

"Good God!"

"You may well say so, ma'am: it was frightful!"

He shuddered.

"And afterwards?" I urged.

"Well, ma'am, afterwards the house was burnt to the ground: there are only some bits of walls standing now."

"Were any other lives lost?"

"No—perhaps it would have been better if there had."

"What do you mean?"

"Poor Mr. Edward!" he ejaculated, "I little thought ever to have seen it! Some say it was a just judgment on him for keeping his first marriage secret, and wanting to take another wife while he had one living: but I pity him, for my part."

"You said he was alive?" I exclaimed.

"Yes, yes: he is alive; but many think he had better be dead."

"Why? How?" My blood was again running cold. "Where is he?" I demanded. "Is he in England?"

"Ay—ay—he's in England; he can't get out of England, I fancy—he's a fixture now."

What agony was this! And the man seemed resolved to protract it.

"He is stone-blind," he said at last. "Yes, he is stone-blind, is Mr. Edward."

I had dreaded worse. I had dreaded he was mad. I summoned strength to ask what had caused this calamity.

"It was all his own courage, and a body may say, his kindness, in a way, ma'am: he wouldn't leave the house till everyone else was out before him. As he came down the great staircase at last, after Mrs. Rochester had flung herself from the battlements, there was a great crash—all fell. He was taken out from under the ruins, alive, but sadly hurt: a beam had fallen in such a way as to protect him partly; but one eye was knocked out, and one hand so crushed that Mr. Carter, the surgeon, had to amputate it directly. The other eye inflamed: he lost the sight of that also. He is now helpless, indeed—blind and a cripple."

"Where is he? Where does he now live?"

"At Ferndean, a manor-house on a farm he has, about thirty miles off: quite a desolate spot."

"Have you any sort of conveyance?"

"We have a chaise, ma'am, a very handsome chaise."

"Let it be got ready instantly; and if your post-boy can drive me to Ferndean before dark this day, I'll pay both you and him twice the hire you usually demand."

The manor-house of Ferndean was a building of considerable antiquity, moderate size, and no architectural pretensions, deep buried in a wood. I had heard of it before. Mr. Rochester often spoke of it, and sometimes went there. His father had purchased the estate for the sake of the game covers. He would have let the house, but could find no tenant, in consequence of its ineligible and insalubrious site. Ferndean then remained uninhabited and unfurnished, with the exception of some two or three rooms fitted up for the accommodation of the squire when he went there in the season to shoot.

To this house I came just ere dark on an evening marked by the characteristics of sad sky, cold gale, and continued small penetrating rain. The last mile

I performed on foot, having dismissed the chaise and driver with the double remuneration I had promised. Even when within a very short distance of the manor-house, you could see nothing of it, so thick and dark grew the timber of the gloomy wood about it. Iron gates between granite pillars showed me where to enter, and passing through them, I found myself at once in the twilight of close-ranked trees. There was a grass-grown track descending the forest aisle between hoar and knotty shafts and under branched arches. I followed it, expecting soon to reach the dwelling; but it stretched on and on, it would far and farther: no sign of habitation or grounds was visible.

I thought I had taken a wrong direction and lost my way. The darkness of natural as well as of sylvan dusk gathered over me. I looked round in search of another road. There was none: all was interwoven stem, columnar trunk, dense summer foliage—no opening anywhere.

I proceeded: at last my way opened, the trees thinned a little; presently I beheld a railing, then the house—scarce, by this dim light, distinguishable from the trees; so dank and green were its decaying walls. Entering a portal, fastened only by a latch, I stood amidst a space of enclosed ground, from which the wood swept away in a semicircle. There were no flowers, no garden-beds; only a broad gravel-walk girdling a grass-plat, and this set in the heavy frame of the forest. The house presented two pointed gables in its front; the windows were latticed and narrow: the front door was narrow too, one step led up to it. The whole looked, as the host of the Rochester Arms had said, "quite a desolate spot." It was as still as a church on a week-day: the pattering rain on the forest leaves was the only sound audible in its vicinage.

"Can there be life here?" I asked.

Yes, life of some kind there was; for I heard a movement—that narrow front-door was unclosing, and some shape was about to issue from the grange.

It opened slowly: a figure came out into the twilight and stood on the step; a man without a hat: he stretched forth his hand as if to feel whether it rained. Dusk as it was, I had recognized him—it was my master, Edward Fairfax Rochester, and no other.

I stayed my step, almost my breath, and stood to watch him—to examine him, myself unseen, and alas! to him invisible. It was a sudden meeting, and one in which rapture was kept well in check by pain. I had no difficulty in restraining my voice from exclamation, my step from hasty advance.

His form was of the same strong and stalwart contour as ever: his port was still erect, his hair was still raven black; nor were his features altered or sunk: not in one year's space, by any sorrow, could his athletic strength be quelled or his vigorous prime blighted. But in his countenance I saw a change that looked desperate and brooding—that reminded me of some wronged and fettered wild beast or bird, dangerous to approach in his sullen woe. The caged eagle, whose gold-ringed eyes cruelty has extinguished, might look as looked that sightless Samson.

And, reader, do you think I feared him in his blind ferocity?—if you do, you little know me. A soft hope blest with my sorrow that soon I should dare to drop a kiss on that brow of rock, and on those lips so sternly sealed beneath it: but not yet. I would not accost him yet.

He descended the one step, and advanced slowly and gropingly towards the grass-plat. Where was his daring stride now? Then he paused, as if he knew not which way to turn. He lifted his hand and opened his eyelids; gazed blank, and with a straining effort, on the sky, and toward the amphitheater of trees: one saw that all to him was void darkness. He stretched his right hand (the left arm, the mutilated one, he kept hidden in his bosom); he seemed to wish by touch to gain an idea of what lay around him: he met but vacancy still; for the trees were some yards off where he stood. He relinquished the endeavor, folded his arms, and stood quiet and mute in the rain, now falling fast on his uncovered head. At this moment his servant John approached him from some quarter.

"Will you take my arm, sir?" he said; "there is a heavy shower coming on: had you not better go in?"

"Let me alone," was the answer.

John withdrew without having observed me. Mr. Rochester now tried to walk about: vainly,—all was too uncertain. He groped his way back to the house, and, re-entering it, closed the door.

I now drew near and knocked: John's wife opened for me. "Mary," I said, "how are you?"

She started as if she had seen a ghost: I calmed her. To her hurried "is it really you, miss, come at this late hour to this lonely place?" I answered by taking her hand; and then I followed her into the kitchen, where John now sat by a good fire. I explained to them, in few words, that I had heard all which had happened since I left Thornfield, and that I was come to see Mr. Rochester. I asked John to go down to the turnpike-house, where I had dismissed the chaise, and bring my trunk, which I had left there: and then, while I removed my bonnet and shawl, I questioned Mary as to whether I could be accommodated at the Manor House for the night; and finding that arrangements to that effect, though difficult, would not be impossible, I informed her I should stay. Just at this moment the parlor bell rang.

"When you go in," said I, "tell your master that a person wishes to speak to him, but do not give my name."

"I don't think he will see you," she answered; "he refuses everybody."

When she returned, I inquired what he had said. "You are to send in your name and your business," she replied. She then proceeded to fill a glass with water, and place it on a tray, together with candles.

"Is that what he rang for?" I asked.

"Yes: he always has candles brought in at dark, though he is blind."

"Give the tray to me; I will carry it in."

I took it from her hand: she pointed me out the parlor door. The tray shook as I held it; the water spilt from the glass; my heart struck my ribs loud and fast. Mary opened the door for me, and shut it behind me.

This parlor looked gloomy: a neglected handful of fire burnt low in the grate; and, leaning over it, with his head supported against the high, old-fashioned mantelpiece, appeared the blind tenant of the room. His old dog, Pilot, lay on one side, removed out of the way, and coiled up as if afraid of being inadvertently trodden upon. Pilot pricked up his ears when I came in: then he jumped up with a yelp and a whine, and bounded towards me: he almost knocked the tray from my hands. I set it on the table; then patted him, and said softly, "Lie down!" Mr. Rochester turned mechanically to see what the commotion was: but as he saw nothing, he returned and sighed.

"Give me the water, Mary," he said.

I approached him with the now only half-filled glass; Pilot followed me, still excited.

"What is the matter?" he inquired.

"Down, Pilot!" I said. He checked the water on its way to his lips, and seemed to listen: he drank, and put the glass down. "This is you, Mary, is it not?"

"Mary is in the kitchen," I answered.

He put out his hand with a quick gesture, but not seeing where I stood, he did not touch me. "Who is this? Who is this?" he demanded, trying, as it seemed, to see with those sightless eyes—unavailing and distressing attempt! "Answer me—speak again!" he ordered, imperiously and aloud.

"Will you have a little more water, sir? I spilt half of what was in the glass," I said.

"*Who* is it? *What* is it? Who speaks?"

"Pilot knows me, and John and Mary know I am here. I came only this evening," I answered.

"Great God!—what delusion has come over me? What sweet madness has seized me?"

"No delusion—no madness: your mind, sir, is too strong for delusion, your health too sound for frenzy."

"And where is the speaker? Is it only a voice? Oh! I cannot see, but I must feel, or my heart will stop and my brain burst. Whatever—whoever you are—be perceptible to the touch or I cannot live!"

He groped; I arrested his wandering hand, and prisoned it in both mine.

"Her very fingers!" he cried; "her small, slight fingers! If so there must be more of her."

The muscular hand broke from my custody; my arm was seized, my shoulder—neck—waist—I was entwined and gathered to him.

"Is it Jane? What is it? This is her shape—this is her size—"

"And this her voice," I added. "She is all here: her heart, too. God bless you, sir! I am glad to be so near you again."

"Jane Eyre!—Jane Eyre," was all he said.

"My dear master," I answered, "I am Jane Eyre: I have found you out—I am come back to you."

"In truth?—in the flesh? My living Jane?"

"You touch me, sir,—you hold me, and fast enough: I am not cold like a corpse, nor vacant like air, am I?"

"My living darling! These are certainly her limbs, and these her features; but I cannot be so blest, after all my misery. It is a dream; such dreams as I have had at night when I have clasped her once more to my heart, as I do now; and kissed her, as thus—and felt that she loved me, and trusted that she would not leave me."

"Which I never will, sir, from this day."

"Never will, says the vision? But I always woke and found it an empty mockery; and I was desolate and abandoned—my life dark, lonely, hopeless—my soul athirst and forbidden to drink—my heart famished and never to be fed. Gentle, soft dream, nestling in my arms now, you will fly, too, as your sisters have all fled before you: but kiss me before you go—embrace me, Jane."

"There, sir—and there!"

I pressed my lips to his once brilliant and now rayless eyes—I swept his hair from his brow, and kissed that too. He suddenly seemed to arouse himself: the conviction of the reality of all this seized him.

"It is you—is it, Jane? You are come back to me then?"

"I am."

"And you do not lie dead in some ditch under some stream? And you are not a pining outcast amongst strangers?"

"No, sir! I am an independent woman now."

"Independent! What do you mean, Jane?"

"My uncle in Madeira is dead, and he left me five thousand pounds."

"Ah! this is practical—this is real!" he cried: "I should never dream that. Besides, there is that peculiar voice of hers, so animating and piquant, as well as soft: it cheers my withered heart; it puts life into it.—What, Janet! Are you an independent woman? A rich woman?"

"If you won't let me live with you, I can build a house of my own close up to your door, and you may come and sit in my parlor when you want company of an evening."

"But as you are rich, Jane, you have now, no doubt, friends who will look after you, and not suffer you to devote yourself to a blind lameter like me?"

"I told you I am independent, sir, as well as rich: I am my own mistress."

"And you will stay with me?"

"Certainly—unless you object. I will be your neighbor, your nurse, your housekeeper. I find you lonely: I will be your companion—to read to you, to walk with you, to sit with you, to wait on you, to be eyes and hands to you. Cease to look so melancholy, my dear master; you shall not be left desolate, so long as I live."

He replied not: he seemed serious—abstracted; he sighed; he half-opened his lips as if to speak: he closed them again. I felt a little embarrassed. Perhaps I had too rashly over-leaped conventionalities; and he saw impropriety in my inconsiderateness. I had indeed made my proposal from the idea that he wished and would ask me to be his wife: an expectation, not the less certain because unexpressed, had buoyed me up, that he would claim me at once as his own. But no hint to that effect escaping him and his countenance becoming more overcast, I suddenly remembered that I might have been all wrong, and was perhaps playing the fool unwittingly; and I began gently to withdraw myself from his arms—but he eagerly snatched me closer.

"No—no—Jane; you must not go. No—I have touched you, heard you, felt the comfort of your presence—the sweetness of your consolation: I cannot give up these joys. I have little left in myself—I must have you. The world may laugh—may call me absurd, selfish—but it does not signify. My very soul demands you: it will be satisfied, or it will take deadly vengeance on its frame."

"Well, sir, I will stay with you: I have said so."

"Yes—but you understand one thing by staying with me; and I understand another. You, perhaps, could make up your mind to be about my hand and chair—to wait on me as a kind little nurse (for you have an affectionate heart and a generous spirit, which prompt you to make sacrifices for those you pity), and that ought to suffice for me no doubt. I suppose I should now entertain none but fatherly feelings for you: do you think so? Come—tell me."

"I will think what you like, sir: I am content to be only your nurse, if you think it better."

"But you cannot always be my nurse, Janet: you are young—you must marry one day."

"I don't care about being married."

"You should care, Janet: if I were what I once was, I would try to make you care—but—a sightless block!"

He relapsed again into gloom. I, on the contrary, became more cheerful, and took fresh courage: these last words gave me an insight as to where the difficulty lay; and as it was no difficulty with me, I felt quite relieved from my previous embarrassment. I resumed a livelier vein of conversation.

"It is time someone undertook to re-humanize you," said I, parting his thick and long uncut locks; "for I see you are being metamorphosed into a lion, or something of that sort. You have a 'faux air' of Nebuchadnezzar in the fields about you, that is certain: your hair reminds me of eagles' feathers; whether your nails are grown like birds' claws or not, I have not yet noticed."

"On this arm, I have neither hand nor nails," he said, drawing the mutilated limb from his breast, and showing it to me. "It is a mere stump—a ghastly sight! Don't you think so, Jane?"

"It is a pity to see it; and a pity to see your eyes—and the scar of fire on your forehead: and the worst of it is, one is in danger of loving you too well for all this; and making too much of you."

"I thought you would be revolted, Jane, when you saw my arm, and my cicatrized visage."

"Did you? Don't tell me so—lest I should say something disparaging to your judgment. Now, let me leave you an instant, to make a better fire, and have the hearth swept up. Can you tell when there is a good fire?"

"Yes; with the right eye I see a glow—a ruddy haze."

"And you see the candles?"

"Very dimly—each is a luminous cloud."

"Can you see me?"

"No, my fairy: but I am only too thankful to hear and feel you."

"When do you take supper?"

"I never take supper."

"But you shall have some tonight. I am hungry: so are you, I daresay, only you forget."

Summoning Mary, I soon had the room in more cheerful order: I prepared him, likewise, a comfortable repast. My spirits were excited, and with pleasure and ease I talked to him during supper, and for a long time after. There was no harassing restraint, no repressing of glee and vivacity with him; for with him I was at perfect ease, because I knew I suited him; all I said or did seemed either to console or revive him. Delightful consciousness! It brought to life and light my whole nature: in his presence I thoroughly lived; and he lived in mine. Blind as he was, smiles played over his face, joy dawned on his forehead: his lineaments softened and warmed.

"Have you a pocket-comb about you, sir?"

"What for, Jane?"

"Just to comb out this shaggy black mane. I find you rather alarming, when I examine you close at hand: you talk of my being a fairy, but I am sure, you are more like a brownie."

"Am I hideous, Jane?"

"Very, sir: you always were, you know."

. . . .

"I am no better than the old lightning-struck chestnut-tree in Thornfield orchard," he remarked ere long. "And what right would that ruin have to bid a budding woodbine cover its decay with freshness?"

"You are no ruin, sir—no lightning-struck tree: you are green and vigorous. Plants will grow about your roots, whether you ask them or not, because they take delight in your bountiful shadow; and as they grow they will lean towards you, and wind round you, because your strength offers them so safe a prop."

Again he smiled: I gave him comfort.

"You speak of friends, Jane?" he asked.

"Yes, of friends," I answered rather hesitatingly: for I knew I meant more than friends, but could not tell what other word to employ. He helped me.

"Ah! Jane. But I want a wife."

"Do you, sir?"

"Yes: is it news to you?"

"Of course: you said nothing about it before."

"Is it unwelcome news?"

"That depends on circumstances, sir—on your choice."

"Which you shall make for me, Jane. I will abide by your decision."

"Choose then, sir—her who loves you best."

"I will at least choose—her I love best. Jane, will you marry me?"

"Yes, sir."

"A poor blind man, whom you will have to lead about by the hand?"

"Yes, sir."

"A crippled man, twenty years older than you, whom you will have to wait on?"

"Yes, sir."

"Truly, Jane?"

"Most truly, sir."

"Oh! my darling! God bless you and reward you!"

"Mr. Rochester, if ever I did a good deed in my life—if ever I thought a good thought—if ever I prayed a sincere and blameless prayer—if ever I wished a righteous wish,—I am rewarded now. To be your wife is, for me, to be as happy as I can be on earth."

"Because you delight in sacrifice."

"Sacrifice! What do I sacrifice? Famine for food, expectation for content. To be privileged to put my arms round what I value—to press my lips to what I love—to repose on what I trust: is that to make a sacrifice? If so, then certainly I delight in sacrifice."

"And to bear with my infirmities, Jane: to overlook my deficiencies."

"Which are none, sir, to me. I love you better now, when I can really be useful to you, than I did in your state of proud independence, when you disdained every part but that of the giver and protector."

"Hitherto I have hated to be helped—to be led: henceforth, I feel I shall hate it no more. I did not like to put my hand into a hireling's, but it is pleasant to feel it circled by Jane's little fingers. I preferred utter loneliness to the constant attendance of servants; but Jane's soft ministry will be a perpetual joy. Jane suits me: do I suit her?"

"To the finest fiber of my nature, sir."

"The case being so, we have nothing in the world to wait for: we must be married instantly."

He looked and spoke with eagerness: his old impetuosity was rising.

He pursued his own thoughts without heeding me.

"Jane! you think me, I daresay, an irreligious dog: but my heart swells with gratitude to the beneficent God of this earth just now. He sees not as man sees, but far clearer: judges not as man judges, but far more wisely. I did wrong: I would have sullied my innocent flower—breathed guilt on its purity: the Omnipotent snatched it from me. I, in my stiff-necked rebellion, almost cursed the dispensation: instead of bending to the decree, I defied it. Divine justice pursued its course; disasters came thick on me: I was forced to pass through the valley of the shadow of death. His chastisements are mighty; and one smote me which has humbled me forever. You know I was proud of my strength: but what is it now, when I must give it over to foreign guidance, as a child does its weakness? Of late, Jane—only—only of late—I began to see and acknowledge the hand of God in my doom. I began to experience remorse, repentance; the wish for reconcilement to my Maker. I began sometimes to pray: very brief prayers they were, but very sincere.

"Some days since: nay, I can number them—four; it was last Monday night, a singular mood came over me: one in which grief replaced frenzy—sorrow, sullenness. I had long had the impression that since I could nowhere find you, you must be dead. Late that night—perhaps it might be between eleven and twelve o'clock—ere I retired to my dreary rest, I supplicated God, that, if it seemed good to Him, I might soon be taken from this life, and admitted to that world to come, where there was still hope of rejoining Jane.

"I was in my own room, and sitting by the window, which was open: it soothed me to feel the balmy night-air; though I could see no stars and only by a vague, luminous haze, knew the presence of a moon. I longed for thee, Janet! Oh, I longed for thee both with soul and flesh! I asked of God, at once in anguish and humility, if I had not been long enough desolate, afflicted, tormented; and might not soon taste bliss and peace once more. That I merited all I endured, I acknowledged—that I could scarcely endure more, I pleaded; and the alpha and omega of my heart's wishes broke involuntarily from my lips in the words—'Jane! Jane! Jane!'"

"Did you speak these words aloud?"

"I did, Jane. If any listener had heard me, he would have thought me mad: I pronounced them with such frantic energy."

"And it was last Monday night, somewhere near midnight?"

"Yes; but the time is of no consequence: what followed is the strange point. You will think me superstitious,—some superstition I have in my blood, and always had: nevertheless, this is true—true at least it is that I heard what I now relate.

"As I exclaimed 'Jane! Jane! Jane!' a voice—I cannot tell whence the voice came, but I know whose voice it was—replied, 'I am coming: wait for me;' and a moment after, went whispering on the wind the words, 'Where are you?'

"I'll tell you, if I can, the idea, the picture these words opened to my mind: yet it is difficult to express what I want to express. Ferndean is buried, as you see, in a heavy wood, where sound falls dull, and dies unreverberating. 'Where are you?' seemed spoken amongst mountains; for I heard a hill-sent echo repeat the words. Cooler and fresher at the moment the gale seemed to visit my brow: I could have deemed that in some wild, lone scene, I and Jane were meeting. In spirit, I believe we must have met. You no doubt were, at that hour, in unconscious sleep, Jane: perhaps your soul wandered from its cell to comfort mine; for those were your accents—as certain as I live—they were yours!"

Reader, it was on Monday night—near midnight—that I too had received the mysterious summons: those were the very words by which I replied to it. I listened to Mr. Rochester's narrative, but made no disclosure in return. The coincidence struck me as too awful and inexplicable to be communicated or discussed. If I told anything, my tale would be such as must necessarily make a profound impression on the mind of my hearer: and that mind, yet from its sufferings too prone to gloom, needed not the deeper shade of the supernatural. I kept these things then, and pondered them in my heart.

"You cannot now wonder," continued my master, "that when you rose upon me so unexpectedly last night, I had difficulty in believing you any other than a mere voice and vision, something that would melt to silence and annihilation, as the midnight whisper and mountain echo had melted before. Now, I thank God! I know it to be otherwise. Yes, I thank God!"

He put me off his knee, rose, and reverently lifting his hat from his brow, and bending his sightless eyes to the earth, he stood in mute devotion. Only the last words of the worship were audible.

"I thank my Maker, that, in the midst of judgment, he has remembered mercy. I humbly entreat my Redeemer to give me strength to lead henceforth a purer life than I have done hitherto!"

Then he stretched his hand out to be led. I took that dear hand, held it a moment to my lips, then let it pass round my shoulder: being so much lower of stature than he, I served both for his prop and guide. We entered the wood, and wended homeward.

. . . .

Reader, I married him. A quiet wedding we had: he and I, the parson and clerk, were alone present.

I have now been married ten years. I know what it is to live entirely for and with what I love best on earth. I hold myself supremely blest—blest beyond what language can express; because I am my husband's life as fully as he is mine. No woman was ever nearer to her mate than I am: ever more absolutely bone of his bone and flesh of his flesh. I know no weariness of my Edward's society: he knows none of mine, any more than we each do of the pulsation of the heart that beats in our separate bosoms; consequently, we are ever together. To be together is for us to be at once as free as in solitude, as gay as in company. We talk, I believe, all day long: to talk to each other is but a more animated and an audible thinking. All my confidence is bestowed on him, all his confidence is devoted to me; we are precisely suited in character—perfect concord is the result.

Mr. Rochester continued blind the first two years of our union; perhaps it was that circumstance that drew us so very near—that knit us so very close: for I was then his vision, as I am still his right hand. Literally, I was (what he often called me) the apple of his eye. He saw nature—he saw books through me; and never did I weary of gazing for his behalf, and of putting into words the effect of field, tree, town, river, cloud, sunbeam—of the landscape before us; of the weather round us—and impressing by sound on his ear what light could no longer stamp on his eye. Never did I weary of reading to him; never did I weary of conducting him where he wished to go: of doing for him what he wished to be done. And there was a pleasure in my services, most full, most exquisite, even though sad—because he claimed these services without painful shame or damping humiliation. He loved me so truly, that he knew no reluctance in profiting by my attendance: he felt I loved him so fondly, that to yield that attendance was to indulge my sweetest wishes.

One morning at the end of the two years, as I was writing a letter to his dictation, he came and bent over me, and said—"Jane, have you a glittering ornament round your neck?"

I had a gold watch-chain: I answered "Yes."

"And have you a pale blue dress on?"

I had. He informed me then, that for some time he had fancied the obscurity clouding one eye was becoming less dense; and that now he was sure of it.

He and I went up to London. He had the advice of an eminent oculist; and he eventually recovered the sight of that one eye. He cannot now see very distinctly: he cannot read or write much; but he can find his way without being led by the hand: the sky is no longer a blank to him—the earth no longer a void. When his first-born was put into his arms, he could see that the boy had inherited his own eyes, as they once were—large, brilliant, and black. On that occasion, he again, with a full heart, acknowledged that God had tempered judgment with mercy.

from Jane Eyre

Questions for discussion

1. What do you think of the portrayal of the two types of disability portrayed in this segment (Mr. Rochester's wife's mental illness, and Mr. Rochester's blindness)?

2. How does Jane react to Mr. Rochester's blindness? How does he expect her to react? How do you think you would react in her situation?

3. When Mr. Rochester married Bertha Mason, she was sane, and later lost her sanity. Mr. Rochester felt obligated to care for her, but he hid his marriage to

her so he could marry someone else. What are the limits of a spouse or family member's duties to a family member that is mentally ill? What if the person is dangerous? What other "family secrets" might be associated with disability?

4. The actual incidence of persons with mental illness who are a danger to others is very low (the National Alliance for the Mentally Ill estimates that the percentage of former mental patients who are dangerous is less than two percent[1]). Do you believe that the dangerousness of mentally ill people is over-represented in literature and film? What examples of these types of characters can you think of?

5. Why do you think the author had Mr. Rochester partially regain his sight at the end? Do you think that was important to the story?

6. Design your own discussion questions for this piece.

For Further Reading

About family members' obligations in caring for someone with a disability

Simon, Rachel. *Riding the Bus with My Sister.* A professor agrees to spend a year with her disabled sister, doing what her sister loves most: riding buses.

Packer, Ann. *The Dive from Clausen's Pier.* Fictional account of a young woman whose fiancee becomes paralyzed.

About blindness

Montalambert, Hugues de. *Invisible.* A man who loses his sight after an assault learns to accept his blindness.

Keller, Helen. *The Story of My Life.* Helen Keller's memoir.

Kleege, Georgina. *Blind Rage: Letters to Helen Keller.* Tired of being asked why she doesn't handle her blindness as well as Helen Keller did, a legally blind woman writes an open letter to the deceased icon, and in the process learns about Helen Keller and herself.

About confining people with mental illness

Gilman, Charlotte Perkins, "The Yellow Wallpaper."

Plath, Sylvia. *The Bell Jar.* Semi-autobiographical novel that includes harrowing episodes of electric shock "therapy" and institutionalization.

---

1. http://www.namigc.org/content/fact_sheets/stigma/web-%20combating%20the%20stigma%20of%20mi%200304.htm.

Harriet McBryde Johnson (1957–2008) was a civil rights attorney from Charleston, South Carolina. She worked for social justice, especially disability rights. She holds the world endurance record (fourteen years without interruption) for protesting the Jerry Lewis telethon for the Muscular Dystrophy Association. She served the City of Charleston Democratic Party for eleven years, first as a secretary, then as chair. She was a frequent contributor to *The New York Times Magazine* and to the disability press.

Too Late to Die Young

I'm three or four years old. I'm sitting on the living room floor, playing with dolls. I look up at the TV and see a little boy. He's sitting on the floor, playing with toy soldiers. Then he's in Little League; he stumbles on his way to first base. He visits a doctor. His parents are sad. He's in a wheelchair. Then a bed. Then I see the toy soldiers. No boy. An unseen narrator says, "Little Billy's toy soldiers have lost their general." It's a commercial for the Muscular Dystrophy Association. As the narrator makes the pitch, a realization comes to me: I will die.

Is it really one of my earliest memories? Or was it manufactured by my imagination? I don't suppose it matters. Either way, it was my truth. It is my truth.

I'm a little girl who knows she will die, but I don't say anything; I don't want to distress my parents. Somehow, though, my mother realizes. "That boy," she tells me more than once, "has a different kind of muscular dystrophy. Girls don't get it." Maybe, I think, but he looks a lot like me. And pretty soon I see little girls on the telethon and hear that girls, too, have "killer diseases."

I don't know the word, but I figure my mother is in denial.

By the time I am five, I think of myself as a dying child. I've been sick a lot. There is some discussion before they decide to send me to kindergarten. I am glad they do.

When I die, I think, I might as well die a kindergartner.

I'm in a courtroom at the defendant's table. I look up at the bench and hear the judge sentence me to death. A gasp rises from a faceless crowd. They're shocked, astonished. I'm not. I've known all along. There's no question of guilt or innocence, justice or injustice. It's simply a fact. It's hard to understand, but true. I will die.

How old am I when that dream first comes to me? Eight, I think.

The death sentence hangs over my childhood like a cloud. Beneath the cloud, I live a happy child's life. Why not? A daughter of graduate students who become teachers, I am well tended by a succession of black women. My sister, Beth, two years old when I arrive on the scene, generally tolerates me with good grace; three brothers come along for me to boss. The TV regularly brings me Dick Van Dyke, Andy Griffith, and Bullwinkle, and one person in a wheelchair, Dr. Gillespie, who fulminates and barks orders at handsome Dr. Kildare. I lay LPs on the turntable and soak up the sounds of Joan Baez and Los Hermanos de Vera Cruz. There are books with beautiful pictures. To try to fatten myself up, I get black beans and fried bananas. To fry my brain, *Alice in Wonderland*. All these things are great pleasures, then and now. But then and now, life has a certain edge. I know it will not last.

When I am thirteen, I read Orwell's *1984* and calculate how old I'll be then. No way, I think. I go to a "special" school and then a "normal" high school and study hard, but I have no fantasies of a future. I study because somewhere along the way I've developed a competitive streak and because studying, too, is a pleasure.

And besides, I think, when I die I might as well die educated.

I'm watching an old Dracula movie on TV. I'm twelve, old enough to know this is cheesy pop culture, and yet it speaks to me. Like any preteen I pick up, without fully understanding, the latent sexual charge: the count's perverse seduction of the Englishman's fiancee is weird sex safely disguised as weird violence. But for me it's not only about strange passions under the moon, bats passing through tight cracks, moaning in canopy beds, or even all that neck-biting. For me, the best part is when Professor Van Helsing, the expert from Amsterdam, taps his pipe and explains, "They are called the Undead." The professor's presentation has the dull rationality of a graduate seminar. Dramatically, it's agony. But I love it. It gives meaning to the crashing ending, that moment when they drive the stake through Dracula's heart. For Dracula, there is no heaven or hell, no rebirth, no haunting. It's dust to dust and vanishing in the wind. Ah! Beautiful!

I've accepted the reality of death so early it's hard to imagine life without it. But figuring out what it means is another matter. I look to conventional religion and try to think of death as a one-way ticket to a perfect place. With a naturally legalistic mind and a smattering of Catholic doctrine, however, I conclude that the odds are against a straight shot to heaven, especially since

Thought Crime counts. And anyway, who would want perfection, having known the gorgeous squalor of the Carolina Low country?

There are mystical and occult alternatives. Hauntings, auras, and energy fields. Reincarnation. Time warps, parallel universes. Returning to the Oversoul. But none satisfies me. It is Professor Van Helsing who speaks to the fundamental tragedy of refusing to Die; it is Dracula's end that shows the way out.

And what of Dracula's bride? The feminist view is that she pays the price of breaking convention in a patriarchal society. For me, her story means something else. When the tale starts, she is beautiful, healthy, engaged to be married—normal in every way. But she, too, gets a stake in the heart. She shows that death is not only for people like me.

It comes in a slow dawning, this idea that death is for normal people, too. In childhood and youth, I am personally acquainted with only a few dead people, but there are lots of them around—they live in family stories. At our Thanksgiving table, my mother speaks of Great Aunt Harriet's dinner rolls, which always came out of the oven just as the family sat down to eat. Great Aunt Harriet died nearly twenty years before I was born; the black people who made those rolls, and timed them so perfectly, are dead, too. As we spoon out the oyster casserole, my grandmother tells how Uncle Oscar found a pearl in his oysters and set it in a gold tiepin. Then someone, maybe someone born after Uncle Oscar died, remarks that of course it happened to Uncle Oscar, because he was rich and drew more riches like a magnet.

So rich uncles and hospitable aunts die. I will die. It is only one more step to infer that everyone at our table will die, too. What amazes me is that the others seem oblivious. They seem to think that dying is only for the terminally ill, only for people like me.

I don't see myself as morbid or obsessed, but I think about death a lot. I know it isn't normal, but my relationship with death becomes part of me. I can handle it, even if normal people can't. I decide to be discreet, like Dracula, and live quietly among normal people. No need to trouble them with details. No need for them to know about the coffin I keep in the basement.

I start being vague about my medical diagnosis. Rather than owning this or that form of muscular dystrophy or this or that type of muscular atrophy, I say I have "a muscle disease." I don't want others to connect me with the dying people on the telethon. I figure if I let people peek in my basement, they'll jump to the wrong conclusion. They'll define me as one of the undead, an unnatural creature, not really alive but feeding on the lifeblood of others. Or, alternatively, they'll make me a pity object, one of Jerry's Kids—someone to make them grateful they are not like me. By setting me apart as a death totem, they can avoid looking in their own basements where their own coffins wait.

I know I am as alive as any of them, and they are as mortal as I. I am set apart not by any basic realities, but by perceptions—theirs and mine. They insist on dividing the world between the living and dying; I insist on both at the same time. Why not?

I study, play, work, find a place in a family and a community, and enjoy the many delights that continue to fall on me. As my body continues to deteriorate, my life looks more and more normal.

At twenty-five I leave the cozy comfort and familiar dysfunctionality of home and family to go to law school. I figure, I'll be twenty-seven when I finish; if I go now, I can probably practice for a couple of years.

By this time, the thought is almost subconscious: when I die, I might as well die a lawyer.

I've just turned thirty. I've been lolling in bed for nearly three weeks; I say I've strained my neck, but really it's major depression. Just before my birthday, my mother had brain surgery; she's come through it beautifully, but I'm terrified to think I could actually outlive my parents. I'm put further adrift by the sudden death of the crazy German doctor who nursed me with pea soup and sausages when I refused to go to the hospital with pneumonia. Now I remember how he kept vigil at my bedside so my parents could sleep and then fell asleep himself. As I listened to his deep barrel-chested rumble, I imagined he was snoring in German. In the middle of the night, in the middle of a medical crisis, that snore made me smile and know again that life is a great gift, worth hanging on to. Now, in my depression, the memory makes me smile again. But then I sink back down.

Maybe "sink" is the wrong word; it feels more like "rising." It has that kind of intensity. Is this a midlife crisis? Should I now take stock? Deal with my disappointed expectations? My thoughts race by, but I manage to grab them and take a look. I find they are coherent. I'm bonkers, but rational. I know what's bothering me: my plan to die young hasn't worked out. I wonder, what would I have done differently if I'd known I would live so long? What do I do now? My thoughts take on the structure of a song, a song with too many verses. But there's a simple chorus, repeated over and over: it's too late to die young.

The time comes and I tell them my neck is better. I go back to work and all of life's routines, but some things have changed. I went in bed agnostic and have come out atheist. When the next medical crisis comes, I find I can hear the death sentence without dread. The lessons of Little Billy and his toy soldiers, of Dracula and his bride have gone from my head to a deeper place. I have taken death into my heart.

I decide to talk about the coffin in the basement. As an experiment, I confide to two nondisabled woman friends that I am genuinely surprised to be alive at age thirty.

"I had no idea," one says. "I've never thought of you that way."

"Absolutely not," the other agrees.

They refuse to believe I am under a death sentence. I am pleased my reticence has been so effective, but I also wonder if it will ever be possible to get real.

Then I reconsider my childhood death sentence and decide I have been the victim of a fraud. Sure, I am mortal. Yes, I will die. But I have never been terminally ill the way I was led to believe. I study the telethon and try to understand its peculiar power. It spews out the same old messages—"killer disease," "life ebbing away," "before it's too late." As I hear the death sentence pronounced on another generation of children, I wonder how many have actually been killed by the predictions. How many have suffered pneumonia without vigilant parents or a crazy German doctor with pea soup? How many have died for lack of a reason, when a reason was needed in the middle of the night, to hang on to life? Worst of all, how many have lived and died without learning to value their own lives?

I join the telethon protest and oppose physician-assisted suicide. I want people to know our culture is playing fast and loose with the facts. While anyone may die young, it's not something you can count on. You have to be prepared to survive.

Among allies in the disability rights movement, I start hearing things I don't expect. "We're not dying," some comrades say. "We're disabled, not terminally ill." Even in the movement, denial rules. It's not only nondisabled people who shy away from what's in the basement.

I decide to embrace the death sentence. No need to fear it; no need to hasten it. Mortality is something all people share, a unifying force. Every life, whether long or short, is a treasure of infinite value. These things are true, I figure, and it's my job to say so.

When I die, I might as well die honest.

I'm thirty-nine. A man has come to my law office for a will. He has advanced AIDS. I start explaining the options: "When you die ..." I'm horrified to realize I've dropped the polite circumlocutions and make a quick substitution. "When your will takes effect ..."

I'm flustered. He looks at me with a wise, weary smile. "It's OK," he says. "I know what's going to happen. That's why I'm here."

He has unlocked the door. He knows about the coffin in the basement. We can get real.

"So explain what happens when I croak," he says.

By the time the final documents come off the printer, we're laughing so hard I wonder what the lawyer in the next office will think. "I can't tell you," he says, "how great it is to work with someone who can deal with this stuff without freaking out. Most people are so … compassionate."

We shake hands. "It's been my pleasure," I tell him. It really has.

Life still demands circumlocutions. Concealing my exact diagnosis—even officially from myself—remains the easiest way to deal with popular fears; I can't hope to bring everyone around to my way of thinking. Sometimes I wish I could do what they do, pretend that death is something that happens to other people. But denial is not an option now.

In youth, I accepted death as the end of all things. Now I know it is more. It is part of all we are, all there is.

An awareness of death fosters appreciation for the stuff of life. Those structures of material creation, webs of relationships, cultural institutions, language, thoughts, memories become marvelous. How extraordinary that they exist, yet are no more permanent than soap bubbles floating in the air! The author of Ecclesiastes said (in arguing a position very different from mine) that everything we undertake is striving after wind. In other translations it's rendered "a vexation of the spirit" but I like striving after wind. It seems a fine description for all the activity of humankind from the beginning to the end. Why do it? Why not?

Now I am unexpectedly middle-aged. In the last twenty years or so, I've lost most movement in my arms and in several fingers; in the last four years, I've lost the ability to swallow most solid foods and lost so much flesh that I am coming to look like the skeleton I will someday become. Yet, day by day, my physical deterioration has been slow, downright gentle. If the next twenty years are like the last, I'll be old. It certainly could happen.

Still, in my heart, the old death sentence remains in force. Sometimes the death-penalty dream comes back, just as I created it in childhood—the same anonymous judge, faceless spectators, nondescript Perry Mason-style courtroom. I wonder, why doesn't the dream story happen in one of the real courtrooms where I work? Why not use a real judge? How about a ghostly visit from the late J.B. "Bubba" Ness? Shouldn't attorney David Bruck be there beside me? He might get me off.

Why is it so plain? I'm not sure. Maybe it's sufficient to keep in my mind a plain truth: I will die.

Now the dream typically comes after a loss. It tells me that death remains mysterious. My mind continues to struggle with what it is, what it means. How can I imagine a world without me? How have I survived so many friends, so many family members, so many heroes? How many more losses will there be? Why can't Mel Brooks live forever? For someone so funny, even two thousand years wouldn't be enough! Death is natural, but not just. It is a random force of nature; survival is equally accidental.

Each loss is an occasion to remember that survival is a gift. I owe it to others to make good use of my time.

When I die, I might as well die alive.

It's late October. Beth and I are coming home from Cuba, on layover in a Mexican airport. She gives me a poke: the Aeromexico counter is decorated with paper skeletons to celebrate the Day of the Dead. We wait in line and I contemplate the skeletons. Our plane might crash. Not likely, but possible. We get on the plane and experience the miracle of an uneventful flight. I remember those skeletons with joy.

I shouldn't care what happens to my bones. When I'm dead I'll be past caring. Yet I think about it sometimes. I like the way it is for wild things. It would be good to be swallowed up in a swamp, feed delicious crabs, nourish the fetid fertility of pluff mud. Over centuries the weight of earth and slow growth of roots could grind my bones to powder. My skeleton might give strength to the cyprus trees.

But I am not a wild creature. There are rules. The rules don't suit me. I don't want my body preserved by chemicals, sealed off in a box, set apart in a graveyard. A body, no longer living but artificially tied to a life that once was, becomes hideous. I don't want that.

Most of all, I don't want my name on a tombstone. It's enough to have my name recorded in dull public records with the names of generations of lawyers filing lawsuits and writing deeds and wills. Let my tale-telling family connect me with a few good stories. That way, Aunt Harriet, though dead, will have a place at the table.

Yet even in my family, memories will fade. I may be confused with the other Aunt Harriet, the one who served the hot rolls. Then, I'll be forgotten. Even ghosts must die to make room for new ones. That's fine. A little immortality—for a little while—is good enough. When the time comes, let my body and mind and memory vanish without a trace.

Between now and that time, there are things I want to do. While I have been expecting to die, my time has become filled with people and places and work and strange undertakings. I have become active and involved with a family and a community and a web of varied beloveds and a number of causes. My calendar is booked with deadlines and appointments and travel and meetings and occasions of celebration. I have stories to tell and retell and stories unfolding that I want to live out.

When I die, I might as well die striving after wind.

Too Late to Die Young

Questions for discussion

1. The author says, "While anyone may die young, it's not something you can count on. You have to be prepared to survive." What do you think she means, and how does she show examples from her life experiences?

2. Do you agree with the author's conclusions? Do you feel that they apply to people with disabilities, or to everyone? Why?

3. The author protests the Jerry Lewis telethons. Why? What do you think she'd have said to someone who advocated the position that telethons raise important funds for research? What do you think about this debate?

4. What did you think of the author's observation that even her own friends wouldn't "get real"? Have you ever felt that a family member or friend was in denial about a real problem? What did you do about it?

5. Design your own discussion questions for this chapter.

For Further Reading

About women with disabilities

Browne, Susan E., ed. *With the Power of Each Breath: A Disabled Women's Anthology.* Collection of personal essays written by women with disabilities.

About living with physical impairments

Hockenberry, John. *Moving Violations.*

Montalambert, Hugues de. *Invisible.* A man who loses his sight after an assault learns to accept his blindness.

About disability rights

Shapiro, Joseph. *No Pity.*

Linton, Simi. *Claiming Disability.*

Jones, Larry A. *Doing Disability Justice*. A history of the disability rights movement in Washington state.

Other works by Harriet McBryde Johnson

You might enjoy her entire memoir, *Too Late to Die Young,* especially the chapter entitled "Unspeakable Conversations" detailing her interchange with Professor Peter Singer. He wrote a eulogy of her after her death in 2008 in *The New York Times*; the eulogy sparked debate.

Politics

Choosing to invest time, energy, and identity in the political process is an expression of hope. If something in our personal experience has informed or inspired us to believe that one direction or outcome is preferable to another, for not only the individual, but society as a whole, we put that belief into action through activism, advocacy, financial support of a candidate, actually running for office, or by simply casting a vote. The American political experience can therefore be viewed as optimism in the collective. Naturally, unanimity is rare, as reasonable (and not so reasonable) people are bound to disagree. Take it from me, things get a little intense when the swords come out and all you're holding is a plowshare.

When I first felt the jab of the swords, [my assistant] Jackie and I had just arrived in Chicago on the morning flight out of New York. We were to head directly to a campaign appearance on behalf of Major Tammy Duckworth, a Democrat hoping to win Henry Hyde's soon-to-be-vacant seat in the staunchly conservative sixth congressional district outside Chicago. The plan was to stay over Tuesday night, attend an unrelated nonpolitical donor luncheon for the Michael J. Fox Foundation, and then return to New York Wednesday afternoon. As we deplaned, we were met by John Rogers, Kelly Boyle, and Alan McLeod. Throughout our handshakes and hellos, the three of them were like multimedia jugglers, responding to the cacophony of buzzes, trills, and ring tones emanating from their cell phones, BlackBerrys, and other various PDAs. Now off the plane, Jackie had activated hers as well, and instantly, it began clamoring for her attention. From the look on everyone's face, the urgent tone of their whispered questions and answers, and the furious flurry of their text messaging, it was obvious that something serious was in the wind.

We met up with a Duckworth staffer who led us to yet another rented campaign minivan. Hustling through the parking lot, John briefed me on the situation. There had been a conservative response to the campaign ads, the McCaskill ad in particular. We had anticipated this, but what we hadn't counted on was that no less an attack dog than Rush Limbaugh was leading the charge. Much of his previous day's broadcast had been devoted to not so much debunking the ad on its merits or plumbing the ethical complexities of stem cell research, but going after me specifically ad hominem and apparently ad nauseam. Up to this point, I had been completely unaware—my radio tastes tend toward classic rock and NPR. He'd been going on about it since the first McCaskill ad interrupted game one of the World Series, while he was no doubt enjoying his hometown Cardinals' domination of the Detroit Tigers. The gist of his complaint, I was learning from John and his staff, was that I was a faker, exaggerating, playing up, and manufacturing symptoms in order to stir sympathy and pity in the hearts and minds of voters.

"What the hell did you get me into, John?" I muttered.

John, who was sitting in the backseat of the latest campaign minivan on our way to our hotel in suburban Chicago, shrugged and said, "Well, pal, I'm not quite sure of that yet myself, but it's gonna be fun."

"For you maybe," I laughed.

"Let's just see where it goes," he said.

We poured the tepid dregs of our Starbucks coffees out of the van's windows as we pulled into the hotel parking lot. We had a busy morning ahead of us. I couldn't think of a more appropriate person than Major Tammy Duckworth to spend the morning with, given that I'd woken up to the fact that I was in for a hell of a fight. Tammy, after all, was no stranger to tough fights. Here she was, a political newcomer, a Democrat, with the guts to compete for the seat Henry Hyde was vacating in this most conservative of Chicago suburbs.

Less than two years earlier, Major Duckworkth, a thirty-eight-year old National Guard pilot, had lost both her legs in Iraq when the Black Hawk helicopter she was copiloting was hit by a rocket-propelled grenade and brought down. Ten days later she woke up in Walter Reed Army Medical Center in Washington, DC, and by August of 2005, she had decided to run for Congress. Not given a chance in the traditionally Republican district, she was now, less than two weeks before Election Day, engaged in an unexpectedly competitive race with her GOP opponent, Peter Roskam.

Before meeting with Tammy, still en route to the rally, I had the standard local interviews, one in print and one televised. My inner circle had moved from the van to a holding room within the hotel, where they would prep me for the interviews. Under normal circumstances this would involve refreshing myself on the issues of research and the point-counterpoint that developed between sides of the debate. But now there was this new element to the discussion. How to respond to Rush?

"Let me get this straight one more time. He said I did what?" I asked.

"That you were either faking your symptoms or that you purposefully didn't take your medication when you shot the ads so that your symptoms would be exaggerated," John answered.

"Wait, let's back up," I said. "Did he say anything about stem cells, about the merits of the research, or any inaccuracies in the statements we made in the ad?"

"Mostly just that you were a fraud," Kelly said. I detected a slight upturn at the corner of her mouth as she said it. *Was she actually smiling?*

"Oh," Alan joined in. "He also said you were pandering to Missouri voters by pronouncing Missouri *Missoura*."

Then I smiled too and half-laughed as I responded, "You've gotta be kidding."

A Duckworth aide tapped on the door. The local NBC reporter was ready to do the on-camera interview in another room of the hotel.

In my role as an advocate for Parkinson's-related issues, my key responsibility is to inform and educate, to promote understanding of what we go through as individuals and as a community. For the first time that I could remember, my message was being countered by someone equally visible and even more vocal than I, and to make matters worse, he was actively and enthusiastically disseminating misinformation, promoting ignorance.

"We don't know for sure that she's gonna bring this up in the interview," John said as I put on my jacket and he instinctively straightened my tie.

"And if she does?" I asked. I mean, this stuff was almost crazy. I decided that I'd just go with the truth, that I hadn't heard or read the exact comments yet and wasn't in a position to respond. As I was being escorted to the interview, I took stock of my physical condition. I was actually feeling pretty good this morning. My meds had kicked in nicely; my gait was smooth, my hands were steady, and as of yet, I had no pronounced dyskinesias. *Great. Or was it?*

I knew of course that to simply dismiss Limbaugh's allegations as crazy would be dangerous. If he was crazy, then he was, pardon the expression, crazy like a fox. It was a classic "when did you stop beating your wife?" provocation, based not on an accusation, but on a presumption that something sinister had been perpetrated. His diatribe had set out an array of traps for me to stumble into if I wasn't careful, the first of which lay immediately ahead.

Like I said, I was feeling good that morning. It's always the goal to be as comfortable as possible, particularly in public situations. But was there now suddenly such a thing as being too comfortable, too smooth—not symptomatic enough? I wasn't going to involve myself with circular thinking, manufacturing symptoms to prove I wasn't manufacturing symptoms.

It turned out that the two reporters I spoke to weren't entirely up to speed on Rush's attack, so his remarks were only referred to in passing and rather obliquely at that.

The morning received a much-need injection of class when I finally met Major Tammy Duckworth, just moments before the rally. Her warm smile and affable nature immediately put me at ease. Very quickly we were exchanging anecdotes about our respective experiences as political neophytes on the campaign trail. She was the first to mention the attention coming my way from the conservative Right; having heard Limbaugh on the radio, she found herself "in utter disbelief," though she had faced similar accusations herself. After brief inquiries about each other's health, she matter-of-factly showed me the prosthetics she wore on each leg, admitting with a smile that any height advantage she held over me, she acquired with her new prosthetic legs.

I had read Major Duckworth's campaign biographical materials and was familiar with her story. Be that as it may, meeting her was nothing short of inspirational. Her example—transforming a tragic circumstance into an opportunity for service—put into sharp relief the character of those detractors who claimed she was using her disability to evoke sympathy. I pity anyone who would make the mistake of having pity for Tammy Duckworth. She's the real deal. Even more obvious than her toughness is her positive spirit. In the first moment of eye contact, it is clear that she believes in what she's doing and has a real hope—an informed optimism—that given the opportunity, she can affect positive change, not only for disabled vets, from whom she drew the inspiration to run, but for people in her district, her country, and the world.

Never a "super-optimistic person" before she was injured, she says, "I'm more optimistic now than I was before." She points out that battlefield triage has advanced over the last ten years to such a degree that "I would not have survived if I had been injured in the first Gulf War."

Unfortunately, advances in our ability to treat victims on the battlefield haven't been matched by our capacity to care for them once they've returned stateside, to heal and rehabilitate. Military hospitals, the Veterans Administration, the entire system, already considered by many to be woefully impersonal and inefficient, are now buckling almost to the point of breaking under the strain. Tammy discovered this firsthand in the days, weeks, and months she spent in the hospital being treated for horrific injuries. "When I was at Walter Reed, I started doing advocacy work for other patients because I was the highest-ranking amputee there for a while," she told me. "So whenever anyone needed to speak as a representative for other patients, they sent me. I started talking about the bureaucracy that existed and how we need to get rid of it. I testified before the Senate and the House, and through that process I was sucked into being politically active even though I never was before. The army had assigned me to this post for the other patients and then I started calling Senator Durbin's office saying, look, we've got a problem here or a problem there, I need help. It was in the late summer when Senator Durbin called me and told me that if I'm this upset about things that are not happening, I should run for office. At that point he mentioned Henry Hyde's district to me."

The rally was held in one of the hotel's large banquet halls. The room was already packed and raucous with cheering and chanting as we entered, gauntlet-style, the Major proceeding through a phalanx of well-wishers and supporters on either side. It was hard to grasp what any individual was saying, but suffice it to say, I was hearing the name "Rush" a lot, usually accompanied by an expletive or two. Metal risers accommodated the media, which was out in force—a dozen or so TV cameras and two or three times as many still photographers. I kept my comments brief, with most of the focus on Tammy and stem cell research. As with the two interviews I had done earlier, I didn't mention Rush Limbaugh specifically. In fact, from that point on, with only one exception, I didn't say the guy's name in any public forum for the remainder of the campaign. I couldn't help but appreciate the enormous roar of approval when I made a passing reference to a certain "less than compassionate conservative" who had spoken out against our efforts. It was a good line, and I'd keep using it for the next two weeks.

That afternoon I checked into a hotel in downtown Chicago; I had a luncheon the next day for some Fox Foundation donors in the Chicago area. The political portion of my junket was now complete. But, of course, my mind was entirely occupied with politics.

There was no question that I was on edge. Having been retired for the most part from acting for the last few years, it had been a while since I had received a bad review, and I don't think I'd ever had one so surgically personal in nature. This was not disagreement, disapproval, or even distaste. This was disgust, that same sort of sharp rebuke I had seen dealt out to those over the past few years who had spoken out against government policy, although their comments had largely been about the war and the administration's actions leading up to it. I was being "Dixie Chicked."

This was new for me, and I suddenly realized how much I had always liked being liked. It is spooky to see that a contingent of society, vocal and connected to power, has worked up an antipathy toward you and is rallying this base to marginalize you and the threat you represent. Would I have still made the ads if I'd had some idea of what the stakes were for my public reputation?

Absolutely. The stakes for me as a patient and an advocate were infinitely higher. My options had been narrowed to the basic "fight or flight," and I wasn't about to run away, but I was anxious and a little unsure as to how to respond.

My immediate plan was to order some room service and watch the baseball game. While I was waiting for dinner time to roll around, I compulsively forged through the contents of the minibar, putting a large dent in the inventory. Not the booze, of course — after fifteen years of being sober, it would take more than a gust of hot air from Rush Limbaugh to blow me off the wagon. I did, however, polish off two bags of peanut M&M's at the inflated hotel price of about eight bucks each, some gelatinous lemon wedge-type things, coated in crystallized sugar, and some salty squares with wasabi peas from a bag labeled entirely in Japanese except for the single English word "SNACK."

There were a number of phone calls. The wider media, smelling blood in the water, were circling and looking for someone to feed them something. John called to gather a statement. I told him I wasn't sure yet.

"Tell ya what, pal, for today, I'm just gonna speak on your behalf and say something general, but accurate — express shock and disappointment at the ignorance of his statements and reaffirm your commitment to continue speaking out on behalf of stem cells."

That was cool with me.

The phone rang again. It was my mom. She didn't even ask if it was me, but instead, immediately led with the question "Are you okay?"

There's a way that people ask that question, teeming with the certainty that you aren't, that makes you do a quick scan of your extremities and put the back of your hand to your forehead just to make sure that indeed, you are, before answering in the affirmative.

"What an idiot that man is. I'm so mad I can't see straight."

"Mom, it's all right."

"He's just ignorant. He has no idea what he's talking about!"

"That's why it's okay. No serious person will take him seriously."

As we talked, it became clear that what had Mom especially fired up, aside from the natural maternal instinct to defend her kid, was her recollection of the day the ads were filmed, how upset she was to see me struggle with dyskinesias.

"I didn't even know you listened to his show."

"I don't," she said. "But other people do, and they've been calling. Then I saw him imitating you on TV and I was so livid."

"You saw him doing what?" I said. This was the first I'd heard of this.

"He was imitating you, making fun of you—wiggling, shaking, squirming around."

Hunter S. Thompson was right. When the going gets weird, the weird definitely do turn pro.

My subsequent telephone conversation with [my wife] Tracy went a long way toward keeping my head in the right place. Sensibly, she was neither as angry as my mother nor as baffled as I still seemed to be.

"Congratulations," she said. "You got their attention."

Tracy, as she so often does, had hit the nail on the head. I had the attention not only of Rush Limbaugh and his "ditto heads," but also of those in the media and general public drawn to the sound of their complaints. The attention had created an opportunity to educate. I'd have to give a little more thought as to how to best capitalize on that opportunity. In the meantime, John's first public comment on my behalf was a step in the right direction: "It's a shameful statement. It's appallingly sad that people who don't understand Parkinson's disease feel compelled to make these comments. Anyone who understands the disease knows that it is because of the medications that Parkinson's sufferers experience dyskinesias."

... I was slack-jawed when I finally caught the video of the Limbaugh show before I left Chicago. He flapped his arms and wiggled his fingers while rocking his body, rolling his shoulders, and bobbing his head. "[Michael J. Fox] is exaggerating the effects of the disease. He's moving all around and shaking and it's purely an act ... This is really shameless of Michael J. Fox. Either he didn't take his medication or he's acting."

If his intention was only to mimic and mock what he maintained was my "shameless" performance, it went well beyond the personal—caricaturing the thousands of Parkinson's patients I'd met and worked with over the years. I saw it as an affront to them and their families, and I felt an obligation to defend them.

Predictably, my reception at the luncheon for the foundation was warm and supportive. Up to now, most of my focus had been on the extent to which Limbaugh and the Right had denounced the ads and the motive behind my involvement in them, but now I was getting a dose of the other side. The pro-research and patient communities were shocked and disgusted by the political attack. On the plane back home and at the airports on both ends of my journey, I discovered that my well-wishers extended beyond those with an interest in Parkinson's or stem cells. At the check-in counter, through security, and at the baggage claim, people approached me with words of encouragement. The consistent message I was getting was that I should fight back. While I appreciated the sentiment, I was wary of letting myself be distracted and engaging in the wrong fight. My battle was not with a conservative radio talk show host, whose intention among other things was to distract me and others from our message, but rather, against those in power who willfully sought to impede the progress of scientific research that could improve the life of millions.

Limbaugh wasn't alone in his objections to the ads and my participation in them. Predictably, representatives of the candidates whose anti-stem cell views I was effectively campaigning against took issue with our message, but what they had no way around was the indisputable effects and ravages of catastrophic illness. It's ironic that one answer for it could very well be the research they so strongly opposed.

Over the course of the few hours that it took to travel back from Chicago to New York, the controversy only intensified. Limbaugh apparently was feeling the force of a backlash. His allegation that I had been manufacturing symptoms to manipulate voters had been effectively countered by John's explanation about dyskinesias.

....

Slightly chastened, Limbaugh allowed that he would "bigly, hugely, admit that I was wrong, and I will apologize to Michael J. Fox if I am wrong in characterizing his behavior in this commercial as an act." Surprisingly, perhaps benefiting from low expectations in general, this was widely regarded as an apology from the talk show host, or as close as he was going to get to one.

His next salvo was, I think, intended to work on two levels. Having already alluded to my being an actor and, therefore, a con man, he now made the next logical connection. If my being an actor didn't necessarily mean that I was faking my symptoms, it was a pretty safe bet that I was a liberal and, therefore, a de facto Democrat. He went on to say, "Michael J. Fox is allowing his illness to be exploited and in the process is shilling for a Democratic politician."

Friends and associates from every corner of my life—professional, personal, and medical—were quick to correct him at every turn, loudly and convincingly. Moreover, members of the media were themselves having fun poking holes in his accusations. Keith Olbermann on MSNBC took glee in responding to the Democratic "shill" comment by pointing out that I had, in fact, supported and campaigned on behalf of pro-stem cell Republicans in the past.

What I needed to do, I decided, more than anything else, was to seize the opportunity that had presented itself, to use this spotlight that had been fixed upon me right up to Election Day. The only acceptable counter to all of this negativity was positivity.

Late in the evening after I returned from Chicago, Tracy found me standing at the fridge, door open, staring vacantly at a jar of mayonnaise, as men are wont to do. Intuiting that I wasn't really looking for anything but just filling the moment with an instinctive activity, she gently closed the door and pulled me in for a hug.

"You must be exhausted," she said.

"Yeah, I guess so," I replied. "But I feel really calm, ya know? This whole thing, the ads, Limbaugh, stem cells, the elections—it's like a perfect storm. And I'm right in the center of it, the eye, I mean. I just feel so weirdly relaxed."

"I know. It's great," she said. "I think this is the first time since I've known you that you haven't worried about ticking somebody off. You're always such a diplomat. But when it comes to this, you have such conviction, you truly don't care about what anybody else thinks—especially Rush Limbaugh."

"I care what you think," I said.

"I think you should get some sleep."

Good thinking.

Wanting me to slam Rush Limbaugh, preferably on their air, requests ran the gamut from talk radio shows—liberal and conservative—to the seeming thousands of cable news programs. Two names that stood out on the list of potential interviewers were Katie Couric and George Stephanopoulos. I have already mentioned George, and besides having been interviewed many times by Katie when she was on *The Today Show*, we live in the same neighborhood and often pass each other as we walk our kids to the bus stop on school-day mornings. I wouldn't characterize either as a close friend, but I knew that they would be intelligent and fair, and were informed on stem cell research.

I'm old enough to remember Walter Cronkite, the most trusted man in America (he had a pretty solid rep in Canada too), so stepping onto the set of the *CBS Evening News* in midtown Manhattan gained me a further appreciation for the history and tradition of the institution. I heard Katie's voice, and turned as she approached to welcome me. I could sense the enormity of the weight that had been placed upon this diminutive but determined broadcaster. I understood that I was the day's hot topic and therefore a good "get," but what Katie and her producers had proposed was extraordinary, the first seven and last six minutes of their broadcast. While we did have a personal connection, I was prepared for her to be as tough as she needed to be.

As if to confirm this, in the seconds before tape rolled—the floor director literally counting down—Katie leaned toward me and quietly allowed, "Now I have to forget how much I like you." After opening remarks to the camera, she turned to me, polite but professional, and asked, "How are you?"

Let's see. I was already sweating; my assistant, Jackie, had talked me into a sports coat over a blue cashmere sweater over a T-shirt. My fashion deference to the women in my life, dating back to Mom laying out clothes at the end of my bed, prevented me from protesting that we were in the middle of a heat wave. Now, under the studio lights, aesthetics became less important than absorbency. Shaking uncontrollably, I sought in vain to establish and maintain a single, consistent physical attitude, like a gate swinging in the wind, waiting for the latch to catch. Partly at my urging, partly on its own initiative, my right arm, in a semi-controlled flail, tried to catch and contain my left leg, the ankle of which crossed my right knee. And I knew that if my hand wasn't there to police it, a violent spasm could cause a painful kick to Katie's shin. If this was distracting to her, she didn't let on. I was also occupied by what I call a "central body tremor"; it feels as though someone has punched through my torso, grabbed a hold of my spine, and is waving me like a flag.

"I'm fine, thank you."

Katie began asking about symptoms, allowing a chance to correct the mistaken ideas and address willful ignorance. It took four questions for Katie to invoke Limbaugh's name and his allegations of fakery. She played the role of devil's advocate, albeit a more polite version, in deference to the sensibilities of others, putting Limbaugh's attack in more reasonable terms.

"Could you have waited to do that ad when you had less dyskinesias, for example?"

My answer was immediate. "Well, when do you know when that's going to be? … It's just not that simple." I saw this as an opportunity to correctly and necessarily take it away from the personal—this was not just about me.

That's why we're doing this. Not only people with Parkinson's. People who have spinal cord injuries. People who have the ticking clock of ALS, where they waste away, kids who are born with juvenile diabetes. I mean, potentially there's answers for those people. We're not interested in being exhibitionists with our symptoms or asking for pity or anything else. We're just resolved to get moving with this science. It's been a long time. It's not a time-neutral situation.

We moved on to explaining the disease, and, more importantly, why I had chosen this moment to speak up. Aside from being the first of several high-profile interviews that I would do over the next couple of weeks, two things about the *CBS Evening News* stand out in my mind. It was my first and only time, on the campaign before or after, that I uttered Rush Limbaugh's name. (I believe the quote was "I don't give a damn about Rush Limbaugh's pity.") And the second was something Katie did later in the interview, as the drugs kicked in and the tremors segued into the jerkiness of dyskinesias. Somewhere in the contortions of making a point, my left arm detached the microphone clip from my jacket lapel. With no fuss and hardly a break in conversation or eye contact, she calmly leaned over and refastened it. Neither of us commented on it, but it was such an empathetic gesture, so far from anything patronizing or pitying, a simple kindness that allowed me the dignity to carry on making a point more important than the superficiality of my physical circumstance.

I was aware of Katie's familial connection to Parkinson's disease—her father had PD. She disclosed this information as well as her previous support for the foundation at the end of the interview. Still, it would be hard for any objective viewer to judge the exchange as anything but fair. One thing was clear though, whether or not she was able to forget how much she liked me: with that single act of consideration, she made it abundantly clear how much she loved her father.

The impact of the Couric piece was immediate and powerful. My voice mail and e-mail were full. Not surprisingly, the Parkinson's and patient advocacy communities were supportive and gratified by the measured tone of our response. By neither appearing defensive nor firing back with inflammatory rhetoric, we were taking the high road, effectively a passive resistance sort of approach. In fact, Meg Ryan, an old friend of Tracy's, called her and jokingly asked, "What's it like to be married to Gandhi?" That's me, Mahatma J. Ghandi.

The show was widely watched and the *CBS Evening News* registered a significant bump in its overnight numbers. (A recent *New York* magazine article chronicling Katie's tenure as a news anchor pointed to our segment as both a ratings and editorial highlight). Personally, I felt a real sense of relief.

I certainly hadn't been at my best physically. I admitted to Katie, "It's not pretty when it gets bad ... but I've had enough years of people thinking I was pretty, and teen-age girls hanging my picture on the wall. I'm over that now." Watching the playback, I was confronted by the physical price I was paying for my efforts and the certainty that it was a bargain for the privilege. The forum Katie provided, to state our position passionately yet with a calm diplomacy, provided a sharp contrast to the belligerence of those attempting to confuse the issue. It helped shift the tone.

Later that afternoon, John and I and our retinue were at ABC's Manhattan studios for the next stop on our schedule of appearances. George Stephanopoulos had flown up from his Washington base, no doubt wishing that I was still on the Vineyard. I anticipated, correctly, that George would be after the political angle more than the personal. As I endured the rituals of paint and powder in the makeup room, George and I kidded around, talking politics and family. Physically, true to formless form, I had given up any pretense of control or calibration of symptoms and went before the cameras feeling at ease, if not anywhere close to being comfortable.

George started off with the rantings of Mr. Limbaugh. Still loose from the joviality of the backstage conversation, I went right away to the ridiculousness of Limbaugh's premise: "When I heard his response, I was like, 'What, are you kidding me?'... It just seemed so 'No, it can't be.'"

"But your mom was mad," George countered.

I said yes, then alluded to "the way Irish moms can get."

"Or Greek moms," he replied.

Much of the remaining conversation was nuts-and-bolts politics, detailing campaign positions, methods, and tactics. But a later reference to Limbaugh returned me to a theme that I had touched upon before and that would become a major part of my message in the coming days—the intrinsic faith we have in ourselves as Americans to do the right thing. I also touched upon how ironic it is that sometimes the greatest believers in the possibilities for the future are the very people who have cause to doubt.

"I'm going to bring up Rush Limbaugh one more time," George warned. "One of the things he says is that when you're talking about all these cures, you're giving people false hope and that is cruel."

"Which is crueler," I responded, "to not have hope or to have hope? And it's not a false hope. It's an informed hope. but two steps forward, one step back, you know? It's a process. It's how this country was built. It's what we do. It seems to me that in the last few years, eight, ten years, we've just stopped. We've become incurious and unambitious. And hope, I mean, hope is ..." My enthusiasm had now carried me to a patriotic reference that would make Emma Lazarus twist in her grave, " ... I don't want to get too corny about it, but isn't that what the person in the harbor with the thing—?" I made an emphatic flourish with my arm and held aloft an imaginary torch indicating the Statue of Liberty, and then finished my point. "To characterize hope as some sort of malady or some kind of flaw of character or national weakness is, to me, really counter to what this country is about."

Even as the interview was winding down, Rush Limbaugh was in the rearview mirror. He had given us a significant push, and we were ready to take to the road. Let's face it, the whole episode, unpleasant though it may have been, was a gift in the same way that I have described Parkinson's as a gift. You suffer the blow, but you capitalize on the opportunity left open in its wake. "The notion of hiding—this is what struck a nerve. Feeling the need to hide symptoms is so key to what patients of all kinds of conditions, but particularly Parkinson's, have to face. We have to hide—don't let anybody see, don't let them think you're drunk, don't let them think you're incapable, don't let them think you're unstable, you're unsteady, you're flawed, you're devalued. Mask it. Hide it. Cover it up ... We'd be better to take other things into account. We take our responsibility as citizens very seriously and our sense of ethics and, again, our spirituality and our participation in government, we take it very seriously. It's not made sinister by the fact that we have an affliction that may drive us down a certain path of activism."

Wrapping up, George inquired, "And you're campaigning next week?"

"Yes," I replied, "I'll be out there."

Politics

Questions for discussion

1. How do disability and politics intersect? How was this evident in this chapter, and in what other areas have you seen it?

2. What did you think of the media's approaches to Michael J. Fox, as reported in this chapter? What did you think of his strategies for responding? What do you think of his statement that he had not realized how much he liked being liked?

3. What did you think of Michael J. Fox's comments to George Stephanopoulos about masking symptoms? What other types of disabilities might have symptoms that people try to mask? What do you think about masking symptoms versus just letting them be obvious?

4. How and why do various celebrities support various causes? What is your opinion about this? Which celebrities come to your mind in this regard?

5. What are your thoughts about stem cell research? What do you think of the argument that it is cruel to raise people's hopes of a cure, and what did you think of Michael J. Fox's response?

6. Michael J. Fox talks of turning a negative into a chance to educate the public. What examples have you seen of this in the media?

7. Tammy Duckworth talked with Michael J. Fox about the plights of disabled veterans. What do you think of these issues?

8. Michael J. Fox views Tammy Duckworth as an inspiration. Some disability rights activists do not like feeling like they have to be "supercrips" or "inspirational people," but just wish to lead their own lives and be seen for who they are. Can you see both sides of this issue?

9. Design your own discussion questions for this chapter.

For Further Reading

About Parkinson's Disease

www.parkinson.org (National Parkinson Foundation)

http://www.michaeljfox.org/. Contains information, podcasts, and links to information about Parkinson's.

About Michael J. Fox's foundation

http://www.michaeljfox.org/

About celebrities supporting disability causes

Baird, Robert M. *Disability: The Social, Political, and Ethical Debate.* This anthology contains five essays about the late Christopher Reeve and the debate sparked among some disability rights activists by his tireless search for a cure.

Memoirs about accepting one's own disability

Hockenberry, John. *Moving Violations.* An NPR reporter with paraplegia recounts important events in his career and life.

Johnson, Harriet McBryde. *Too Late to Die Young.* A civil rights attorney in South Carolina recounts her life with mobility impairments. She also weighs in on the Christopher Reeve debate.

Walker, Cami. *29 Gifts.* A young businesswoman with MS recounts her journey toward giving.

John Hockenberry (1956–) was born in Ohio and grew up in New York and Michigan. He attended the University of Chicago and the University of Oregon. While in college, he was injured in a car accident and became a paraplegic. He was one of the original innovators of public radio, and has had an extensive career in television news. He has covered the Middle East extensively. He is the author of three books and lives in Brooklyn with his wife and children.

Public Transit

If you use a wheelchair and you want to avoid cabs in New York City, you can pay ten thousand dollars a year in parking to have your own car, or you can try your luck at public transit. There are para-transit wheelchair vans which are bookable far in advance. Then there is the subway, which has only twenty elevator sites out of hundreds of stations. And there are the buses.

The buses in New York have wheelchair lifts, and if the driver is carrying a key to operate the lift, and the lift has been serviced recently, and the bus is not too crowded, and the driver notices you at the stop, then you have a chance of getting a ride. Because the fare box is at the front of the bus and the lift is at the back, you can ask the driver to put your bus token into the box, but he will refuse. "I'm not allowed to touch your money," is what they usually say, and so they hand you instead a self-addressed stamped envelope for you to mail a check for a dollar and twenty-five cents to the Transit Authority. The bus lifts are better than nothing, except that when the city buys new buses, the new wheelchair lifts don't work properly, so there is a period of months when a bus drives up and the driver shrugs and says that his bus is one of the new ones. Only in New York would the new buses be the ones you can count on not to work.

Attempting to use public transit involves taking the risk of finding no bus lift, no elevator, or that either one will stop working while you are in the middle of using it. The transit system in New York sometimes seems like an elaborate trap for people in wheelchairs, lured like mice to cheese with promises of accessible transportation. For years, in New York's Herald Square there were signs indicating an accessible subway station with an elevator. The space for

241

the elevator was a large cube covered with plywood that looked as though it hadn't been disturbed for years. Wheelchair signs had arrived before the elevators, but that didn't keep the Transit Authority from putting the signs up even when there was no way to use the train at this stop. While they waited for the long-delayed elevator, the Transit Authority covered the little wheelchair symbols on the Herald Square subway station to prevent confusion. Today the elevator works, but the signs for it are still covered. The Transit Authority apparently wants it to be a surprise.

When I returned to New York City from the Middle East in 1990, I lived in Brooklyn, just two blocks from the Carroll Street subway stop on the F train. It was not accessible, and as there appeared to be no plans to make it so, I didn't think much about the station. When I wanted to go into Manhattan I would take a taxi, or I would roll up Court Street to the walkway entrance to the Brooklyn Bridge and fly into the city on a ribbon of oak planks suspended from the bridge's webs of cable that appeared from my wheelchair to be woven into the sky itself. Looking down, I could see the East River through my wheelchair's spokes. Looking up, I saw the clouds through the spokes of the bridge. It was always an uncommon moment of physical integrity with the city that ended when I came to rest at the traffic light on Chambers Street, next to City Hall.

It was while rolling across the bridge one day that I remembered a promise to Donna, my physical therapist, how I would one day ride the rapid transit trains in Chicago. Pumping my arms up the incline of the bridge toward Manhattan and then coasting down the other side in 1990, I imagined that I would be able physically to accomplish everything I had theorized about the subway in Chicago in those first days of being a paraplegic back in 1976. In the Middle East I had climbed many stairways and hauled myself and the chair across many filthy floors on my way to interviews, apartments, and news conferences. I had also lost my fear of humiliation from living and working there. I was even intrigued with the idea of taking the train during the peak of rush hour when the greatest number of people of all kinds would be underground with me.

I would do it just the way I had told Donna back in the rehab hospital. But this time I would wire myself with a microphone and a miniature cassette machine to record everything that happened along the way. Testing my old theory might make a good commentary for an upcoming NPR radio program about inaccessibility. Between the Carol Street Station and City Hall there were stairs leading in and out of the stations as well as to transfer from one line to another inside the larger stations. To get to Brooklyn Bridge/City Hall, I would make two transfers, from the F to the A, then from the A to the 5, a total of nearly 150 stairs.

I rolled up to the Brooklyn Carroll Street stop on the F train carrying a rope, a backpack, and wired for sound. Like most of the other people on the train that morning I was on my way to work. Taking the subway was how most people crossed the East River, but it would have been hard to come up with a less practical way, short of swimming, for a paraplegic to cover the same distance. Fortunately I had the entire morning to kill. I was confident that I had the strength for it, and unless I ended up on the tracks, I felt sure that I could get out of any predicament I found myself in, but I was prepared for things to be more complicated. As usual, trouble would make the story more interesting.

The Carroll Street subway station has two staircases. One leads to the token booth, where the fare is paid by the turnstiles at the track entrance; the other one goes directly down to the tracks. Near the entrance is a newsstand. As I rolled to the top of the stairs, the man behind the counter watched me closely and the people standing around the newsstand stopped talking. I quickly climbed out of my chair and down onto the top step.

I folded my chair and tied the length of rope around it, attaching the end to my wrist. I moved down to the second step and began to lower the folded chair down the steps to the bottom. It took just a moment. Then, one at a time, I descended the first flight of stairs with my backpack and seat cushion in my lap until I reached a foul-smelling landing below street level. I was on my way. I looked up. The people at the newsstand who had been peering sheepishly down at me looked away. All around me, crowds of commuters with briefcases and headphones walked by, stepping around me without breaking stride. If I had worried about anything associated with this venture it was that I would just be in the way, but I was invisible.

I slid across the floor to the next flight of stairs, and the commuters arriving at the station now came upon me suddenly from around a corner. Still, they expressed no surprise and neatly moved over to form an orderly lane on the side of the landing opposite me as I lowered my chair once again to the bottom of the stairs where the token booth was.

With an elastic cord around my legs to keep them together and more easily moved (an innovation I hadn't thought of back in rehab), I continued down the stairs, two steps at a time, reaching the chair at the bottom of the steps. I stood it up, unfolded it, and did a two-armed, from-the-floor lift back onto the seat. My head rose out of the sea of commuter legs, and I took my place in the subway token line.

"You know, you get half-price," the tinny voice through the bullet-proof glass told me, as though this were compensation for the slight inconvenience of having no ramp or elevator. There next to his piles of tokens the operator had a stack of official half-price certificates for the disabled users. He seemed thrilled to have a chance to use them. "No thanks, the tokens are fine." I bought two, rolled through the rickety gate next to the turnstiles and to the head of the next set of stairs. I could hear the trains rumbling below.

I got down on the floor again, and began lowering the chair. I realized that getting the chair back up again was not going to be as simple as this lowering maneuver. Most of my old theory about riding the trains in Chicago had pertained to getting up to the tracks, because the Chicago trains are elevated. Down was going well, as I expected, but up might be more difficult.

Around me walked the stream of oblivious commuters. Underneath their feet, the paper cups and straws and various other bits of refuse they dropped were too soiled by black subway filth to be recognizable as having any connection at all to their world above. Down on the subway floor they seemed evil, straws that could only have hung from diseased lips, plastic spoons that could never have carried anything edible. Horrid puddles of liquid were swirled with chemical colors, sinister black mirrors in which the bottoms of briefcases sailed safely overhead like rectangular airships. I was freshly showered, with clean white gloves and black jeans, but in the reflection of one of these puddles I too looked as foul and discarded as the soda straws and crack vials. I looked up at the people walking by, stepping around me, or watching me in their peripheral vision. By virtue of the fact that my body and clothes were in contact with places they feared to touch, they saw and feared me much as they might fear sudden assault by a mugger. I was just like the refuse, irretrievable, present only as a creature dwelling on the rusty edge of a dark drain. By stepping around me as I slid, two steps at a time down toward the tracks, they created a quarantined space, just for me, where even the air seemed depraved.

I rolled to the platform to wait for the train with the other commuters. I could make eye contact again. Some of the faces betrayed that they had seen me on the stairs by showing relief that I had not been stuck, or worse, living there. The details they were too afraid to glean back there by pausing to investigate, they were happy to take now as a happy ending which got them off the hook. They had been curious as long as they didn't have to act on what they learned. As long as they didn't have to act, they could stare.

I had a speech all prepared for the moment anyone asked if I needed help. I felt a twinge of satisfaction over having made it to the tracks without having to give it. My old theory, concocted while on painkillers in an intensive care unit in Pennsylvania, had predicted that I would make it. I was happy to do it all by myself. Yet I hadn't counted on being completely ignored. New York was such a far cry from the streets of Jerusalem, where Israelis would come right up to ask you how much you wanted for your wheelchair, and Arabs would insist on carrying you up a flight of stairs whether you wanted to go or not.

I took the F train to the Jay Street-Borough Hall station. The train ride was exhilarating. I had a dumb smile on my face as I realized that the last subway ride I had taken was in February 1976, when I went from Garfield on the Dan Ryan train in Chicago to Irving Park on the north side to visit a friend. The Chicago trains had a green ambient light from the reflection off the industrial paint on all the interior surfaces. The New York trains were full of yellows and oranges. But the motion and the sound of the train was familiar. The experience was completely new and just as completely nostalgic.

The Jay Street station was a warren of tunnels and passageways with steps in all of them. To get to the A train track for the ride into Manhattan I had to descend a flight of stairs to the sub-platform; then, depending on which direction I was going, ascend another stairway to the tracks. Because it was a junction for three subway lines, there was a mix of people rushing through the station in all directions, rather than the clockwork march of white office-garbed commuters from Brooklyn Heights and Carroll Gardens on their way to midtown.

I rolled to the stairs and descended into a corridor crowded with people coming and going. "Are you all right?" A black lady stopped next to my chair. She was pushing a stroller with two seats, one occupied by a little girl, the other empty, presumably for the little boy with her, who was standing next to a larger boy. They all beamed at me, waiting for further orders from Mom.

"I'm going down to the A train," I said. "I think I'll be all right, if I don't get lost."

"You sure you want to go down there?" She sounded as if she was warning me about something. "I know all the elevators from having these kids," she said. "They ain't no elevator on the A train, young man." Her kids looked down at me as if to say, "What can you say to that?" I told her that I knew there was no elevator, and that I was just seeing how many stairs there were between Carroll Street and City Hall. "I can tell you, they's lots of stairs." As she said good-bye, her oldest boy looked down at me as if he understood exactly what I was doing, and why. "Elevators smell nasty," he said.

Once on the A train I discovered at the next stop that I had chosen the wrong side of the platform and was going away from Manhattan. If my physical therapist, Donna, could look in on me at this point in my trip, she might be a bit more doubtful about my theory than I was. By taking the wrong train I had probably doubled the number of stairs I would have to climb.

I wondered if I could find a station not too far out where the platform was between the tracks, so that all I had to do was roll to the other side and catch the inbound train. The subway maps gave no indication of this, and the commuters I attempted to query on the subject simply ignored me or seemed not to understand what I was asking. Another black lady with a large shopping bag and a brown polka-dotted dress sitting in a seat across the car volunteered that Franklin Avenue was the station I wanted. "No stairs there," she said.

At this point, every white person I had encountered had ignored me or pretended that I didn't exist, while every black person who came upon me had offered to help without being asked. I looked at the tape recorder in my jacket to see if it was running. It was awfully noisy in the subway, but if any voices at all were recorded, this radio program was going to be more about race than it was about wheelchair accessibility. It was the first moment that I suspected the two were deeply related in ways I have had many occasions to think about since.

At Franklin Avenue I crossed the tracks and changed direction, feeling for the first time that I was a part of the vast wave of migration in and out of a Manhattan that produced the subway, all the famous bridges, and a major broadcast industry in traffic reporting complete with network rivals and local personalities who have added words like "rubbernecking" to the language. I rolled across the platform like any other citizen and onto the train with ease. As we pulled away from the station, I thought how much it would truly change my life if there was a way around the stairs, and I could actually board the subway anywhere without having to be Sir Edmund Hillary.

The incoming trains were more crowded in the last minutes of the morning rush, and back at the Jay Street station there was a roar of people rushing to catch that lucky train that might make them not late after all. As I was sliding my folded chair toward the steps down to the platform, a young black man with a backward baseball cap walked right up to me out of the crowds. "I can carry the chair, man," he said. "Just tell me where you want me to set it back up." I looked at him. He was thin and energetic, and his suggestion was completely sensible. I didn't feel like giving him my speech about how I didn't need any help. "Take it to the Manhattan-bound A train," I said. "I'll be right behind you."

One train went by in the time it took to get up the flight of stairs, but going up was still much easier than I had imagined. My legs dragged along cooperatively just as my theory had predicted. At trackside, the boy with my chair had unfolded it and was sitting in it, trying to balance on two wheels. A friend of his, he explained, could do wheelies ever since he had been shot in the back during a gang shooting. "Your chair has those big-ole' wheels," he said, commenting on the large-diameter bicycle wheels I used, as if to explain why he was having some trouble keeping his balance. "I never seen those kinda wheels," he said as I hopped back into the chair.

As the train approached, he asked me for some cash. I thought that I must be some kind of idiot to go through all this and end up spending more to get into Manhattan than anyone else on the subway that day. The smallest bill I had was a five. I handed it over to him and boarded the train, laughing to myself at the absolute absurdity of it all. When I looked up, I could see commuters looking up from their newspapers. They cautiously regarded my laughing, as though I had just come from a rubber room at Bellevue Hospital. I let out a loud, demented shriek, opening my eyes as wide as I could. The heads bobbed quickly back behind the newsprint.

On the last flight of stairs leading onto City Hall Plaza at Centre Street and Chambers, the commuters in suits poured into the passageway from six trains. There was not a lot of space, and people began to trip over me. One gray-suited man in headphones carrying a gym bag nearly fell down, but he caught himself and swore as he scrambled up to street level, stepping on one of my hands in the process. A tall black man in a suit holding his own gym bag picked up my chair and started to carry it up the stairs. In a dignified voice he said, "I know you're okay, right?" I nodded.

Behind him a Puerto Rican mother with two identically dressed daughters in fluffy flowered skirts with full slips holding corsages offered to take my backpack and cushion up to the top so that I could haul myself without worrying about keeping track of the loose things. At the top, as I unfolded the wheelchair, the mother told me that she was on her way to get married at the Manhattan municipal building. Her two daughters were bridesmaids. She said she was going to put on her wedding dress, which she had in her gym bag, in the ladies' room before the ceremony. I wished her good luck and hopped back up into the chair as the commuters streamed by. It was a familiar place, the same spot I always rolled to so effortlessly off the Brooklyn Bridge.

I turned to roll away and noticed that the two little girls had come back. In unison they said, "We will pray for Jesus to bring back your legs, mister." "Thank you," I said. As though I had just given them each a shiny new quarter, they ran back to their mother, who was waiting for them with her hand outstretched to take them across busy Center Street. It was not the sort of thing I ever cared to hear people say, but after the ordeal of the subway, and the icy silence of what had seemed like every white person I met, I didn't mind at all. For once, I looked forward to riding home in a cab.

Since 1976 I had imagined the trip on the subway. I knew it was possible, while my physical therapist back in Michigan had known it would be utterly impractical as a form of transportation. We were both right, but neither of us could have imagined the America I found down there. The New York subway required only a token to ride, but on each person's face was the ticket to where they were all really going, the places they thought they never had to leave, the people they thought they never had to notice, or stop and apologize for stepping on them. Without knowing it, I had left that America behind long ago. I discovered it alive and well on the F train.

Public Transit

Questions for discussion

1. What did you think of Hockenberry's attempt to ride the inaccessible subway? What did you think of other people's responses to him? If you had crossed his path during this endeavor, what might your reaction have been? Why?

2. What do you think Hockenberry was hoping to learn from this endeavor? What other things do you think he ended up learning?

3. What accessible and inaccessible places have you noticed as you have traveled? What accessibility features have you noticed with regards to public transportation? Do you think our current system of public transit provides "good enough" accessibility? Why or why not? How could we, as a society, improve physical accessibility? Stricter laws? Better enforcement? More awareness?

4. Design your own discussion questions for this chapter.

For Further Reading

About public transportation and accessibility issues

http://www.ada.gov/cguide.htm ("A Guide to Disability Rights Laws")

"Denver Crips Win Bus Suit." www.raggededgemagazine.com/drn/10-01
    .shtml#320

About John Hockenberry's work

www.johnhockenberry.com. His memoir *Moving Violations* covers a multitude of subjects from living among the Kurds, to attempting to become an astronaut, to meeting Stephen Hawking, to the accident that led to his paraplegia, to his love life, and everything in between. Many of his journalism clips are available at youtube.com.

Other memoirs from authors with mobility impairments

Johnson, Harriet McBryde. *Too Late to Die Young.*

Walker, Cami. *29 Gifts.*

About reporters with disabilities

O'Brien, Mark. "The Unification of Stephen Hawking," in *Staring Back: The Disability Experience from the Inside Out.*

About recovery from an accident

Packer, Ann. *The Dive From Clausen's Pier.* Fictional account of a young woman whose fiancé becomes paralyzed, and of his struggle to accept his situation.

Westmacott, Mary (a pseudonym for Agatha Christie). *The Rose and the Yew Tree.* A young man is injured in a car accident and tries thereafter to find his place in society.

Wharton, Edith. *Ethan Frome.* A sad novella about two lovers injured while on a wild ride.

Fear of Bees

My seven-year-old niece, Sarah, was once sitting on my lap, having long ago gotten used to Uncle John never walking. As a child whose notions of normal had not solidified in concrete, she was free to think far and wide about the implications of my physical condition. Much farther and wider than even I. She grabbed my thigh and looked into my eyes with a questioning, probing gaze that only a child can give. "Can you feel that, Uncle John?" she asked.

"No," I told her incredulous, shaking head. She was deep in thought, examining the implications of such a truth. She was satisfied that I had no sensation, but she still needed further elaboration. She suddenly burst out with a last question: "So if a bee stung you right here, Uncle John ..." She pointed to a place on my thigh where one summer she had been stung. It was her ultimate test, her ultimate definition of pain. I shook my head. "Nothing, Sarah. Ten bees could sting me there."

Sarah was lost in thought until she said triumphantly, "Then you aren't afraid of bees."

In a future world where the thoughts of little girls can matter as much as those of presidents and generals, the fear of bees as a metaphor for spinal-cord injury might even be an appropriate topic for "Oprah." It would truly be an indication of the millennium if in supermarket parking lots in the twenty-first century the signs on the parking spaces in the front said: *Reserved for People Unafraid of Bees.* If you need a name for me, call me John. If you want to know one more thing about me, you may comfortably note that I am a person not afraid of bees.

Fear of Bees

Questions for discussion

1. What examples have you seen of children looking at differences in ways that an adult might not?

2. The author seems to like the idea of the fear of bees as a metaphor for spinal-cord injury. What progress has been made in discourse about disability, and about particular words that are used to describe it? How is such progress made? Has there been enough progress in this regard? Why or why not?

3. The author says that his niece's notions of normal had not yet solidified into concrete. Is it important for children to be exposed to differences before a certain age? If someone's notions of normal have solidified, how can they be changed?

4. Design your own discussion questions for this passage.

For Further Reading

About disability labeling

Shapiro, Joseph. *No Pity* ch. 1, "Tiny Tims and Supercrips." A discussion about labeling and stereotypes, and the negative consequences thereof.

Linton, Simi. *Claiming Disability.*

Rosen, S.L. "I Call Myself Survivor."

Jennifer Graf Groneberg lives and writes in the mountains of Montana with her husband of twenty years and their three "ABC" boys, Avery, Bennett and Carter. She's the author of the award-winning memoir, *Road Map to Holland: How I Found My Way Through My Son's First Two Years with Down Syndrome* (NAL/Penguin 2008).

First Words

On the fifth day of our son Avery's life, I learned the two words of his story that separated him from his twin brother, Bennett, from his older brother, Carter, from his father, Tom, and from me.

Our pediatrician was in the NICU in the afternoon. I remember thinking how odd it was, seeing her then. She always made her rounds in the mornings, the opposite of most other doctors. "She does things in her own way," one of the nurses explained to me. And here she was, watching me hold the babies. It finally dawned on me: she was waiting to see me. It was a setup. When I'd returned Avery to his isolette, had tucked Bennett back into his purple and white knit cap and handed him to his nurse to be weighed, she came over. "I have the results of the genetic karyotype," she said. I barely remembered her ordering it. She'd had some concerns about Avery, little things, like a crease in the palm of his left hand, or the placement of his ears in relationship to his eyes. I knew, then, that whatever she had to tell me would not be good.

She sat down next to me, reached out and touched my forearm, then showed me the results of the FISH test. In front of me was a photocopy of pairs of squiggly lines representing chromosomes. One from the father, one from the mother, a map of genetic destiny. At the twenty-first pair of chromosomes, Avery had one extra.

"Down syndrome," she explained.

Down syndrome is the most common disabling genetic condition, happening about once in every 730 births. Down syndrome occurs among people of all races and all economic levels and affects more than 350,000 American families. I didn't know these statistics at the time of Avery's diagnosis—all I knew was that the hopes and dreams we had for him were lost, and I didn't know what, if anything, would replace them. One well-meaning nurse told me, "You'll get used to it. You'll get a thick skin." I didn't want thick skin. I wanted my dreams back, I wanted my baby back, the one I had felt twist and kick inside me, the one I had joked would be a soccer player.

When Tom and I spoke about it later, alone in our bedroom, I could see the summer light coming through the blinds so clearly, so sharply. Here was a man I had known and loved for fourteen years, but I didn't know what these words would mean to him, the first two words of Avery's life, words that had redefined him in my eyes, words that might redefine us. Our little family might be ending, imploding, and I thought I might be set adrift, alone.

I could hear sounds coming out of my mouth, my voice hoarse and choked and unrecognizable to me even as I watched the dust settle around us, the light shift imperceptibly toward the west. Sundown. I'd never seen a look of such anguish on his face before. His fear, his love, twisted together in sadness. The comforter cover glowed a color from my childhood. Burnt Sienna. Tom reached out to me, and we held each other. We stayed like this for a long time, holding on to each other in the fading summer light. It's funny the things you remember. I was wondering if Avery would ever be able to color; if he would ever be able to even say the word "crayon."

All the possible children a woman will bear are present inside her even before she is born. They are created while she is still just a tiny form twisting and floating in utero. For a short while, three generations—mother, daughter, and child—live as one, each a link, one to another, in the long, twisted chain of my son's DNA. If you stretch it end to end, it would reach to the moon and back. A son I had wished for, yearned for, prayed for, and yet when he arrived, I was wholly unprepared.

When I think of that time now, I think of hands. Hands working for us, some belonging to people I'd known for years, like my parents, or Tom's, or my friends Phyllis and Sarah, Emily, Carrie. Others were strangers to me— nurses whose names I could barely keep straight, social workers, doctors, neighbors I knew just by sight. Hands folded in prayer, hands lifting baby clothes fresh out of the dryer and folding them into boxes for us, hands dialing phone numbers as our news spread, as others called and offered help. A woman whose name I will never know helped me find my car when I was sobbing so hard I couldn't see straight; another offered the phone number of her sister, who had a child with Down syndrome. Hands holding mine, hands helping me up when I could not help myself. One to another, slowly. Wherever I went, it seemed I was never alone. I felt cradled, loved; led by so many that it became one, one love, one light, leading me home.

When Avery was first diagnosed, we were told many things, mostly about how hard our life would be, how difficult. There might be heart defects, or thyroid problems; growth issues and developmental delays. He was presented to us as a set of complications. What they left out was Avery. No one told me how beautiful he would be. No one told me how sensitive he would be. No one told me he would hug me with his whole body, wrapping arms and impossibly nimble legs around me at once, such a strong embrace. No one factored in love.

Avery is three. He has a shy smile and a gentle personality. Hair the color of wheat, eyes blue like a river, like his brother's, like mine. He will eat pears with gleeful abandon, but when I hold up a green bean, he turns his head away in disdain. He plays the piano, making up his songs with heartfelt seriousness. At our house, people take their shoes off and leave them in a line by the door. When no one is looking, he puts things into the empty shoes, like parting gifts—a toy car, a tiny horse, a pilfered spoon. Despite the stubbed toes, the lost cutlery, the startled guests, it's hard for me to be mad at him. He is the child that I wanted, that I did not know I wanted. He is my son.

Last night I was tucking the little boys in bed, Bennett in the bottom bunk, Avery in a twin mattress on the floor next to him. Sometimes Bennett climbs down and joins Avery and I find them curled into each other, a tangle of arms and legs in a nest of blankets. I made sure Avery had his little puppy, Bennett his stuffed monkey. I gave each boy his blanket. Each a kiss, then "I love you" to Bennett, "I love you" to Avery. I turned toward the door, making my way by the light of the glowing turtle on the dresser, when I heard a soft voice that I didn't recognize.

"ahluvyou."

I swung around and there was Avery, smiling at me.

Until now, there had been no actual words, no "mama" or "dada." I had come to think of him as my quiet boy, though I would sometimes catch him saying his sounds in the stillness of the early morning, his blanket over his head so no one could see. He was saving them up until he was ready, saving them up for me. Before the tiniest of smiles, before the blink of an eyelash, before the first sweet breath, there was a heartbeat, echoing a twin heart, one to another, together, in the watery bed my body created beneath my ribcage, just below my heart. We started as three points of a triangle, close as could be, and though we have widened, we are a triangle still, connected no longer by blood and muscle and tissue but by one simple word: Love.

My hurt has softened into a small, quiet wish—for the world to see Avery without the almond-shaped eyes, the looseness of joints, the wide grin—to see him instead as he is inside, a pure spirit, a brave soul. It is my wish for

Avery, and it is my wish for us all. Words have the power to separate us from each other. Words like disabled. Handicapped. Retarded. There are other choices we could use: Acceptance. Encouragement. Love. The power is ours. We can build our lives with words that devastate, or words that heal, giving hope and support as real as the hands that lifted me up. The choice is ours. Choose love.

First Words

Questions for discussion

1. The author says she was told mainly about the difficulties her son would bring to her life, and nothing about the joys. Why do you think this was so? What problems does this raise? What do you think about the ethics of doctors making such predictions in the early stages of a woman's pregnancy?

2. The author pleads for the world to see her child as he is inside. How could this be accomplished?

3. Have you known anyone with Down Syndrome? What was the person like? What are the stereotypes that you have heard or seen portrayed in the media or in literature?

4. The author says that we can choose to use words that devastate or words that heal. What do you think of this idea? Which words can you think of on both sides of this divide?

5. Design your own discussion questions for this piece.

For Further Reading

About physicians' reactions and explanations of disability

Parens, Erik, ed. *Prenatal Testing and Disability Rights.*

About parenting a child with a disability

Meyer, Donald J., ed. *Uncommon Fathers.* A collection of essays by fathers of special needs children.

Stimpson, Jeff. *Alex: the Fathering of a Preemie.* A father's memoir about his premature baby.

Park, Clara Claiborne. *The Siege.* A mother's memoir recounting her young daughter's autism.

Soper, Kathryn Lynard, ed. *Gifts: Mothers Reflect on How Children with Down Syndrome Enrich Their Lives.* Jennifer Graf Groneberg's story is one of many in this anthology.

Ryan, Joan. *The Water Giver: The Story of a Mother, a Son, and Their Second Chance.* Simon & Schuster, New York: 2009. Memoir of a child who injures his head and his mother who cares for him.

The Five-Sensed World

The poets have taught us how full of wonders is the night; and the night of blindness has its wonders, too. The only lightless dark is the night of ignorance and insensibility. We differ, blind and seeing, one from another, not in our senses, but in the use we make of them, in the imagination and courage with which we seek wisdom beyond our senses.

It is more difficult to teach ignorance to think than to teach an intelligent blind man to see the grandeur of Niagara. I have walked with people whose eyes are full of light, but who see nothing in wood, sea, or sky, nothing in city streets, nothing in books. What a witless masquerade is this seeing! It were better far to sail forever in the night of blindness, with sense and feeling and mind, than to be thus content with the mere act of seeing. They have the sunset, the morning skies, the purple of distant hills, yet their souls voyage through this enchanted world with a barren stare.

The calamity of the blind is immense, irreparable. But it does not take away our share of the things that count—service, friendship, humor, imagination, wisdom. It is the secret inner will that controls one's fate. We are capable of willing to be good, of loving and being loved, of thinking to the end that we may be wiser. We possess these spirit-born forces equally with all God's children. Therefore we, too, see the lightnings and hear the thunders of Sinai. We, too, march through the wilderness and the solitary place that shall be glad for us, and as we pass, God maketh the desert to blossom like the rose. We, too, go in unto the Promised Land to possess the treasures of the spirit, the unseen permanence of life and nature.

The blind man of spirit faces the unknown and grapples with it, and what else does the world of seeing men do? He has imagination, sympathy, humanity, and these ineradicable existences compel him to share by a sort of proxy in a sense he has not. When he meets terms of color, light, physiognomy, he guesses, divines, puzzles out their meaning by analogies drawn from the senses he has. I naturally tend to think, reason, draw inferences as if I had five senses instead of three. This tendency is beyond my control; it is involuntary, habitual, instinctive. I cannot compel my mind to say "I feel" instead of "I see" or "I hear." The word "feel" proves on examination to be no less a convention than "see" and "hear" when I seek for words accurately to describe the outward things that affect my three bodily senses. When a man loses a leg, his brain persists in impelling him to use what he has not and yet feels to be there. Can it be that the brain is so constituted that it will continue the activity which animates the sight and the hearing, after the eye and the ear have been destroyed?

It might seem that the five senses would work intelligently together only when resident in the same body. Yet when two or three are left unaided, they reach out for their complements in another body, and find that they yoke easily with the borrowed team. When my hand aches from overtouching, I find relief in the sight of another. When my mind lags, wearied with the strain of forcing out thoughts about dark, musicless, colorless, detached substance, it recovers its elasticity as soon as I resort to the powers of another mind which commands light, harmony, color. Now, if the five senses will not remain disassociated, the life of the deaf-blind cannot be severed from the life of the seeing, hearing race.

The deaf-blind person may be plunged and replunged like Schiller's diver into seas of the unknown. But, unlike the doomed hero, he returns triumphant, grasping the priceless truth that his mind is not crippled, not limited to the infirmity of his senses. The world of the eye and the ear becomes to him a subject of fateful interest. He seizes every word of sight and hearing because his sensations compel it. Light and color, of which he has no tactual evidence, he studies fearlessly, believing that all humanly knowable truth is open to him. He is in a position similar to that of the astronomer who, firm, patient, watches a star night after night for many years and feels rewarded if he discovers a single fact about it. The man deaf-blind to ordinary outward things, and the man deaf-blind to the immeasurable universe, are both limited by time and space; but they have made a compact to wring service from their limitations.

The bulk of the world's knowledge is an imaginary construction. History is but a mode of imagining, of making us see civilizations that no longer appear upon the earth. Some of the most significant discoveries in modern science owe their origin to the imagination of men who had neither accurate knowledge nor exact instruments to demonstrate their beliefs. If astronomy had not kept always in advance of the telescope, no one would ever have thought a telescope worth making. What great invention has not existed in the inventor's mind long before he gave it tangible shape?

A more splendid example of imaginative knowledge is the unity with which philosophers start their study of the world. They can never perceive the world in its entire reality. Yet their imagination, with its magnificent allowance for error, its power of treating uncertainty as negligible, has pointed the way for empirical knowledge.

In their highest creative moments the great poet, the great musician cease to use the crude instruments of sight and hearing. They break away from their sense-moorings, rise on strong, compelling wings of spirit far above our misty hills and darkened valleys into the region of light, music, intellect.

What eye hath seen the glories of the New Jerusalem? What ear hath heard the music of the spheres, the steps of time, the strokes of chance, the blows of death? Men have not heard with their physical sense the tumult of sweet voices above the hills of Judea nor seen the heavenly vision; but millions have listened to that spiritual message through many ages.

Our blindness changes not a whit the course of inner realities. Of us it is as true as it is of the seeing that the most beautiful world is always entered through the imagination. If you wish to be something that you are not,—something fine, noble, good,—you shut your eyes, and for one dreamy moment you are that which you long to be.

The Five-Sensed World

Questions for discussion

1. What do you remember learning about Helen Keller when you were a child? What legacy do you think she has left?

2. Helen Keller writes that "The bulk of the world's knowledge is an imaginary construction." What do you think of this idea? What link does Helen Keller suggest between disability and imagination?

3. How does Helen Keller suggest that disabled and non-disabled people find common ground? Do you have suggestions for how this can happen, and why is it important?

4. What does this piece say about different kinds of learning and wisdom?

5. Design your own discussion questions for this piece.

For Further Reading

About Helen Keller

Keller, Helen. *The World I Live In* and *Story of My Life.*

Kleege, Georgina. *Blind Rage: Letters to Helen Keller.* Tired of being asked why she doesn't handle her blindness as well as Helen Keller did, a legally blind woman writes an open letter to the deceased icon, and in the process learns about Helen Keller and herself.

About sensory impairments

http://www.flatrock.org.nz/topics/odds_and_oddities/bump_lets_lisa_see.htm. Story about a blind woman who regained some sight after bumping her head.

Mango, Karin. "Christmas Cheer." A woman who is losing her hearing considers how to spend her holidays.

Montalambert, Hugues de. *Invisible.* A man who loses his sight after an assault learns to accept his blindness.

Kate Silver (1977–) is a freelance journalist living in Chicago. Her work has appeared in *People* and *Spirit* magazines, Pauline Frommer's *Las Vegas 2007* and *2009*, *Mobil Travel Guide, Chicago Tribune, Luxury Las Vegas* and more. She is also a former editor at *Las Vegas Life* magazine. She has two cats and a dog, none of whom listen to her very well.

How Mya Saved Jacob

Mya [Jacob's dog] senses something wrong. Sitting in the back of the SUV as they barrel down a back road, she detects a change in the air. Jacob is driving, on their way to camp in the Grand Canyon. Though Mya met Jacob only a month ago, she knows him better in some ways than he knows himself. With his "yes ma'am" Southern twang and lanky, broad-shouldered, 6-foot-3-inch frame, he can seem like a big, easygoing guy. But there are times, urgent times, when Jacob needs Mya.

Outside the window, the desert hills that stretch as far as the eye can see might as well be in the Middle East. A car comes up behind their SUV—the first car they have seen for many miles—and it passes them, kicking up a whirlwind of dust. Mya doesn't even look to see Jacob's shoulders tighten. She leaps into the front seat just before Jacob slams on the brakes. They skid to a stop, and in an instant Mya is on top of Jacob, licking his convulsing body so hard she almost seems to smother him. In reality, this highly trained black labrador accomplishes just the opposite. Her care leads him out of his dark terror and back to the dusty road.

Bedford Hills Correctional Facility in New York consists of commanding, institutional-looking brick buildings enclosed with fences topped with spools of razor wire. The only women's maximum-security prison in New York State, it holds 840 inmates, some of them notable. Pamela Smart, Amy Fisher, Jean Harris, and Kathy Boudin have all been housed here. And so was Mya. Her mother, a breeding dog owned by an organization called Puppies Behind Bars, conceived the dog and bore her inside the prison walls in January 2008. Mya and her siblings trained for two years, two of them at bomb detection, Mya and a fourth helping veterans with psychological disorders. Gloria Gilbert Stoga, the president and founder of Puppies Behind Bars, chose the training venue. Puppies Behind Bars got its start 13 years ago, after Gilbert Stoga read about a veterinarian in Florida named Thomas Lane who had begun enlisting inmates as dog trainers. Prison gave inmates plenty of time to work with the dogs, and the rigid schedule proved ideal for a strict training regimen. What's more, the cost was a fraction of the $26,000 it can take to train a service animal. In 1997, Gilbert Stoga's new organization placed its first five puppies in the Bedford Hills prison, where the inmates trained them to work with the blind. A few years later, Puppies Behind Bars added explosive detection; and in 2006 it launched a unique program, "Dog Tags: Service Dogs for Those Who've Served Us," to train service dogs for veterans returning from Iraq and Afghanistan.

Inmates look after the puppies when they reach between six and eight weeks of age. Laurie had written a letter explaining why she wanted to be a "puppy raiser." The prison confirmed that Laurie met the requirements —a clean prison record for the previous 12 months, a reputation for being reliable and trustworthy, no history of any sex offense or of harm to a child or animal. Then Laurie and other qualified inmates interviewed with Puppies Behind Bars instructors, who explained the program's expectations: in addition to mandatory attendance at weekly puppy class and successful completion of reading assignments, homework, and exams, the puppy raiser must always put the needs of the puppy before her own. Instructors selected the candidates who responded best. Laurie learned she'd made the cut.

After Mya was born, the inmates fitted her with a red cape that identified her as a service dog in training. Then they took Mya to Laurie's cell to meet her new puppy raiser. When Laurie saw Mya for the first time, the short, thin brunette's usually stoic demeanor shattered. She immediately created a scrapbook, documenting everything the puppy did from day one and preserving every tag from every toy. Over the 16 months Laurie had Mya, the scrapbook grew to nearly three inches thick. The first page contains a photo of Mya standing in the prison yard. Words cut out of a magazine read, "Our first day together." Across from the opening page, Laurie wrote, "Today is March 25, 2008, and several hours ago, I had a 15-pound fluff ball of black fur placed into my arms. She is 'Mya' and she is beautiful!" Like a doting mother, Laurie dedicated an entire page to "Firsts": fur from Mya's first brushing, Mya's baby teeth, Mya's first nail clippings. Laurie wrote on the page beside the nail clippings, "took several attempts while she slept."

Mya spent most of her time with Laurie, but two days a week a different inmate would train her while Laurie took on another puppy. Mya learned that a command is a command, no matter who it comes from. And there were so many commands to master. First, Mya learned how to respond to her name, along with the standard "sit," "leave it," "heel," and "stay." The more Mya learned, the more complex the orders became. She worked on the 82 basic commands that service dogs know (turning on the lights, closing the door, unzipping a zipper, tugging socks off feet, picking up a pen, retrieving keys), in addition to a repertoire created specifically to help a veteran with a psychological disorder. Over a number of months, Mya learned how to "block" her puppy raiser by casually standing two feet in front of her in order to keep anyone who might approach at a safe distance. She learned "got my back," sitting behind her master to provide space from other people while they were waiting in line. Mya would "pop a corner," walking ahead of her puppy raiser and looking to the right and left to communicate that the coast was clear. And she could dial 911 on a special phone if a human fell and became unresponsive.

Besides the training, Mya attended regular services with Laurie in the prison chapel, and she received blessings from both the chaplain and a Catholic priest. She accompanied Laurie to discipleship training classes and choir rehearsal, earning the nickname "The Church Puppy." That's how she learned her 88th command: when someone says "Praise the Lord!" she leaps several feet off the ground.

Even the other puppy raisers thought Mya was special. She showed a remarkable ability to sense the mood of any human around her. Before she had turned five months old, Laurie would take the pup into a room full of people and let her off the leash. Mya immediately headed toward the one who was having the worst day, mentally or physically, and lie at the person's feet. This skill couldn't be taught. It would prove invaluable to a veteran whose bad days seemed to outnumber the good.

Other days, Mya left prison to spend time with volunteer families and Puppies Behind Bars staff. They took her on all kinds of adventures and introduced her to a wide variety of sights and smells. By her first birthday Mya had been to Manhattan, visited the aircraft carrier USS *Intrepid*, participated in a charity walk for cancer, spent time in a residential treatment center for adolescents, and frequented Dunkin' Donuts, K-Mart, gas stations, banks, grocery stores, coffee shops, post offices, parks, meadows, and many other human habitats. Along the way, she met countless people and pets and practiced her commands in every setting. The volunteers wrote letters to Laurie to tell her what a wonderful job she was doing with Mya, calling the dog "confident," "intelligent," "charming," "loving," "playful," a "pure delight to be around."

Finally, after 16 months with Mya, Laurie had to let her go. She wrote the dog a letter:

You be my good girl, and you make sure your soldier knows that they are special and loved every day; and you do everything you know how, to make their life fuller and richer, and better, even if it's just by being there. Loving is your strong suit so I know you'll be on point, no matter how much they need!

I'll always love you, Mya Bug! Always your PBB Mom.

Jacob used to go by Jake. That was six years ago, a lifetime, before he joined the military. A smart, punk kid in Winston-Salem, North Carolina, he had no goals, drank too much, and worked too little. He lived with his parents and took classes at the University of North Carolina at Greensboro, quitting after a few months. One day, at 19, Jake saw battlefield footage of Iraq during CNN's coverage of the presidential election. He had never thought about joining the military, but maybe it would give his life some direction. He talked to a recruiter and signed up. The Navy gave him 11 months' training as a Fleet Marine Force hospital corpsman, or medic, including instruction in assisting with battlefield surgery. In August 2006, they sent him to Iraq. He served for eight months at combat outposts in the Euphrates River Valley, a hotbed of insurgents. Several minutes after he got to his first post, an Iraqi military vehicle dropped off the bodies of two Marines. Hi, welcome to Iraq, Jake thought. Two days later, an ambulance brought two teenage Iraqi sisters to the makeshift clinic with gunshot wounds. Jake had been well trained for the physical part of his job, but nothing prepared him for the look in the eyes of the girl he worked on. As he cut off her clothes, the look of terror and mistrust that flashed made him feel her shame. Both girls survived, but Jake never got over that look.

During those eight months, he couldn't let his guard down. As he talked to Iraqi kids on the street or had dinner with other Marines in the homes of Iraqis, he would wonder whether they were the enemy. Once, he escaped a pair of mortars that exploded ahead of him as he was walking. He didn't have time to think of the horrors of war that he witnessed and literally touched. He and his fellow corpsmen dealt with a constant stream of wounded men and women that flowed into the clinic. Breaks from clinic duty meant patrolling the streets or standing watch in a guard tower. Sleep meant catnaps, a couple of hours at a time.

Throughout it all, he liked the work and formed powerful friendships with the other Marines. He got promoted to first assistant to the base's physician. But he missed his girlfriend—they'd been dating for four years—and he felt ready for college, to become a physician assistant. When his tour of duty was near an end, he got accepted at Hofstra University and returned to the States. He would live with his girlfriend in New York City. In June 2007, he loaded up the car to start his new life. It was a big deal, he thought, a country boy going to the big city.

The first panic attack hit while he was driving through the Baltimore Harbor Tunnel. Something was happening to him; he didn't know what, exactly, except that he felt overwhelmed with anxiety. His girlfriend was driving behind him, and he called her, saying, "I don't know if I can make it through the tunnel." He started to hyperventilate, the car slowed, and he reached the end of the tunnel and had barely pulled over when he passed out.

More attacks hit him over the following weeks—moments when he couldn't move, couldn't even breathe. His entire body would clench, convulsing, as tears streamed from his eyes. Between attacks, even in his sleep, the memories kept coming: the mortars, the suffering, the look in that Iraqi girl's eyes. He drank heavily, got into terrible moods, was always on edge. His life began to seem just too painful, and he even went so far as to buy himself a gun and hide it from his girlfriend. Three months after Jake and his girlfriend moved to New York, she walked in one night as he was loading the gun. She panicked and rushed him to the VA hospital's emergency room. There he told the doctor and his girlfriend about his suicidal thoughts. He talked about the memories and the nightmares, and the doctor diagnosed him with post traumatic stress disorder—a disease that affects roughly one in eight returning soldiers, according to the Army. Jake shrugged off the diagnosis at first, thinking he wasn't disabled. Then he talked to his two closest friends from his unit. They reported similar problems: panic attacks, moodiness, nightmares. The diagnosis began to make sense. So after mulling it over for a couple of months, he began therapy. His psychiatrist put him on five medications totaling 11 pills a day.

They seemed to help, but not that much. The symptoms continued. He switched to another therapist, then another, then another. Jake's disorder became his whole life. He and his girlfriend broke up. New York was too much for him, so he transferred to Southern Utah University, in the quiet mountain town of Cedar City, about two hours northeast of Las Vegas. One night, while reading about police dogs on the Internet, he learned about Puppies Behind Bars and applied for a service dog. And without ever really knowing why, he began referring to himself as Jacob.

It was a brooding Jacob who flew to Colorado last August to meet the puppies and their instructor. His face flushed when he spoke, and his eyes narrowed with suspicion. You could almost smell the anxiety. His teeth chattered as he walked toward the baggage claim in Denver International Airport. He had waited six months, but he still knew just how lucky he was: only 20 percent of veterans who apply get a service dog. He spotted the instructor from the distance. She was waiting with two black labs. He hung back, taking a few deep breaths before he could bring himself to approach. That's when Mya's eyes met his and she flopped onto her back for a belly rub.

They all drove to Loveland, Colorado, a mountain town about 45 minutes outside of Denver. The whole way there Mya sat on the floor between Jacob's legs. Jacob and three other veterans stayed in a hotel for two weeks as they trained with the dogs. The first four days were introductory. Each vet worked with a different dog each day, learning their commands, how to feed and groom them. Jacob tried not to play favorites, but he found that no matter which dog he was paired with, he kept slipping and calling it Mya. At night, the dogs would return to the instructors' home and the veterans would return to their rooms. At the end of day four, the instructors disappeared to decide who would get which dog. Jacob wanted Mya—he really, really wanted Mya. He went back to his room to wait and couldn't shut his mind off. He tried watching TV but couldn't concentrate. He thought about calling a friend, but knew he was too on edge even for that. His stomach was upset, and he felt like he might be on the verge of a panic attack, when there was a knock on the door. This is it, he thought. He opened the door, where an instructor stood, alone. She told him to follow her to the conference room, and the three other veterans joined in.

As soon as she opened the door Mya rushed over to Jacob, her tongue out, brown eyes lit up. As Jacob reached down to pet her, his eye caught a list posted on the wall: Mya was his. "Is there anything else we have to do today?" he asked, giddy. When they told him no, he took Mya back to the hotel room and wrestled with her on the floor for more than an hour, beaming the whole time. He called his parents: "It's a girl!" he told them. He hadn't been this happy in the two years since he'd been back from Iraq.

For the next week and a half, Mya and Jacob were immersed in dog training. Jacob discovered that he could take Mya into Whole Foods, and through a series of commands he could get her to pick up a can of creamed corn and put it in his basket (that's not a skill that his disorder demands, but it's something she was taught in case she had an owner with physical limitations). He could drop his Visa card at Home Depot and Mya would pick it up for him. He could usher her under his table at P.F. Chang's and she would rest quietly while he ate lunch.

It was hardest to adjust to all the attention. She was like an advertisement for the walking wounded, a bandage on his formerly invisible disorder. Since coming back to the United States, Jacob had learned to camouflage himself, sitting silently in class, walking unnoticed across campus. Mya was about to change all of that, and it made Jacob nervous.

The dogs and veterans learned all they could over two weeks, and then it was time to leave Colorado. Jacob and Mya graduated as a team, Mya wearing her new blue cape, adorned with an American flag patch that said "Puppies Behind Bars Service Dog" on the top and "Veteran" on the bottom. Then the two flew to Las Vegas and drove two hours to Cedar City, their home.

As much as Jacob had to learn about Mya, Mya had to learn about Jacob and the world without prison bars. She was used to her routine: getting up at 6:00, going to the yard, eating breakfast, following Laurie to work, playing in the yard, eating lunch, following Laurie back to work, recreation, eating dinner, getting groomed and massaged, and going to bed. She was used to working with women who knew her commands and had very defined roles and expectations. They led. She followed. Jacob's world wasn't nearly so structured.

Jacob had never had a dog before. Prior to meeting Mya, he had always assumed service dogs were like robots, creatures that could perfectly complete a series of simple commands, but possessed few other capabilities. They were high-functioning untouchables in a separate category from "real" dogs, he thought.

But Mya was never a robot. A bouncy ball of energy, she'd eye his muffin on the Starbucks table as longingly as any dog. When visitors came to the house she'd pant and jump up to greet them, spinning in rapid circles and running around the house. She'd whine while he was rock climbing, growing antsy as he grew more and more distant. She was still a dog. She just happened to be a dog that could open the refrigerator and bring him a soda, or retrieve his Blackberry and the TV remote control. She could also rescue him from the panic attacks that laid him flat.

A major panic attack knocked him off his feet just days after Mya joined Jacob and his roommate in the three-bedroom home they rent on the edge of the Dixie National Forest. It started with a feeling of doom. Jacob collapsed, fell into the fetal position, and his body locked, shaking uncontrollably, hyperventilating. Mya straddled him, climbed right on top of him and started licking his face. The panic attack went on for a couple of minutes, and she just stayed there, licking. Before Mya came along, Jacob would come out of his three- or four-times-a-week panic attacks wanting to die. The experience was so horrendous and so painful that he didn't think he could bear to go through it again. Since he'd moved to Utah he'd even begun rock climbing without equipment, daring death to come for him.

This time was different. Sweating and spent, Jacob just put his arms around Mya and held her close. Things didn't seem so bad anymore. He had something to live for.

He'd been haunted by nightmares since he got back from Iraq. They were the war images that were still in active combat in his brain—that Iraqi girl, that exploding bomb, all accompanied by night sweats, and the taste of fear.

Once Mya arrived, those changed, too. Rather than fears of the past, they turned into fears of the future: at first he had nightmares about someone stealing Mya. Gradually they became more gruesome—someone was cutting Mya up and handing him her limbs. He would awaken, drenched in sweat, screaming in terror, and Mya would be on top of him licking his face.

Even an act as simple as petting Mya had the power of setting his mind at ease. He found that with her along, he could handle being in crowded spaces, the kind of areas he'd spent two years avoiding. With Mya at his side things just got better. Immediately. She was a reminder that he was still actively living his life—he wasn't stuck in a state of flashback, or a world of paranoia, and he wasn't still fighting the war.

Those first few months he thought a lot about Laurie. He'd flip through Mya's scrapbook, reading every word this woman wrote about her. Sometimes he'd go online to the Puppies Behind Bars website and listen to the video clips of the inmates talking about the program. He didn't know which voice was hers, but he watched Mya, hoping her ears would perk up and give him a clue into the life of this stranger who has helped him in so many ways.

In the six months since Jacob brought Mya home, his psychiatrist lowered his drug dosages by a third. Jacob also committed to living a responsible life— no more high-risk behavior, no more rock climbing without proper equipment. If something happened to him, who would take care of Mya?

As fall semester of his senior year flew by, Jacob could see the end in sight. His days were filled with psychology classes, and his nights were filled with homework and grad school applications. All his time spent with therapists— he went through eight before finding one he clicked with—inspired Jacob to pursue his doctorate in psychology. But it's not just for him. The plan is that Mya will join him every step of the way as a therapy dog, when and if Jacob no longer needs her every day. If she can just help others a fraction of what she's done for him, then he feels as though the two of them, as a team, have done something right.

On a chilly afternoon in November, the two walked into the Pastry Pub in Cedar City, where he bought a sandwich for himself and a bottle of water for the dog. They'd just gotten out of statistics class, and Jacob wanted to give Mya a treat for being so good during such a boring class. Sandwich in hand, he drove fifteen minutes up a mountain in the Dixie National Forest to play. The snow was six, maybe eight inches deep at the top, and untouched. When Jacob stopped the truck, Mya leaped into the front seat, staring at the white powder with excitement. Jacob took off her blue cape. Mya knew that when the cape was untied, she was off-duty. This was Mya time. The door opened, and she squeezed out just as fast as the hinges let her. She bounded through the snow, picking up speed as she ran circles around trees, jumped over mounds of white, tucked her tail and reached full gallop.

"Hey c'mere!" Jacob's voice took on a special tone just for the cape-free Mya. The sound was high-pitched and playful, like a Muppet. "What're you doing?" he yelled in that falsetto. Mya was in hyper drive, zipping around him, acting like any playful puppy. "Snow dog! Snow dog!" Jacob's whole face was smiling, from the eyes to the lips, like a kid. As he scooped up a snowball, his clenched shoulders relaxed, his eyes stopped darting and followed her. The sound of Mya's panting filled the quiet, pine-scented mountain air as she sprinted through the snow, carrying a stick in her mouth that was nearly the length of her body. "Gimme that!" he said, pitch still high. "Good girl! Drop. Leave it. Ready?" He hurled it, those smiling green eyes following her and the tracks she left in the snow. "Get it. Bring it. Good girl! Good girl!" This, it seemed, was Jake.

Mya and Jacob have been apart only once since she arrived in Cedar City. It was a hot day in September, and between classes he'd taken her to swim in a creek near his house. He didn't calculate enough drying time, though, and felt bad taking a wet dog into class, so he dropped her off at his friend Jesse's house. Jacob couldn't focus for the entire class. He was irritable, shifty, kept staring at the clock. Mya was the same way. She stared out the window and cried the whole time he was gone. The two stuck together ever since. Every night, Mya slept in Jacob's bed (and insisted on using his pillow), she accompanied him to all of his classes, and she was at his side for every peppermint mocha he purchased at the city's only Starbucks.

Out in public he slowly grew to accept the attention that bothered him so much in the beginning. On days when he was feeling good, he'd even open up to people who asked and tell them what it was like to live with PTSD. People were not shy about asking personal questions or giving him The Look. The Look starts with a hint of surprise, as the passerby eyes Mya, and then scrutinizes Jacob, before returning to Mya. He knows what a woman in a bar must feel like.

One evening, he got The Look for the fifth time that day. Jacob was studying the menu at Starbucks while a young girl working behind the counter was studying him. Tall, brunette, and plain looking, her eyes scanned Mya, then moved to Jacob with a slow, skeptical up-and-down probe, then back to Mya.

"So are you training her?" She didn't sound so much curious as accusatory.

Jacob reached down and touched Mya, subconsciously, as if to glean some calmness or inner strength, and then fell into his lines. "No, she's already been trained. She's working for me now."

❦

How Mya Saved Jacob

Questions for discussion

1. What are your views about service animals for purposes other than vision? What do you think of the idea of prisoners training guide dogs?

2. What supports do you believe should be afforded to former soldiers who have become disabled as a result of their service?

3. This article was originally published as part of Southwest Airline's magazine, available to passengers in their seat pockets. What do you think the author of the article was trying to do by selecting this subject material, this particular subject, and this audience? How would you describe the tone of this article?

4. People with disabilities often get stared at or asked the same questions over and over. Is this avoidable, or is it desirable to avoid this behavior? How much should a person feel obligated to explain about his or her own personal condition?

5. Design your own discussion questions for this article.

For Further Reading

About PTSD

http://www.helpguide.org/mental/post_traumatic_stress_disorder_symptoms_treatment.htm

http://www.nimh.nih.gov/health/publications/post-traumatic-stress-disorder-ptsd/complete-index.shtml

About service animals

http://www.nh.gov/disability/information/community/serviceanimals.htm

About veterans with disabilities

http://www.ptsd.va.gov/

About Puppies Behind Bars

www.puppiesbehindbars.com

To see pictures of Jacob and Mya

www.spritmag.com/features/article/how_mya_saved_jacob/

from Thinking in Pictures

Autism/Asperger's and Careers

I am very concerned about careers for people with high-functioning autism or Asperger's syndrome. Since *Thinking in Pictures* was written, more and more really gifted students are being labeled as having Asperger's. I am worried that some of these students will have their careers hindered by the label. The students I am most concerned about are the very bright students who are not being challenged at school and who misbehave because they are bored. In some schools these students are kept out of gifted and talented classes due to the Asperger's label.

I was a miserable, bored student and I did not study until I was mentored by Mr. Carlock, my high school science teacher. Over the years I have observed that the high-functioning autistic individuals who became successful have had two important factors in their lives: *mentoring and the development of talents*. The students who failed to have a good career often had no mentors and no development of their talents. I ended up in a career where I could use my visual skills to design cattle-handling facilities.

I have observed that there are many successful undiagnosed people with Asperger's working in many jobs. One man is a plant engineer who keeps a gigantic multi-million-dollar meatpacking plant running. In another plant, I met a head maintenance man who was clearly an undiagnosed Asperger. The man who fixed my copier had Asperger traits. I have also been interviewed by several journalists who were on the spectrum. Some college professors are also Aspergers. The computer industry is filled with Asperger people. These are the happy people on the spectrum. One Asperger computer programmer told me that he was happy because he was with his own people.

Many of these successful people are my generation now in their forties and fifties. How were these people able to get and keep their jobs? All of us were raised in the '50s and '60s where it was standard to teach all children social skills. When I was a child, I was expected to sit through formal Sunday dinners and behave. Most of the time I did. Rudeness was not tolerated and I was taught to say *please* and *thank you.* Normal family activities provided structured opportunities to learn social skills. Sit-down meals and activities such as playing cards and board games like Chinese checkers taught turn-taking and patience.

Today many children lack this structure. Video games and time on the computer are spent solo. Many of my favorite childhood activities *required* participation with another child. I played with other children in board games, bike races, softball, and building tree houses. The other kids were fascinated with the kites and parachutes that I built.

Even the normal children today are growing up with more social problems. Later on they do not know how to behave at work. In the '90s, the *Wall Street Journal* started publishing more and more articles on how normal people should conduct themselves. The articles cover topics such as gossip, use of e-mail, and behavior at office parties. In the '70s and '80s these articles were rare, yet now there are one to three of them in most issues. In the '90s, MIT, the prestigious engineering school, started a course in social skills. Many engineering students have mild Asperger's. Social skills training is extremely important for people on the spectrum. I am not suggesting turning "Aspies" into social beings. People with autism and Asperger's are seldom interested in socializing for the sake of socializing. However, they need to have good manners and not be viewed as total slobs who wear the same dirty shirts for a week.

Portfolios to Show Your Work

When I started freelance design work, people thought I was weird. I had to sell my work, not my personality. People respected the accurate articles that I wrote for the *Arizona Farmer Ranchman* and they were impressed with my drawings and photos of completed cattle-handling facilities.

The successful people on the spectrum often get in the back door by showing a portfolio of their work to the right person. That often means avoiding the traditional front door with a job interview or the normal college admission process. One student circumvented the strict New York state testing requirements by sending a portfolio of her creative writing to an English professor. Her work was so good that he got her excused from the exams. I sold many jobs by sending portfolios of pictures and drawings to plant engineers. I contacted them after I read in a trade magazine that their plant was expanding.

Portfolios must be professionally and neatly presented. The person on the spectrum may need help choosing the best items to put in the portfolio. More information is in my careers book *Developing Talents.*

Getting in the Back Door

The computer field is full of people with Asperger's or Asperger's traits. Many of these individuals followed their parents into the field. When they were eight, their parents taught them computer programming. In other cases, the person started at an entry-level job and then worked his/her way up. This is how many of the Asperger's people who work in construction or in factories get good jobs. They start out as laborers and then they hang around the computers. The *Wall Street Journal* has many articles about people who started highly specialized niche businesses. Parents and teachers need to think creatively to find mentors and jobs. A mentor might be a retired electronics specialist who lives next door. Mentors are attracted to talent. Talents should be developed into skills that can turn into careers. Individuals on the spectrum need to learn that high standards are required to be successful but having perfect work is impossible. I remember almost quitting livestock equipment design when one of my early customers was not completely satisfied. My friend, Jim Uhl, a building contractor, explained to me that satisfying everybody is not an attainable goal. Explain to the individual that getting 90 to 95 percent of the answers right on a test is excellent, A-grade level work. In a job your work has to be at the 90 to 95 percent level. The concept of a percentage may be easier to understand with a bar graph or pie chart. The individual needs to understand that in some jobs 90 to 95 percent is an acceptable standard but in jobs such as computer programming the error rate has to be lower. However, absolute perfection is like absolute zero in physics: it is impossible to attain.

High school and college students must get work experience and learn basic skills like punctuality. They also must learn to do what the boss tells them and to be polite. Working for a seamstress helped teach me work skills when I was a teenager. When I was in college, I had summer volunteer jobs at a school for autistic children and at a research lab. The best work experiences use the individual's talent. A volunteer job in a career-related field may be better preparation for adult life than a paying job that is not career related.

Other Sources of Learning

High-functioning teenagers on the spectrum often get bullied in high school. I was kicked out of a large girls' high school after I threw a book at a girl who teased me. High school was the worst time in my life. Going away to a specialized boarding school where I could pursue interests such as horseback riding, roofing a barn, and electronics lab was the best thing that happened to me. It is a shame that some high schools no longer have classes in art, auto mechanics, woodworking, drafting, or welding. Some students need to be taken out of the social obstacle course of high school to attend a university, community college, or technical school. Online classes are another option. There are now some special high school programs for Asperger's that help develop strengths. Valerie Paradiz, a mother of a child with Asperger's, started one of the first programs—the Aspie School in New York. I really like their slogan, "reengaging students in learning." Their program emphasizes hands-on learning in areas such as movie making and graphic arts.

Exposing Children to Interesting Things

Students need to be exposed to many different interesting things in science, industry, and other fields so they learn that there is more to life than video games. Talents can be developed and nurtured when children have different experiences where they can use their special skills. Scientists have fabulous programs for visualizing organic chemistry molecules. At MIT, John Belcher developed a computer program that turns mathematical equations into beautiful abstract designs. Getting a student hooked on this could motivate a career in chemistry and physics. Other fascinating areas are distributed computing projects, statistics programs, and computer graphics. The journal *Science* has a section called "Net Watch." It provides descriptions and links to interesting science websites. Reviews of the best sites are in the magazine or on www.sciencemag.org/netwatch. Large bookstores have a full selection of computer programming books that can be used to educate and motivate students. Commercially available simulation software such as *Sim City* and *Spore* can stimulate an interest in science, biology, or design. Children have to use their intellect to play these video games. Parents should bring trade journals and publications about their profession or business into the school library for students to read. Every industry from construction to banking has its own journal. The *Wall Street Journal* is another good resource. Old medical and scientific journals, computer industry magazines, and general interest publications such as *National Geographic* and *Smithsonian* could also be given to the library. Parents could also direct teachers to the websites of their professional organizations and interesting sites related to their careers. Parents could show a PowerPoint presentation with lots of pictures of what they do at work to get students interested. Trips to fun places like construction sites, TV stations, control rooms, factories, zoos, farms, backstage at theaters, a graphic design studio, or architectural computer-aided drafting departments can help get students motivated.

When I was a child I spent lots of time outdoors watching ants and exploring the woods. Kids today miss out on these experiences. I loved collecting shells on the beach and finding different weird rocks for my rock collection that lived on a shelf in our toolshed. Another fun activity I shared with other children was stick racing in the brook. We would drop sticks off the bridge into the brook and run to the other side to see which one came out first. Richard Louv's book *Last Child in the Woods* has many practical suggestions on how to get kids engaged with nature. A strip of woods or a vacant overgrown field can be used to get kids interested in biology, insects, conservation, ecology, and many other careers. There is a big world out there of interesting things and kids need to be exposed to them.

Autism/Asperger Advocacy

Many individuals with high-functioning autism or Asperger's feel that autism is a normal part of human diversity. Roy, a high-functioning autistic, was quoted in *New Scientist*, "I feel stabbed when it comes to curing or treating autsim. It's like society does not need me." There are numerous interest groups run by people on the autism/Asperger spectrum and many of them are upset about attempts to eliminate autism. A little bit of the autism trait provides advantages but too much creates a low-functioning individual who cannot live independently. The paradox is that milder forms of autism and Asperger's are part of human diversity but severe autism is a great disability. There is no black-and-white dividing line between an eccentric brilliant scientist and Asperger's.

In an ideal world the scientist should find a method to prevent the most severe forms of autism but allow the milder forms to survive. After all, the really social people did not invent the first stone spear. It was probably invented by an Aspie who chipped away at rocks while the other people socialized around the campfire. Without autism traits we might still be living in caves.

❧

from Thinking in Pictures

Questions for discussion

1. Which parts of this material did you find the most interesting? Why?

2. The author says that people with high-functioning autism who become successful have two things in common: mentoring and development of talents. Do you agree with this analysis? Do you think it applies to all people, or particularly to those with disabilities? What mentors have you had, and how have you developed your talents with a career in mind?

3. The author states that all children used to be taught social skills, and that today such training is lacking. Do you agree? How do you think that things are different for children now than they were 50 years ago? Are the changes positive or negative?

4. The author states that high school was the worst time of her life and that many students with high-functioning autism are bullied. How can we teach tolerance among teens for people with disabilities, even for those with impaired social skills? The author also expresses worry that some very bright children are being labeled and then kept from challenging curricula. What could be done about this problem?

5. What did you think of the section about "Exposing Children to Interesting Things?" What would you add to the author's discussion of that topic?

6. Design your own discussion questions for this chapter.

For Further Reading

About Asperger's syndrome

http://www.ninds.nih.gov/disorders/asperger/detail_asperger.htm

About Temple Grandin

www.templegrandin.com

http://theenvelope.latimes.com/news/la-et-emmy-temple-20100830,0,376
0606.story. News story about the Emmy awards won for the movie depicting Temple Grandin's life.

About autism

http://abcnews.go.com/WN/software-company-hires-people-autism/story?id=
10260617. Article about a Danish software company that only hires people with autism.

Park, Clara Claiborne. *The Siege.* A mother's memoir recounting her young daughter's autism.

Tammet, Daniel. *Born on a Blue Day.* A man with autism's memoir, including a fantastic chapter about his fascination with the mathematical constant Pi.

Moon, Elizabeth. *The Speed of Dark.* A futuristic novel about a possible cure for autism and the narrator's dilemma: to cure or not to cure?

About children with disabilities in school

Palladino, Lucy Jo. *Dreamers, Discoverers, and Dynamos: How to Help the Child Who Is Bright, Bored, and Having Problems in School.*

Tim Lefens received his BFA from Virginia Commonwealth University and did graduate work at Rutgers University Mason Gross School of the Arts. His paintings have been exhibited frequently in New York City. He is the founder of A.R.T. (Artistic Realization Techniques) and lives in Belle Mead, New Jersey.

from Flying Colors

When you get to the top of the hill there are two ways to go: straight, which will take you into the woods, and left, which will take you to the hospital.

I had been told it was a school. The car slows to a crawl past the fancy wooden sign. It seemed like a nice enough thing, an abstract painter being invited to a school, but I, like you, am not anxious to go into a hospital, no matter what the reason.

The last acres of rising fields behind me now, the building appears; low, one-story, brick. It sits up on the top of this high hill: alone; quaint little towns and farmlands in the valley far below. A cardboard box under each arm, I wait outside the automatic glass doors of the main entrance. With a pneumatic exhale, the door rumbles open, and I step into the building. The receptionist is on the phone. When she gets off, she places a piece of paper and a blank ID badge on the counter, pushes them toward me.

"Fill these out," she says, then turns back to her work. Clipping the blank ID badge to my shirt, I hoist my slide projector and portable screen. Halfway down the main hall, fluorescent lights, gloss white cinderblock walls, shining linoleum floor, I have to step quickly to my right. Three doctors in white lab coats sweep past, behind them a child on a stretcher. The doctors, the child, and the man pushing the stretcher make a hard right turn and disappear.

The kid had not been on the stretcher the normal way. The stretcher had been rigged so it stood vertically, pushed ahead on a set of four wheels, the child lashed to the stretcher by a wide nylon belt that ran across his chest, up under his armpits, the little arms extending out and away from his body, fingers splayed, eyes glazed, tiny feet hanging above the rushing floor.

My stomach tightens. Further down the hall, two women stand together. A third, younger, sits in a wheelchair. As I move past them I hear their conversation.

281

"You're going to see a movie today." One of the standing women speaks singsong to the woman sitting in the wheelchair. "A movie. Yes, you are. Do you like movies?"

The young woman in the wheelchair stares vacantly at the floor.

"Anyway, like I was saying"—the standing woman turns to her co-worker—"I am definitely getting that place down the shore this year."

Well past the women, I am drawn for some reason to stop, to look back, and am startled to see the young woman in the wheelchair watching me. She smiles, her eyes warm with the pleasure that we, at least our eyes, have met. Turning away, I blink. One moment the young woman looks brain-dead, the next completely alive. A little light-headed, the experience becoming surreal, I order my legs to move.

At the end of the hall, a set of glass doors with a warning: EMERGENCY EXIT ONLY, ALARM WILL SOUND. SALIDA DE EMERGENCIA SOLA-MENTE. ALARMA FUNCIONARA. To the right of the fire-door alcove, a short unlit corridor. At the end of the corridor, an open door. I look back at the landscape outside the emergency exit, then turn to step into the dark.

...

"Are we about ready?" the doctor asks me, then moves to the center of the splattered floor. Beneath the fluorescent lights, his lab coat glows white. "Tim," he addresses the class, "is a professional artist. He has had some shows in New York City. He is here today to show us some of his work and to share his ideas with us."

What ideas? I ask myself. Getting free of the limitations of the physical world? That was the point of my paintings. I'm supposed to share this zeal for freedom with them as they sit strapped in their wheelchairs? The urge to get back outdoors is overwhelming, if not for my exit at least to clear my head. I glance at the redheaded boy. Livid with anger, he glares down at his Plexiglass laptray. Feeling my eyes on him, he glares up out me, glares out the window, then back down at his tray.

The doctor pulls the door shut. The room goes black. My mind hovers.

Plip, plip, plip, droplets fall from the tap into the water in the sink. I hear the wrenching sobs of a child out in the main hall, muffled by the closed door.

"Tim?" the doctor asks.

I feel for the projector's on-off switch.... In the light that escapes the ventilation grate on the back of the projector, I see the intense face of the boy. The incandescent light plays off the stainless steel wires that hold up the man's head. The young woman appears in silhouette, backlit by the dim light of the gray sky outside the recessed window. No sound now other than the water droplets and hum of the projector's fan.

"Tim?"

I reach out to press the button; the first of my paintings drops into view. It is tall, and quite narrow. A randomly slathered coating of cream-colored acrylic gel, three inches thick, had been laid down first, then in the bottom left corner the outline of a square, crudely brushed in wide strokes of metallic rust and crimson. Rising up off the square is the furtive outline of a rectangle painted in four wispy thin strokes. It claims the greater space above the square, it is looser, freer. The awkward square, held down by gravity; the tracery of the thin rectangle, above it, dancing in the wind.

I glance down at the red-haired boy. How intensely he is looking at the image. I mean, he is really staring at it.

Stripped down, his life is raw, his energy: keen ...

I reach for the projector. The second painting drops into view. As the rest are shown I manage to say a little something about how each was made. When the last one has been up for a few minutes, I say, "That's it."

A switch clicks, a buzzing sound, the fluorescent lights turn pale blue, then fill the room with white light. I know the doctor is speaking, but I do not take in his words. I look at the woman. Her head sways gently from side to side, her eyes holding mine.

"... Thank Tim for coming up today," the doctor is saying, "and maybe he will come up and see us again. What do you say, Tim?"

I look at the floor, then up at the man with the wired head. When our eyes meet, he nods, an inch, the metallic spokes of his wire crown drawn downward with this slight movement of his head. I look at the fierce little redheaded boy. I look at the three. They look at me.

"See you," I say.

...

Home, I rest my forehead on the kitchen table. For some time, I think of nothing. Then I see the man with the wired head. Not so much his body, but his eyes, that look he gave me when I first saw him. Clear, with a steely light, not at all sad or weak as you might expect. He had a second or less to connect with me before I looked away. He gave this second everything he had; his gray eyes open to me as he hoped I would be to him. This stays in my mind.

Making a drink, I sit back down at the kitchen table. I wonder what it is like for him not to be able to talk with anyone. As I sit here, he sits up there, on top of that hill, in that building, silent, motionless, looking straight ahead, at whatever wall they parked him toward....

I think of the young woman. She was flirting with me. She was not the zombie I saw in the hall. And the angry little red-haired kid. Fierce and determined as a wolf I had once seen, in a dog's pen. The next few nights, I lie awake.

There is something worse than their bodies not working. It is difficult to imagine anything harder than the restrictions they endure. But there is something worse—if they, as it appeared to me, are as alive as you or me and they are being treated like idiots ...

Trapped first by their bodies, then again by the people around them. One massive barrier wall stacked on top of another. Quite a height to overleap. The isolation must be crushing. Yet there is that light in their eyes. How had they kept their spirits alive? What would they tell us if they had the power?

In the morning after a cup of black coffee and some walking around, I call the school.

"Matheny School and Hospital. How may I help you?" ...

"I was up there, at the school ..."

The receptionist speaks with someone. I can tell when she puts her ear back to the phone.

"Who do you want to speak to?"

"The head of the art program."

"Do you have a name?" she asks.

"Do you have a list there or something?"

"Who runs our art program?" she asks her friend.

"I didn't know we had an art program," her friend says ...

She finally connects me to the woman who runs the art program. "Suzanne."

"Hi. I was up a week ago, showed slides of my paintings in Ron's class. I was wondering if there was any way I could come back to the school."

"To help with the class?"

"No," I say. "To start a new one."

A couple of weeks after I got the green light from Suzanne to start up a new class, I went up for employee orientation day....

The students' bedrooms line either side of the long halls. All the doors are kept open; I saw the rooms were small. Some have two, some three, hospital-style beds; the bedroom walls, like the halls, cinderblock painted gloss white. There was none of the stuff kids tape up, no posters, stickers, pennants ...

All the halls have sources of natural light. Many open onto a courtyard. I opened a door to one of the courtyards. It required pressure be placed on a spring-loaded aluminum bar, installed too high for a student to reach. The door would not stay open. When I let it go, it returned quietly, the latch making a clack, then a thunk. The only way I saw for students to get outdoors on their own was to go down past the main desk and out the automatic glass doors. This would bring them to the edge of the parking lot. Yet the school owns eighty acres of land on top of the hill; some of it woods, some fields. I think about the high quality of the clinical care the students get. Then I think about the bedrooms devoid of privacy and the doors to the outside that will not open.

When I called the school about the possibility of running a class, it had been a tentative inquiry. I did not think they would say yes. When they did, and a date was set for the class to start, I had no idea of any technique that would allow the students to paint. Very few could hold a brush. Others I met at the orientation day might be able to hold one, but could not control the movement of their arms. The technique I finally came up with would not give the students the ability to do realistic work, but could be used by them to make decisive abstract painting.

It is hard to anticipate what will happen tomorrow with the first class. I am not sure how many students will be there or if those who are will want to be there. Without any teaching experience, I have no clear idea how to run a class. My plan will be to offer them the technique. The rest will be up to them.

…

"Well, I see you've met the gang," Suzanne smiles my way.

"Not really," I tell her.

"Well then," she nods to Chet, "this is Chester Cheesman." The wild teen shoots up, waits until I nod back before slamming back down.

"This is James Lane."

"Hey, James Lane," I smile in return of his sneer.

"This is Eric Corbin." Suzanne nods to the older student with the down-turned mouth. Eric's eyes are closed, his head resting on his right shoulder.

"And this is Tammy Heppner," she says.

"Tammy and I have met," I say.

"I'll be right back," Suzanne informs us.

With her disappearance, I sit on one of the five-gallon pails, breathe in, look at each of the students, then stand up.

"Let's get started," I say. "I have a way you guys can paint, a way you can make a real painting. Let's look at the materials. This is canvas. This"—I pry the lid off one of the five-gallon pails—"is acrylic gel. It is what they make artists' paint from. It comes clear. You add your own color to it. It is thick, so you can create textured paintings. Put it on thin, water it down, it comes out clear, like a sheet of glass, shiny, see-through. You with me?" I ask.

In fact, they are. My martial tone of voice has them on alert. "Today," I say, "we have only two colors, black and white." I pry the lid off the black, scoop out a handful, hold it out for them to see, invert my hand to demonstrate its viscosity. James snorts. I smile at him before he regains his sour puss.

"Okay." I whip the gleaming gel back into the pail, wipe my hand on my jeans. Chet whoops, James snorts, Tammy laughs. It is a move I make unconsciously; for me it is nothing. For them it is wild. Bohemia meets the institution.

To regain the seriousness of the presentation, I give them a hard look, to ask, "What's so funny?" But it's not that easy to keep from smiling at the intense kick they got out of it.

"Here is how it works," I say. "Your canvas goes on the floor. It gets coated with black, over the whole thing. A thick coat of white goes over that, over the whole thing. Then we lay down a sheet of clear plastic. We tape it down. Then," I pause for effect, staring at each of the students in turn, "You drive right onto it."

from Flying Colors

Questions for discussion

1. The author worries that his students are trapped first by their bodies, then by the people around them. What examples of both types of situations have you seen? What might a disability rights advocate say about using the term "trapped" to describe someone's body?

2. What features of the institution did the author notice? What supports might have allowed the individuals with disabilities to live in the community?

3. As the book *Flying Colors* progresses, the students become better and better at producing art, and eventually their art is exhibited at an elite gallery. The author is dismayed to learn that the staff at the institution refuse to guarantee transportation for the students to attend their own art show. After a lot of advocacy, he gets the staff to change their minds. How can the attitudes of staff affect the lives of residents? What examples of this have you seen in the media or in literature? What examples have you seen of advocacy that helps change outdated ideas?

4. The author found a project that he was personally passionate about, and helped build and expand it. Is there such a project that you would enjoy? What obstacles might interfere with your project's success?

5. Design your own discussion questions for this story.

For Further Reading

About Tim Lefens's work and about his organization
www.timlefens.com

www.artrealization.org

About institutionalization vs. community living

Shapiro, Joseph. *No Pity,* chapter 10: "Crossing the Luck Line." The author's autobiographical account of befriending someone with developmental disabilities who lives in an institution, and the advocacy efforts required to get his friend moved to a community setting.

Lakin, Charlie. Charlie Lakin has produced a body of work about successful community living for people with intellectual disabilities. He is with the University of Minnesota's Institute on Community Integration, and his work can be accessed on their website: http://ici.umn.edu/index.php?staff/view/ybgjekxj7.

Jeff Stimpson (1962–) is a native of Bangor, Maine, and lives in New York with his wife Jill and their two sons. He is the author of *Alex: The Fathering of a Preemie* and *Alex the Boy: Episodes from a Family's Life with Autism*. He maintains a blog about his family at jeffslife.tripod.com/alextheboy and is a frequent contributor to various sites on special-needs parenting, such as *Autisable* and *TheFasterTimes*.

The Looks

I got my first sense of how people reach for labels when Alex was born: 27 weeks gestation, 21 ounces, living in the plastic box of an isolette in a gigantic hospital, wires stuck on his every limb and across his chest that was slightly smaller than a deck of cards. I learned the word "preemie." Soon after, I learned that society often likes to glue the word "miracle" to the word "preemie." To people who said such things I gave the Shocked But Hanging In There New Parent look.

Alex spent his whole first year in the hospital, wearing more wires than hang in the average hardware aisle in Duane Reade. I remember one afternoon, visiting him and playing a pinball game in the patients' lounge. I love pinball, and have probably dropped three months' mortgage in quarters down those slots. This game in the lounge was free, however, and I remember thinking that I hoped Alex would work his way down the road of miracles to the point where he'd go somewhere where the games of pinball didn't have to be given away.

And he has. He's played skee-ball in arcades with his younger brother Ned, my other son. Ned, who is typically developing, stood at the foot of the game and rolled the ball up the ramp and into the little holes under the metal grill, earning his points. Alex picked up a ball, ran up the ramp, and tried to place the ball under the screen and directly into one of the little holes. Makes perfect sense! People marveled. I gave them the That's Not the Way My Son Should Play Skee-Ball And We Both Know It look.

Last weekend, Alex kept trying to scoot through an open door in the basement of our neighborhood supermarket. The store wasn't crowded and hardly anyone noticed me hauling him back to the checkout line except a young lady working the register. I saw her looking at Alex with the small smile and direct eyes that I've learned mean: *she knows someone with autism.* She stroked his head once. I appreciated the gesture; she might have stroked his head out of understanding the kind of life Alex is likely to have. Funny, though, how I wish she'd maybe felt comfortable yelling at him for trying to go into the basement, comfortable because he was normal and he shouldn't be trying to run in the basement of a grocery store. I gave her the Tired Slightly Angry Parent look. That is rapidly becoming my favorite look because so many parents of the typically developing wear it half the time.

People—at least the people I'd like to have around Alex—seem to need to think there's something beyond vulnerability to those with autism. Something special or beneficial to society, or at least likable and warm, like the message of movies like *Rain Man,* lessons tied up in what Richard Yates disdainfully called "a neat little dramatic package." Yeah, there's autism. But they can count cards, too!

Some of them can count cards. Some can paint. Some with autism can do all sorts of things, just like some of all of us can, and of course the verdict is still a long way off when it comes to Alex's real abilities. I want people to stroke his head someday because he helped them, because he contributed in a way that brought him fulfillment at the end of his working day. And I just want to live to see him get that. I call that my Hopeful Outlook.

The Looks

Questions for discussion

1. What do you think this author is saying about responding to others' reactions to disability? What such reactions have you had or experienced?

2. Do you agree with the author's statement that some people need to think there is something "special or beneficial" about autism or other disabilities? If so, why do you think this is the case?

3. What does this author want for his son? Do you think parents of children with disabilities want the same things for them as do parents of "typically-developing" children, or do you think there is a difference in expectations and goals?

4. Design your own discussion questions for this piece.

For Further Reading

About staring

Hathaway, Katharine Butler. *The Little Locksmith.* Autobiography about a woman with a disability (perhaps polio) who, in the early 1900s, meets a man, the local locksmith, who also has a bent back. As she stares at him, she develops both a sense of kinship and a fear of him.

Thomson-Garland, Rosemarie. "Staring at the Other."

About prematurity

http://www.cdc.gov/Features/PrematureBirth/

Sears, William. *The Premature Baby Book: Everything You Need to Know About Your Premature Baby from Birth to Age One.*

About children with autism

Park, Clara Claiborne. *The Siege.* A mother's memoir recounting her young daughter's autism.

About parenting a special needs child

Meyer, Donald J., ed. *Uncommon Fathers.* A collection of essays by fathers of special needs children.

Soper, Kathryn Lynard, ed. *Gifts: Mothers Reflect on How Children with Down Syndrome Enrich Their Lives.* Jennifer Graf Groneberg's story is one of many in this anthology.

Rachel Simon (1959–) is the critically acclaimed author of six books, the best known of which is the memoir *Riding The Bus With My Sister* (2002). She was born in New Jersey and has a degree in anthropology from Bryn Mawr College. She has taught creative writing, and currently writes full time. She lives in Wilmington, Delaware.

It Takes a Village to Help a Sister

Last Wednesday, two weeks before my sister Beth's fiftieth birthday, my phone rang. I saw her name on the caller ID and was baffled. It was only nine thirty in the morning, and she rarely takes her lunch break so early. I snatched up the phone, expecting her usual, sing-songy "Hi, Sis. Thiz Chatty Beth."

Instead she said, "My side hurts." Her voice had a gasping, panicky tone, as if she was holding back tears.

I sat up at my desk, on full alert. This is the opening to a call you do not want to get from someone you love, and especially not someone who needs a little more help to get through life. My sister Beth has an intellectual disability, and although she's confident and self-reliant, has a boyfriend and an apartment of her own, and has carved out a very social life riding buses all day, every day, I know I need to help when she needs me.

I've always known that. She's eleven months younger than I am. On her birthday we'll be twins for the next month.

I kept my voice calm. "Does it hurt a lot?" I said.

"A *lot*. And I've been throwing up all morning."

"That doesn't sound good."

"My aide's coming to take me to the doctor." She pushed the words out through what were obviously volleys of pain. "At ten."

"Do you want me to come to you?" Beth lives a couple of hours away, even if I broke speed limits all the way there.

"You don't have to. She's taking me."

"Maybe you should go to the hospital."

"I'm going to the doctor!"

"Will you call me as soon as she sees you?"

"Yeah."

"Do you want to stay on the phone until your aide gets there?"

"She's gonna call so we can't."

"Then tell her to call me, okay?"

"Yeah," she said, and she hung up.

I sat there, my heart pounding. I have no medical training, but these sounded like serious symptoms. I wanted to do right by her, but she didn't tell me to come. My friends with kids have told me about calls like these, when their daughter or son phones in the midst of a crisis, not knowing what was happening, wanting to connect but not wanting their parents' help, and maybe living too far away for help to come galloping immediately there anyway. My friends have told me about the fear, the feelings of powerlessness, the time-stopping descent into hell of not knowing how bad this might be.

Having a sibling with a disability is not like having a child. For one thing, Beth has always been there; unlike parents, I knew no Before.

For another, everywhere you look, a substantial number of the adults you'll see are parents, so, as singular as your problems with your child might be, you can take comfort in knowing that you're far from alone. But special siblings, far less common, might know few, if any, others like themselves, so the sense of aloneness, of having to figure it out on your own, of having no one except a handful of other siblings who truly understand, can be profound.

There are many other distinctions between having a child and being a sibling to someone like Beth, but the one I have the opportunity to notice most often is that sometimes Beth wants to me to do the things a parent might do, like pay for her meals when we go out, attend meetings with her aides, answer questions she's too embarrassed to ask anyone else. But other times she wants me to be only a sofa-sharing companion while watching DVDs, a supermarket chauffeur who lets her buttons get pushed, an engaged listener to endless bus-related gossip, a tireless back scratcher who expects to get teased for eating soy yogurt, agrees to watch *Shark's Tale* for the thirtieth time, notices that each toenail is painted a different color, and knows not to step on the purple rug—i.e., she wants me to be a sister.

Being the sibling of a person with special needs means being a shape-shifter. Which is why, when she didn't ask me to come meet her at the doctor's, I didn't just don my parent cape, jump in my car, and fly up to see her. I stayed dressed as an ordinary sister and waited by the phone at home.

Years ago, I struggled with just about every aspect of our relationship. Then I rode the buses with her, and came to terms with many things about her, about myself, about the unique nature of the special sibling relationship. I recounted my experiences in a book, *Riding The Bus With My Sister*, which became a movie. But my story with Beth has, of course, continued after the last page and the final credits. That's the real difference between being a sibling of someone like Beth and being a parent. The lifelong worry of After.

When I was a kid, After meant after our parents passed away. I knew, as did my brother and other sister, that we were expected to step in and be there for Beth after they were gone. As a child, I just accepted this as a fact of my life, but by my college years I'd come to dread it. How would I know what to do? What if we weren't getting along, as was the case then? Why wasn't I free to live my own life without this responsibility?

Then Beth entered the world of adult services, and we were lucky enough to find an agency that treated her well. They got her an apartment when she didn't like the group home. They gave her good training in independent life skills. They hired aides who often stayed with Beth for years. With their support, I no longer had the worries I'd had about After. I could choose to be there After, but it wasn't a requirement.

I chose to be there.

And then I started to realize there was another kind of After.

What happens After one of us begins to lose the vigor and health we've both enjoyed through our half century together? I hate to say this, but I've always hoped she would lose it first, so I could—if she wanted—accompany her to doctor appointments and keep her company if she grew weak. Yet she's always seemed so robust, so unstoppable; even with a cold, even in a blizzard, nothing will keep her off the buses. What will it be like to watch the decline of the willful, energetic, Croc-addicted, Winnie-the-Pooh-adoring, always-in-my-life force of nature known as Chatty Beth? (She was Cool Beth for a long time, but switched to Chatty Beth when a new, favorite bus driver was amused by her talkative ways.)

I haven't wanted to think about it. Not only can't I imagine her not being there, always eager for a visit, a call, a letter, and money to buy her ice-cream. But I've known siblings who've lost their Beths, and have told me that the absence and grief is made all the harder by people who just don't get it. One friend told me that, soon after her sister's funeral, people said to her, "You must be so relieved." She wasn't relieved at all; without her sister, she felt forlorn, and given that kind of reaction, she felt abandoned.

It's ironic. Being a sibling of a person with a disability means always feeling connected to someone else. Yet because of the way our society thinks of that someone else, it also means feeling far apart from others.

Fortunately, because of my book, there are hundreds of thousands of people who do think about Beth. Many of them are also siblings, or parents, of people with disabilities. Or they have disabilities themselves. And they know her life is worth as much as any other life, and would never dream of saying, "You must be so relieved."

Yet there I sat, after she'd hung up, feeling all alone. I wasn't at her side as she hurried to the doctor. I wasn't speeding down the highway to meet her at the hospital.

Only later did I learn that I wasn't alone at all. When the day had begun, and she'd insisted on getting on the bus despite the pain in her side, her bus drivers took stock of the situation. When she began to throw up, they urged her to go home, call her aide, see the doctor. When her aide came, they rushed to the doctor. When the doctor saw her, she sent them to the emergency room. When Beth called her boyfriend from the hospital, he rode his bike right there.

I learned most of this a few hours later, when another one of Beth's aides began calling me with updates. Over and over she called, as every little piece of news developed. That's when I found out that Beth had many people who'd been ready to help out. That's when I found out that, after an early suspicion of diverticulitis and the discovery of an excess of white blood cells, and then a CAT scan, an IV, and morphine for her pain, her aide and her boyfriend stayed by her side. She wasn't alone.

And, because of the kindness of her friends on the buses, and the professionalism of the people who work at her agency, and the devotion of her boyfriend, neither was I. I might have been sitting alone at home, holding my breath. But I was one of many who encircled her, waiting for the answer, hoping for the best.

Finally, at seven o'clock, she called. This time there was excitement in her voice. They were releasing her, she said, and she couldn't wait to get home. Her aide got on the line and explained that Beth had had a kidney stone, which she'd passed while she was in the hospital. She was also found to have a slight case of pneumonia. Oh no, I thought, imagining her blasting onto the buses the next morning. But then I learned that, when Beth called a bus driver to tell her, she was told she simply had to stay home the next day and fill the prescription the hospital gave her and take it easy and that was that. And so, Beth told me, she would.

I went to see Beth a few days later. She seemed a little lower in energy than she often does, though I'm not sure if that was because of the pneumonia. In fact, one of her drivers said to me, while I was there, that maybe it was a misdiagnosis, because, after her one day off, Beth had gotten back on the buses and ridden with her usual gusto. The downshift I saw in her energy was probably more related to her having fallen over an uneven sidewalk when she went out to get the prescription filled. She'd hit her forehead and gashed her knee, which still hurt. I felt a surge of worry, then learned that she'd applied Neosporin and bandages.

"How did you know to do that?" I asked.

"A driver told me."

So as of today, it seems we've pulled through. There will be other times ahead, I know that. And maybe the next one will hit me instead of her. But right now, when I think about the Afters that will come, I know she won't be alone—so I won't be, either. Some people just get it. They might not be siblings, or even parents. But whoever they are, they know what matters. They know not to step on the purple rug. They know not to ignore the many-colored toenails. They know not to toss around words like "relieved."

It Takes a Village to Help a Sister

Questions for discussion

1. What do you think is different in sibling dynamics when one sibling has a disability? Why do you think this? What other books or articles have you read on this topic, and how was the subject addressed?

2. The author talks about worrying about After. What do you think of this idea? How can you relate it to other worries someone might have about the future?

3. In many states, there is inadequate funding for supports like the author's sister has. How might it change this situation if Beth had no funding for an agency or an aide to support her?

4. The author mentions feeling consoled by the other people who have cared for her sister. Have you ever had to entrust a loved one's care to others? Have you provided care for someone whose loved ones are far away? Can community ever be a substitute for family? Why or why not?

5. The author has written a book, *Riding the Bus with My Sister*. In that book, the author describes her sister Beth's love of riding buses. While the author, her family, and Beth's service providers would rather she try to work at least part-time, Beth does not want to. The author then discusses "self-determination," the idea that people with disabilities should make their own decisions. What do you think of this concept? If someone decides to ride buses full-time, is that a decision that should be accepted or resisted? If you had a sibling that made that choice, how do you think you'd react? Would it matter whether the sibling had a disability or not?

6. The author decided to ride the buses with her sister for a year, working it into her schedule whenever she could, and thereby learned a great deal about her sister and her world. Have you ever spent time doing something for someone else's sake? What did you learn? Do you think you would have been willing to ride the buses?

7. Design your own discussion questions for this piece.

For Further Reading

About siblings with disabilities

Hurst, James. "The Scarlet Ibis." Short story about a pair of brothers, one with a disability.

Byars, Betsy. *Summer of the Swans.* A young-adult novel about a girl whose beloved brother becomes lost, and her search to find him.

http://www.thearc.org/page.aspx?pid=2661ity. (information from The Arc, a national disability advocacy agency, for siblings of those with developmental disabilities.)

Cris Matthews is a disability rights activist. She has muscular dystrophy and was an MDA poster child in 1961. She has been active in ADAPT[1] actions and, with her brother, started a group in Chicago called AccessAbility Associates. The following selection comes from *The Ragged Edge: The Disability Experience from the Pages of the First Fifteen Years of The Disability Rag* edited by Barrett Shaw.

Giving It Back

Two years ago Gail Linn—my best friend through most of grade school—died. Yet I found out only a week ago—accidentally. Taking a nostalgia drive through the old neighborhood, I noticed the wheelchair ramp that had taken up most of her parents' yard was gone. I was unprepared for the news that my old friend was gone too.

We were diametric opposites, she and I. She was blonde; I have dark hair. She was shy at school, not popular; I was outgoing and had lots of friends. My parents were divorced; her family even included a live-in grandmother! She excelled at everything academic, including perfect penmanship. I was smart but struggled with math; my writing was a more "distinct" scrawl. She was 5 months older than me. Throughout grade school we were best friends.

Freshman year of high school meant different homerooms, different classes and even different bus routes (yes, in those days we were bused to "special" schools). Most of the friends we'd made in grade school still hung out with me; Gail Linn could be with my crowd at recess after lunch. By then I was a hippie. Gail Linn was still Gail Linn.

When I transferred to yet another gimp school, my ties to my former friend ended in the blur of adolescence and the unrelenting roll into adulthood. Through grapevines and assumptions I knew our lives had taken quite different paths. I had been on an adventure with thousands of experiences in my

---

1. According to its website, "ADAPT is a national grass-roots community that organizes disability rights activists to engage in nonviolent direct action, including civil disobedience, to assure the civil and human rights of people with disabilities to live in freedom."

catalog and twice as many lessons learned. I struck out on my own and sometimes paid dearly for it, but ended up richly rewarded. I'd traveled a bit, been involved in disability civil rights confrontations in the streets of our city and was now managing to live on my own.

Gail Linn's academic brilliance brought her an offer of a full scholarship, including room, board and attendant service at a Big Ten University, at a time when gimps like us just didn't go to college. She turned it down though, because she couldn't bear to leave home. There she stayed until she died.

When I returned to my hometown after having been away for several years, I'd once made an effort to call her, curious to see if the woman who had always had the best of everything was still on top.

We chatted, and I learned her grandmother had died, her brother moved away and sister had married—and that Donna's husband really liked Gail Linn. Poor Donna, I thought: even marriage hadn't given her an escape from her demanding older sister. Gail Linn told me that she and Donna would go to an occasional Barry Manilow concert or this or that. I saw Gail Linn was still insulated from my harsh realities.

I didn't tell her how hard it was for me to find someone to get me up in the morning. I glossed over the last broken heart I'd had; I didn't mention how I was afraid of getting old. I told her, instead, about my job. I told her I was learning to drive, and that I was now volunteering at the same summer camp that 18 years ago she'd gone home from after two days.

I realized I still knew her. I remembered the look of uncomfortable disagreement she'd wear when you knew she just didn't get it. She'd kind of shrink into herself when something seemed too much for her, in all her academic brilliance, to think about. She'd smile weakly, divert her eyes. "Oh, uh-huh," she'd say.

There wasn't much to say after that conversation. We'd hit a wall, reached an impasse even nostalgia couldn't penetrate, leaving me searching for what it had been that had held us together so long ago.

She called only once after that; I don't remember what it was we talked about. When I moved to my own place, I entertained the idea of inviting her and her parents over for dinner, to show them what people with disabilities could accomplish in these modern times. But I knew my purpose was only to gloat, so the invitation was never extended.

When I met my beloved Dave, the thought of calling Gail Linn occurred to me. But then I recalled a tearful conversation we'd once because a neighbor boy hadn't liked her. She'd been crazy about him and he knew it. He'd told me privately once that he didn't like Gail Linn much, but that he'd come over because her mother had always been nice to his widowed mom. He'd proceeded to point out to me the things I'd thought only I noticed. He'd mocked, while I'd sat numbly, divided inside between loyalty to my defenseless friend and relief that I wasn't alone in my view of her. Through all the nights Gail Linn had weepingly prayed for Joey's conversion, I writhed in guilt, knowing the truth.

I couldn't tell her about Dave. I was afraid I'd be gloating—over finally having the one thing Gail Linn didn't.

When Gail Linn's mother told me about her daughter's death, she revealed a few things that underscored for the final time the differences that had helped us drift apart.

Gail Linn was involved in her church's young adult club. On overnight trips, her brother would go along and handle her care, because he could still lift her. The family knew nothing of attendant services—or even lifting devices that would help other women to lift her.

Her mother told me that Gail Linn, when she went down the block, would take along a cordless phone to call home in case she got in trouble. At the end of her block is an accessible bus route; Gail Linn probably never knew it existed. She would not go on her own any farther than the cordless phone would work. A beautiful city, a calm neighborhood and an accessible bus route at her door—she turned them all down. A free ticket to higher education, summer camp and access to all kinds of interesting other adventures. She couldn't cope.

I took comparatively wrong roads; traded common sense for intrigue so often it became habit. I opted for the gravel road instead of the yellow brick one. I spent so much time on self-loathing that I nearly became a burnout who could only identify friends by which barstool they sat on. My physical health and mental attitude were so poor that I almost lost my life. Much of my experience has been a voluntary boxing match. But the victory has come in a life richer than I could have predicted. Still, Gail Linn's death has made me examine my life as I've never done before.

I feel rage when I think of her life, and its lurking, stereotypic "happy cripple" motif, used as a standard for the rest of us. In school Gail Linn was demure and quiet. She followed instructions, did what she was told and never deviated from the path others presented to her. So pleased were they with her gentility! They always asked me why I couldn't "be like Gail Linn."

They didn't see the after-school side of Gail Linn. They didn't see that the instant she was lugged up the stairs to the main floor of her family home, Gail Linn became the queen of all she surveyed, using her disability to lord it over her siblings. Donna came third even though she was the middle child (Jack, her brother, was the youngest, but his gender granted him household priorities.). Once home, Gail Linn became loud, bossy and spoiled. The transformation was practically unbelievable.

Is the rage I feel resentment? It would have been so much easier for me had I never gone away to school, never gotten a job; if I'd never done anything more than was offered me within the two-block radius of my mother's home. The stresses of recruiting and managing attendants, paying bills or even figuring out what to eat each day could have been traded for a comfortable, predictable life with my mother. Maybe I resent Gail Linn for taking the cushy route.

Could my rage be frustration? Frustration at knowing that Gail Linn had been in a unique position for someone with a disability at that time in society—that her brain could have opened countless doors for her? Frustration knowing that she might have written her own ticket, and still ended up with a cushy life—that she had earned herself? Frustration thinking that, had she done that, she could have given something back?

She had a chance to bust a stereotype. Instead, she accepted it. That she had a life of relative ease is not what so enrages me; it's the way she accomplished it.

A major roadblock to our community ever gaining power is that we're handed things. Gail Linn's family handed her a life; Social Security handed her a check. Gail Linn handed back the cute, acquiescent gimp routine that telethons are so fond of promoting. Thus she got her needs met.

Are we better for living this kind of life? Did she make a difference in anything in the time she spent on earth?

I can't begin to judge the worth of a person's life, particularly when I so often question my own. And who can actually fault someone for the harmless, innocent choices they make as they move across the continuum? But why have we made it so easy for gimps to do nothing? And why do we as a community allow so many of us to do so damn little?

My mother says there can be only one Albert Schweitzer. But each of us has the chance to make some little impact on our world. It doesn't mean that every person with a disability has to have a job or be involved in politics. It simply means that individually we should find something to get interested in that reaches beyond our dwellings, more than two blocks away. Instead of allowing others to keep us content by feeding us, providing us shelter and care, let us find a way to return something.

This seems particularly important for those of us who don't work, whose hours aren't taken up in work and work-related activities. There's endless opportunity to find ways to give back. Volunteers are needed everywhere. In a volunteer situation it's often easy to see the results of your efforts. If transportation is a problem, find out what you can do where you are. Go to the library and help another person learn to read. Get out the phone book and pick out a few organizations that look interesting and call to see if you can do something from your home. Take a class. Get a pen pal. Do something. Turn off the television and do something.

There is nothing wrong with accepting benefits the government has designed for us. Such benefits help many of us stay out of institutions. But to spend our days and nights doing nothing with our lives is pure selfishness. Those of us who do are simply taking advantage of the still-popular opinion that people with disabilities needn't worry about anything; that someone will take care of it all and we don't have to lift a finger to do anything about it— that we can simply take our checks, meet our immediate needs and vegetate.

Employed gimps are not above reproach. There's plenty of time to do nothing after hours. Even if we accept that the stress of preparing for, traveling to and from work and being on the job are compounded by the presence of a disability, most of us can find an occasional hour or two to do something for someone else.

Organizers complain that there are never enough people to do all that needs to be done. They then pile so much work on themselves that they end up getting nothing done. Maybe we should turn our attention to those who benefit from the sweat of activism and find out why there is so much inactivity among us. Perhaps we should be thinking of ways that make surrender to the happy cripple role less attractive. It might take coming out of our high-and-mighty leadership modes and really listening to those in our community like Gail Linn whom we write off because they don't fit our expectations.

Involvement of any kind makes a statement that's unmistakably clear. It says that our lives are not defined by entitlements, public assistance programs or others' definitions of who we should be. When we immobilize ourselves we're affirming what Jerry Lewis has claimed is gospel—that we have nothing in our lives worth mentioning. That our lives as people with disabilities are devoid of productivity or goals; that nothing should be expected of us.

When we get outside ourselves, though, even for an instant, we not only enrich ourselves as individuals and as a community, but we strengthen a world which is in desperate need of help.

Look at ADAPT. Whether one agrees with their tactics or not, the fact is that they are able to mobilize more of us than any other organization has ever been able to. This is largely due to the fact that they reach out to those of us who have been considered by others with and without disabilities as valueless and shown us our worth.

Not everyone can be a leader. But ADAPT leadership understood a long time ago that leadership is meaningless without folks who are willing to fight the battles. And by having the sense to include all kinds of us with disabilities, they have built a power base that made even Bill Clinton take notice. Every person at an ADAPT action is made to feel his or her own worth. They know that their efforts as individuals count, that their being at an action makes a difference. And they all share in the victory.

All ADAPT members reach outside themselves whenever they confront the issues ADAPT takes on. No non-disabled person who ever encounters an ADAPT action will ever look at people with disabilities in the same way again. Even if they disagree with ADAPT's tactics, they'll be changed—ADAPT has underscored for them in a big way what many of us preach: that individuals with disabilities are not all willing to be "Jerry's Kids." ADAPT makes people who have disabilities think about themselves again, and think about where they fit in the world. Even if they don't agree with what ADAPT does, or how it does it, they at least have been forced to think about why they disagree. For once they're not numbly accepting someone else's dictates.

ADAPT folks have done more with their lives than suck up resources. Along with others, they laid the groundwork for what would become the Americans with Disabilities Act. So did many people with disabilities who grew up before the days of access. Instead of staying home, they got out and rolled down driveways and into streets, because there were no curb cuts. They went to college; they did things that none of us could begin to know about, things that began to change the face of disability and make it possible for activism to start. Most didn't sit in front of government offices or block buses, but they did something.

So can each of us. Gail Linn may not have ever joined ADAPT, but had I taken the time to understand her, maybe we could have hit a common chord that might have encouraged her to use that marvelous brain of hers for some good cause. Maybe not; but it would have been more difficult for her to ignore the world around her had some of us activists planted the seeds.

It boils down to who controls our lives. We might think we do; but every time Jerry Lewis snivels his way across America, he takes away our control. Every time one of us decides it's easier to just take what we can take, Jerry Lewis wins. If we let people like him win, then we have no business complaining when we can't get jobs, or the services we need, or even access to the local grocery store.

It isn't up to me to decide what Gail Linn's life amounted to. But as long as I can, I will continue fighting anyone who sees our lives as pitiable—including those of us with disabilities who hold that view. I will do my best to help battle the forces that keep people like Gail Linn from doing just one little thing for someone or something outside themselves. And I will never ever again entertain the thought that I could possibly have been happy on the same road that Gail Linn chose.

A popular country song speaks to the choices we make. He could have made different, less complicated, easier choices in life, the singer croons; but he would have missed a lot in the process: "I could have lived without the pain, but I'd have had to miss the dance."

Some of us are dancers. We fly across the floor in our wheelchairs, turning them, moving them, spinning them around to the music around us. Sometimes there are patterns, sometimes it's freeform. Onlookers may not consider this dancing, but it is to us. It is celebration. This is why we dance.

Some make it to the dance, but then wait for someone to lead them through the steps. Few realize that it's OK to invent the steps. They often leave without fully enjoying all the dance has to offer. If someone had encouraged them from the floor, they might have danced a little, once in a while.

Others simply don't come to the dance at all, because they can't imagine how such a thing is possible. Since they can't conceive of the dance, it doesn't exist for them. They live and die without making any difference—to anyone or anything. They sat back and took all the favors, all the handouts, all good deeds done for them, without ever trying it for themselves. Whether they lived or not seemed to make no difference.

Had that song been popular when I was a kid, I might have told those so anxious for my conformity why I couldn't be like Gail Linn. "'Cause I gotta dance," I would have said. "And Gail Linn won't learn how." They couldn't have understood. But 25 years later, I am so glad I didn't change. What a stunningly beautiful dance I would have missed!

Gail Linn's mother summed up her daughter's life: "Well, at least all her sufferings are over." I didn't ask, but I kind of figured that she wasn't talking about the short illness at the end. My life has to be more than a testament to suffering. Existence on this earth must, in some small way, be better for my time here. Gail Linn convinced me of this. Maybe that is the meaning I've been searching her life for.

Giving It Back

Questions for discussion

1. Why was the author so frustrated with Gail Linn?

2. What do you think of the author's comments about the "happy cripple" stereotype? Why do some people feel comfortable living within society's ex-

pectations while other people feel compelled to push the boundaries? Which way are you? What regrets or successes have you had based on your outlook?

3. What does the author say about making one's own way in the world? How could you apply this advice to other situations?

4. Should all people be expected to contribute to their communities? What if someone (disabled or not) prefers to stay home and do very little?

5. What does the author say about leadership in the disability community?

6. Design your own discussion questions for this piece.

For Further Reading

About self-determination

Simon, Rachel. *Riding the Bus with My Sister*. A woman wonders about her sister's decision to ride buses all day long.

Lahiri, Jhumpa. "The Treatment of Bibi Haldar." A young woman from India fights against stereotypes.

About contributing to society

Fox, Michael J. *Always Looking Up*. The author discusses his diagnosis of Parkinson's disease and his establishment of a charitable foundation.

Hockenberry, John. *Moving Violations*. The author recounts his various contributions to society through his career in journalism.

Johnson, Harriet McBryde. *Too Late to Die Young*. A civil rights attorney tells stories of her life of advocacy.

Walker, Cami. *29 Gifts*. A memoir about MS and establishing a foundation that seeks to bless the world.

About ADAPT

www.adapt.org

Georgina Kleege (1956–   ) was born in New York City. Her collection of personal essays, *Sight Unseen* (1999) is a classic in the field of disability studies. She has also written *Blind Rage: Letters to Helen Keller* (2006). Her current work is concerned with blindness and visual art: how blindness is represented in art, how blindness affects the lives of visual artists, and how museums can make visual art accessible to people who are blind and visually impaired. She has lectured and served as a consultant to art institutions around the world including the Metropolitan Museum of Art in New York and the Tate Modern in London. Kleege joined the English department at the University of California, Berkeley in 2003 where, in addition to teaching creative writing classes, she teaches popular courses on representations of disability in literature and disability memoir.

Disabled Students Come Out: Questions without Answers

Once, in an undergraduate fiction-writing workshop, a student wrote a story about a Deaf woman. The woman was married to a hearing man and had two hearing children. In the central scene, the couple was discussing having a third child, and the woman announced that she hoped the child would be Deaf. A distinctive feature of the story was the way the author handled the characters' dialogue. The characters were using American Sign Language, and the author had, in effect, transcribed their conversation without translating it. She was trying to capture the flavor of ASL while making the language comprehensible to an English-speaking reader.

The story generated a lot of discussion. It turned out there was another student in the class who knew ASL because her mother was deaf. The story's author had learned ASL in high school so she could interpret at assemblies and theatrical events. Together they introduced the class to basic elements of the language and did an impromptu performance of some of the story's dialogue as a demonstration. As we discussed this dialogue, I reminded the class of discussions we had previously about how such authors as William Faulkner and D. H. Lawrence rendered dialect. Was this the same or different?

A student said that he found the story convincing because he'd heard on a segment of "Sixty Minutes" that all Deaf people want to have Deaf children so they can all speak the same language. The generalization made me uneasy, so I asked, "Can we say all Deaf people?" This question sparked some discussion about deafness, the physical condition, versus Deafness, the linguistic and cultural minority.

I was pleased that the class wanted to talk about these issues but felt compelled to guide the discussion back to the student's story. This was a fiction-writing workshop after all, not a class in disability studies. I kept asking questions about elements of fiction we'd discussed all term. We talked about the sequence of scenes (Did that flashback work?), about narration (Could she have written the story in the first person?), about characterization (Was there a need for more background information and, if so, how much and where?).

As the discussion was beginning to wane, a student, who had been uncharacteristically quiet so far, began a sentence with the phrase "Speaking as a disabled person" and raised the question of whether a hearing person could or should write from the perspective of a Deaf person. We'd talked about similar issues before: Could a male author write from a female point of view? Could an African American represent an Asian American's experience? Was this the same situation or different?

Naturally class ended before we could answer all the questions we'd raised. Still, I felt the story's author had received some useful feedback. I left the classroom making a mental list of additional points I wished to bring up at our next meeting. Distracted by these thoughts, I was a little surprised when the student with the disability followed me back to my office. He seemed agitated, a little out of breath. Before we even sat down, he said, "That's the first time I ever did that."

"Did what?" I asked, because I genuinely did not know.

"You know," he said. "The first time I ever said it in front of people like that. The first time I ever called myself disabled."

Many people might have been startled by his statement. His disability was readily apparent to everyone in the class. Everyone but me, that is, because I am legally blind. Still, I knew he was disabled. He rocked from side to side when he walked, and he dragged one foot. I could not tell if he used a cane or wore leg braces and would not hazard to put a name to his condition. Even if I had been unaware of these traits, however, I knew he was disabled because we'd talked about it. He'd explained to me that sometimes he used a wheelchair, in museums or the grocery store, but generally he did not. He'd also referred to operations he'd undergone and mentioned that he'd been a poster child and appeared on a telethon. On these occasions we'd also talked about my disability: When did my condition develop? How did I handle all the reading I had to do? And we talked about the differences between having a visible disability like his and an invisible one like mine, which is apparent only when I use a white cane or read Braille.

These conversations were always comfortable—matter-of-fact exchanges of information. Furthermore, I knew he'd talked about his disability with other instructors. So why was it such a big deal for him to identify himself as disabled on this occasion? The question I asked was "Why haven't you ever said it before?"

"I don't know," he said. "I guess I didn't want to be one of those whiny wheelies."

His reluctance reminded me of the reluctance of some women to identify themselves as feminists even though they have beliefs and expectations that could be defined as feminist, for fear they would seem strident and unfeminine. Was he worried that calling himself disabled would make him appear abrasive and militant? In fact, he had a chip on his shoulder and could be rather edgy, argumentative, defensive. He was also smart, quick-witted, prone to make ironic asides. These were all traits that conform to a stereotypical disabled personality—the cranky cripple rather than the cheerfully stoic kind. These facets of his personality may well have evolved as ways to counter playground taunts or to repel patronizing pity. But he might have turned out this way because he'd grown up without a father or for some other reason I didn't know.

In any case, he did not seem like someone who worried about offending people. Before I could ask another question, he said, "You should have seen the way they looked when I said it."

I almost cautioned him against being oversensitive, but I stopped myself. I had noticed a pause after he spoke, but since I can't make eye contact or read people's expressions, I had no idea what sort of nonverbal communication might have occurred. Still, I told him that I didn't think his classmates' response to his word came from hostility or prejudice. Rather, they had been brought up not to stare at people with disabilities, not to call them names, not to ask rude questions. For him to bring it up forced them to violate all those parental admonitions, to look at his disabled body and give it a name.

Of course they should have been used to this simply because they had a professor with a disability. From the first day of class my presence challenged many of their assumptions. In my class, they were obliged to break the cardinal rule of classroom decorum and speak without raising their hands, since I cannot see this gesture. Also, since I read tape-recorded versions of their written work, they were obliged to think about how their writing would sound out loud. Eventually they'd got used to what's different about my classes; they even learned to tease me about it. When I asked, "Who's not here today?," someone was bound to say, "Please raise your hand if you're absent."

Although my students had a greater awareness of disability issues than the general nondisabled public, when the student with the disability "came out" in my class, it was still startling, subversive, perhaps even revolutionary. For many, a disabled person is a unique individual with a specific physical, perceptual, or cognitive problem marked by a distinct set of characteristics or behaviors. Thus, a person with a mobility impairment seems to have little in common with someone who is visually impaired. The student in my class was not merely identifying an obvious physical fact about himself. He was claiming identity with the Deaf woman in the story; with me, his blind professor; and with numerous other people who had various deficits, impairments, and anomalies. He was saying, "I speak for all these."

Did he have the right to do this? Is there really such a thing as a disabled perspective? Did this student and I share common beliefs and values that transcended all other identity categories? I admit these questions make me uneasy. Every female is not a feminist. Similarly, every disabled person is not a disability rights activist or an expert in disability studies. I write and think about disability issues, but I write and think about a lot of other things too. Of all the adjectives I can use to describe myself, disabled is only one of many and not always the first I mention. When I encounter such phrases as "blind lust" or "lame response" in a student's writing, I will probably mark it as a cliche. When I encounter a disabled character in a work of literature, I may analyze the cultural attitudes connected to that representation. A nondisabled instructor could do the same. Do my students find it more memorable when I do it, because they perceive me as speaking from personal experience? Did this student feel comfortable coming out in my class because I have a disability, or would he have done it anywhere? Did the student who wrote the story about the Deaf woman feel I would be more receptive to it than a nondisabled teacher?

I don't have all the answers. I do resent any inference that the mere fact of my disability augments my teaching qualifications or that there is a pedagogical value in exposing my disability to nondisabled students. This practice smacks too much of the freak show and casts me in the role of goodwill ambassador sharing the quaint beliefs and customs of my alien world.

While I resist displaying myself as an exotic species, I am also a reluctant role model for students with disabilities. I'm unconvinced that the ways I deal with my disability are worthy of emulation. Furthermore, I am not always as sensitive and sympathetic as I could be. I have a chip on my shoulder too. Like many disabled people who went through school before IDEA (Individuals with Disabilities Education Act) and ADA (Americans with Disabilities Act), I must quell the urge to say, "You kids today have it so easy." While they may enjoy the advantages of legally mandated access and new assistive technologies, the world continues to be far from perfect.

Still, my disabled students and I have much in common. We do not, for instance, take for granted that the university environment and practices were designed with us in mind. This can make us cranky, but it can also make us resilient and adaptable. These are qualities we need, since legally mandated access does not eliminate all barriers. The student who came out in my class had told me on a previous occasion that another professor once asked him, "What's wrong with you?"

"I didn't know what he meant at first," he said. "I thought maybe my nose was bleeding or something."

"What did you tell him?" I asked.

"I told him what he wanted to know," he said. "I should have told him it was none of his business. I mean, if I was blind or deaf, I would have had to explain things to him. What's 'wrong' with me makes no difference to how I read or write or talk."

I asked him if he wanted me to do something, to speak to the professor or take some other action. He said he did not. Perhaps he sensed that my anger with my colleague would have made me an ineffective advocate. Instead, we talked about what we found wrong with the question, articulating a response for the next time it was asked. What was wrong with the question was not the way it violated contemporary codes of political correctness, not to mention older codes of common courtesy. What was wrong with the question was the way it assumed that we people with disabilities perceive ourselves to be defective, deficient, substandard, that we long for the abilities we lack, experiencing eye envy, leg envy, ear envy. A better though more challenging answer to the question would be to say, "There is nothing wrong with being disabled." Disability is a fact of life for some of us. It demands our attention and effort in certain situations. If we long for anything, it is better assistive technologies, better architecture, better attitudes among the nondisabled.

When this student came out in my class, it was unclear how the event would affect his future life. Had he now appointed himself official spokesperson for disability issues? Would his spin on things be the same as mine? We disagreed about many things. I told him that a lot of Deaf people reject the disability label, preferring to be identified as a linguistic or cultural minority. Then we argued about identity politics. I said, "I don't think it's a question of whether a nondisabled person has the right to write about a disabled person.

It's a matter of whether or not the writing seems genuine and doesn't conform to stereotypes."

"I hate the way they always want us to be inspirational," he said.

I wanted to caution him against divisive generalizations and thought of asking, "Can we really say always?" But in this instance I found myself on his side of the divide, so I said, "I hate it, too."

Sometimes, the consequences of coming out as disabled are more practical than philosophical. In a sophomore-level literature class, a student stayed after the first session to ask a question. From the way she let other students go before her, I sensed that she wanted to speak to me privately. When everyone else was gone, she pointed to a line in my syllabus and said, "It says here that this is available in large print."

I noticed that she was making a statement, not a request. I also noticed that she made no mention of herself, as if she were asking for a friend who wasn't there. I gave her the large-print syllabus and explained that I could produce all the course materials—handouts, quizzes, exams—in this or other formats.

I had already explained to the class about my disability. Now I told her that to the extent that I can read print at all, it must be very large. I showed her some pages of notes I had and some other materials, naming the different font sizes. She seemed a little overwhelmed by the range of options. Although we were still not talking about her or her disability, I finally asked, "Which one would you prefer?"

"Whatever's easiest," she blurted, as if it required extra effort to produce a text in 18- rather than 14-point type. I surmised she was new at this, perhaps newly disabled. She was uncertain how to ask for what she needed, uncertain how much was permitted. But the ice was broken now, and she volunteered that she was in her forties, a returning student. She'd dropped out of college when she was twenty to get married and raise her children, and now she was back. Then finally, she told me that she was deaf in one ear and blind in one eye, which was why she was asking about the large print. She could read standard print, but it was a slow and difficult process. So for my course she'd bought the textbooks as soon as they showed up in the campus bookstore and had been reading ahead during the term break.

I asked her if she'd ever been to the university's Office of Disability Services. Perhaps they could offer some additional assistance.

"But I'm not disabled," she said.

I guessed it was the word disabled that made her balk. Yes, she had "something wrong" with her, but she was not disabled. She was normal, a normal person with a problem.

Though "deaf in one ear and blind in one eye" sounded like a disability to me, I wasn't going to argue with her. Instead, I gave her some basic information about what an office of disability services does. I said it was a resource, a place to ask questions, to try out technologies and techniques. I also said that it could be helpful to make contact with other students with disabilities, who might offer additional advice, even if they had different disabilities. I have learned a lot about reading audio books from a dyslexic and about crossing streets from a paraplegic. I sensed the phrase "other students with disabilities" was presumptuous on my part. It forced her to picture herself as part of a group she'd always perceived as alien—people in wheelchairs, people with garbled speech, people with missing limbs. So I hastened to add that many people with disabilities develop their own adaptive strategies without others' advice, such as buying the textbook early in order to give themselves extra reading time.

"Or like sitting in the front row," she said. "And I always sit on this side, so I can use my good ear to hear."

I was pleased that I hadn't offended her, but I sent her to Disability Services with some trepidation. At their worst, such offices exist merely to protect the institution from lawsuits. In other cases they may offer only those accommodations experts deem appropriate for a particular disability without fully assessing the student's individual needs. A student who fails to benefit from the prescribed accommodation or asks for something else can be labeled a malingerer or troublemaker. I didn't tell her all this, however. She was an adult and could decide for herself. I didn't want to poison her with my paranoia. My own bad experiences with the Evil Custodial Oppressor might scare her away from possibly valuable services.

Two weeks later she was back, breathless with gratitude. "Disability Services was so helpful," she told me. They had calibrated and certified her impairments and offered all sorts of visual and audio aids. She was going to try a hearing aid, magnification devices, audio books. I offered to share the taped versions of my texts and gave her a few tips about aural reading.

"It's such a relief," she told me. "I've been this way all my life, but I never really talked about it before." Because she had always thought of herself as an individual with a unique problem, it was a revelation to discover not only that there were other people with similar conditions but also that there were others who had thought up ways of dealing with them. She was learning to shift her attention from what was wrong with her to what was wrong with the educational environment that barred her access to it. I was glad for her, glad that coming out was a positive experience, glad that her transition from "normal person with something wrong" to "person with a disability" was going smoothly.

But by the end of the term she was angry. There was trouble with Disability Services. They refused to order recorded books for the next term until all the other students had turned in their requests. I gave her a phone number and told her she could order the books on her own, warning that if she did this, she might be viewed as subversive.

She took this advice without comment. Was she developing a chip on her shoulder? She was still angry, about something else. "When I dropped out of college, I thought there was something wrong with me," she said. "If I'd known all this before, I never would have dropped out of school. Why did I have to wait so long for this help? Why did everybody think it was better to say I was 'not college material' than to say I was disabled?"

I had no answer to this question. I offered some personal history, telling her that though I was diagnosed as legally blind when I was eleven, I didn't really talk about it until I was well into adulthood and first started teaching. We talked about the nature of an invisible disability, about stoicism, about the temptations and risks of passing. I did not presume to advise her about dealing with her past, but I wanted her to know that my own disabled identity has evolved over many years and continues to evolve.

I was reminded that I had only one disabled professor during my entire college career, though he did not identify himself as such. His disability affected his use of one arm, and, as far as I could tell, he was able to write, type, and carry things with the other, so he did not need to speak about his disability to his classes as I do. He was not the sort of person who invited personal disclosures, and though I must have had a conversation with him about my disability, I cannot imagine the possibility of any discussion of our shared experiences as disabled people. I had "something wrong" with my eyes, he had "something wrong" with his arm; we had nothing in common. For me to claim otherwise would have been as shocking to him as it was unthinkable to me.

The world has changed a lot since then, and the change manifests itself in university classrooms. As more and more students with disabilities pursue higher education, disability becomes a central topic for scholars not only in the social sciences, medicine, and law but also in history, literature, even creative writing. Social evolution seldom follows a smoothly linear path. It can create discomfort and discord. It can raise more questions than it answers. And while I have few answers, I believe that as long as disability remains a taboo topic, progress is impossible. When disabled students come out, they assert that there is nothing wrong with being disabled. We have a right to a place in the classroom, as students and teachers. As we come out, we demonstrate that there is more than one way to move through space, to access a text, to process information, to communicate—more than one way to be a human being.

"It's better now than it used to be," I told my student. "Now at least there are more of us around."

"Us" was presumptuous, pushing her to the other side of the us/them divide. But I sensed she was moving in that direction anyway.

Then she said, "I guess sooner or later they'll have to get used to us."

Disabled Students Come Out: Questions without Answers

Questions for discussion

1. Why do you think the student in the story decided to "come out"? Why do you think he had not "come out" before?

2. What might be the pros and cons of asking for accommodations versus hiding a disability?

3. What stories have you heard from students who have asked for various accommodations from either professors or disability services' offices?

4. The author's class had a discussion about whether a hearing person could or should write from the perspective of a deaf person. What do you think about this issue? Also, what about the issue that is raised by this piece about whether a disabled person can speak for people with all kinds of disabilities, not just their own particular kind of disability?

5. What did you think of the student's other professor asking him "what's wrong with you?"

6. What did you think of the female student who was visually and hearing impaired saying that she wasn't disabled? What did you think of her interactions with Disability Services?

7. What did you think of the author's views of herself as a mentor?

8. Design your own discussion questions for this piece.

For Further Reading

About disabilities in higher education

Ben-Moshe, Liat, ed. *Building Pedagogical Curb Cuts: Incorporating Disability in the University Classroom and Curriculum.*

About disability labeling
Shapiro, Joseph. *No Pity*, ch. 1, "Tiny Tims and Supercrips."
Linton, Simi. *Claiming Disability.*

from 29 Gifts: How a Month of Giving Can Change Your Life

It is 4 a.m. and I am wide awake—again. I have not slept in sixty-three hours. Visions of myself crippled, unable to move my arms and legs, flash like red fire-exit signs in my mind. Thoughts spin uncontrollably, running in the same tired circles as I work myself into a full-fledged panic attack. Here I go again.

I'm going to end up in a wheelchair. I'll never be able to walk normally again. I'll never find a way to earn a living again. I'll never be able to write again. My friends and family will abandon me. My husband will get tired of taking care of me and leave me locked up alone in a nursing home before I'm 40, where I'll be ignored day after day and die before I'm 45 from infected bed sores.

I'll never get to be a mother.

Why have I been cursed with this horrible disease? Why can't the doctors cure multiple sclerosis ... or at least give me some drugs that actually help? My life sucks. My life is over.

I want to die.

I try to lie quietly, not wanting to wake up Mark, my exhausted husband, who snores loudly beside me.

....

My diagnosis of MS came just one month after my wedding day. Three neurologists in white coats took turns looking into my right eye and commenting on the degradation they could see on my optic nerve. They took me through a few standard neurological tests. Tap your index finger and thumb together. Walk heel to toe. Touch your nose with your index finger. One of the top neurologists at the UCSF Medical Center confirmed the diagnosis for me by showing me pictures of my brain from the MRI scans they took.

"You see this hook-shaped white lesion here?" he asked, pointing to his computer screen. "That's a classic MS lesion. Judging from your history of symptoms, I'd estimate you've had MS for more than a decade."

"A decade!" exclaimed Mark, stunned. "Shouldn't someone have caught this sooner?"

"I don't think she's ever had enough symptoms present at one time to lead to an accurate diagnosis," replied the doctor. So there really wasn't anyone to blame, but that didn't stop me from being angry at all the doctors I saw over the years who told me I was suffering from nothing more than stress.

Now I sit here on the phone with [my friend] Mbali. It is the night before my psych ward stay to detox [off some painkillers], and she listens intently and lets me cry for a while. Then, in her British lilt, she attempts to pull me out of my self-pity.

"Cami, I think you need to stop thinking about yourself."

For a few seconds, I'm shocked silent. I imagine Mbali on the other end of the phone, sitting near her unique altar, her silver hair and bronze skin reflecting in the soft light of her apartment. She's probably wearing one of the beautiful, colorful necklaces she makes and smiling at my stunned reaction.

"Thinking about myself?" I howl. I start in on her about what a wreck I am, what a wreck my body is, telling her I don't have room to think about anything except myself right now.

"I know, that's the problem," she says. "If you spend all of your time and energy focusing on your pain, you're feeding the disease. You're making it worse by putting all of your attention there."

I absorb this information quietly.

"Cami," she says, her voice soft and soothing but her words hitting me hard, "you are falling deeper and deeper into a black hole. I'm going to give you a tool to help you dig yourself out."

"What should I do?" I ask.

"I have a prescription for you. I want you to give away 29 gifts in 29 days."

I blink and consider this for a moment before deciding it is stupid. For one thing, I'm going into the hospital for eight days—how can I give anything away there?

"There will be others at the hospital with you," Mbali counters. "You can give to them. These gifts don't have to be material things."

I continue to insist that I need to focus all my energy on my own healing, while Mbali calmly points out what I'm forgetting: "Healing doesn't happen in a vacuum, Cami, but through our interactions with other people. By giving, you are focusing on what you have to offer others, inviting more abundance into your life. Giving of any kind is taking a positive action that begins the process of change. It will shift your energy for life."

I'm starting to tune out, wallowing in thoughts of what I am about to endure. *I'm in pain and I can't freaking walk! Are you telling me that giving away spare change or doing someone a favor will make me better? Come on!*

Mbali tells me about the effects the "challenge" or giving 29 gifts had on her when she first did it. It makes sense in a way, but I'm not really taking it in. She's saying how giving can make you humble, keep your heart open, revitalize you, that kind of thing.

In addition to giving the gifts, you're supposed to keep a journal for those 29 days. If you skip a day for some reason, she's saying it's best to start over, to release the energy that is building and allow it to begin building again.

Now, I've been into alternative medicine and spirituality for a long time, but even I have no patience for all this. And I'm in the midst of a medical crisis. Without any intention of following through, I grab my journal and write a note: "Give away 29 gifts in 29 days." I close the journal and politely say goodnight to Mbali.

....

After less than a week of giving, despite my early skepticism, there's no denying that something intangible has relaxed inside me. Last time I spoke with Mbali I tried to explain this to her, but she already understood. "It's weird. It's like I'm being supported everywhere I look," I told her. "And the more I give little things, the easier it's become for me to accept assistance and love from others. Instead of being tied up in knots all the time." Mbali had seen this effect many times and wasn't surprised.

"You did something very brave by finally making a choice to answer the call to give your gifts, Cami," she said. "It is a profound moment in all of our lives when we can let go of control and surrender to something bigger."

When I hung up I felt proud to know her. And after giving only four gifts, I have even begun to feel a little proud of myself, something I haven't felt in a very long time.

Today is Easter Sunday. Habib is meowing to be fed, so I follow her to the kitchen. As I pour the kibble into her bowl, I start to think of all the people who could benefit from the giving challenge, as I have. A seed of an idea takes hold, and I start to play around with it.

What if everyone started giving one small thing each day? How different would our world look?

I scratch Habib behind the ears. Her brother, Abu, a large black cat who is less than graceful, rambles in and begs for equal treatment. So I pet him until he loses interest and begins to lap up water from his yellow ceramic bowl.

What would happen if thousands ... or even millions of people committed to give away 29 gifts in 29 days?

The spring equinox just passed. It's the time of rebirth and renewal. Crocuses are bursting through thawing snow in other parts of the country, and women are breaking out their white shoes and floral prints. It's the perfect time to start imagining what a movement like this could do on a grand scale.

....

Today marks my 365th consecutive day of giving. I am in the midst of my thirteenth 29-day giving cycle. My life looks completely different today than it did one year ago.

I wish I could say that giving 29 Gifts cured my multiple sclerosis, but that would be dishonest. I still live with the effects of this disease, but the difference is that I cope a lot better. I now get through most days with only two prescription pills. I still inject myself daily with a drug that slows the progression of my MS, and it seems to be working, according to my doctors. In fact, my latest MRI scan shows there has been no new disease progression in the past year. Chronic pain is still a part of my life, and I sometimes take over-the-counter pain medication. Other than that, I take a few vitamin supplements and herbs to help support my immune system, and I try my best to eat well.

Though physical pain is still a constant in my life, it doesn't control me anymore. I'm able to work a little bit each day—usually about two hours. I am productive again and really enjoy the work I do.

Most days, I can walk on my own. I have had a few rough patches in the past year that required me to get a new cane. Once in a while—if I get overtired or push myself too much—I need the cane or an arm to hold on to when I walk. I no longer see this as a sign of weakness, but rather view my determination to continue walking as a source of strength. The distance I'm able to walk differs each day. Sometimes it is up and down my hallway at home. Other times, I'm able to go outside and walk anywhere between six and twelve blocks. When I'm not feeling my best, I still use the trick of walking laps around my block so I can stay close to home.

My relationships with my husband, family, and friends are more intimate and fulfilling. Mark and I get along better than ever. We still aren't parents but are again considering adopting a child. Mark and I are also discussing the possibility of becoming foster parents to provide shelter and stability to children who need it during times of family crisis.

In the meantime, we've added a dog to our family, an adorable little 5-pound Chihuahua named Charlie that we rescued from a bad living situation. Nursing Charlie back to health and rehabilitating him from a scared, shaky little dog into a confident, loving, sociable pooch has been rewarding for us. Charlie rarely leaves my side and I think of him as my baby.

Sadly, I recently lost my big, black cat Abu, who had been with me for fourteen years, since he was a tiny kitten. Habib is still healthy, but I miss Abu every day. Eventually we may get another kitten or a little dog to keep Charlie company.

My relationship with money has also changed dramatically. Though we still owe my father a large sum, we continue to make our payments to him each month. But I no longer worry about whether we have enough money. I've come to view money as an endless resource that exists in the world, and I trust that God will provide us with the funds to meet our needs.

Today I have a large community of friends in L.A. and I continue to stay close to my extended community of friends in San Francisco and the Midwest through regular phone calls and interaction online.

One of the biggest differences I see in my life today is that people tell me they love me several times a day and I tell them I love them, too. One year ago, I was in too much pain to allow love to be part of the picture.

I still cry sometimes when I have a hard day, but more often, I find myself tearing up because I'm overwhelmed with gratitude or moved by an amazing story from one of the givers on the 29 Gifts website.

Today, I'm part of a large group of people committed to the vision of a worldwide goodwill movement. Our collective mission is to create a grassroots revival of the giving spirit in the world. As of this writing, nearly 5,000 people in 38 countries have committed themselves to the 29-Day Giving Challenge by signing up on our website at www.29Gifts.org. More than 8,000 stories and 2,000 pieces of art have been posted.

Together as a community we have done some powerful work, proving that we can do together what we cannot do alone. We helped one of our fellow young 29Givers, Elysia Skye—who was recovering from breast cancer—raise more than $10,000 in only thirty days to help pay for a much-needed surgery. Hundreds of hungry South African children living in poverty have been fed through our support of Operation Teddy Bear Care, an organization that evolved out of one blog post from a fellow 29Giver named Maureen Forbes. Most recently we helped Mbali raise nearly $5,000 to fund a humanitarian trip to South Africa with Vukani Mawethu, the choir she sings with, an award-winning, nonprofit multiracial choir that sings the freedom songs of South Africa and also gospel, spirituals, and civil rights songs linking people in the

United States, South Africa, and around the world. During their South African tour, Mbali and the choir raised money for many worthy causes in her homeland and they had the distinctive honor of giving a private concert for Nelson Mandela.

I've found the new voice I yearned for during my first divination with Mbali, and I write almost every day now. When people ask me what I do, I always reply, "I'm a writer." I've even managed to write a whole book, with a lot of help from my friends!

I couldn't be more grateful to the people who have chosen to take part in the 29-Day Giving Challenge. I see our community as a place where we can all come to strip away the masks we tend to wear in our day-to-day lives. Most important, it's a place where we can all shine our collective light out into the world through the power of story and art.

Giving mindfully and being actively grateful for all I am receiving has become a part of my daily spiritual practice. Each day, I practice a simple series of actions that have developed into a formula for happiness that works for me without fail … I have learned much about myself over the past 365 days. I've discovered that I am a good person at heart. I've learned that my value as a person isn't measured by how much I accomplish. I've embraced that I am so much more than the physical; the limitations multiple sclerosis imposes on my body do not stop me from living a purposeful life. I discovered that I have the power to touch other people and move them to action.

So today, on my 365th day of giving, I want to send out a sincere thank you to every person who has chosen to take part in the 29 Gifts Movement and to invite all of you to visit the site at www.29Gifts.org and sign up, too. And once again, I wish to express my deepest gratitude to Mbali Creazzo and the many other teachers who have passed on their wisdom and given me the inspiration to move forward with my life.

from 29 Gifts: How a Month of Giving Can Change Your Life

Questions for discussion

1. What did you think of the "prescription" the author's friend gives her (to give away 29 gifts in 29 days)? What things might you do if you took the giving challenge?

2. What if you only had energy two hours each day? How do you think you would spend your time?

3. The author seems to contend that there is a correlation between a positive attitude and health. Do you believe in that correlation? Why or why not?

4. What must it be like to know you have a progressive disease? Do you have experience with yourself or a loved one getting such a diagnosis? How was it handled?

5. What do you think of the author's idea that you don't have to measure your value by what you can accomplish?

6. Design your own discussion questions for this piece.

For Further Reading

About multiple sclerosis

www.nationalmssociety.org

About the 29 Gifts foundation

www.29gifts.org

About accepting life with a disability

Hockenberry, John. *Moving Violations*. A reporter with paraplegia discusses the ups and downs of his career.

Rubio, Gwyn Hyman. *Icy Sparks*. Fictional account of a young girl who grows to accept her Tourette's Syndrome.

de Montalambert, Hugues. *Invisible*. A man who loses his sight after an assault learns to accept his blindness.

Packer, Ann. *The Dive from Clausen's Pier*. Fictional account of a young woman whose fiancé becomes paralyzed, and of his struggle to accept his situation.

S.L. Rosen is a pseudonym.

I Call Myself "Survivor"

"Is he dead?" they whispered, lifting me onto the stretcher and shoving me quickly into the ambulance.

"No. He's one of the survivors."

I call myself a "survivor." I have survived death. Survived in a world that doesn't know what to make of people like me, true; but survived, nevertheless. That should be worth something.

A lot of people use the word "survivor" today. There are survivors of bad economic times. Survivors of divorce. People survive layoffs, psychological traumas, deaths of spouses.

The word "survivor" is uniquely suited to one group of people. People who survive accidents, diseases, who survive what would have been almost certain death just a few short decades ago. And people deformed, born with cerebral palsy, with stutters, cleft palates, open spines. People whom society has trouble imagining at all; the sideshow people: freaks, geeks, crips, gimps, people who look funny, talk funny, walk funny. The halt, the lame and the blind, as the Bible says.

In much earlier times many of us were killed. The ones of us who weren't exist as survivors. Sometimes, we were saved for a purpose: to provide entertainment, perhaps, or to serve as an omen, or token, of the Other. We have been ridiculed, tortured, locked in chains, locked out of sight of day. We survived—perhaps because we had no other choice. But nonetheless, we survived.

No other word could unite us quite as clearly as the word "survivor."

It finds common bonds among so many different people, in so many different physical conditions. For it does not deal with the state of our bodies, but with a political reality: survivorship.

"Survivor" unites us politically and socially. We are not alike in our physical conditions—as we know too well when looking for coalition. But we are alike in experiencing oppression—an oppression focused on the status our bodies signal to our oppressors. We are different because of our bodies: but for that reason we are also alike. And we are all oppressed the same way, for the same reasons: our bodies are different; therefore we are not normal. This one fact unites us. Our status throughout our oppression is as survivors.

Attempts have been made before to unite us with a word that recognizes the social reality of our status. That's how "handicapped" was born. It attempted to unite us by stating that we were all "handicapped" (or put at a disadvantage) by society. But it had a negative ring to it. It has made us sound like so many social service cases. And the fact that it is an adjective—"handicapped"—didn't help things either. "Handicapped what?" That has always been a problem. The solution has always been to call us "the handicapped"— something that grates on our ears and means, really, nothing at all.

"Disabled" was our own way of fighting this label. But "disabled" is in many ways even worse: it is, itself, a negative word. True, we can look to the success of "Black" which was also originally a pejorative term. But Black, as a word, is neither negative nor positive. It's only a color. But you cannot get away from the fact that "disabled" means "not able." There is no other meaning.

Thus there has been continuing disagreement among us. Some of us hate being called "handicapped" and want to be called "disabled." Others hate the word "disabled" because it seems so negative. The division really exists because neither word is right, and we know it.

"Survivor" is a real word. It is not negative; it always conveys a sense of wholeness, of skill in just those ways we have had to be skillful. And it defines us both socially and politically within the framework we have had to live all these years. We have survived medically, morally, and politically. Those of us who are involved in the struggle to end our oppression are, simply, survivors.

There is no better word to define the reality that belongs uniquely to us. We persist in enduring continuous medical humiliation, lack of privacy, lack of respect, constant tooling around on our bodies; blithe promises of cure, prohibitively expensive devices for moving about, confinement in nursing homes, confinement in back rooms, dependence on the mercy and good will of people who take care of us (because we are not allowed the technology to take care of ourselves), deplorable economic conditions, life on SSI, blockage from buildings. And yet we continue to work for change. What are we if not survivors?

There has been a move recently to coin "cute" words: "handicappers," "exceptional" and "physically challenged" come to mind. What are we trying to do? The intention is good: we're looking for a way to make it all sound so positive. But it ends up sounding like pablum.

"Survivor" does not sound like pablum.

It is no good to invent an identity. If we do not choose an identity freely, it has no meaning to us. We will still be defined by the oppressors. And how can we build a pride if we are defined by our oppressor, if our existence is plotted by our oppressors?

Until we define our existence, in a word we have chosen, we will never be free.

I Call Myself "Survivor"

Questions for discussion

1. What do you think of all of the terms used to describe disability? Which terms do you think are preferable, and why? What do you think of the term "survivor"? Would it work well in most situations? Why or why not?

2. Have you ever felt uncomfortable when speaking with someone about disability issues, because you did not know which words to choose or even whether to mention the disability at all? What happened?

3. What do you think of the last sentence, "Until we define our existence, in a word we have chosen, we will never be free"? What do you think the author is trying to say? What oppression is the author referring to? Who are the "oppressors"?

4. Design your own discussion questions for this piece.

For Further Reading

Shapiro, Joseph. *No Pity* ch. 1, "Tiny Tims and Supercrips." A discussion about labeling and stereotypes, and the negative consequences thereof.

Linton, Simi. *Claiming Disability.*

Karin Mango (1936–   ) is a writer and editor. She has had a hearing loss since her teens, and now wears bilateral cochlear implants. She grew up in England and received her M.A. from Edinburgh University, U.K., and, after moving to the U.S., received her M.L.S. from Pratt Institute, N.Y. She has written 15 books, chiefly for children and young adults, and numerous articles. She is a member of *advocates for better communication (a.b.c.)* affiliated with the Center for Hearing and Communication, NYC. She is married with two children and two grandchildren.

Christmas Cheer

Maybe the best idea would be to pack a small bag with books and Hershey bars and go away to an isolated cottage somewhere in the wilds. Peacefully alone over Christmas. It was tempting, even if I were accidentally to pack junk mail and Proust instead of James Michener and Agatha Christie.

No straining to hear above a hubbub of voices. No explaining: "I have a hearing loss—would you say that again, please? And again? Just one more time, in different words?" No resentment over yet again being the "odd man out" in a holiday group of chatting people. What good was "Hark, the Herald Angels Sing" when you couldn't hark to them yourself? And when all the family was gathered together so rarely and it was so important to hear them, not to understand two connected sentences. Christmas cheer? Not that way.

It wouldn't have to be anywhere exotic like Bermuda or the Bahamas. I'd even take New Jersey—a stone's throw from home in New York—if it was quiet.

The feeling started soon after Thanksgiving. "Panic" was too strong a word, and it wasn't depression. "Mixed feelings" was more like it. Very mixed. I love festivals and traditions, and Christmas has always been my favorite. But with my hearing loss creeping annually down the scale from mild to moderate to severe and now severe to profound, all the things I had loved—people, festivities, carol-singing, getting together—were being slowly and inexorably pulled from my resisting grasp. As I saw the signs of Christmas appearing all around, in store decorations, Christmas tree vendors with their "forests" at street corners, the first cards arriving ... the sensation intensified in my mind—and in my stomach—as I thought, How will I manage with so little intelligible sound? I miss such a lot. It's not worth the effort. Why not just say, "See you after the New Year" and even leave my TT behind?

I have thought about it quite seriously. First, I would leave the festive food ready for my husband and for Nick and Helen when they arrived from out of town. Then, we simply wouldn't give a party that year. I wouldn't get angry and resentful at the various gatherings of the season. I wouldn't have to be frustrated by the carol service at the church—a small thing, but emblematic of the whole season. I wouldn't get so tired by the sheer effort to communicate that all I wanted was escape.

Escape from the thick glass wall behind which so many of us hearing impaired people live. On the other side we see the lips moving, the easy communication, the connections with our fellow men and women, the laughter, the conversation, the discussions. All the things we sweat to get a mere inkling of. Outsiders at the window, looking in.

If you allow yourself to look at it that way.

It can be very easy to get into that frame of mind. It does seem a solution to escape and be safely, quietly alone. But as I went on thinking, it was clear I had to look at it differently. Not "escape," because it wasn't that at all. What I might be starting was the easy, deadly path to withdrawal and isolation, losing the ground so carefully achieved through adapting to the hearing loss and learning to live with it as best I could.

And what I'd been thinking of certainly wouldn't do much for my family's Christmas spirit. Not a brave "escape," merely a self-centered, cowardly running away.

Now that I was no longer looking through a haze of anxiety, common sense started to reassert itself. I didn't have to hear everything or struggle beyond reason. People would help me. What I didn't hear, I wouldn't hear. It wasn't only words that were important.

I sat down with my husband, Tony, and we planned our party. "Let's make it an open house," he suggested. "People will come in smaller groups and that will mean less noise to try to hear through. Easier for everyone." It was easier already.

It was a good party, with neighbors from our brownstone area. Truthfully, I didn't hear much, and yes, I did read a lot. But it wasn't either junk mail or Agatha Christie. It was the conversations carried on in writing to supplement my hearing aids and keep my friends from going mad with repetition. I had also forgotten that they were friends, who knew about my hearing loss, knew how to help me and were willing to do so.

Before Christmas, my son Nick brought his girlfriend to dinner. She is thoughtful and patient and in the quiet of home we managed quite passably.

Then my daughter Helen brought her new boyfriend for us to meet. I looked at the beard hopelessly. How would I ever lipread him? I wanted to be at least minimally intelligent and communicative with someone who's important to her.

"What can I do to make conversation easier?" He asked the perfect question.

"Shave off the beard!" was my sincere but unspoken wish. But that was not what he meant and anyway it looked good on him. Instead, I took him into good light, asked him to speak slowly, Helen helped, and we could—sort of—talk. And "sort of" didn't matter.

The carol service is on Christmas Eve. Poinsettias were on the altar, a huge Christmas tree beside it; candles filled the church with their gentle light. Over the past years I have been going for the family company and the beauty of the scene. Forget the service, forget the minister speaking, forget the carols.

Well, this year it was still forget the first two items (and now I thought, common sense uppermost at last, how about getting a loop installed?), but surely carols are meant to be sung! The music, distorted and cacophonous to my damaged ears, was still familiar inside my head. I sang along, inaudible to myself, but no heads turned. I went on singing happily.

Christmas Day. We always take the festive lunch to a tetchy and touchy old aunt who never leaves her house. We all helped her celebrate in spite of herself, heading off her impatience with my hearing difficulties. She has her own problems of failing hearing and sight and arthritic legs. I have only one thing wrong with me.

But still, the next evening, invited to a gathering across the street from our house, with people overflowing the rooms, with the noise and effort and straining to catch a minimal something, I nearly despaired. I couldn't hear Tony's familiar voice trying to help me, no quiet place, no room for paper messages. I reminded myself firmly of a couple of things. Sometimes it's not a defeat to withdraw, but common sense. You don't have to be a part of everything—and you can also be part in various ways. It isn't only words that matter; it's people. I rested my ears and relaxed.

On the day both Nick and Helen had to leave, we all sat around the kitchen table eating Christmas leftovers. I looked at the faces around me. I no longer wanted to be in New Jersey or wherever it was by myself. With gratitude, love, and a small but definite feeling of success, I raised my glass: "*Christmas cheers!*"

Christmas Cheer

Questions for discussion

1. What does this piece say about withdrawing versus putting forth effort to interact with others? What do you think of the author's philosophy on this subject?

2. Assume that you had profound hearing loss and could hear very little. What situations in your life would be difficult to adapt to? Which might not be so challenging?

3. The author says escaping for the holidays might start her on "the easy, deadly path to withdrawal and isolation." Do you agree or disagree, or why?

4. Near the end of the story the author comments, "Sometimes it's not a defeat to withdraw, but common sense. You don't have to be a part of everything—and you can also be part in various ways. It isn't only words that matter; it's people." Do you agree or disagree, and why?

5. Design your own discussion questions for this piece.

For Further Reading

Shapiro, Joseph. *No Pity*, ch. 3. A fascinating discussion about the deaf community and the debates that rage within it: those who advocate living in separate deaf communities, and those who advocate learning to adapt to the hearing world; those who favor "cures" such as cochlear implants and those who spurn them, and other important topics.

Conley, Willy. "The Hearing Test." A short play anthologized in *No Walls of Stone*. A satirical piece about a child who is visiting his doctor for his periodic hearing test. He endures the boredom of the test, the condescension of the doctor, and the discussions about him, but puts his foot down when the issue of a cochlear implant arises.

Bibliography

Baird, Robert M, Stuart E. Rosenbaum and S. Kay Toombs, eds. *Disability: The Social, Political, and Ethical Debate.* Amherst: Prometheus Books, 2009.

Ben-Moshe, Liat, et al., eds. *Building Pedagogical Curb Cuts: Incorporating Disability in the University Classroom and Curriculum.* Syracuse: Syracuse University Press, 2007.

Bradford, Arthur. "Texas School for the Blind," in *Dogwalker: Stories.* New York: Random House, 2001.

Bratt, Kay. *Silent Tears: A Journey of Hope in a Chinese Orphanage.* Las Vegas: Amazon Encore, 2008.

Brontë, Charlotte. *Jane Eyre.* New York: Penguin Group, 2010.

Browne, Susan E., Debra Connors, and Nanci Stern, eds. *With the Power of Each Breath: A Disabled Women's Anthology.* Berkeley: Cleis Press, 1990.

Byars, Betsy. *Summer of the Swans.* New York: Penguin Group, 1970.

Cohen, Brad and Lisa Wysocky. *Front of the Class: How Tourette Syndrome Made Me the Teacher I Never Had.* New York: Macmillan, 2008.

Conley, Willy. "The Hearing Test," in *No Walls of Stone: An Anthology of Literature by Deaf and Hard of Hearing Writers.* Washington DC: Gallaudet University Press, 1992.

Dillard, Annie. *The Maytrees.* New York: HarperCollins, 2007.

Dubus, Andre. "Dancing After Hours," in *Staring Back: The Disability Experience from the Inside Out,* by Kenny Fries, ed. New York: Penguin Group, 1997.

Fox, Michael J. *Always Looking Up.* New York: Hyperion, 2009.

Gilman, Charlotte Perkins. "The Yellow Wallpaper," in *Herland and Selected Stories.* New York: Penguin, 1992.

Gloss, Molly. *Hearts of Horses.* New York: Houghton Mifflin, 2007.

Grandin, Temple. *Thinking in Pictures.* New York: Random House, 1995.

Grisham, John. "Quiet Haven," in *Ford County.* New York: Random House, 2009.

Groneberg, Jennifer Graf. "First Words," in *Gifts: Mothers Reflect on How Children with Down Syndrome Enrich Their Lives* by Kathryn Lynard Soper, ed. Bethesda: Woodbine House, 2007.

Hathaway, Katharine Butler. *The Little Locksmith*. Coward McCann & Geoghegan, 1943.

Hockenberry, John. *Moving Violations*. New York: Hyperion, 1995.

Hurst, James. "The Scarlet Ibis." Mankato: Creative Education, 1998.

Huxley, Aldous. "Jacob's Hands." New York: St. Martin's Press, 1998.

Johnson, Harriet McBryde. *Too Late to Die Young*. New York: Henry Holt, 2005.

Jones, Larry A. *Doing Disability Justice*. Lulu Press, 2010.

Kafka, Franz. *The Metamorphosis*. New York: Random House, 1972.

Kaysen, Susanna. *Girl, Interrupted*. New York: Random House, 1993.

Keller, Helen. *The Story of My Life*. New York: W.W. Norton & Company, 2003.

———. *The World I Live In*. Mineola: Dover Publications, 2010.

Kleege, Georgina. "Disabled Students Come Out," in *Disability Studies: Enabling the Humanities*. New York: Modern Language Association, 2002.

Lahiri, Jhumpa. "The Treatment of Bibi Haldar," in *Interpreter of Maladies*. New York: Houghton Mifflin, 1999.

Lefens, Tim. *Flying Colors: The Story of a Remarkable Group of Artists and the Transcendent Power of Art*. Boston: Beacon Press, 2002.

Le Guin, Ursula K. *The Lathe of Heaven*. New York: Simon and Schuster, 1971.

———. *The Ones Who Walk Away from Omelas*. Mankato: Creative Education, 1993.

Linton, Simi. *Claiming Disability: Knowledge and Identity*. New York: New York University Press, 1998.

Mango, Karin. "Christmas Cheer," in *No Walls of Stone: An Anthology of Literature by Deaf and Hard of Hearing Writers*. Washington DC: Gallaudet University Press, 1992.

Matthews, Cris. "Giving it Back," in *The Ragged Edge: The Disability Experience from the Pages of the First Fifteen Years of the Disability Rag*. Louisville: Advocado Press, 1994.

Meyer, Donald J. *Uncommon Fathers: Reflections on Raising a Child with a Disability*. Bethesda: Woodbine House, 1995.

Montalambert, Hugues de. *Invisible: A Memoir*. New York: Simon & Schuster, 2010.

Moon, Elizabeth. *The Speed of Dark*. New York: Random House, 2002.

Nabokov, Vladimir. "Signs and Symbols" in *Vintage Nabokov*. New York: Random House, 2004.

O'Brien, Mark. "The Unification of Stephen Hawking," in *Staring Back: The Disability Experience From the Inside Out* by Kenny Fries, ed. New York: Penguin Group, 1997.

Packer, Ann. *The Dive from Clausen's Pier*. New York: Random House, 2002.

Palladino, Lucy Jo. *Dreamers, Discoverers, and Dynamos: How to Help the Child Who Is Bright, Bored, and Having Problems in School*. New York: Ballantine Books, 1997.

Parens, Erik, and Adrienne Asch, eds. *Prenatal Testing and Disability Rights*. Washington, D.C.: Georgetown University Press, 2000.

Park, Clara Claiborne. *The Siege: A Family's Journey into the World of an Autistic Child*. Boston: Little, Brown and Company, 1967.

Plath, Sylvia. *The Bell Jar*. New York: HarperCollins, 1971.

Poe, Edgar Allan. "The Man That Was Used Up," in *The Unabridged Edgar Allan Poe*. Philadelphia: Running Press, 1983.

Porter, Katherine Anne. "He," in *The Collected Stories of Katherine Anne Porter*. Orlando: Harcourt Brace & Company, 1972.

Rosen, S.L. "I Call Myself Survivor," in *The Ragged Edge: The Disability Experience from the Pages of the First Fifteen Years of the Disability Rag*. Louisville: Advocado Press, 1994.

Rubio, Gwyn Hyman. *Icy Sparks*. New York: Penguin Group, 1998.

Ryan, Joan. *The Water Giver: The Story of a Mother, a Son, and Their Second Chance*. New York: Simon & Schuster, 2009.

Sacks, Oliver. *An Anthropologist on Mars*. New York: Random House, 1995.

Sears, William. *The Premature Baby Book: Everything You Need to Know About Your Premature Baby from Birth to Age One*. Boston: Little, Brown and Company, 2004.

Shapiro, Joseph. *No Pity: People with Disabilities Forging a New Civil Rights Movement*. New York: Random House, 1993.

Silver, Kate. "How Mya Saved Jacob." *Spirit* (June 2010): 102–118.

Simon, Rachel. "It Takes a Village to Help a Sister." http://www.rachelsimon.com.

———. *Riding the Bus with My Sister: A True Life Journey*. New York: Houghton Mifflin, 2002.

Smith, Alexander McCall. *Tears of the Giraffe*. New York: Random House, 2002.

Soper, Kathryn Lynard, ed. *Gifts: Mothers Reflect on How Children with Down Syndrome Enrich Their Lives*. Bethesda: Woodbine House, 2007.

Stimpson, Jeff. *Alex: The Fathering of a Preemie*. Chicago: Academy Chicago, 2004.

———. "The Looks." http://www.yaiautismcommunity.org/blog/?p=56.

Tammet, Daniel. *Born on a Blue Day: Inside the Extraordinary Mind of an Autistic Savant*. New York: Simon & Schuster, 2006.

Tan, Amy. "The Opposite of Fate," in *The Opposite of Fate*. New York: Penguin Group, 2003.

Taylor, Jill Bolte, M.D. *My Stroke of Insight.* New York: Penguin Group, 2006.

Thomson-Garland, Rosemarie. "Staring at the Other," *Disability Studies Quarterly* (Fall 2005), Volume 25, No. 4.

Tolstoy, Leo. *The Death of Ivan Ilych.* New York: Tribeca Books, 2011.

Walker, Cami. *29 Gifts: How a Month of Giving Can Change Your Life.* Philadelphia: Perseus, 2009.

Wells, H.G. "The Country of the Blind," in *The Complete Stories of H.G. Wells.* London: Orion Books, 1999.

Westmacott, Mary [Agatha Christie]. *The Rose and the Yew Tree.* New York: HarperCollins, 1997.

Index